THE RISE OF HOUSTON AS A GLOBAL CITY

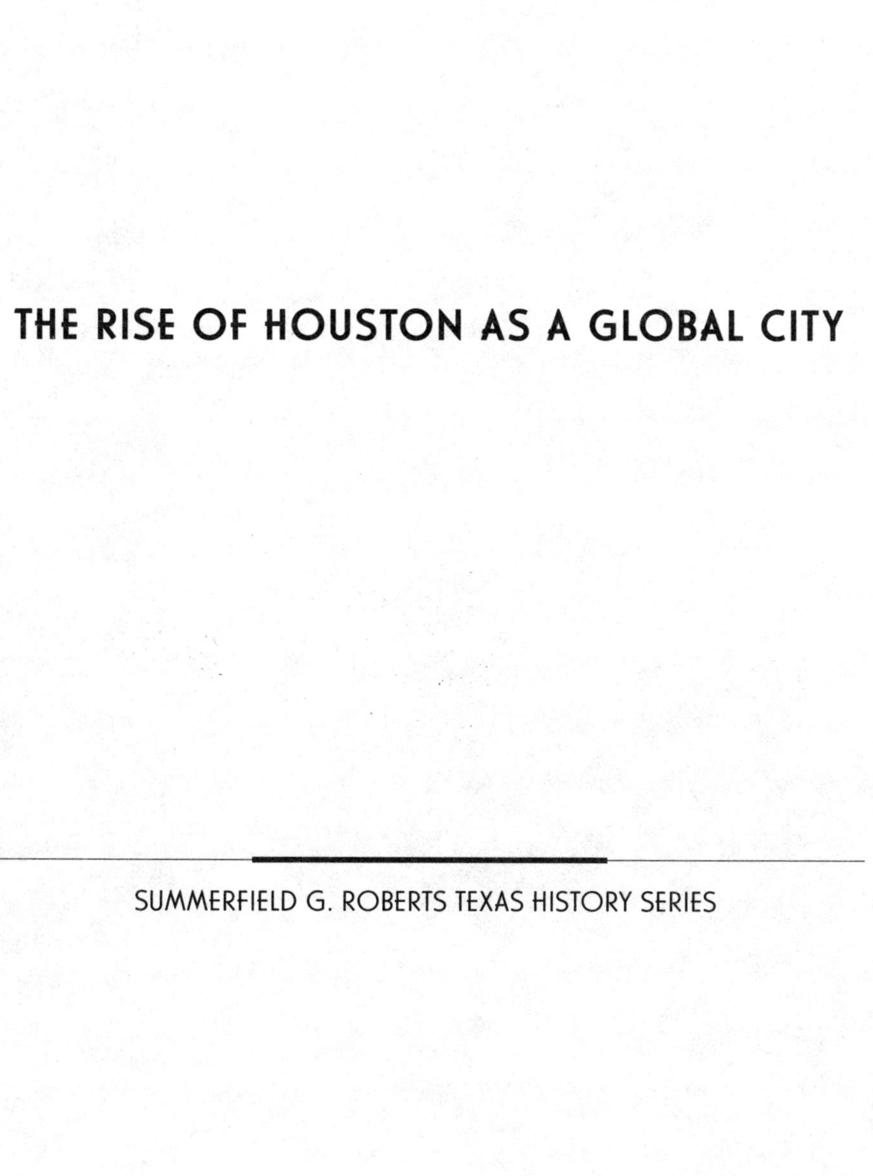

SUMMERFIELD G. ROBERTS TEXAS HISTORY SERIES

THE RISE OF HOUSTON AS A GLOBAL CITY

Geoffrey Scott Connor

Foreword by **Cecilia Abbott**

TEXAS A&M UNIVERSITY PRESS

COLLEGE STATION

First edition

∞ This paper meets the requirements of ANSI/NISO Z39.48–1992 (Permanence of Paper).
Binding materials have been chosen for durability.

LIBRARY OF CONGRESS CATALOGING-IN-PUBLICATION DATA

Names: Connor, Geoffrey S., 1963– author | Abbott, Cecilia, 1959– writer of foreword
Title: The rise of Houston as a global city / Geoffrey S. Connor; foreword by Cecilia Abbott.
Other titles: Summerfield G. Roberts Texas history series
Description: First edition. | College Station: Texas A&M University Press, [2025] | Series: Summerfield G. Roberts Texas history series | Includes bibliographical references and index.
Identifiers: LCCN 2025022222 (print) | LCCN 2025022223 (ebook) | ISBN 9781648433092 cloth | ISBN 9781648433108 ebook
Subjects: LCSH: Globalization—Texas—Houston | Medical Innovations—Texas—Houston—History | Space sciences—Texas—Houston—History | Entrepreneurship—Texas—Houston | Houston (Tex.)—Commerce—History
Classification: LCC HF3163.H8 C66 2025 (print) | LCC HF3163.H8 (ebook) | DDC 381.09764/1411—dc23/eng/20250806
LC record available at https://lccn.loc.gov/2025022222
LC ebook record available at https://lccn.loc.gov/2025022223

To my parents, who have always loved and supported me

Contents

Foreword

CECILIA ABBOTT
First Lady of Texas

The amazing city of Houston has played such a large role in my life as it has for so many Texans. I was not born in Houston, now the nation's fourth-largest city and among the most diverse, but I lived there for almost two decades. My husband, Greg, and I grew to love the city and felt energized by its business community, welcomed by its social circles, and excited by the city's palpable prodding to always do more—and do it better.

As a young couple, we enjoyed the city where Greg began his legal and political career and where I completed both undergraduate and graduate studies at the University of St. Thomas in the Montrose area. We enjoyed so many of the opportunities that Houston provided for quality education, the launch of new careers, and the vast number of beautiful neighborhoods, parks, museums, restaurants, performing arts venues, and other attractions that are still the enduring legacy of generations of Houstonians. It is an exceptional city that I believe could easily have been our permanent home but for the pull of public service in Austin.

Geoff Connor and I have been friends for over twenty years. We first met when he was appointed as the secretary of state of Texas. He writes informatively and entertainingly in this book about how Houston has achieved all that we admire in the city. He explains the factors, people, and circumstances that made Houston a global city, a metropolis that has established itself on par with the great cities of the world—while remaining a livable, welcoming, and ever-fresh urban home.

His book explains the original vision of Houston as a trading center that grew rapidly to become a leading international port. That port then enabled Houston to become the center of the Texas oil boom, created a myriad of corresponding industries, and led to its designation as the "Energy Capital of the World." The skills and resulting prosperity created by the trade and energy sectors then led to the establishment of the Texas Medical Center in the 1940s, the world's largest medical complex. And of course, the Manned Space Center in 1961 remade Houston into "Space City," with all the technology businesses that flowed from the nation's space exploration program.

As a Texan, and a Houstonian in my heart, I am proud of Houston's accomplishments and prominence, and I am in awe of the breadth and scale of each succeeding new height the city reaches. But I am particularly proud of the generosity and farsightedness of Houstonians over the years who have given back to their city and sought to make it more than just an economic miracle.

Geoff recounts the history of William Marsh Rice, whose fortune established Rice University; of Monroe Dunaway Anderson, who funded the state's first cancer hospital and sparked the Texas Medical Center; of Ima Hogg, who established the Houston Symphony and later left her Bayou Bend estate to the Houston Museum of Art. He writes of Jesse Jones, who built hotels and office buildings, promoted the port, and brought international attention to the city before eventually leaving a legacy to establish the Houston Endowment. He also writes of many other prominent Houston leaders who did not succeed just for themselves but reinvested their labor and wealth back into their beloved community—building parks and museums, providing health care, funding education, and creating an atmosphere of opportunity and support for each new generation.

I love Texas and I love philanthropy; together they make what I call Texanthropy—volunteerism and service to others. What a beautiful, historic example Houston has been in that regard. This book shows how a sense of Texanthropy has pervaded Houston from its early days and is now a recipe for ongoing opportunity and success for the community.

Reading history is fun, and this book is full of fascinating stories. It is also full of inspiration for how we can all serve to build a society built on compassion and opportunity. And I thank Geoff for bringing this incredible story to the printed page and to life.

Preface

In 2012, I began a four-year course of study at the University of Texas at Austin to obtain a PhD in history. I focused on US diplomatic and national security history, and I expected that I would write a dissertation on some traditional aspect of the field, perhaps especially related to my primary interest in British hegemony and its decline and how that might be instructive on continued American power.

However, the cochairs of my dissertation committee, H. W. Brands and Jeremi Suri, encouraged me to think about my previous role as Texas secretary of state, the chief international officer of Texas. Since I was a returning, nontraditional student, they advised that I need not feel bound to a traditional dissertation path and should instead draw on my career experience to find a dissertation topic that was both academically sound yet a more specific fit for me.

We spent several months discussing various events and individuals important to Texas who had international roles that had perhaps not been sufficiently researched and explored. However, it was Jeremi Suri who remarked one day that the city of Houston was so amazing in its global reach and presence and why didn't I think about writing a biography of the city? H. W. Brands agreed but helped me sort through differing approaches until we finally all agreed that a dissertation that tracked the city of Houston's rise as a global city and focused on the growth of its international connections and influence would fill a gap in historical writing on the city. At the same time, it allowed me to make use of my personal expertise on Houston developed from my many years of personal and professional interactions there.

There were so many times that I had spoken at international business conferences in Houston, gone to diplomatic parties, and attended society events filled with the foreign crowd that always seems so prevalent in the city. As a state official, I had greeted heads of state on their arrival in Houston, toasted royalty on their official tours in Houston, and signed trade and cultural promotion agreements with foreign leaders. As I began researching the historical background of the city's global rise and the many fascinating details of past business, political, and social leaders, I realized I was on the very best track with my academic work.

Once the dissertation project was completed and I received my PhD, I began rewriting the manuscript into a more suitable book format. I was excited to share with others what I had learned about Houston and how I believe the city was destined from its inception to be one of the great cities of the world.

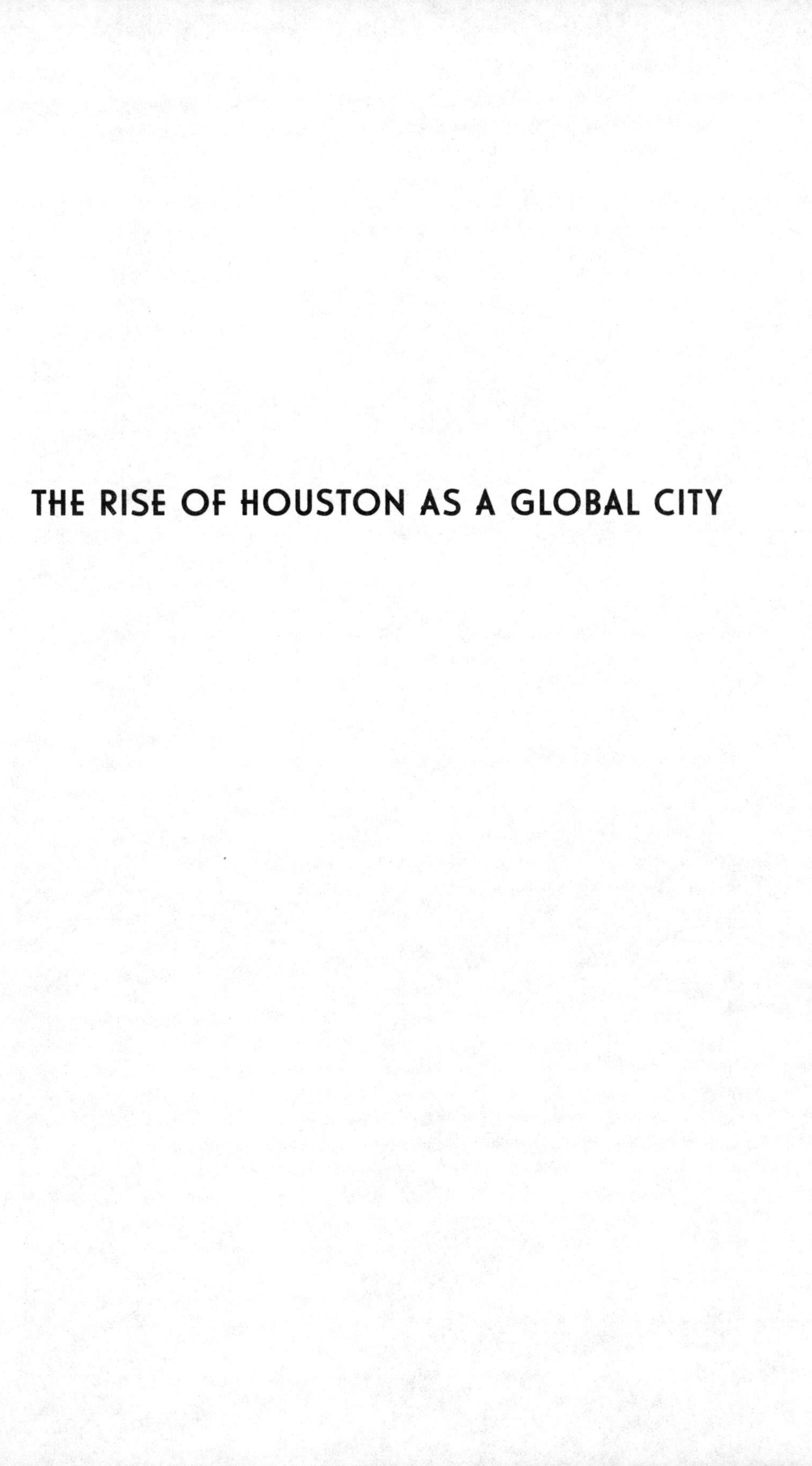

THE RISE OF HOUSTON AS A GLOBAL CITY

INTRODUCTION

THE UNITED STATES hosted the 16th G7 Summit in July 1990 in Houston, Texas. President George H. W. Bush invited the leaders of the other six major industrialized nations to his hometown for the three-day summit. Prime Minister Brian Mulroney of Canada, President François Mitterrand of France, Chancellor Helmut Kohl of Germany, Prime Minister Giulio Andreotti of Italy, Prime Minister Toshiki Kaifu of Japan, and Prime Minister Margaret Thatcher of the United Kingdom all came ready for an agenda focused on international economic issues against the backdrop of a declining Soviet Union. These leaders not only represented the most industrialized nations but were also among the wealthiest, diplomatically influential, and militarily powerful.

Houston rolled out the red carpet, both literally and figuratively, for the arriving world leaders and their entourages. The business community, jointly chaired by Ken Lay and George Strake Jr., raised funds, organized committees, planned venues, and deployed teams of workers.[1] The city gleamed from the dedicated attention of over five thousand volunteer citizens who cleaned, repaired, and planted vast areas of urban landscape.[2] The city ordered custom cowboy hats for each leader as well as custom cowboy boots with the seven flags of the participating nations and the name "Houston" stitched along the bottom. Local hosts organized a barbecue, a rodeo, and country and western singers. Barbara Bush wrote admiringly of the city's hospitality and recorded in her diary, "I am so proud of Houston."[3]

The most daunting challenge was simply the weather. Stan Musial, of the St. Louis Cardinals, while playing baseball in Houston for the first time in 1962, observed that the city had only three seasons, "Summer, and then July and August."[4] Barbara Bush admitted that "one might question the wisdom of choosing our hometown for a summit in July."[5] But the G7 Summit is always held in the summer, so there was not any flexibility on timing. City organizers, facing reality, simply adopted the slogan "Houston's Hot" and were determined to make it work.[6]

Houstonians, long before the rest of the country, figured out how to control the heat and humidity for homes, offices, churches, and shopping malls, as well as the Space Center and the Astrodome. They were fully in control to ensure that every building, car, and corridor used by the G7 Summit leaders and attendees was perfectly dry and chilled. However, part of every G7 Summit at the time was a group photograph in a picturesque venue, *outside*.

Rice University, as the official summit headquarters, determined that the courtyard in front of Lovett Hall was the right spot for the arrival ceremony and photographs. To make it comfortable, they then buried a ten-ton air-conditioning unit under the sidewalk with ground vents to blow cold air up the legs of the assembled leaders so they could stand in the hot sun for official and media photographs without melting.[7] This idea seemed ingenious and also consistent with Houston's reputation as the most air-conditioned "Tower of Babel" in the world.[8] Then someone remembered that the British prime minister would be wearing a skirt, because she never, for any reason, wore pants and certainly not for a formal arrival ceremony for the G7 Summit.[9]

The contractor who installed the underground air-conditioning system briefed British protocol representatives on the air volume and speed coming from the vents at maximum capacity. An engineer in London then calculated the lift such air would cause and told the prime minister's seamstress the right amount of lead weight to sew into the hem of the skirt. The weight needed to be sufficient to prevent lift but not so much that the skirt drooped low and looked slouchy.[10] Houstonians did not fear conquering their own environment, but they had no desire to embarrass the woman who was arguably the most prominent guest by turning her into an undignified Marilyn-Monroe-esque figure with skirt blowing up in front of the international press corps.

The first official day of the summit began on Monday, July 9. As expected, it was a typical hot, sunny day in Houston. By early afternoon it was nearing its high temperature of ninety-five degrees and a humidity reading of 87 percent. There was almost no wind at all. Instead, the air reached that heavy, sultry feeling that has led people to compare Houston to Saigon or other wet,

In 1990, President George H. W. Bush hosted the political leaders of the Group of Seven leading industrial powers in Houston for their annual summit. The representatives of the United States, United Kingdom, France, Canada, Germany, Italy, and Japan all posed on the lawn at Rice University. Courtesy of the National Archives and Records Administration.

hot tropical locales. The seven motorcades arrived, and the leaders assembled in Lovett Hall for a short reception before being led onto the lawn for the ceremony. Barbara Bush recorded that "it was hot!" as they stood for all seven national anthems, marching colonial fife and bugle corps, firing cannons, and welcoming remarks by President Bush.[11] The ground air-conditioning worked without a hitch or incident.[12]

Over the next several days the world leaders conducted meetings and negotiating sessions at Rice University. They enjoyed dinner at Bayou Bend, the legendary Rivers Oaks home that once belonged to Ima Hogg. The next evening they enjoyed dinner at the Houston Museum of Fine Arts with its spectacular art collection. Some leaders went to the Space Center, some went to the Texas Medical Center, and some toured the Houston Ship Channel. All could see the amazing, rich, international city that Houston had become. The G7 Summit was a culmination of all the dreams and hard work of Houstonians over a century and a half, made all the more special that the hosting president of the United States had invited these world leaders to his hometown.

President Bush was a Houstonian but not native born. He was from the East Coast, and even when he came to Texas, it was first to Midland to work in the oil industry. But once he achieved some level of success in oil, the move to Houston was inevitable. George Bush knew his company, Zapata Oil, could grow and flourish better in Houston, the "Energy Capital of the World." Additionally, Bush had political ambitions, and Houston was a draw for that as well because it represented a secure base for the projection of power and a platform from which he could build a political career. Having done so, and having reached the pinnacle of American political leadership, he reveled in being able to host his global counterparts in Houston. He wanted to show them not just the cowboy boots, the Stetson hats, the barbecue, and other trappings of Houston culture. He also wanted to show them that Houston was a solid and genuine base for modern wealth, political power, prestige, and a cosmopolitan and sophisticated culture that was a match for, if not better than, anything his guests' home countries could offer. Being the host city for the G7 Summit confirmed Houston's place in the world and its importance to the president and the other world leaders who gathered there.

The Houston at the center of the world in 1990 was, of course, a stark contrast to the Houston of 1837, when Francis Lubbock recorded that he had completely missed the town while gliding up Buffalo Bayou and had to double back to look for some markings of civilization.[13] Much had happened over the years that transformed Houston from a small settlement with big dreams to the reality of a modern international city. My book recounts that story but in a way that emphasizes the international connections of the city and the choices that the community itself made, or choices by its leading citizens, to project the city into the global business, political, and social world.

Review of Literature

In preparing my book, I have reviewed the work of many others who have written about Houston or specific aspects of the city's extraordinary history. In 1969, David G. McComb published *Houston, the Bayou City*. The book began as his doctoral dissertation at the University of Texas in 1968 and was converted into a book the following year. McComb writes his history of Houston chronologically and divides the narrative into what he views as three major blocks of the city's urban evolution. From the founding of the city in 1836 until 1875, McComb believes it was a "commercial emporium" depending on extraction of raw materials and agricultural production, but with minimal commercial activity such as milling lumber or grinding flour. McComb sees the period of 1875–1930 as a time of industrialization with much greater trade, oil production and gasoline refining, and extensive building and population growth. Finally, he terms the whole period of 1930–68 as "Space City," in which Houston suddenly "took off" in terms of technology, medicine, and the space program. McComb concludes that Houston is a great city with an outstanding future, but he spends little time distinguishing any aspect of Houston's history as internationally related or not.

Marguerite Johnston wrote a lengthy and very informative book titled *Houston, the Unknown City, 1836–1946* in 1991. Johnston was a longtime journalist for *The Houston Post*, including years as assistant editor when she wrote foreign affairs commentaries. Johnston was very informed about Houston's global role, and she provides many details and interesting stories along those lines. For example, she describes a naval officer, Edwin Fairfax Gray, from Houston who served with Commodore Perry in Japan and writes of Jesse Jones at Buckingham Palace and Colonel House at Versailles. However, Johnston ends her narrative immediately after World War II and uses the phrase "unknown city" in the title because she believed that Houston was an important city but not widely known and recognized as such until after World War II.[14]

A Houston Legacy, by Marie Phelps McAshan and published in 1985, is also attentive to Houston's international ties. She writes about the legacy of her hometown in trade, oil, medicine, and space, tracing the story of accomplishment and achievements to the early 1980s. McAshan speaks of many important events from her personal experience as well as the historical record but writes with the confidence that Houston is a global city in the modern era.[15]

George Fuermann was a journalist with *The Houston Post* for forty-nine years and was very engaged in community affairs. He wrote prolifically about Houston. His best-known volume, *Houston: Land of the Big Rich*, was published in 1951. Fuermann tells the story of Houston as a Midas land where "big money flows like water." Fuermann recounts the serious side of Houston when he describes people like Jesse Jones, Will Clayton, and Oveta Culp Hobby, who applied their business acumen to service in Washington and abundant local philanthropic activities.

Fuermann also writes about the flamboyant Glenn McCarthy, the exceptionally generous Hugh Roy Cullen, and other leaders of the oil crowd. Fuermann believed Houston to be a city of very distinct personality and culture. Fuermann wrote other shorter books on Houston, including *Houston: The Feast Years* (1962); *The Face of Houston* (1963) with Owen Johnson; and

Houston: The Once and Future City (1971), all focused on the many impactful achievements and events of the city.

Other writers have explored Houston through books about particular institutions. In *But Also Good for Business*, authors Walter Buenger and Joseph Pratt recount the history of Texas Commerce Bank and its preceding institutions that brought modern banking concepts to Houston beginning in 1886. Focusing on leaders such as Jesse Jones and Ben Love, the authors explain how the banks of Houston financed important portions of the ship channel, the downtown infrastructure, and housing that enabled Houston to succeed, without the selfish divisions that sometimes affected banks and cities, and facilitated a community-wide approach to growing and improving Houston. *Baker and Botts in the Development of Modern Houston*, published by Kenneth Lipartito and Joseph Pratt in 1991, tells a similar story of a growing Houston from the perspective of one of the city's leading law firms. The firm originated in 1840 when the nascent city was only three years old. As Houston expanded in international business over the years, the firm of Baker Botts grew with it, assisting with international trade matters, a new and growing body of law associated with the oil industry, and the challenges of the Depression and the modern era of medicine, technology, and space.

Marilyn Sibley, a history professor at Houston Baptist University, published an authoritative book, *The Port of Houston: A History*, in 1968. She describes the early history of the area and the original purposes for trade envisioned by founders John and Augustus Allen. Sibley traces the expansion of trade and the continuing quests for deep water coupled with competition from Galveston. Sibley shows that the success of modern-day Houston is inextricably linked with the port and ship channel.

There are many famous individual Houstonians and many books written about them. But in my focus on Houston as an international city, I was especially informed by the biography *Jesse H. Jones* by Bascom Timmons and *Unprecedented Power* by Steven Fenberg, also a biography of Jones. Both of these books make clear the impact Jesse Jones had in making Houston a modern city with a diversified economy. Robert Cotner's *James Stephen Hogg: A Biography* and Kate Kirkland's *The Hogg Family and Houston* both illustrate the political and philanthropic power behind the Hogg family and how they brought it to bear, transforming Houston into a city of arts and culture. In a similar vein, *Colonel House: The Texas Years*, by Rupert Richardson, and *Colonel House*, by Charles E. Neu, carefully explore the early history of Edward M. House, perhaps the most famous Houstonian of his day, and how his success abroad reflected well on his hometown. But more important, they examine his continued connections to leaders in Houston even after he began to spend more time in New York and Washington. Other biographies of Houstonians that have particular bearing on my examination of the city's international position include *William Marsh Rice and His Institute*, by Andrew Forest Muir; *Hugh Roy Cullen: A Story of American Opportunity*, by Ed Kilman and Theon Wright; and *Joseph Stephen Cullinan: A Study of Leadership in the Texas Petroleum Industry, 1897–1937*, by John O. King.

I have also examined writings that, while not about Houston, are informative in considering how a city shapes its environment, and vice versa. In his 1991 book, *Nature's Metropolis: Chicago and the Great West*, the scholar William Cronon writes a history of Chicago that is very different from a typical urban history. Cronon writes a chronological history of Chicago that focuses on how the city's growth was intertwined with the environment around it. Cronon tells the urban history and the environmental history of the surrounding countryside as one narrative. Chicago grew because of where it is located, a crossing point of rail and water traffic. As it grew, it affected the land around it, and vice versa, in an ongoing cycle of evolution. Chicago could grow because it drew to itself the commodities around it, such as cotton, grain, and livestock, for processing and shipping. The growing demand for these commodities caused better and more widespread transportation, further changing the landscape around Chicago.

Cronon also speaks to the relationship of people with time and space. While Chicago was once remote and far from the "civilization" of the East Coast, the demands of trade coupled with the changes of transportation technology eroded that distinction of time and space until people and perishable goods could easily move back and forth across the distance. From being an originating city sending commodities to the East Coast, Chicago's growing population and wealth began to pull consumer and luxury goods back the other way.

Finally, Cronon's writing undermines some of the Frontier Thesis of Frederick Jackson Turner from the previous century. Turner essentially believed that the great western frontier allowed continued expansion of American prosperity as settlers rolled out across open and available land. As they did so, the agricultural use of the land would become increasingly urban with a changing economy. By contrast, Cronon viewed city and country as evolving together in a reciprocal cycle of influence.

Cronon's ideas illustrate similarities in the ways that Chicago and Houston evolved into the major national and later international cities that they both became. Both cities positioned themselves as transit points for shipping. Both cities improved their positions as trading cities by improving water transportation projects: Houston by dredging Buffalo Bayou to create the Houston Ship Channel, and Chicago by first dredging the Illinois and Michigan Canal, and later the Illinois Waterway, to connect the Great Lakes with the Mississippi River. Both cities depended on railway connections to make them transportation and trading hubs.

Cronon's presentation of Chicago shows a certain sense of inevitability about the city as, once the railroads are established, people and goods simply had to move through Chicago in order to connect the East and West Coasts. Houston is not so inevitable in its evolution as a major international center and seems much more a created, human-made center.

Michael Rawson, a professor at City University of New York, wrote *Eden on the Charles: The Making of Boston,* in 2010. Similar to Cronon's writing in *Nature's Metropolis,* Rawson writes about the evolution of Boston and its effects on the countryside around it, and vice versa. However, Rawson focuses more on the power of Boston's government in his examination of parks, public water systems, planned housing developments, and the harbor. Like Houston, Boston was founded as a commerce city on the water, albeit better-connected water than Houston originally had. But the emphasis on government action and leadership does not square as well with Houston's history, where the most robust projects in its international development were either private-sector-led initiatives, such as the oil industry and early shipping, or they were very much public-private partnerships, such as the Medical Center, Space Center, and the later development of the port and ship channel.

Gotham: A History of New York City to 1898, by Edwin G. Burrows and Mike Wallace, published in 1999, explores the history of New York City in detail almost to the beginning of the twentieth century. The authors emphasize New York as a settlement founded on trade by Dutch merchants. So focused were early New Yorkers on international trade that they were unfazed by the conquering British in 1664, as long as their trading businesses could proceed as usual. New York was on the water, but the city dug the Erie Canal to further its waterborne trade. Railroads completed the national trade loop with international shipping. By the end of World War I, "New York began to vie with London as the fulcrum of the global economy."[16] *Gotham* particularly stresses the acts of individuals and families in the extraordinary development of New York. Names like Vanderbilt, Morgan, and Astor were important in New York and beyond for creating wealth and power for themselves as well as their home city. Likewise, Houston had certain individuals and families, such as Hogg, Jones, Rice, Anderson, Baker, Cullen, and Brown, that seemed to particularly direct the city's destiny.

In this book, I examine these same themes as applied to Houston and its evolution from early trading center to global commercial center, energy capital, and international hub of medicine and technology. I also examine how much of this evolution to international city was intentionally planned or sought, that is, did city business and political leaders want to become an international city or was that a by-product of lesser or more individualistic goals? In *Atlanta Rising: the Invention of an International City 1946–1996*, Frederick Allen posits that a small group of public and private Atlanta leaders determined in the post–World War II era that they were going to transform the city from what they considered to be an underperforming, racially divided, and often violent community into an internationally recognized and appreciated city. Allen credits the leadership of progressive white businessmen like Coca-Cola president Robert Woodruff and black intellectual leaders like Atlanta native Martin Luther King Jr. with establishing a new paradigm for the city. Over the course of a half century, a succession of both black and white community leaders transformed Atlanta from a poor and scorned center for the revived Ku Klux Klan to a city that could host the 1996 Olympics and show off its international airport, downtown skyscrapers, CNN headquarters, and biracial business and political community. Atlanta is not an international city on the same economic and political level as Houston, but there are excellent parallels with Allen's emphasis on individual leaders, that is, people who sought to unify, build up, and improve the city even in the face of strong opposition or at the risk of personal ruin.

Joel Kotkin writes in *The City: A Global History* that cities are mankind's greatest creation and that they serve the purpose of uniting people into cohesive economic and political unity essential for security and prosperity. Kotkin compares ancient cities in Mesopotamia and North Africa to modern urban areas, finding that the successful ones incubate concentrated talent and wealth to create more wealth, security, and power. Kotkin notes that while many planned communities do not work out well, there are instances of unplanned ones, such as Pudong, that are enormously successful. Most fall in between with a plan that, for various reasons, morphs into a greater plan.

The urbanism intellectual Lewis Mumford wrote in his greatest work, *The Culture of Cities*, that the world's culture, and prosperity, would be guided by what happened at the local levels with technology, intelligent planning, modern housing, and a spirit of community. Writing in 1938, Mumford does not mention Houston and probably would have frowned on the city's lack of zoning and somewhat haphazard development. Nevertheless, Mumford would have admired the well-thought-out plans to create a deep-water port, link it with rail and road, coordinate it with oil and gas, and then use the resulting wealth and political power to harness new technology-based businesses.

Why Houston Is an International City

Modern Houston is the largest city in the South and the fourth largest in the nation, behind New York, Los Angeles, and Chicago. It is the nation's largest port for international cargo and the second-largest port for overall cargo. Houston's international airport, George Bush Intercontinental, is one of the busiest in the nation, handling over forty-eight million passengers in 2023 (in addition to another fifteen million, mostly domestic, passengers at Hobby Airport). The city has a broad industrial base in manufacturing and technology in addition to its core businesses in oil and gas, international trade, space technology, and medical services. There are more Fortune 500 companies headquartered in Houston than any other city except New York. Houston is consistently designated as a Global City in the A. T. Kearney Global Cities Index as an urban area of global influence, and it is ranked by the US Department of Commerce as the top US market for exports, ahead of rivals New York and Los Angeles. There is great individual wealth in Houston as well, with over 120,000 households ranked as millionaires.

Houston is culturally rich with a professional Houston Grand Opera, Houston Ballet, Houston Symphony Orchestra, and the Alley Theatre. Its internationally famous museums include the Houston Museum of Fine Arts, the Rothko Chapel, the Menil Collection, the Museum of Natural Science, the Holocaust Museum, and Bayou Bend.

Houston is demographically diverse with a population that is barely 49 percent white with the rest being Hispanic, black, and Asian. With one of the highest Asian populations of any US city, Houston is required to print ballots in Vietnamese and Mandarin, as well as English and Spanish. The city maintains sister-city relationships with nineteen other global cities. Some of these foreign cities are linked to Houston because of oil, such as Baku, Luanda, Stavanger, Abu Dhabi, and Tampico. Others are linked to Houston because of a common connection as global trade ports, such as Istanbul, Karachi, Shenzhen, Nice, and Taipei. Ninety-two nations have consular representatives in Houston, the third-largest concentration of consulates in the nation. Some of these are only one-person representative offices as in the case of Belize, Trinidad and Tobago, and Ghana. Others are very large operations, such as the consulates of Indonesia, France, Mexico, Italy, and India. Some of the consulates are also paired with trade offices and economic development personnel, such as those of Japan and the United Kingdom.

All of the aforementioned statistics and information describe what makes Houston an international city. But how did that evolution occur from the barely perceptible settlement of Houston in 1836 to the Houston that hosted the G7 Summit of 1990? How did Houston become not merely a large city, or even a large and wealthy city, but one that had such an amazing international reach in business, culture, and politics?

I believe Houston's modern status as an international city rests on four primary pillars: international trade, oil and related industries, medical treatment and research, and space and related high technology. They arrived in the same chronological order, each building on the previous one. As the four pillars were constructed over time, they provided a platform upon which a fifth important dimension of Houston's international presence could develop and project itself: political and social leaders. As the number and girth of each pillar grew, the platform for the development of politics and society grew proportionately until finally Houston could be regarded as a true global city.

The following describes how each pillar of international presence began and grew and how each area influenced, aided, attracted, or enhanced others as Houston increased in size, stature, wealth, and power.

International Trade

International trade was the first pillar, and most important base, upon which Houston built its global standing. From the founding of Houston in 1836, the early Houstonians envisioned a city that would be a center for trade. Houston was established on the banks of Buffalo Bayou, a slow-moving stream of water that flows easterly and then southeast to Galveston Bay. The founders, brothers Augustus Chapman and John Kirby Allen, realized that agricultural commodities produced by farmers in Southeast Texas needed to move to market, and that supplies and consumer goods needed to come to the farmers. There were no roads to speak of at the time, and shipping overland was subject to delay and danger. The only real option for a settlement as remote as Houston, and those farther inland, was to ship by water down the bayou to Galveston Bay where oceangoing ships could move goods onward to New Orleans, the Caribbean, the East Coast, or Europe.

The Allen brothers relied on marketing and promotion to initiate that first bit of trade in Houston. First, they named the city Houston after the most famous Texan of the day, thereby capitalizing on a famous and popular name. Second, they printed propaganda materials, directed at investors in New York and other major cities, extolling the virtues of Houston and seeking their participation in the venture.

From the outset, Houston's trade was international in nature. Cotton was abundantly produced in Texas and had to be shipped to the East Coast or Europe where textile mills could produce the fabrics so much in global demand. Other crops might be partially shipped after the farmers had consumed some of it themselves. In the case of cotton, however, virtually all of it left the farm to be ginned, cleaned, dyed, and woven into fabrics in an industrial setting. The great demand for Texas cotton provided opportunity for the individuals and community who could facilitate that trade.

The fledgling Republic of Texas government was headquartered for a time in Houston before the village of Waterloo was renamed Austin and built into the new capital city. Even afterward, Houston's economy benefited as the new Republic of Texas established consulates in France, the Netherlands, the United Kingdom, and other places, in part for diplomatic protection against Mexico but also to facilitate foreign trade.

Texas trade in cotton grew and continued even during the Civil War as some merchants tried to run the blockades and reach Mexico or other Caribbean locales to reload the goods. After the war, the proliferation of railroads and better communications encouraged more people to move to Houston and created even greater shipping opportunities. Rather than the railroads being a competition to shipment by water, they brought even more agricultural commodities to Houston for shipping to overseas ports while also transporting consumer goods back to the interior markets.

Realizing the increasing demand for international trade and benefits to be gained, Houston began a process of improving its port and canal. At first, this process meant simply straightening curves, dredging sandbars, removing overhanging trees, and keeping the waterway free of fallen trees or other debris that would impede ships. Later, Houston secured federal technical and financial help to make the port and ship channel incrementally deeper and wider. Finally, by the late 1890s, Houston secured federal assistance to dredge its channel sufficiently to make it a true deep-water port that allowed large oceangoing ships to come to the Turning Basin very near the city itself.

Houston repeated this cycle over the years, constantly partnering with the federal government to dredge the channel ever deeper and wider to allow for larger and more numerous ships to call. The Houston business and political community joined together to seek state or federal help with a program to match outside funding with local support, both public and private. Houston built the infrastructure needed for the port, including rail connections, wharves, storage, and other facilities. Houston supported the Intracoastal Canal project seeking to link Houston shipping with other ports throughout the Gulf of Mexico all the way to Florida. Houston's political leadership also advocated a canal across the isthmus at Nicaragua and then finally at Panama. Houston could see how such a canal would bring it business from Asia to supplement what it already had from Europe.

Once the Texas oil boom began in the early twentieth century, Houston was quick to see the linkage between that new industry and its port. Houston quickly became a major shipping point for tankers of crude so abundantly produced in the region to be loaded for shipment to the East Coast and Europe. Soon thereafter Houston facilitated construction of refineries and other petroleum-related chemical plants along the ship channel, enjoying the enhanced value of refining the crude oil locally but also building an industrial base along the entire extent of the ship channel. Ultimately, the ship channel would be the home of the Space Center announced in 1961 and completed by the following year. With each new generation of business and technology, Houston has successfully improved the ship channel and its global network of customers to continually expand its international economic base.

Oil and Related Industries

Oil is closely linked nowadays with the ship channel because of oil exports by huge tanker ships and the presence of so many refineries and petrochemical plants along the ship channel. However, oil originally emerged as its own separate industry and is a distinct second pillar in the global reach of Houston. The Texas oil boom began with Spindletop in 1901 soon after Houston committed itself to seek a deep-water channel all the way to Galveston Bay. As more discoveries of oil were made in the Houston region, people and wealth poured into the city. In the same time frame, the Great Hurricane of 1900 struck Galveston, so badly damaging the city, and so undermining the confidence of many of its business leaders, that the city could never fully recover. Houston easily filled that void as oil wealth created layers of new jobs and launched new businesses in real estate, banking, roads and bridges, hotels, restaurants, retail, and more.

Soon after the Texas oil boom began at Houston, the automobile became mass-produced and available to millions of working-class Americans. The Wright brothers invented the airplane, and within the decade, all the major military powers of the world had airplanes as a part of their weaponry, while civilians flew on growing numbers of passenger airlines. The abundance of oil also revolutionized the railroad industry, so important to Houston's position as a transportation and shipping center. Trains converted to oil-fueled engines that ran better, cleaner, and with fewer employees than were required for the coal-dependent trains.

Major oil companies formed in Houston in the early days of the boom. These included Gulf Oil; the Texas Company, which later became Texaco; and Humble Oil, which later became Exxon. These homegrown companies were later joined by foreign oil companies, such as Royal Dutch Shell, British Petroleum, and Total, who all realized the global market required them to have a presence in Houston. Houston-based companies expanded into many parts of the world, especially the Middle East, led by Texaco, who convinced the Roosevelt administration to assist its efforts in Saudi Arabia. It would be the first of many Texas oil companies to go overseas.

The image of the rich Texas oilman began to form during this period and was amplified in the 1930s when the lavish lifestyles of many oilmen stood in sharp contrast to the lives of those who were suffering through the Depression. But just as many struggling Depression-era people were buoyed by the glamour of golden-age Hollywood films, so people were also entertained, inspired, and motivated by stories of rags-to-riches Texas oilmen and the adventurous, sometimes risky, lives they led. It was an era of the swashbuckling Glenn McCarthy, who inspired the movie *Giant*; Hugh Roy Cullen with his famous "Big White House"; H. L. Hunt's re-creation of Mount Vernon; and Jim "Silver Dollar" West, who threw out money by the fistfuls. It did not matter that the majority of the new oil millionaires actually lived elegant but quiet lives. It was the big personalities that the public wanted to read about and whose image was imprinted on Houston.

The oil industry in Houston gave rise to the chemical industry and the production of fertilizers, antifreeze, pharmaceutical products, synthetic rubber, and most important, plastics. The plastics industry became the crucial building block of American consumer demand, supplying toys, car interiors, jewelry, fabrics, furniture, and home decor.

Medical Treatment and Research

The vast wealth created in both international trade and oil was the source of many fortunes used philanthropically by leading Houstonians to launch the third pillar of Houston's global reach, medical treatment and research through the Texas Medical Center, which began as the M. D. Anderson (now MD Anderson) Cancer Hospital, named for Monroe Dunaway Anderson, whose fortune came from cotton shipping. His family company, Anderson, Clayton and Co. of Oklahoma, relocated to Houston when the city developed its deep-water port. From there, the company opened offices around the world to control much of the world's cotton beyond the United States, including prolific production from Egypt and India. Anderson's fortune established MD Anderson Hospital, but importantly, it also facilitated the move of Baylor Hospital to Houston to form the nucleus of a medical center. When that happened, philanthropists who had derived their fortunes from oil stepped in and financed additions to the medical center with new hospitals, including St. Luke's Episcopal, Methodist Hospital, and Children's Hospital. The Cullens gave money for Baptist, Hermann, Episcopal, and Methodist Hospitals. The Fondrens also gave to Methodist Hospital. The Abercrombies gave to Children's Hospital. The Texas Medical Center brought in the brightest minds of the world to provide world-class treatment, as well as the first air ambulance service, comprehensive cancer treatment, open-heart surgery, artificial heart, and organ transplant.

The Texas Medical Center (TMC) attracted the world's elite because health is the most important factor in lives everywhere, and the TMC could do things no one else could. The publicity of various stars, royalty, and heads of state who visited brought more income, more patients, and more charity dollars to support the TMC and its continued expansion. The shah of Iran, the Duke of Windsor, President Lyndon Johnson, and King Hussein were all patients. Even those not needing treatment visited because the TMC became a tourist attraction for international visitors to the city, including elites such as the king and queen of Spain, the king and queen of Sweden, and Prime Minister Gandhi. The TMC also went out in the world to train and consult other medical experts, with heart surgeon Michael DeBakey's trip to examine Boris Yeltsin in Moscow perhaps the most famous example. Houston's own business and social leaders were its best ambassadors to promote the TMC to the world.

To make the TMC a success, Houston followed its earlier pattern of harnessing its local wealth and power to project influence in Austin and Washington for funding and program support. The TMC successfully united leading Houstonians for a great cause. It was a spectacular success in itself, but it also worked to recast the public view of Houston. The remarkable feats of medical skill and the high level of sophisticated treatment created a new image of Houston as not just big and rich but also smart. This revised impression of Houston helped position the city for its next big accomplishment, the Space Center.

Space and Related High Technology

In 1957, Houston was positioned well in the world as an international shipping center, the heart of a sustained oil boom, and the location of the largest medical center. But that year was also a time of Cold War stress that grew especially acute when the Russians successfully launched Sputnik, the first artificial satellite to orbit the earth. Suddenly, US exceptionalism was called into question, and the nation feared that the Soviets were winning the technology race and might soon deploy weapons from space. Senator Lyndon B. Johnson (D-TX) passed the 1958 Space Act and became Washington's leading figure on space policy. Three years later, President John F. Kennedy placed him, as the new vice president, in charge of the Space Council and charged him with planning how the United States could gain supremacy in space. Putting a man on the moon was the top priority, and that required a Space Center from which to direct the Manned Spaceflight program.

In a familiar pattern, Houston's business and political leaders determined their city could be the location of the space center and put together a local package of land and money. Then with their considerable influence, they got the attention of President Kennedy, the administrator of the National Aeronautics and Space Administration (NASA), and their own Texan, Lyndon Johnson. Overcoming a series of obstacles, Houston was selected in 1961, and the Space Center opened in 1962. By 1969, man walked on the moon in an operation controlled from Houston. This new status as Space City brought the world to Houston for new reasons and spawned a technology boom in the city that carried over into the modern computer age.

Political and Social Leaders

Throughout the development of these four main pillars there have been individuals who brought international recognition to Houston and who projected Houston into the world. Modern society is familiar with George H. W. Bush, who moved to Houston because of the oil business but then represented the city in Congress before continuing a remarkable public service career culminating in his election to the presidency. The public is also very familiar with James Baker III, who served in two cabinet posts as well as White House chief of staff to both Ronald Reagan and Bush. Baker's ancestral home was the first site for the MD Anderson Cancer Center. His grandfather was instrumental in establishing Rice University, and his great-grandfather began the international law firm Baker Botts, which figures so prominently in the development of Houston as an international trade and energy center. Also serving in the Bush era was Houstonian Robert Mosbacher Sr. as the secretary of commerce.

An earlier secretary of commerce is Jesse Jones, who served in the Franklin D. Roosevelt cabinet but previously worked for President Woodrow Wilson. Besides his political service, Jones was a successful banker, builder, and newspaper publisher. He brought the first Democratic National Convention to Houston in 1928, although he later supported Republicans when it was good for Houston. Jesse Jones's estate formed the Houston Endowment, one of the great philanthropic foundations of the nation.

People such as Ima Hogg, daughter of a Texas governor and sister of the founders of River Oaks, was the grande dame of Houston for many years. Her home, Bayou Bend, holds one of the finest collections of American antiques in the nation and is now a well-known museum. She established the Houston Symphony in 1913 after studying music in Europe and came back determined that Houston should also have a world-class music program. She spent decades building up the organization, raising money from her fellow Houston elites, and bringing the best talent from the nation and world.

Joanne Herring was among the modern social leaders who projected her influence from Houston to Washington, Pakistan, and Afghanistan to orchestrate resistance to the Soviet occupation of Afghanistan and hasten the end of the Cold War. Lynn Wyatt, once described as the socialite of the century, brought many of the great names of twentieth-century society to her River Oaks home and made Houston a fashionable destination for the international jet set. Her brother, Robert Sakowitz, ran the toniest stores in Houston and promoted Space City by bringing the miniskirt to Houston in 1967 for its American debut along with all the new minimalist Space Age fashions.

Houston: A Southern City or a Western City?

Part of understanding Houston's position as a global city is to understand its place in the United States. Geographically Houston is in the south of the nation, but whether it is in the South is debatable. Likewise, Houston is west of the Mississippi, but whether it can be considered part of the American West is also unclear.

Some people believe Houston to be a Southern city because of the plantation-style homes in the older neighborhoods; the lush landscape of azaleas, dogwood, and magnolia; and a passion for bourbon, barbecue, and Cajun dishes. Some believe it is a Western city because of the Houston Livestock Show and Rodeo, the biggest such event in the world. Either answer is plausible, but the fact that both have support shows how unique Houston really is and how hard it is to categorize it as is done with other cities. Denver seems clearly a Western city, and Atlanta seems clearly a Southern city. However, geography alone is not determinative since Kansas City, in the same longitudinal lineage, is famously Western. And New Orleans, in the same latitudinal line, is indisputably Southern.

Historically, the Allen brothers were thinking in Southern terms when they platted the city in 1836. It was not established as a city to serve ranchers or to be a gathering point for cattle and other livestock in the way that Ft. Worth was or the way that Chicago later evolved to be. Rather, Houston was focused on trade: moving goods from the Eastern United States and from Europe, Latin America, and beyond into Texas through Buffalo Bayou and to take the goods of Houston and its surrounding area out to these same markets. Cotton was a chief commodity, moving through Houston in the early years and for many decades to come, and what could be more Southern than King Cotton? Houston often looked to other Southern cities like New Orleans as a good role model for a city thriving on its trade port.

Some commentators believe that the reason for Houston's shift away from the original Southern identity to a Western one may be political in nature. Southern culture projected a refined image both before and after the Civil War: plantations, lush landscapes, ornate furniture and accessories, riding clothes, and an aristocratic lifestyle of genteel country living—as though a fine English country house had been transported to the Southern United States along with its horses, hunting dogs, hand-painted china, billiard room, and conservatory, all maintained, of course, by an army of uniformed servants, or in the case of the South, by slaves until 1865.

Even after the Civil War, the Southern culture did not really shift. The slaves may have been freed, but they were still mostly there and worked as before often for little wages or no wages at all but simply room and board and a chance to share in part of the agricultural production. The South may have actually reinforced its culture in some ways in the postbellum era, including naming many schools, streets, cities, and other public places after the leaders and heroes of the Confederacy. Statues of Confederate heroes were erected everywhere from local villages to major universities and the State Capitol. Pride in the South and its culture was openly celebrated. The shift really came with political and cultural concerns about the South's image, especially in the post–World War I era when the Ku Klux Klan grew in strength and the enforcement of Jim Crow laws and even lynchings grew in frequency and in publicity. Leaders began to question "Texas' essential Southerness."[17]

Some historians have examined the general shift of Texas from its identity as a Southern state to a Western one. The issue is "rooted in the subtle relationship between history and memory."[18] Volumes have been written about history based on archival research and facts that can be proven, rather than history as it exists in a society's culture, collective memory, and perceptions of certain issues and events. The transition of Texas from an identity as a Southern, former Confederate, state into one with a Western and frontier-oriented personality is truly one of the most fascinating examples of societal reinvention. Former Texas state historian Light Cummins has written, "It is my opinion that, by scholarly standards as held by historians, Texas remains southern and does so without historical debate."[19] Yet he goes on to acknowledge that modern Texans do see themselves as Western, "drawing on a collective memory that, although it has a basis in fact, is not the essence of Texas."[20]

By the 1930s, wallowing in the nostalgia of the antebellum era was growing stale, and the later generations did not like to think about slavery, military occupation, racial violence, squalor, and a general sense of backwardness. Not that these characteristics told the entire story of the South, but there was enough of it to make some business, social, and political leaders uncomfortable. At the same time, the resurgence of the Ku Klux Klan in the 1920s was identified less with the prominent civic leaders of an earlier era and more with the uneducated, coarse, and rough-edged persons on the fringe of white society.

James Allred of Wichita Falls was one such Texas leader who opposed the Ku Klux Klan and, as district attorney, gained a statewide reputation for his fearless prosecution of the Klan and efforts to end its political influence. He was elected attorney general of Texas and later governor from 1935 to 1939. It was during his term as governor that the Texas Centennial of 1936 was celebrated and is regarded by many scholars as a turning point in the image of Texas, a "deliberate rebranding."[21]

The 1930s saw an intellectual rebranding of Texas by scholars as well. University of Texas (UT) history professor Charles W. Ramsdell "had successfully established the southern heritage of the state in his teaching."[22] But that shifted with Walter P. Webb, also a UT history professor, who published *The Great Plains*, making the case for the state's Western heritage. Webb's most important publication was *Texas Rangers*, which not only made a strong case for the state's Western heritage but also "interpreted Texas history as a contest of three civilizations: Native American, Spanish and Anglo-American pioneer folk, not southerners."[23] J. Frank Dobie, a "tireless proponent of the western, ranching heritage of Texas," decorated his UT office as a ranch headquarters filled with Western art and cowboy memorabilia.[24] Dobie was not alone, since many Texas intellectuals of the time preferred to revere a past focused on "the frontier, the west, and the images of the cowboy who, 'in all his mythic grandeur, served as a symbol of a simpler, more rugged frontier age.'"[25]

Texas regionalism and the westernization of Texas in the 1920s and 1930s were apparent in literature, movies, politics, painting,[26] sculpture,[27] and music.[28] But it was in architecture that a particular point is brought home regarding Houston. As late as the 1920s, John Staub was designing classical Southern plantation homes, especially in the prestigious River Oaks neighborhood of Houston. Indeed, his most famous commission was the design of Bayou Bend in 1928, a plantation-style home for Ima Hogg, which is now owned by the Houston Museum of Fine Arts. As ranch-style architecture swept the nation, and even overseas, Staub continued to churn out classical styles, including an emphasis on Greek Revival homes with two-story white pillars.[29] Part of the reason for this may be that Staub was designing principally for River Oaks and other high-end neighborhoods in Houston, whereas the ranch-style architecture of the post–World War I era was first popular with the middle class and first-time homeowners. Staub's clients were building large, two-story (or taller) homes intended to impress, which was hard to do with the low, flat, more modestly styled ranch home. Historian Light Cummins calls River Oaks "the last great bastion of southern residential architecture in the 1920's."[30]

All of this raises the question of whether Houston and River Oaks were just resistant or slow to respond to the new westernization of Texas. Or did they embrace the Western image, but in River Oaks they were simply rich and needed a more elaborate architectural style to display their wealth? Houston as a whole "billed itself as the Magnolia City from about 1870 until 1920, and their local festivals focused on cotton, mardi gras and other Southern oriented themes."[31]

Polyglot from the outset, Houston only became more cosmopolitan and international as it matured. As the city passed through phases of being a frontier community, a trading town, a Southern city, a Western city, Energy City, Space City, Medical Center City, and so forth, it developed in a way overall that incorporated design elements and themes from a national and international pool of ideas.[32]

At least one Houstonian, Louis Wiltz Kemp, was fully on board with rebranding the state's image. Kemp was a native Texan who studied engineering at the University of Texas at Austin. He made his career with Texaco based in Houston. He was an excellent historian of Texas history and served on the board of the Texas State Library as well as president of the Texas State Historical Association. He was principally responsible for the San Jacinto Monument and for the refurbishment of the Texas State Cemetery. In particular, he served as chairman of the Board of Historians for the Texas Centennial, the board that would decide what the official history of the state was and "which personages and events from Texas history would be commemorated."[33] Also on the board of historians were J. Frank Dobie and Reverend Paul Foik.[34] Although there were disagreements among the men on some issues, they were all disposed to westernization of Texas in recommending historical markers and commemorations. This was pivotal "for changing public memory in Texas, because history written in stone by its nature is more durable than history written in ink."[35]

I personally believe Houston to be an international city that is primarily Southern in nature but has effectively rebranded itself as Western and international. The story of how Houston evolved from a concept in 1836 to its modern state as a global city is a fascinating historical account. First, international trade fueled the city's growth until it was later supplemented by the oil boom. The wealth and power created by trade and oil provided the tools needed to make the Texas Medical Center possible. The medical center then changed the image of Houston to one of innovative technology. Using this new image, and relying further on its plenitude and political reach, Houston was awarded the Space Center. All of these things in turn provided the platform for an array of fascinating social and political leaders who furthered Houston's international stature.

STANDING AT THE G7 Summit arrival ceremony that hot afternoon in 1990, Joanne Herring was flushed with pride and a sense of awe. "It was the most spectacular sight seeing all those world leaders arrive in motorcades with flags and flashing lights. And Rice and all of Houston looked so beautiful. I was so proud of President Bush bringing all these people to our city. And there was Jimmy Baker, who I'd known since kindergarten, standing there as the nation's top diplomat. I have always known what a great city Houston is, but today, I knew the world knew it too."[36]

CHAPTER ONE

VISIONS OF A GLOBAL TRADE PORT

1836

THE HOUSTON SHIP Channel may be the single most important factor in the development of Houston as an international city. The watercourse is now generally regarded as a human-made structure, but it largely follows the course of natural streams, especially Buffalo Bayou, which begins well west of Houston and meets with White Oak Bayou, flowing through modern Houston, including its most posh area, River Oaks. It is joined by Brays Bayou, near Harrisburg, then Sims Bayou, and finally Greens Bayou before merging with the San Jacinto River. It is at this point where General Sam Houston defeated General Santa Anna at the Battle of San Jacinto, and it is also at this point where the modern ship channel begins and continues to Galveston Bay.

Early History of the Houston Area

The modern Houston Ship Channel is one of the great commercial wonders of the world, but such a status seemed unlikely to early Europeans. Houston and its surrounding area was a part of the Spanish Empire for centuries, and it is believed that the explorer Álvar Núñez Cabeza de Vaca passed through the region.[1] Cabeza de Vaca was part of the Narváez expedition sent by King Charles I of Spain in 1527. By November 1528, the group shipwrecked on or near Galveston Island, and native tribes reportedly enslaved Cabeza de Vaca for a time until he was able to reach Mexico City and then return to Europe.[2]

The French explorer René-Robert Cavelier, Sieur de La Salle, also came to the region and claimed all of the Mississippi River basin for France. When the United States purchased Louisiana in 1803, it was not clear exactly where the boundary lines were drawn. From then until the Adams-Onís Treaty of 1819, both Spain and the United States claimed the area. After 1819, the Houston area was regarded as Spanish and then later as Mexican after Mexico gained its independence.

During these times of disputed sovereignty and lax or nonexistent oversight, "the Texas coast became the special province of renegades and outcasts," including most notably Jean Lafitte.[3] Lafitte, originally a legitimate warehouseman in New Orleans, became a famous and opportunistic pirate who first helped the Spaniards against the Mexican revolt and later assisted Andrew Jackson defend New Orleans from the British. Lafitte established his pirate colony on Galveston Island and made raids in the area until he was eventually killed in a sea battle with a Spanish ship.[4] In 1818, before Lafitte was killed, the United States sent George Graham as its emissary to Galveston Island to determine what Lafitte was doing, whether he was a front for a French colonization of the area and whether the region should be, and could be, subjected to American jurisdiction. Of course, the matter was mooted by the Adams-Onís Treaty the following year, but Graham was impressed with Galveston Island and the economic possibilities of the region. "Graham concluded that the United States had underestimated the importance of the Texas Gulf Coast."[5] In fact, Graham recommended the United States "occupy Galveston Island without further quibbling with Spain," opining that "it is the key to the greatest and best part of the province of Texas."[6]

After Mexico obtained independence, the new nation granted rights to landmen to seek colonists and bring them in to settle and develop the area. One such entrepreneur was Stephen F. Austin, who received a grant "that encompassed the entire length of Buffalo Bayou."[7] As settlers began to fill the area, they enjoyed the natural benefits of Buffalo Bayou, including its width and depth, making it easily navigable, at least for the ships of the time period.[8] More ships began to use the area, and in 1830, "the first steamboat on Texas waters, the *Ariel*, made its way up Buffalo Bayou, arriving at the Harrisburg landing."[9] Another larger steamship, the *Cayuga*, came up Buffalo Bayou in 1833 at the instigation of Brazos Valley planters who sought a better way to bring in supplies and to ship out their products.[10]

General Sam Houston reached Buffalo Bayou on April 18, 1836, as he maneuvered away from General Santa Anna and the Mexican army, waiting for an opportune time to make a stand for Texas. Three days later Houston was able to surprise Santa Anna on the banks of Buffalo Bayou at the San Jacinto River. In one of the most famous battles in the world, the Texian army defeated a Mexican force almost twice their size in a short battle. General Santa Anna escaped but was captured two days later. New settlers and towns would pop up quickly in the aftermath of the battle. Almost a century later, and before the San Jacinto Monument was erected, many ships would pass by as they made their way up the ship channel to Houston. Many of the ship captains would "dip the colors of their vessel in honor of those who fought and won such a great victory."[11]

Founding of the City of Houston

The city of Houston was born in August 1836 in the Republic of Texas, a new nation itself established only a few months earlier.[12] The founders were brothers, Augustus Chapman Allen and John Kirby Allen, who were real estate developers and pioneering entrepreneurs from New York. They selected a parcel of 6,642 acres of land along the banks of Buffalo Bayou, paying $9,428 or slightly under $1.42 per acre.[13] Although the Allen brothers had enjoyed some modest success in their land business, even this purchase of under $10,000 was a sizable amount for them at the time and would not have been possible but for Augustus's wife, Charlotte, who inherited some money from her father. Their intent was to lay out a new city beginning at what became Allen's Landing at the point of a natural turning basin where White Oak Bayou comes into Buffalo Bayou.

From the very outset, the Allen brothers "imagined a great city" arising from their initial, humble plat.[14] Interestingly, the parcel of land the Allen brothers purchased came not only from the original Austin land grant but from an Austin family member. John Austin befriended his distant cousin, Stephen F. Austin, in 1822 when John was just twenty-one years old. He assisted Stephen in settling colonists in Texas, eventually owning land himself and operating a cotton gin on Buffalo Bayou. In 1833, he succumbed to a cholera outbreak that swept the area and that also killed his children. His surviving wife remarried in 1834, and in 1836, she sold the southern half of her late husband's land grant to the Allen brothers.

Many would find it surprising in hindsight that the area of modern-day Harris County was so sparsely visited until shortly before the settlements of the 1820s–1830s. Spain politically controlled the area for centuries, administering the territory as a part of New Spain. However, Spain's New World possessions were so vast that permanent settlements in most areas were simply not possible. Spain established cities at Bexar, modern-day San Antonio, and at Laredo on the Rio Grande. However, it was not until Mexico rebelled against Spain that a few revolutionaries discovered the advantages of Galveston Island as a place from which to launch attacks against Spanish ships. Presumably, some early individuals may have cursorily scouted the area of Harris County, but there is no reliable record in this regard.

Before Spain lost Mexico to independence, the Spanish Crown bestowed a large land grant on Moses Austin with the intent that he would bring Catholic Americans into the areas of Texas to settle and become subjects of Spain. This land grant area was in the Colorado and Brazos River basins and did not include the port of Galveston or the flatlands and bayous of Harris County. Moses Austin would be paid 12.5 cents per acre for land by the settlers, which was a good price compared to the average $1.25 per acre for most available land in the United States. After the revolution, the Mexican government reaffirmed the arrangement with Austin except that they withdrew the authority to collect a fee, leaving as his only compensation the right to receive grants of land himself for every hundred families he could settle in the area.

Moses Austin died in June 1821 even before Mexico was actually independent from Spain.[15] His son, Stephen F. Austin, took over the land broker business and continued bringing in new families, eventually being authorized for up to twelve hundred families. Early settlers in the Colorado and Brazos River valleys faced frequent danger from Indians, including stolen livestock, damaged property, and even death. By contrast, the Harris County area was not permanently settled by Indians in the 1820s and presented a much lower risk.[16] "In 1826, the state government of Coahuila-Texas gave David G. Burnet and Joseph Vehlein permission, as empresarios, to settle six hundred families northeast of what is now Houston." A few months later, it authorized Lorenzo de Zavala to settle five hundred families in the vicinity. Finally, after being ignored for three hundred years of Spanish rule, "the region in which Houston would rise suddenly became hot real estate—a quality it has never seemed to lose."[17]

These new land grantees, however, were really straw men who transferred their rights to a land company composed of prominent businessmen from New York and Boston.[18] The company, the Galveston Bay and Texas Land Company, advertised in the United States and Europe and managed to find buyers. These buyers bought rights to settle in Texas subject to colonization rights, but the price paid did not actually include the land itself. The Allen brothers were among the buyers who jumped at the chance to settle a new and promising area.

Stephen F. Austin established the first settlement of Anglo-Americans in the Mexican territory of Texas. Courtesy of the National Portrait Gallery, Smithsonian Institution.

The Allen brothers combined both good business sense and good political sense wrapped up with strong ambition. John Kirby Allen seems the boldest, and he packed a lot into his brief life. From a young age, John was more interested in work and making money than in school. He got a job as a bellboy at the age of seven when he could hardly have been big enough to manhandle travelers' luggage, especially the large trunks of the day, which were usually heavy even when empty. He moved on to retail sales before accumulating enough money and experience to open a hat store with a partner. Augustus Chapman was quite different from his brother. The more academically inclined, Augustus finished school and began work as a mathematics professor at the Polytechnic Institute of Chittenango, New York. Eventually, John sold his interest in the hat store and Augustus left his academic position. They went to New York City, where the two investors lived until 1832, when they made their way to Texas.

Like most people of the day, the Allen brothers arrived in Texas by ship at Galveston. Travel by land would have taken months and been fraught with danger, especially from Indians and bandits. From Galveston, the brothers went first to San Augustine and then to Nacogdoches to open a land speculation business. When hostilities broke out between Texas and Mexico in 1836, neither brother joined the Texian military but did assist the war effort by running supply lines around the Mexican blockade. Of course, this contribution was also personally profitable to the Allens and caused some controversy at the time. There were rumors of piracy by the brothers, and ultimately they decided to sell their supply ship to the Provisional Government of Texas as a naval ship. This purchase doubled the size of the Texas Navy, which theretofore had only a single ship.

In August 1836, at about the same time the Allens bought the land on Buffalo Bayou, John Kirby Allen announced his candidacy for the new Congress of the Republic of Texas. He won the September election for a seat representing Nacogdoches and immediately set about getting a charter for their proposed new city as well as approval of their proposed name, Houston. The historical record does not reveal what issues of public policy or concern John worked on in Congress, but building his land investment into a profitable enterprise was certainly a priority. And naming his development project for the hero and celebrity Sam Houston could not hurt in either business or political circles. Apparently, it was his sister-in-law, Charlotte, who first suggested naming it for Houston.[19]

The Allens took some risk in even selecting the parcel of land they chose. Foremost, the city of Harrisburg, named for John Richard Harris, had already been established on Buffalo Bayou and surveyed in 1826. It was closer to the Gulf and more conveniently situated. The city had grown and was even suitable to be named the capital of Texas by the Provisional Government of Texas in 1835.[20] Some senior members of the Provisional Government headed to Harrisburg for safety and to await the expected clash between General Santa Anna and General Sam Houston in central Texas. However, after the fall of the Alamo and the Runaway Scrape at Gonzales, Santa Anna moved toward the bayous.[21] The earlier allocation of prestige and recognition made Harrisburg a target, and General Santa Anna burned it in April 1836 as he made his way to San Jacinto. Santa Anna allowed his soldiers to loot the town as well, which included the Harris family home after the Provisional Government had fled.[22] Certainly, the citizens of Harrisburg expected to

Sam Houston was the military hero of Texas and the first president of the republic. The Allen brothers sought to honor him by naming their newly established city Houston and also hoped his popularity would help draw settlers and investors to the promising settlement. Courtesy of the Library of Congress, LC-USZ62-13459.

rebuild after Texas won its independence soon thereafter; however, the Allens purchased their competing land only four months later and soon, with John Kirby's election to the Texas Congress, had their own land investment named Houston, officially chartered and on its way to ultimate success.[23]

In hindsight, the decision by the Allen brothers to establish their new city on Buffalo Bayou seems somewhat odd and even aggressive and hostile toward Harrisburg and the Harris family. The brothers were opportunistic, perhaps even ruthless, in seeking to take advantage of Harrisburg's unfortunate sack and plunder at the hands of General Santa Anna. Additionally, naming their new city Houston was a clever, but calculated move to appeal to sentimentality and patriotic exuberance.

To be fair, there is another aspect of the story of Houston and Harrisburg that could explain the seemingly harsh competition.[24] John Richardson Harris worked hard to build commerce at Harrisburg but simply did not live long enough to see the ultimate potential of his city. In 1829, he traveled to New Orleans to buy supplies for the town but was struck with yellow fever and died within five days.[25] Some accounts state that as a result of his death and the later destruction by Santa Anna, when the Allen brothers came along looking for a place to buy, they could not acquire Harrisburg, even though it was a more desirable location, because they could not obtain clear title. Even with a will, there was no established court system, and while there was a semblance of "frontier legal process," the Allens, accustomed to the neat and tidy system of business and legal certainty of New York, would have been understandably reluctant to buy an enterprise with a possibility

The San Jacinto Monument on the Houston Ship Channel marks the battleground where General Sam Houston defeated Santa Anna in 1836. MSS 1220-1131-01, Houston Public Library, Robert L. Browning Photographic Collection.

of legal dispute arising later. No doubt, they would have weighed that possibility against purchasing another settlement farther up Buffalo Bayou, less convenient perhaps, but without the nagging, ongoing possibility that a legal challenge could arise.

The establishment of Houston probably also simply followed the classic line of American expansion explained only decades later by Frederick Jackson Turner. In 1893, Turner sought to explain the establishment and evolution of American democracy and culture as being rooted in what became known as the Frontier Thesis. The gist of his argument was that American social and political structure was not inherently carried by the early explorers and colonists, but rather it grew in the atmosphere of a "frontier"—a vast area of land free for the taking that offered opportunity to people of all classes and backgrounds.[26] What was required was bold self-confidence, willingness to assume risks (including risks to life and personal safety besides other financial, social, and health issues), hard work, innovation, entrepreneurial spirit, and faith in oneself and the nation.

Turner used his Frontier Thesis to explain the particular way in which American society had grown over time by relying on continually available new frontiers of land and opportunity such that each generation could generate new wealth for their immediate families and the nation as a whole. Turner acknowledged at the time that the American frontier was really gone by about 1890 with American expansion having taken in all of North America between Canada and Mexico. Of course, large areas of wilderness still existed, but they were not unknown in a political or legal sense, and title to those properties were recorded for either government or private citizens. Turner worried about what this change would mean for the future of the United States, given that all of American history to date had occurred within the framework of a frontier and open opportunities for expansion. However, even as Turner expressed such concerns, entrepreneurs found new "frontiers" within already known geographical areas. Certainly, Houston later became a prime example of continually finding new frontiers and opportunities for development within the same city.

Houston in 1836 was undoubtedly a frontier establishment. There were few European inhabitants in the area and rarely an Indian presence. For entrepreneurs like the Allen brothers, the banks of Buffalo Bayou represented a golden opportunity to establish a new settlement that could be a center for neighboring farming and ranching operations, as well as a shipping point for agricultural goods going out to the Port of Galveston, to the

Gulf of Mexico, and onward to the Caribbean, the East Coast, or Europe. By the time the Allen brothers founded Houston, the usefulness of the location was already realized by the Harris family and others in nearby Harrisburg. When considered from this perspective, the Allens really were not even original in their thinking but were nevertheless "frontiersmen" in the sense that they shrewdly took advantage of a political and economic vacuum created by the recent destruction of Harrisburg. One distinction is that the land the Allens platted was not exactly free frontier land since they did actually pay for it with money from Augustus Chapman Allen's wife, but it was nevertheless quite cheap, even by the standards of the day, and was virgin territory open to many possible uses.

The Allens' establishment of a new city essentially in competition with an existing settlement was not itself a new phenomenon in American frontier history. In fact, American settlement of the frontier was, in general, an uncoordinated, spontaneous, and competitive process. Some settlers established not only their own farms and ranches but also took it upon themselves to build mills and open dry goods stores, funeral parlors, schools, and the like. Sometimes a business entrepreneur or professional, such as a lawyer, doctor, or accountant, would find a grouping of new landowners and open a business in the midst, thereby creating a hub and contributing to the growth of a town. Of course, these new towns did not always work out regardless of their nature of origin. The history of the American West is replete with examples of ghost towns, settlements completely abandoned when the inhabitants found the conditions either unbearable, as in the case of Indian attacks or natural disaster, or simply because another, more appealing, settlement evolved elsewhere and acted as a magnet to draw people away from their original settlements.

The massive expansion of railways into the American frontier was also a powerful factor in determining the staying power of many settlements. Often the location of a rail line would spur the establishment of a new town, buttress the fortunes of an existing town, or reduce or eliminate the attraction of a town that was nearby but not so conveniently located to the line. In the case of Houston, there were no rail lines in the area and certainly no roads in the vicinity. Instead, the settlement, like Harrisburg, was located there because of the water transportation afforded by Buffalo Bayou and was otherwise reached only by horse through largely untamed wilderness. Presumably, the Allen brothers would have had an expectation that rail lines and roads would be forthcoming if they could just make their settlement a success.[27]

John Kirby Allen and his brother, Augustus Chapman Allen, founded the city of Houston in 1836 at a turning point on Buffalo Bayou. Courtesy of the San Jacinto Museum of History.

The Allens themselves personified the frontier spirit in many ways. They did not come from money and had no particularly impressive education. John, in fact, possessed only a very basic education. But they were entrepreneurial in spirit from an early age, making the best of what they had, gambling on a move to New York City, and then really taking a risk in coming to Texas. Running a supply ship in wartime circumstances and then betting their future on the seemingly unlikely success of the Texian rebels against the Mexican army took determination and a great tolerance for risk. Finally, using the one windfall to come to them, in the form of Charlotte Allen's inheritance, they promptly speculated on the Buffalo Bayou land purchase, knowing they faced competition from Harrisburg, notwithstanding its recent difficulties. The capacity of the Allens to see a vision, take risks, and boldly try to move forward is certainly admirable in their individual case but really is consistent with a broader movement of frontierism and the personalities of most successful settlers in the American West.

The frontier appeal of Houston and its capacity to draw in bold new entrepreneurs and people of vision would be repeated many times and in many variations in the years ahead. But this original settlement by the Allen brothers was obviously the cornerstone of all that was to come and was perhaps the only real exercise in Houston of the genuine Frontier Thesis as Frederick Jackson Turner would later explain. New frontiersmen would arrive in Houston, but they would arrive on more established trails, then roads, and then railways until the modern era of Houston developed with interstate highways and international airports.

The early days of Houston were, of course, a far cry from the modern civilization and transportation to come. "[Galveston] Islanders sniffed that the state was getting what it deserved—a mudhole, populated by thieves."[28] The famed ornithologist John James Audubon led a group of explorers to the region in 1837, first to Galveston and then to newly established Houston. Audubon described a scene in Houston of a landing "littered with cargoes of hogsheads and barrels" with "drunken Indians" and a capitol building with a "cluster of half-finished houses and tents" and merchandise "sold from booths along mud streets," including "skulls of Mexican soldiers gathered from the battleground of San Jacinto."[29] Even so, the city of Houston was more of a city from the outset than a simple crossroads that developed over time into a city. The Allen brothers "hired Gail Borden, Jr. and his brother Thomas to survey the property and lay out the town" properly and with sufficient streets, squares, and planning that a city of obvious organization could evolve according to a planned vision.[30]

Geography and Climate of Houston

The geography and climate of Houston that made it so undesirable to Indians and unpleasant to Europeans was less problematic to later American settlers. By the time the Allen brothers came along, the principal focus was on trade, which required good water connections. Other problematic conditions could be managed or eventually conquered.

Geographers describe the city of Houston as being situated in the Coastal Plains area of Texas. The term describes a vast geographical area stretching inward from the Gulf of Mexico to the Balcones Fault of Central Texas. The area runs as far northeast as the Piney Woods of East Texas and as far southwest as the present city of Del Rio on the Rio Grande at the border with Mexico. The term "Coastal Plains" obviously describes a varied area that includes diverse landscapes, flora, and fauna. However, the term also distinguishes the area from other more distinct regions such as the North Central Plains area of Abilene and Dallas, the High Plains of Lubbock and Amarillo, and the dry, often mountainous region of the Chihuahuan Desert area of Laredo, Ft. Stockton, and El Paso.

Houston's particular locale in the Coastal Plains is a flat terrain that includes forested areas and grassy prairies but has a particularly large number of rivers, creeks, streams, bayous, and terrestrial masses associated with water, such as marshes and swamps. The famous Buffalo Bayou runs through downtown Houston and becomes the Houston Ship Channel. However, Buffalo Bayou is also supplemented by White Oak Bayou, Brays Bayou, and Sims Bayou. The tributaries combine to flow through the modern Houston Ship Channel and thence into the Gulf of Mexico.

The term "bayou" is unique to the southern United States and comes from a Creole French word *bayuk*, which refers to a small, tributary watercourse that feeds into another one, and can be generally used to refer to slow-moving bodies of water that are often marshy, swampy, or otherwise sluggish. Such areas are found throughout the southern United States, but especially in Mississippi, Louisiana, and Southeast Texas, where bodies of water, moving generally southward, flow into each other and eventually into the Gulf of Mexico.

The geology of this region of the country has developed from millions of years of river flow carrying sediment from the Rocky Mountains and layering it upon organic materials that were buried and decayed in pools wedged between sedimentary rocks. Of course, it is these pools of decomposed plant and animal material that eventually produced the massive oil and gas

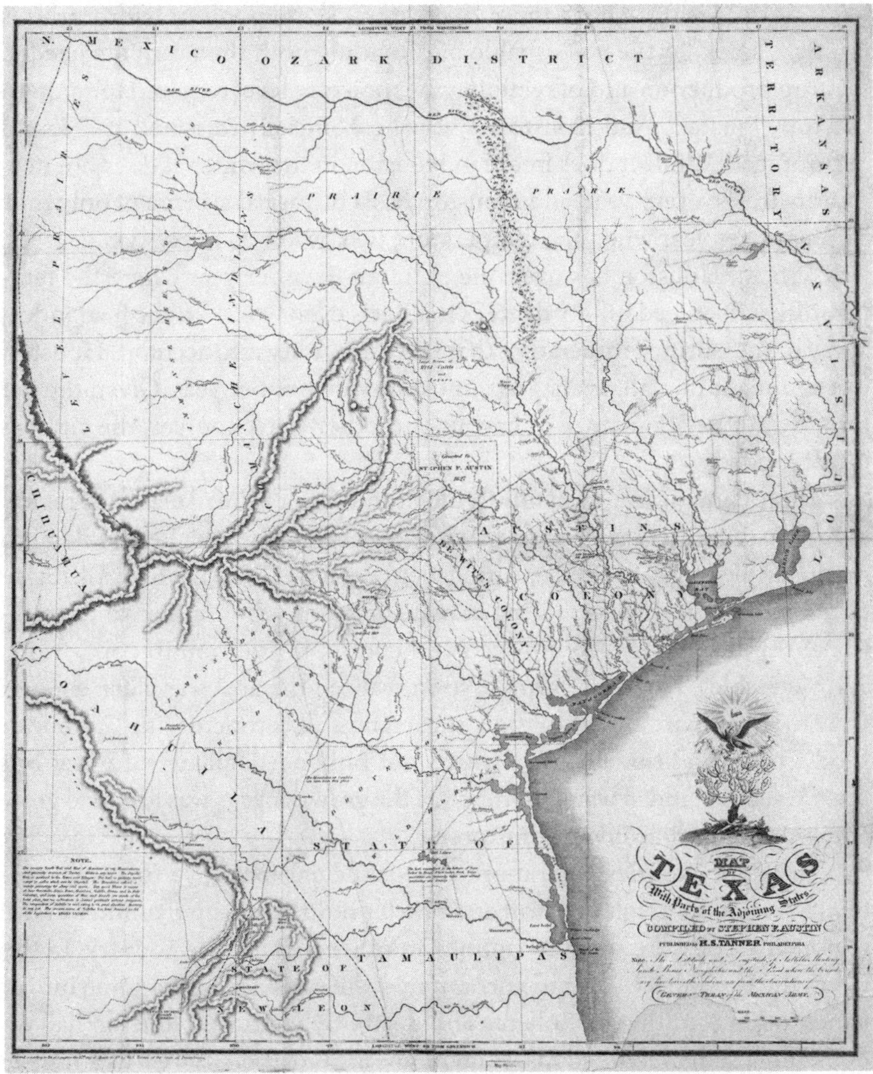

Map of Texas showing Austin's Colony and the settlement of Harrisburg near Buffalo Bayou, 1830. Houston would be established nearby in 1836 following independence from Mexico. Stephen F. Austin, Cartographer, and Henry Schenck Tanner, Map of Texas with parts of the adjoining states (Philadelphia, PA: Published by H. S. Tanner, 1830). Courtesy of the Library of Congress, Geography and Map Division.

fields of the region. Above these layers of rock and pools of hydrocarbons is a rich, black, fertile soil capable of providing both the nutrients needed for crop production and of retaining the moisture level required for growth in a hot climate.[31] And Houston is very hot, officially classified as "Humid Subtropical." While it does freeze in Houston in the winter, it does not necessarily freeze every year, and Houston has a historical average of only thirteen days per year when the temperature falls as low as thirty-two degrees. By contrast, Houston has over one hundred days per year where the temperature will exceed ninety degrees that feels even worse on the heat index, a way of measuring temperature that takes humidity into account. Houston has abundant rainfall, averaging almost fifty inches per year. Given the flat terrain and the abundance of bayous and other water sources, the city has often flooded.

These climatic factors of mild winters and ample rainfall made the region attractive to farmers seeking to maximize yields and to ranchers looking to minimize feeding cattle and ensuring plenty of water for them to drink. Early farmers in the region found the climate and soil very conducive to traditional southern crops like tobacco and cotton, in addition to corn, fruits, and vegetables. However, farmers soon realized the area was close enough to a tropical environment to grow sugarcane and compete with Caribbean production. Additionally, rice, which not only needs plenty of water but must actually stand in water for much of the growth cycle, was found to grow and produce prolifically in Houston.

The opportunities were more than sufficient incentive to attract settlers who had to weigh the farm and ranch production opportunities of the region and compare them to options in other parts of the country. In the 1820s, the land rush westward encountered stiff resistance from some Indian tribes, often resulting in violence and death. By contrast, Houston had no permanent Indian settlements. While some areas of the Midwest had already greatly reduced the Indian threat, there were also the climatic problems of harsh winters and periods of drought. Additionally, land was more expensive where there was greater competition, whereas in Houston, there was much more land than there were settlers.

The opportunity in Houston centered around trade, specifically trade structured to move interior agricultural crops to the Gulf of Mexico and thence to the United States, Caribbean, Europe, and elsewhere, as well as to move refined and manufactured goods from those foreign locations back to Texas and the remote interior regions. Buffalo Bayou was the key to this vision that occurred to the Allen brothers and others.

Early Development of Houston

Even "before the last Mexican Army had withdrawn from Texas soil, in 1836, men with an eye for business had taken steps to exploit the water route from Galveston to the interior."[32] Everyone seemed to realize that trade with the United States and foreign powers had to occur through the Port of Galveston given that the inland routes were so vast, underdeveloped, dangerous, unreliable, and slow. Finding the best water route from the interior of Texas, both the areas developed and those expected to be developed, was not so clear. Different interest groups who sought land rights at various strategic points heavily lobbied the Congress of Texas. One fear was that "if the Brazos River were made generally navigable—as many still expected it to be—then the Buffalo Bayou route to the interior would lose much of its significance."[33] This was important because many new communities were established in the Brazos River valley in the same time period as Houston.

In this plethora of new communities, it was the Allens' promotion skills that made the difference for Houston. They stressed the fact personally, and in numerous newspaper advertisements, that "not only was Houston convenient to interior points . . . but it was connected by water with the coast and foreign countries."[34] They further stated that "vessels from New Orleans or New York can sail without obstacle to this place, and steamboats of the largest class can run down to Galveston Island in 8 or 10 hours, in all seasons of the year."[35] Their statements were, of course, promotional advertising since the waterway at that time had stretches that were "narrow and tortuous, with overhanging trees along the banks and dangerous snags in the water."[36]

The Allens boldly asserted a grand vision for Houston: "In a few years the whole trade of the upper Brazos will make its way into Galveston Bay through [our Buffalo Bayou channel]."[37] Only Harrisburg was geographically positioned to be a real trade competitor with Houston, and "Houstonians regarded that place as their chief rival in the Galveston Bay area during the Republican era."[38] However, "Harrisburg never [was able to recover] its position after its destruction by Santa Anna."[39] Many people had already moved away, litigation tied up clear title to land, and outsiders derided the city either to negotiate a better price on property or to quell competition. Not only did Houston have the Allen brothers to aggressively promote the city, but the town merchants did their part by "establishing trade routes to their town, extending attractive credit to customers, and providing a good selection of goods at the best prices possible."[40] In the end, Harrisburg was left far behind.[41]

In the early days, the trip from Galveston to Houston was a long and difficult journey. Some travelers reportedly passed time by hunting alligators, which were plentiful in the bayou environment. Courtesy of the Woodson Research Center, Fondren Library, Rice University.

Given the heavy industrialization of the broad urban setting of modern Houston, it is difficult to imagine the truly remote, untouched nature of what would quickly evolve into a global city. Houston & Texas History Research Collection, University of Houston Libraries Special Collections, George Fuermann "Texas and Houston" Collection.

Galveston was the other, and later more vigorous, competitor to Houston. Even so, there was a surprising lack of competitive action or spirit between the two cities for the first few decades. Houston was specifically located on Buffalo Bayou to make itself a funnel for trade between the Texas inland and the Port of Galveston, not really to replace it. It would take time for Houston to become a place where the city could realistically think in terms of being able to supplant Galveston.

The Allen brothers, however, had land to sell, and they immediately sought to prove their new city to be a true "port," just as they advertised in their many promotional materials and newspapers.[42] In fact, in 1837, less than a year after Houston was formed, platted, and announced, "they hired the steamboat *Laura* to take a load of investors and potential investors to the lots purchased in Houston."[43] John Kirby Allen himself was on board to personally guide his guests and investors. Also on board was businessman Francis Richard Lubbock,[44] later governor of Texas and namesake of the Panhandle city.[45] The *Laura* was the "smallest steamboat in Texas" at the time and made an easy voyage up Buffalo Bayou to Harrisburg. However, the onward journey from Harrisburg to Houston, a distance of only five miles, took three days due mainly to obstructions in the water and the very careful navigational maneuvers the crew had to take in order to safely negotiate the bayou.[46] But the important point was that a steamship carrying passengers and cargo had actually called at Houston, and the Allens used this to successfully advertise for still more people and goods to come calling by water. "The *Telegraph and Texas Register* . . . headlines boldly proclaimed 'The Fact Proved,' upon the *Laura*'s arrival."[47]

The Allen brothers were aided in their promotional efforts by the Republic of Texas government, which sought diplomatic recognition abroad even before achieving victory over Mexico simply to obtain political support and the survival of the nascent nation. Besides representation in Washington, the republic established consulates-general in London and Paris with additional consuls posted to "Marseille, Bordeaux, Cette, Rouen, Bayonne [as well as] Liverpool, Falmouth, Plymouth, Kingston-upon-Hull, Newcastle-upon-Tyne, Dublin, Glasgow, Greenock, Amsterdam, Rotterdam, Antwerp, and Bremen."[48] While the initial posts overseas primarily sought security against Mexico through diplomatic recognition, the later openings in European industrial centers were obviously more focused on international trade. Besides helping secure business, the Texan diplomatic presence abroad "inspired British and European immigration in a strong, steady flow."[49] Once the new European immigrants settled in Texas, they naturally thought of their homelands when considering trade, thus feeding a circular flow of international business with Houston as the center point of that relationship.

Transportation Challenges and Competition with Galveston

Houston and Galveston began a commercial city codependency in the early years that continued for some time despite occasional competitive outbursts. "The port of Galveston was Houston's outlet to deep water" in the early years before Houston eventually constructed its own deep-water channel. "Almost all the cotton and grain harvested in the Brazos Valley came down the river to Houston before being shipped to Galveston for export." But without Houston, Galveston did not have a link to inland commerce, and Houston was rapidly growing to be the "center of Texas' consumer market." Hovering over all of this was a thought too awful for Galvestonians to contemplate: "If Houston ever got its own deep-water port, there wouldn't be much reason for Galveston to exist."[50]

Criticism of the new city of Houston came from some quarters, as well as skepticism from the press that one really could carry on trade up the narrow bayou. To counter this, the Allens arranged for a much larger steamship, the *Constitution*, to come up from Galveston to Houston.[51] The narrowness of Buffalo Bayou and the obstructions in the water that had hindered the *Laura* were even more problematic for the *Constitution*, the largest steamboat in Texas and almost double the length of the *Laura*. There was simply not enough room "for the vessel to turn around, and it was forced to back up until it reached a wide spot where it could turn. The spot became known as Constitution Bend, and it is the site of the present Port of Houston's Turning Basin."[52]

The steamship traffic, once jump-started by the Allens, increased rapidly until it was a daily service between Houston and Galveston by 1840.[53] The capital moved from Houston to Austin in 1839, and "Houston's newly formed Chamber of Commerce realized Houston's growth and prosperity depended on its sea route [and] in the spring of 1840, the chamber began clearing the bayou of wrecked boats to make the waterway safer and more appealing."[54] "In 1841, the Houston City Council passed an ordinance establishing the Port of Houston, giving it authority over wharves, landings, slips and roads on Buffalo Bayou within city limits."[55] In 1842, "the Republic of Texas's legislature authorized Houston to remove wrecked steamers from Buffalo Bayou and permitted a tonnage tax on ships entering the port."[56]

As Houston grew and prospered, it only proved more valuable to Galveston as a trade funnel for the inland areas. Certainly, "merchants often

The well-publicized voyage of the steamboat *Laura* was very important to demonstrate the feasibility of travel by water between Galveston Bay and Houston. Courtesy of the University of North Texas Libraries, Portal to Texas History, Heritage House Museum.

had business interests in both towns and considered the two as terminal points of a single trade route rather than competitors."[57] The Houston media happily greeted the arrival of foreign ships in Galveston, since they knew the goods on board would soon be in Houston for sale or for onward shipping. They also knew that Texas goods would be passing through Houston to be loaded for a return trip to an overseas market.[58] Cotton was the primary early commodity to move through Houston for loading onto ships in Galveston. "In 1839, only eight bales of cotton were shipped from Houston"; this had increased to 4,260 by 1842 and 11,359 by 1845.[59] Thus, "by the time Texas became a state, Buffalo Bayou was the only stream in Texas that was dependably navigable, and Houston was permanently established as a way station where water and land routes met."[60] In 1846, George Stealey, an engineer, wrote a report to General Sidney Sherman extolling the virtues of the waterway between Houston and the bay and recommending that a full harbor be constructed there.[61]

Competition did eventually arise between Houston and Galveston, but much of it grew out of a dispute over railroads and how they would be planned and developed. Houston developed its then modest port with attendant wharves, docks, and related shipping and trade facilities. Galveston did the same but with accommodation for larger, oceangoing cargo ships. However, land transportation remained a problem for movement of raw goods to Houston in the first place. Some commodities, especially cotton, could be taken in modest amounts by small vessel downriver from various points of the Brazos River valley to Buffalo Bayou. But as the population of Texas grew and more farms and ranches were established farther inland, the practical availability of water transportation diminished. That left interior roads as the only option, although a poor one in the early days of statehood. An early visitor to Houston commented on ground transportation to Houston, saying that "it is scarcely accessible by land in the rainy season, being surrounded by low, wet prairies to a considerable extent."[62] The German historian Ferdinand Roemer "noted that in bad weather much of [the Houston area] flooded, presenting so dismal a sight that many immigrants who intended to settle in Texas returned home after seeing it."[63]

The original plan for the city of Houston shows the importance of navigable water for shipping goods. Special Collections, University of Houston Libraries, University of Houston Digital Library.

Transportation of goods to and from Houston by wagon was slow and unreliable and added considerably to the expense, in addition to the greater risk of damage or loss. The ability to compete in a world market and become a real economic power meant solving all pieces of the trade transportation puzzle from origination to final outbound shipping. "Thus, in the first decade after annexation the economic and political life of the state centered around transportation problems."[64]

Railroads were very much needed in Texas, and early political leaders understood this. However, there were many challenges that made the solution elusive. First, Texas was so vast that railroad costs for even a portion of the state were as much as those for several other states combined. The geographical terrain of Texas required a railroad line to cross mountains, rocky outcroppings, a seemingly endless prairie, a swamp, and other obstacles while addressing issues such as building-material transportation, workers, and hostile Indians. Moreover, the Texas population was comparatively low

Houston was heavily marketed to foreign investors by the mid-1800s but not always accurately. This engraving by a French artist portrays Houston with rolling hills behind a quaint old world bridge and village setting. Courtesy of the Houston & Texas History Research Collection, University of Houston Libraries Special Collections, George Fuermann "Texas and Houston" Collections.

As a growing trade center, Houston was able to position itself as the capital of the new Republic of Texas. This building constructed by the Allen brothers served as the Capitol Building from 1837 to 1839 and again from 1842 to 1845 when the seat of government returned to Austin. The Rice Hotel was built on this site in 1913, which was refashioned into luxury apartments by 1998. Courtesy of the Houston & Texas History Research Collection, University of Houston Libraries Special Collections, George Fuermann "Texas and Houston" Collection.

and very spread out in a primarily agriculture-based economy. The financial capital required for an adequate railroad system in Texas was staggering and unattractive to most investors. None of the railroad companies chartered by Texas were successful.

In the early 1850s, Galveston "proposed a network of railroads leading 'fan-like' to Galveston and bringing the produce of the state to wharves for shipment."[65] A rival vision was "the Corporate Plan, supported by railroad capitalists in the United States and by Houston merchants [by which] Texas railroads would become a part of the transcontinental system."[66] In this way, Texas would not be as insular as under the Galveston plan but would be integrated into the entire US railway system. The advantage to

Houston was really twofold in that the railways would bring goods more easily, more cheaply, and in greater abundance from the nation to be loaded onto ships in Houston for forwarding to Galveston. Additionally, Houston would become the "railroad center of Texas" so that even goods not bound for overseas shipment would still benefit Houston as they passed through the railroad terminal center.[67] Stated a different way, "there was only one way to reach Galveston by rail, but Houston could be reached from many directions."[68]

Politically, the nationally oriented plan was much more sellable everywhere in the state. The political and business leadership of Houston at the time, "including Francis Richard Lubbock, Thomas William House, and William Marsh Rice—toured the state" to support Texas being a part of a national rail link and to fight the efforts to have a rail system oriented toward Galveston and financed with state dollars.[69] The Texas legislature favored the national plan and provided "generous assistance in the form of loans and land grants to private builders. The decision gave Houston a clear-cut victory over Galveston in the battle for interior routes and, in large measure, determined the future of the two cities."[70]

This 1873 engraving shows the head of navigation on Buffalo Bayou where steamboats transported passengers, livestock, crops, and manufactured goods and quickly built Houston as a center for trade in Texas and the South. Courtesy of the San Jacinto Museum of History.

New railroad charters were granted, and new lines and connecting spurs began to appear linking Houston to agricultural towns farther inland in Texas. Galveston became directly linked to Houston by rail, and rail service was built between Houston and New Orleans. "By the eve of the Civil War, Houston was established as the railroad center of Texas [bringing about] an era of unprecedented prosperity to the town in the late 1850's."[71] Once again, cotton was the most important commodity, and the volume moving through the Port of Houston was a good indicator of the city's growth and prosperity. "For 1854 the number was 39,923 [bales]; by 1858 it was 63,453; and by 1860 it had jumped to 115,010."[72]

Houston in the Civil War

The election of Abraham Lincoln as president of the United States, and the outbreak of the Civil War the following year, interrupted the economic rush of Houston. Texas seceded from the Union in 1861, over the objection of state hero Sam Houston, who had led the state to independence from Mexico, served as president of the republic, became a US senator from Texas, and by the time of secession was governor. Because Sam Houston refused to recognize the legitimacy of secession, and likewise refused to swear allegiance to the Confederacy, the Texas legislature removed him from office in 1861, and Texas moved, along with the rest of the South, into a devastating and ultimately unsuccessful war with the North.

The great battles of the Civil War were not fought in Texas, and the widespread destruction familiar to the history of the Old South was not a part of the Texas story. Texas was remote enough that it did not suffer serious damage, but it is certainly true that the prosperity of the state, and of its trading centers in Houston and Galveston, was hurt by the interruption of commerce.

The Union imposed a blockade of the coastline, which included the Texas Gulf Coast. The Union had more and better-armed ships than the Confederacy, making it impossible for all but the boldest blockade runners to move any goods in any direction. Additionally, the larger Confederate ships capable of carrying significant supplies or heavy armaments were slower and more cumbersome and therefore more likely to be captured by the Union. Over time, smaller, swifter boats proved the most adept at slipping past the blockade or escaping once detected. The most important commodity moving through Houston and Galveston was cotton, and the demand for cotton in Europe, particularly the United Kingdom, made it worth the risk to keep some of it moving abroad to secure money, as well as supplies and weapons, to fight the war.

"Foremost among those engaged in the trade was Thomas William House, whose mercantile interests at Galveston and Houston dated back to the days of the Republic."[73] There are reports of House's ships running the blockade to bring arms and ammunition up Buffalo Bayou to be unloaded in Houston, then going back out carrying cotton, running the blockade again, and selling the merchandise abroad.[74] Income to House, or any merchant, depended on the cotton reaching a European buyer before being intercepted by the Union.

Galveston, as a relatively safe base for blockade running, was only briefly interrupted in the Civil War. The Union captured Galveston on October 4, 1862, disabling the one big gun the Confederate forces still had on the island but allowing Confederate forces to withdraw.[75] Soon thereafter, a Confederate force led by Major General John McGruder launched a surprise attack on January 1, 1863, forcing the surrender of Union occupiers, but he was unable to stop a number of Union ships from sailing away to safety.

The Confederacy held Galveston for the remainder of the war until surrender by the South in 1865. In this way, the area enjoyed a special quietness during the conflict, and with Galveston occupied by Confederate protectors, a Union force would not be coming up the bayou to Houston. Furthermore, a land force coming across a vast swath of Confederate territory to reach across the Deep South to Houston was virtually impossible. Thus, Houston sat in relative security. "Indeed, Texas as a whole saw so little of the war that one observer commented at its end that 'Texas was never whipped in spirit, only nominally whipped.'"[76]

E. N. Gray, a resident of Houston at the time of the Civil War, later recalled the experience of the Union victory. Gray was born in 1861 and was only a small boy when the war ended. His father was publisher of the *Houston Telegraph,* one of the earliest newspapers of Texas. He recalled a June day in 1865: "I was playing in the yard when I heard a noise—or music, if you could call it that—of a drum and fife corps, and knew soldiers were coming." He recounted that the soldiers had darker uniforms than any he had seen before, shiny guns, a different flag and were the first Yankee soldiers to enter Houston. They came up from their landing at Galveston to take possession of the courthouse."[77]

In the end, the Civil War interrupted the prosperity of Houston, but it did not destroy it. Although Galveston saw at least some measured level of damage with the initial Union invasion of the port in 1862 and the Confederate recapture in 1863, Houston saw no battles at all and no military damage to its basic infrastructure. To be sure, there was a lack of maintenance during the Civil War period and a certain level of cleanup and refurbishment that needed to be done. And Houston did experience some looting damage both from retreating Confederate forces and from the entry of Union troops at the end of war. However, it was an altogether different circumstance than faced many Southern cities. Not only did Houston bounce back quickly, but Houston and Galveston were able to rather quickly resume their intense competition to be the center of trade and global access for Texas.

Seeking a Deep-Water Port for Houston

Houston's leadership worried that "should technology offer improved overland access to Galveston, Houston could find itself bypassed, [and in fact] in the 1870s, Houston's port lost its passenger traffic after railroad access to Galveston improved."[78] Houston hit upon the idea of seeking to bypass Galveston in the cargo business by establishing the "Houston Direct Shipping company, created in 1869, [for] loading and unloading oceangoing vessels in Bolivar Roads at the mouth of Galveston Bay and transporting cargoes to and from Houston on barges."[79] As a further incentive, the ships would thereby avoid the harbor fees incurred by using the Port of Galveston.

This was only an interim step, however, as Houston sought to create a deep-water channel of its own so that ships had the further option of coming directly to downtown Houston if business necessity or convenience made it undesirable to offload at Bolivar. The dream of a deep-water port, with the capacity to support heavy ships from the ocean to the foot of Main Street in downtown Houston, was not new. In fact, "the idea of converting the bayou into a ship channel was considered as early as 1845 and never abandoned."[80]

The Buffalo Bayou Ship Channel Company was chartered in 1869 with the goal of creating a nine-foot channel that would reach Main Street,"[81] the goal being to bring the ships right up to the business center of the city as was already done in such major ports as New York and New Orleans. "Houston is so intent on so deepening and straightening her bayou that any vessel that can pass at the bar at Galveston may discharge at her wharves, fifty miles inland."[82] As a further boon to Houston's desire to be a real deep-water port, the United States made Houston a port of entry in 1870, permitting international cargoes.[83] The Buffalo Bayou Ship Channel Company began work to implement these plans, but government and private money soon dried up in the Panic of 1873.

In the post–Civil War era, Houston was helped by its own initiatives and by others who had problems with Galveston. The 1873 setback proved

Charles Morgan, the New York–based shipping and railroad magnate, was one of the first American business leaders to see the enormous opportunities of the Houston region. From Nathaniel H. Morgan, *Morgan Genealogy: A History of James Morgan, of New London, Conn., and His Descendants; from 1607 to 1869* (1869).

to be short-lived because of the aid of Charles Morgan, who was angered by the policies of Galveston. Because Galveston was a port city, many business and political people really only knew the city through the Galveston Wharf Company, "or the Octopus of the Gulf as they called it, a convenient scapegoat for all the economic ills of the state."[84] Charles Morgan was the individual who proved to be the most important catalyst of conflict and competition between Houston and Galveston.

Morgan was born in Connecticut in 1795 and by the 1850s had built a large and successful steamship company. He came to monopolize the Texas Gulf Coast trade because he found a way to engineer around a perpetual

Galveston Bay problem: sandbars. Although cargo ships were perfect in so many ways, the challenge was the deep keel that made it difficult for them to navigate around sandbars that could be as little as five feet below the surface.[85] Morgan successfully used shallow-hulled schooners in concert with his larger ships to quickly and cheaply transport cargo.[86] Additionally, lightering of cargo in Galveston Bay was often to the advantage of Houston, because if the lightered cargo was destined for Houston or Galveston anyway, it made no sense for the smaller ships to then proceed to Galveston but instead to haul their cargo directly up the bayou to Houston.[87] "By 1876, Morgan had completed digging a canal across Morgan's Point, named for an earlier and unrelated Morgan, and built a 250-foot turning basin where Sim's Bayou met Buffalo Bayou."[88] "In April 1876, the *Morgan*, an oceangoing side-wheeler that drew nine and a half feet, entered . . . making Houston a seaport—at least for smaller vessels."[89]

Houstonians who were trying to grow their own port and related wharves and freight-forwarding operations originally viewed Morgan with disfavor as a monopolist. But in time, the Galveston Wharf Company's monopolistic practices hurt its own image and played "a leading role in driving Houston to seek deep water."[90] Houston determined that if it could not break the business monopoly, the city would have to make its own port so much more attractive that the monopolists would come to Houston. Over time, and with some twists and turns, this worked.

Charles Morgan began to feel the heat of competition himself with the entry of the Mallory Line, a steamship company operating cargo between New York and Galveston. Morgan and Houston business leaders found it mutually convenient to establish the Port of Clinton on Buffalo Bayou, dredged twelve feet deep and connected to Houston with over seven miles of railroad track.[91] At about this time, the Houston Direct Navigation Company was established to provide expert piloting and navigation services on Buffalo Bayou but also to facilitate a way for merchants to avoid wharfage charges at the Port of Galveston.[92]

Houston, with a growing and diverse economy, had many reasons to seek ever-better water transportation. Although cotton was king, it was not the only commodity important to Houston. In 1880, traffic in cotton reached over thirty-seven thousand tons, but there were also thirty thousand tons of lumber, ten thousand tons of coal, sixty thousand tons of iron rail, and thousands of tons of other goods.[93] The port was important to agriculture, the backbone of the economy, but also to the many goods associated with it, as well as the trade in consumer goods flowing from agricultural profits.

Houston relied on being an equal to Galveston in international shipping because any ship that "could cross the outer bar at Galveston could proceed to Houston."[94] But in 1880, "army engineers selected Galveston as the Gulf port for the American West" as part of a national plan to facilitate better and cheaper transportation for a burgeoning post–Civil War economy.[95] As part of this national recognition, the federal government began work to remove the major sandbar at Galveston and thereby improve Galveston's position as an international port for larger oceangoing ships. A further problem for Houston at this time was a report by the army engineers that Houston's own channel "was filling badly and that it could be maintained only by expensive revetments or continual dredging."[96] Houston business and political leaders organized to leverage federal help. This effort was at least partially successful because Congress appropriated funds in 1881 "for the improvement of the bayou between Clinton and Houston."[97] This at least kept Houston relevant both businesswise and politically, although the value of shipping cargo began to decline in the late 1880s.

A further impediment was that although Houston had real ocean access as of 1876, it was dependent on the Morgan's Point Canal, which was privately owned and constructed with private money. There was actually a chain across the entrance so that it could be used only by Morgan Line ships or by ships that paid a usage fee.[98] Eventually, the Morgan's Point Canal was acquired from Morgan's heirs, but that process was not completed until 1892.[99]

Congressional support for Galveston continued, and in 1890, federal money arrived to complete a series of jetties in Galveston Bay, thereby increasing docking facilities, mitigating the effects of wave action and silting, and raising the water farther over the natural sandbar of the harbor.[100] This had "dire implications" for Houston since its own barge traffic would become obsolete once ships could go directly to portside in Galveston and not have to unload in the bay.[101] Meanwhile, only small ocean ships could get up the bayou to Houston since the depth was not sufficient to support truly large, heavy cargo ships. With the literal survival of the city at stake, "Houstonians launched a deep-water movement of their own in the late 1890's."[102]

In 1896, "Joseph C. Hutcheson introduced a bill requesting a survey for a twenty-five-foot channel to Houston." The bill passed the House and the Senate, and Hutcheson, who was not seeking reelection, "arranged for members of the Rivers and Harbors Committee to visit Houston and inspect

Buffalo Bayou the following winter."[103] The committee's visit to Houston was a success, and federal support for an enlarged and improved Houston Ship Channel was approved.[104]

A new army board of engineers headed by Colonel Henry Martyn Robert met in Houston in 1897 to determine the best plan for the ship channel.[105] The next challenge for Houston was how to have any political influence on the appropriation of federal funds. Tom Ball had replaced Hutcheson in Congress, which by 1898 was Republican-controlled and led by Speaker Thomas B. Reed. Congressman Ball requested to be assigned to the Rivers and Harbors Committee but saw little chance of that happening. In the end it did happen, aided in part by political pressure from some influential Houston Republicans who boosted their new Democrat congressman for the advantage of their hometown.[106]

A delegation of prominent Houstonians arrived in Washington to speak to the committee and lobby the decision-makers. This delegation included former Congressman Joseph C. Hutcheson along with William D. Cleveland (a former Confederate officer and president of the Cotton Exchange), and H. W. Garrow (a founder of the Cotton Exchange).[107] However, things did not go well for Houston's ambitions. The committee chairman, W. B. Hooker of New York, had been among the delegation well entertained and impressed in Houston; however, he left Congress to assume a judicial position. The new chairman, Theodore Burton of Ohio, "emerged as the villain of Houston's deep-water story during the next few years."[108]

In fairness, Burton's hostility was actually based on conversations with some technical experts involved in the project who conceded that although the project was feasible, it might be more costly than it was worth. If ships could unload properly at Galveston, and there were good roads and rails there, there was not a need for ships to go the extra distance to Houston. The counterargument was that there remained the need for a more inland port better protected against wind and wave action in bad weather.

"In 1899, the barge *Jackson* transported the largest cotton cargo ever to travel Buffalo Bayou. The barge was loaded with . . . 5,300 bales of cotton weighing 1,285,861 pounds and journeyed to Bolivar Roads, where it was loaded on the steamship *Catania* for Boston."[109] Promoters of a deep-water port for Houston used this famous load of cotton to purchase newspaper advertising promoting the advantage of deep water at Houston. The advertising copy stated that "had the steamship *Catania* been able to come to Houston, the producer would have saved $2,500 in freight charges." The ad

The channel of Buffalo Bayou allowed Texas cotton to be moved cheaply and reliably to port for shipping to US and foreign destinations. MSS 0087-0268, Houston Public Library, Postcard Collection.

concludes, "With deep water in Buffalo Bayou, this cotton could have been loaded onto a steamer at Houston."[110]

Lumber also became an increasingly important commodity shipped from Houston. The region had vast, lush forests of mostly conifers but many other hardwoods as well. The immense size of the trees made transport by land to Galveston difficult, so shipping directly from Houston was important and added further impetus to the deep-water movement even beyond the demands of the cotton industry. John Henry Kirby founded his famous lumber company in 1901, the same year that Spindletop blew in.[111] Kirby Lumber Company became the largest lumber company in Texas and the southern United States.[112] He was known as the "Prince of the Pines" and figured prominently in Houston for decades.[113]

The Great Hurricane of 1900

For decades, Galveston admirably fulfilled the role of major port of Texas and most important commercial center. Galveston was not only the busiest seaport in Texas, but the city also ranked at the top in terms of population and political and cultural importance. Both France and the United Kingdom operated consulates in Galveston before and after the Civil War, deeming it to be the best and most important place to establish a physical presence in Texas. But Galveston's circumstances were suddenly and radically altered by the Hurricane of 1900, often called the Great Hurricane.

Striking on September 8, 1900, the Category 4 storm remains the deadliest storm in US history, killing somewhere between six thousand and twelve thousand people. Most estimates place the number of dead at approximately eight thousand, but the lack of records, the nature of society at the time, and the passage of time make a precise number impossible. Still, even the lowest estimates of six thousand far exceed the twenty-five hundred deaths in the 1928 Okeechobee Hurricane and eighteen hundred in the 2005 Hurricane Katrina.[114] Beyond the horrific death toll, there was widespread and often complete destruction of homes and businesses. Cleanup took years, and the stench of so many dead bodies could likely be smelled miles away. The vulnerability of Galveston, which was only eight feet above sea level, was suddenly realized.

After the Great Hurricane, some businesses moved to Houston permanently, and others who had initially moved to Houston temporarily then decided to make the move permanent. Of course, those were the lucky ones, because some businesses and their owners were utterly destroyed. The exposure of Galveston was literally laid bare to see, as the hurricane revealed that Galveston could not be protected against hurricanes and no amount of seawall or durable construction could withstand such force, and it was difficult to rebuild confidence. Even the consulates of France and the United Kingdom were permanently relocated to Houston, signaling both unease with the safety of Galveston and confidence in the future of Houston.

The timing of the Great Hurricane also broke down enough political barriers in Washington to enable funding to increase for the Houston Ship Channel. The Turning Basin was designed, as well as cuts in various bends, to allow larger ships to move and pass each other with greater ease and safety. Eventually by 1914, the city dredged a canal between the Turning Basin and the foot of Main Street in downtown Houston that was sufficient for barge traffic but not oceangoing vessels. The long-held dream of oceangoing vessels coming right into downtown was never to be. First, the cost of real estate had already increased so much that it made no sense to use public dollars to acquire enough acreage to make this possible. Second, there was a water connection for barges sufficient to bring to downtown what was not better offloaded to trucks or trains. And third, Houston continued to expand outward until areas suitable for oceangoing vessels were actually within the city limits even if not in the historic downtown.

The cleanup from the hurricane lasted for years and was permanently imprinted on the psyche of surviving Galveston residents. Courtesy of the Rosenberg Library, Galveston, Texas.

The Great Hurricane of 1900 remains the deadliest storm in US history. Courtesy of the Rosenberg Library, Galveston, Texas.

Many businesses and individuals moved permanently to Houston after the Great Hurricane. Special Collection #63, A. O. Rollfing 1900 Storm Collection, 1, Courtesy of the Rosenberg Library, Galveston, Texas.

As Houston moved into the early twentieth century, new community leaders emerged, such as Horace Baldwin Rice, who had a particular passion for Houston's deep-water movement.[115] "Horace Baldwin Rice served as mayor of Houston from 1896 to 1898 and again for four terms from 1905–1913. Rice purchased a large yacht, the *Zeeland,* that was used principally to show the channel to prominent visitors."[116] In this way, Rice served as both mayor and as a one-man chamber of commerce to show off the city from the best view and to highlight one of its greatest features: easy water transport for both people and goods through the channel and into the world.

However, it was Houston's congressman, Tom Ball, who having already done so much to build the deep-water attraction, took things a step further by proposing the creation of a navigation district. The Texas legislature first authorized navigation districts in 1909 to provide for the construction and improvement of waterways. It also gave the districts authority to acquire rights-of-way for improvements. In the case of Houston, this was usually for straightening a bend or removing heavy vegetation that impeded the easy flow of traffic.[117]

Not only did Congressman Ball see the need for such a district in Houston, but he proposed creating it with the power to issue bonds to collect the level of capital needed for a truly deep-water channel and the necessary infrastructure to operate a world-class shipping port. Additionally, Ball reasoned that Congress could then be more easily leveraged to supply generous federal funding that was assisting Houston but was not wholly responsible for the project. Houston embraced the idea, and in "December, 1909, another large delegation from Houston again went to Washington to appear before the Rivers and Harbors Committee. Mayor Rice headed the delegation, and it included many veterans of the cause who had made a similar journey in 1898."[118] The city's proposals were well received by Congress, and the "Houston Plan of sharing the cost of projects with the government set a precedent" that was copied nationwide and was to become a standard for the way the American system would operate in other areas, including highways, parks, airports, and other significant infrastructure development projects.[119]

Harris County voters approved a bond issuance totaling $1.25 million and later approved another $250,000 for additional canal work all matched by the federal government.[120] Selling the approved bonds to a buying public was another problem, but that is where Jesse H. Jones came into the picture.[121] Jones proposed that Houston banks take the bonds "in proportion to their capital and surplus," and in fact, he was able to secure commitments from

Tom Ball was a hardworking congressman for Houston who successfully gained federal recognition of the value of Houston's port and ship channel and support for its massive expansion. Courtesy of the Library of Congress, Prints and Photographs Division, C. M. Bell Studio Collection.

the Houston banks, including his own, to take the bonds within twenty-four hours of making the proposal.[122]

The Harris County Commissioners Court appointed the first three commissioners of the newly established, and now funded, Harris County Houston Ship Channel Navigation District: Charles Dillingham, Camille G. Pillot, and Ross S. Sterling.[123] Tom Ball served as counsel to the commission and eventually became a board member, replacing Colonel Dillingham, who resigned because of ill health.

The navigation district had the right to improve the waterway, but a different agency was needed to manage the waterfront. In 1913, the City of Houston authorized the creation of a city harbor board with Jesse H. Jones

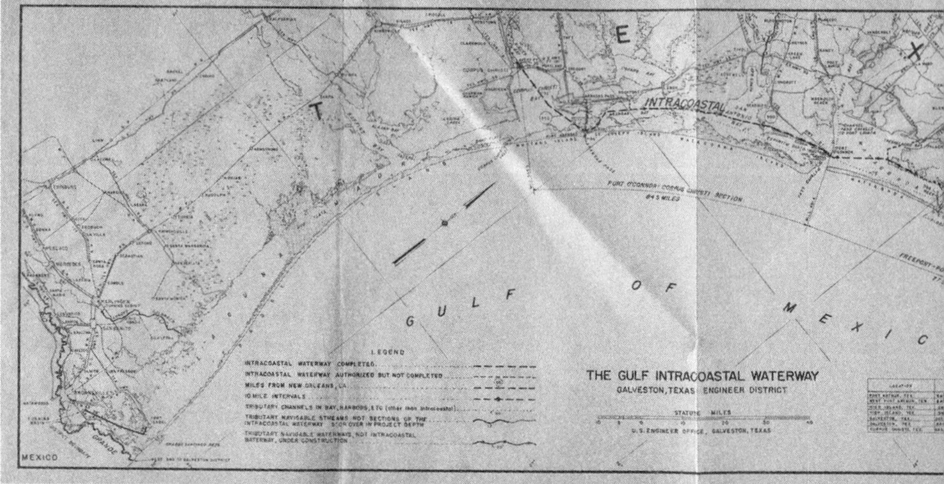

as chairman, and funded by a new bond issuance. Because of some overlap between the county-created navigation district and the city-created harbor board, as well as some inevitable conflicts, the boards were eventually merged.[124]

When the Houston Ship Channel became a deep-water port into Houston, it was extremely important for its own substantial, and continuing, impact on Houston and the region. However, it was also important because of its connection to two other massive water projects of the same time period, the Intracoastal Waterway and the Panama Canal.

The Texas Gulf Intracoastal Waterway is an inland passage that now extends from the Port of Brownsville at the southern tip of Texas to Fort Myers, Florida. It is what was eventually constructed as part of a grand national coastal canal system envisioned by US Secretary of the Treasury Albert Gallatin in a report to the US Senate in 1808. Many factors hindered the realization of this vision, but substantial parts were finally realized.[125]

(*right*) National Geographic Society (US) Cartographic Division, "The Countries of the Caribbean, Including Mexico, Central America, the West Indies, and the Panama Canal" (Washington, DC: 1922). Houston was quick to capitalize on the opportunities afforded by the opening of the Panama Canal in 1914. Courtesy of the Portal to Texas History, University of Texas at Arlington Library, https://texashistory.unt.edu.

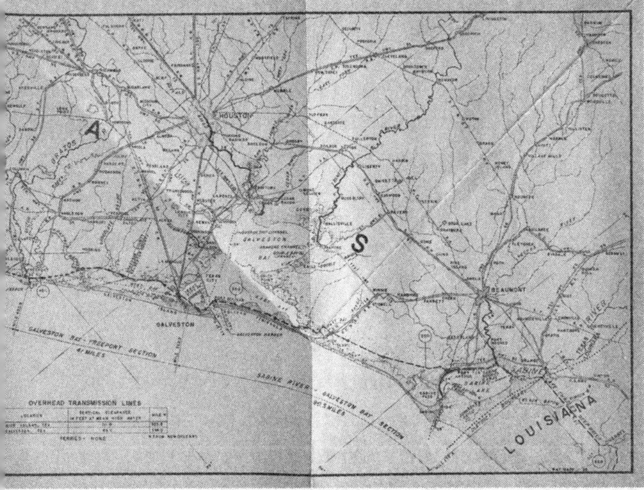

(*left*) Galveston, Tex. Engineering District, "Map of the Texas section of the Gulf Intracoastal Waterway" (1940). The Intracoastal Waterway extends from Texas to Florida, providing a natural route of protected channels and canals. Courtesy of Rice University.

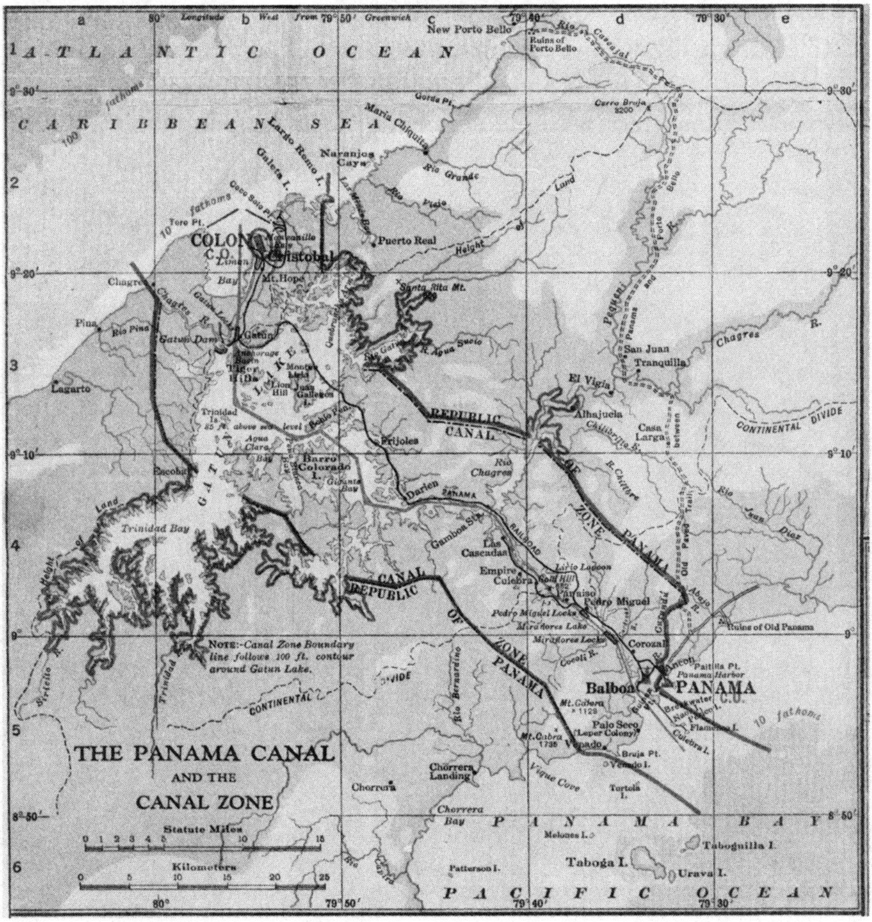

"A two hundred mile segment below Galveston was completed in 1913 [that was] connected with the Houston Ship Channel and developed simultaneously with it."[126] The inland waterway used natural waterways as much as possible to remain inland far enough from the open ocean to be protected by barrier islands and reefs yet be far enough from shore to allow faster shipping and connections along a string of ports and docks stretching along hundreds of miles of American trading centers.[127] Houston lobbied Congress to appropriate funds for the continued dredging and maintenance of the Intracoastal Waterway, recognizing that it was a "tremendous advantage" to the city when connected to its own port and ship channel.[128]

The Panama Canal was the second major water project to complement the Houston Ship Channel in the same time period. Although more remote from the Houston Ship Channel than the Gulf Intracoastal Waterway, the Panama Canal would link the "Atlantic and Pacific oceans and gave the Gulf of Mexico ready access not only to the Pacific Coast states but also to the Far East."[129] Originally begun by France in 1881 and then abandoned, the project was resumed by the United States in 1904 and completed in 1914 in a remarkably parallel time track with the expansion of the Houston Ship Channel,

and with corresponding benefits. "The men working on the channel read monthly reports from the Canal Zone with interest and were sometimes pleased to learn that they had excavated more dirt during a certain length of time than workers on the Isthmus."[130]

It was obvious to Houstonians that large cargo ships that could cross the Pacific Ocean and then transit the Panama Canal needed to be able to come right up the ship channel to Houston. If there were not sufficiently deep water and width, it would necessitate lightering and offloading, which would add costs and delays. In that event, they might just as well sail on to New Orleans or some other port so there would be no interruption between an Asian port and arrival at a US unloading port. The thoughts of capturing such business invigorated Houston to press forward to complete the ship channel as quickly as possible.

The ship channel was finished in 1914, and along the way Houston realized that having the large ships come right to the foot of Main Street downtown was not feasible or even necessary. Instead, the upper reach of the deep-water channel stopped two miles south of downtown but farther north from Galveston than Harrisburg. The upper reaches of Buffalo Bayou

By the late nineteenth century, the growth of Houston reflected its dependence on the bayou/ship channel to connect it economically to domestic and global trade (Houston, TX: n.p., 1891). Library of Congress, Geography and Map Division.

By 1864, Houston already had a well-developed rail system to complement its shipping industry and support the efficient movement of goods to and from the interior of Texas and domestic and foreign ports. From J. H. Colton, *Colton's Rail Road and County Map of the Southern States Containing the Latest Information* (New York: J. H. Colton, 1864). Courtesy of the Library of Congress, Geography and Map Division.

became a better spot for smaller commercial boats, private yachts, or ferries. Houston constructed bridges and pedestrian rails over the downtown areas of the bayou, thereby making the central district more unified and convenient to pedestrians and cars, secure in the knowledge that this would not now be harmful to ever-larger cargo ships.

The official opening of the Houston Ship Channel occurred on November 10, 1914, with much celebration on the banks of the Turning Basin. "Governor Oscar B. Colquitt, Governor-elect James E. Ferguson, and Lieutenant Governor–elect William P. Hobby" were among the prominent dignitaries assembled for the event.[131] In a show of advancing technology and communication, the City of Houston "arranged that President Woodrow Wilson push a pearl-topped button in Washington, to set off a cannon on the banks of the Turning Basin and thus signal the opening of the channel."[132] A telegraph company and a railroad company had cooperated in arranging the link. The president interrupted a cabinet meeting to go push the button at the appointed time, and by exchange of wires, the White House and City of Houston confirmed with each other that the plan had worked.[133] Sue Campbell, the daughter of Mayor Ben Campbell, performed the role of official christener by "sprinkling white roses into the water from the top deck of the United States Revenue Cutter *Wisdom*" and saying, "I christen thee Port Houston; hither the boats of all nations may come and receive hearty welcome."[134]

The Houston Ship Channel in World War I

With all the time and effort to make Houston a real deep-water port and the fortunate timing with regard to the Gulf Intracoastal Waterway and the Panama Canal, it is unfortunate that the vast new opportunity was immediately oppressed by world events. The Deep Water Jubilee of Houston was overshadowed by news of the war in Europe and its effect on global trade, the fulcrum of a modern deep-water port. "For example, on November 9, 1914, the *Daily Post* carried dual headlines: "King Retaw Will Open Jubilee Today," and "Allies' Position Is Said to Be Hopeless."[135]

Many other instances would follow as Houston both celebrated the first arrivals of deep-draft vessels in the ship channel and noted a drop in overall US trade due to the war. Likewise, the local press would proclaim the happy news of regular coastwise service to Houston yet also report that the United Kingdom had placed cotton—so crucial to Houston ship cargo—on the contraband list.[136] Houston businessmen made the best they could of the situation, however, even going to the trouble of traveling to New York to familiarize steamship companies with the Houston Ship Channel and lobby them to utilize its availability. Coal and coke dealer Joseph H. Carroll made such a lobbying trip to New York, and as a result, the first two ocean vessels made use of the new channel in September and October 1914.[137] Further ocean ships arrived but in a slow manner and with varied cargo, showing the global reach the new ship channel provided. In December 1914, a steamer arrived from Central America loaded with coconuts just in time for the Christmas season.[138] Significantly, in June 1915, the first tanker ship with a cargo of foreign oil (from Mexico) arrived in Houston.

To escape the overall slow start, Houston's leaders began devising ways to lure more cargo to the city. First, to establish regular service, a committee from the Houston Chamber of Commerce traveled to New York and in addition to touting the advantages of Houston, they offered to indemnify any losses incurred in providing the services. The Southern Steamship Company "refused the bond, and inaugurated services without it. The company's first vessel to Houston, the *Satilla,* left New York in early August, loaded with seventy-five carloads of general merchandise."[139] It was the beginning of a long relationship between Houston and Southern Steamship. By 1925, the company had added additional ships and Houston had become its most important destination. The company named one of its new vessels *City of Houston* in 1923 in recognition of its large commerce in Houston. In 1920, during a labor strike in New York, Southern Steamship ferried goods from Houston to Philadelphia instead.[140]

The city of Houston was very excited about the arrival of the *Satilla* and regular service from Southern Steamship Company. The mayor led the community in planning a huge arrival ceremony for the ship on August 19 and declared a local holiday. Huge barbecue pits were dug, entertainers lined up, fairgrounds prepared, and, of course, speakers and dignitaries engaged, including the governor and lieutenant governor. The problem was that another big hurricane was brewing in the Atlantic. The Galveston Hurricane of 1915, while not as severe as the Great Hurricane of 1900, still had a devastating impact.[141]

In the years since the 1900 hurricane, Galveston had used fill material to raise its elevation and constructed a solid seawall. While the seawall held during the 1915 hurricane, ships and boats broke up upon smashing into it and water poured over the top into the city, causing widespread flooding. The entire three-hundred-foot city beach was washed away, although much of it reappeared as a sandbar several hundred feet offshore. The storm surge lasted over forty hours with a crest of twenty-one feet. There was widespread damage and loss of life with a total of 275 deaths, mostly in Galveston.[142] By contrast, Houston had approximately $1 million in damage but only 3 deaths. The worst fear in Houston had been whether the surge and churning action of the storm might cause shoaling in the ship channel. Immediately after the storm, a crew worked the channel, taking soundings to determine depth, and reported, to everyone's immense relief, that the channel depth had been unaffected.[143] Meanwhile, the *Satilla* "rode out the storm in the Gulf" and then arrived a few days later to a subdued welcome.[144]

The Galveston Hurricane of 1915 was a stark reminder of Galveston's precarious position on the Gulf and the ever-present risk of storm damage. It also helped reinforce the notion of Houston as being both more protected and, with continually improving transportation and communication, not really much farther from the ocean. The tension with Galveston sometimes flared into the open as Houston postured itself as an international deep-water port and Galveston tried with greater difficulty to maintain its image as the major seaport of Texas and the region. One Galveston defender declared, "If you people at Houston could turn the channel into a pipeline and suck as hard as you can blow, you'd have deep water at Houston."[145]

Expansion in the 1920s Boom and 1930s Depression

Trade in commodities, especially cotton, as well as consumer goods continually drove merchants to seek bigger ships to more efficiently carry the goods. In turn, Houston continually sought an ever-deeper port and ship channel to

Before becoming governor of Texas, Ross S. Sterling was a champion of Houston's development as a major port and shipping center. 1975/070-4945, William Deming Hornaday photograph collection. Courtesy of the Archives and Information Services Division, Texas State Library and Archives Commission.

accommodate the bigger ships, it being obvious that it must grow or be relegated to the side as Galveston had been. However, by the end of World War I, the concern was not just about ships for agricultural products and dry goods but a new and urgent concern about how to accommodate larger oil tankers to move the growing supply of petroleum.

A group of oilmen headed by Joseph Cullinan and Ross Sterling sought and received federal approval in 1919 for a new depth of thirty feet in the channel, which would allow larger ships to call on Houston, and by 1921, Congress had funded the project.[146] Ross Sterling made many contributions to Houston and its port and ship channel,[147] but one of his greatest achievements was recruiting Benjamin Allin to work for the port in 1919. Allin served in the US Army and was stationed in Texas for a while. He sought out Sterling because he wanted to work in the oil business and "was promised employment by him."[148] However, Sterling told him when he arrived in Houston that the port was the better opportunity. What Sterling really focused on was the surplus of warships left with the government. He "proposed to put these to work in the United States merchant marine and encourage the development of American ports."[149] Sterling wanted Allin to guide the port in grabbing all the shipping business they could bring to Houston. Sterling and others in the oil business also directed Allin's attention to the petroleum industry and how it could be developed further, along with related petrochemical plants along the channel. These plans, along with expansion of port facilities for cotton and other products, would enable Houston to enter world-class status as a port city.[150]

Private citizens joined public leaders in efforts to build businesses along the ship channel as a supplement to the business of transportation of goods. One remarkable example was Rosa Allen, widow of Samuel E. Allen, who owned the enormous Allen Ranch. The ranch had made a fortune in the cattle business, including a lucrative shipping arrangement to New Orleans and Havana. Rosa Allen sold seven hundred acres of the ranch at below value as part of a deal to "bring the Sinclair Refining Company to the channel."[151] Other types of industries were also built on the Houston Ship Channel, including flour and fertilizer mills and cotton gins.[152]

Cotton, long the most important commodity, and then after the oil boom, still a very important one, made history again in 1919 when "the first export cargo of cotton was shipped out of Port Houston on the Steamship *Merry Mount*, which carried over 22,000 bales to Liverpool."[153] At the time, Houston was the fourth-largest port in the nation for cotton export but within four years was in second place behind New Orleans. This was accomplished,

Benjamin Allin was recruited to the Port of Houston in 1919. He guided the port in a huge expansion of shipping and the opportunities in petroleum and chemicals alongside the ship channel. MSS0302-032, Houston Public Library, Benjamin C. Allin Papers.

in part, by aggressive building programs to construct the largest complex of wharves, elevators, storage facilities, rail connections, roads, and other infrastructure for both public and private facilities. The private facilities included Anderson, Clayton and Co. with twelve acres of cotton storage and other industries such as Armour Fertilizer, Tex-Cuban Molasses Company, and Texas Portland Cement Company.[154] A new cotton record was set in 1923 when the steamship *Abercos* left Houston for Liverpool carrying 18,810 bales of cotton insured for $4 million, all from the Texas Farm Bureau Cotton Association. It was the largest amount ever shipped at once by a single individual cotton shipper, and the global news stories helped advertise Houston as the place for large-scale cotton shipping to foreign ports.[155]

On April 3, 1924, William L. Clayton, of Anderson, Clayton, spoke to a Houston banquet celebrating the one-millionth bale of cotton shipped through the port in just that one season. Clayton reminded the audience that cotton opens world vistas for Houston. Although it can be successfully grown in only a few places, it is used in every "nook and corner of the world" because "85% of the world's clothing comes from cotton." Clayton went on to compare modern Houston with Renaissance Venice, which owed much of its stature to "the cotton trade between India and Europe." Clayton recounted the many advantages Houston possessed for global shipping and emphasized the need to continue building new and larger facilities to attract more business.[156] Later that year on September 8, Houston got another boost in cotton shipping when the Chicago Board of Trade voted to designate Houston as the delivery point for cotton contracts traded on the Chicago Exchange. The trade units were established at five thousand pounds of cotton or approximately one hundred bales.[157]

As oilmen such as Sterling and Cullinan directed the port's attention to encouraging refineries and chemical plants along the ship channel, they demonstrated that the "ship channel foretold a basic and significant change in Houston's commerce." From being a distribution center to handle goods going elsewhere, Houston became an industrial center itself while continuing to be the most important distribution center.[158] As wealth and population coalesced around it, Houston necessarily became a large consumer center.

William Farish spoke to a Houston crowd in 1924 in his capacity as president of Humble Oil and Refining Co. about the importance of the port to the oil industry.[159] He reminded the audience that although oil permeated conversations and newspaper headlines, it was a very young industry. He spoke of how automobiles had quickly become an indispensable asset to most Americans. However, he also said it was essential to national security, quoting Lord Curzon, that "the allies floated to victory on a sea of oil."[160]

In 1924, the Port of Houston chartered the French Line steamer *Lafayette* to come to Houston, pick up a group of 150 trade promoters, and take them on a Caribbean cruise. The *Lafayette* was 562 feet long, making it the largest passenger vessel to have entered any Gulf port at the time. The cruise made stops in Cuba, Puerto Rico, Dominican Republic, and Jamaica to promote the use of the Port of Houston for international shipping.[161] Port of Houston promoted itself aggressively, stating in marketing materials that it was "anxious to educate the far corners of the world with its advantages, its possibilities, and its facilities."[162] The cruise was successful at bringing in new business and became an annual event for Houston business. In the years ahead the port added stops in Haiti, Colombia, Venezuela, Panama, and the Dutch West Indies.[163]

The Houston Ship Channel began to surge in the 1920s with "new wharves, a grain elevator, additional channel railway, and other channel improvements . . . a continual building program without ever quite catching up with demand."[164] Using a 1922 bond issue, the port facilities were designed for huge increases in international trade with "reinforced concrete" and "structural steel" all wired for power with the belief that in addition to lighting purposes, electric conveyers, loaders, and other mechanical equipment would become the norm.[165] Additionally, the railroad tracks at the port were designed in such a way that each ship berth could be switched independently, allowing up to "thirty cars opposite a ship" at any time day or night for continuous activity.[166] By 1926, Houston had constructed the largest cold-storage facility in the South, big enough to "hold the contents of a train 10 miles long that employed the best chilling technology for the storage, sorting and repackaging of fruits, flowers and vegetables."[167] The fact that Houston was hot and humid was not going to affect the type of goods that flowed through its port.

In the mid-1920s there were over two million wheat farmers in the United States who produced far more wheat than American consumption required. As a result, almost half of the crop was exported, primarily to Europe. Houston sought to become the principal shipping point for wheat. To do so meant not only having the rail and shipping capacity but also the storage capacity to keep wheat in prime condition when surplus needed to be stored to wait for better market conditions or to maintain a supply to cover a short contract while awaiting shipments from the Midwest. Port Houston built a million-bushel capacity grain elevator at the Turning Basin. Additionally, Houston subscribed to uniform grades on grain and employed its own inspector to ensure that grains handled through its facility could be confidently purchased by traders anywhere in the world.[168]

By 1924, steamship commercial lines operated from Houston to places such as Le Havre, Antwerp, Ghent, Southampton, Barcelona, Venice, Trieste, Liverpool, Dublin, Belfast, Bremen, Rotterdam, Amsterdam, [Yokohama], Copenhagen, and Naples. Oil tankers transported vast amounts of Texas crude to East Coast facilities as well as European ports.[169] The Houston port published charts showing the favorable distance to Houston from the Panama Canal, only 1,549 nautical miles, where cargo could be immediately stored or offloaded onto truck or rail. By comparison, it was 1,901 nautical miles to ship to Baltimore, 1,946 to Philadelphia, and 1,974 to New York. Houston advertised its geographic advantages to overseas shippers, showing that it was closer to ship from Hong Kong, Honolulu, Manila, Yokohama, or other Asia-Pacific ports to Houston for overland shipping than to continue on to the East Coast ports with less robust ground transportation options.[170]

An early success of this new approach came in 1927, when a US Department of Commerce official opined that Houston would become one of the great ports due to imports as well as exports, citing the increasing importance of agricultural trade.[171]

International passenger service also expanded greatly in the 1920s with service to Germany, France, Spain, and the United Kingdom. The French Line, operating three passenger luxury liners, stated, "The Port of Houston has a brilliant future," and it is where we can serve "the middle western and western portions of the United States."[172] This statement revealed that the passenger market to Europe looked not just to Houston or Texas, but cruise lines believed that many passengers would travel by rail from Chicago, St. Louis, or Kansas City to board a ship in Houston for their overseas vacation or business trip. Likewise, many passengers apparently traveled from the West Coast by rail to Houston for the same purpose rather than cruise out of Los Angeles or San Francisco and then have to traverse the Panama Canal to reach a port for onward sailing to Europe.

Port Manager Benjamin Allin found a "build it and they will come" sort of attitude in Houston and generally around the country at port facilities he visited. He and the port commissioners determined that such an approach was too risky and that a promotional campaign was essential, starting with the establishment of a "Houston Port Bureau under the sponsorship of agencies interested in the Port's development, among them the City of Houston, the Port Commission, Houston Merchants Exchange, Houston Chamber of Commerce, Houston Cotton Exchange, and the Maritime Committee of the Houston Cotton Exchange." The new "Houston Port Bureau began operations on June 1, 1929, by establishing offices at New York, Kansas City, Dallas, and Houston."[173]

The volume of cotton moving through the Port of Houston continued to grow until by 1930, over two million bales a year were exported through Houston, comfortably exceeding the volume at all other US ports, including the old rival in this area, New Orleans. Also by 1930, the movement of petroleum had grown tremendously, with twenty-seven tanker lines operating to move over 3.9 million tons of petroleum products.[174] Before 1919, no grain shipped from Houston, but then small amounts began to appear in the loading dockets. But once the new grain elevator was opened in 1926, the movement of grain surged to the point that in just the nine-month season of 1929–30, Houston handled almost five million bushels.[175] By the end of the 1920s, Houston was so far ahead of Galveston in terms of facilities, volume of trade, and tonnage of cargo that Houstonians no longer considered Galveston a

A Port of Houston inspection boat in 1919 still patrolled relatively narrow and wild passages in some parts. These rural circumstances would not last much longer. MS 0302-197, Houston Public Library, Benjamin C. Allin Papers.

serious competitor but looked to New Orleans and other major US ports as the real competition.[176] The humorist Will Rogers said in the 1930s that "Houston dared to dig a ditch, and bring the sea to its door."[177]

Private interests in the Gulf region came to understandings before the public officials did. For example, the leading "cotton interests of Houston, Galveston and Texas City" met in 1931 to resolve their points of conflict and settle into a plan designed to promote themselves collectively against competition farther afield.[178] This served as an example to other private businesses and public officials and by 1933 resulted in the Houston-Galveston Equalization Agreement, which "was based on recognition of the common interests of the area." It was regarded as "inevitable that in the course of time the cities of Houston, Galveston and Texas City will be physically merged, and that these three ports are already merely one shipping district serving the same territory."[179] The agreement gave Galveston the equalization it had long sought, although Houston did not really lose anything given its growing paramount position.

Commentators have offered many explanations for Houston's capacity to outdo Galveston. One reason is geography. Houston could continue to sprawl out across the prairies and pine forests, but Galveston was an island hemmed in by a seawall. Related to that issue was weather, where time and circumstance had demonstrated that bad weather might affect Houston but not in the apocalyptically destructive way it could hit Galveston. Politics also played a role, with Houston aggressively seeking favor in both Austin and Washington and doing so at a time when Galveston suffered from great storms, lack of vision and unity, or a combination of bad factors. Houston first surpassed Galveston in population in 1900, but afterward it grew very rapidly while Galveston actually began to decline. Galveston seemed comfortable with the role, however, and became a "solidly established, conservatively and semi-privately operated port whose directors did not seek a mounting volume of traffic, but only the maintenance of its steady level of operations."[180]

On the contrary, Houston embraced its growing role and could boast by 1930 that its port had not only surpassed those of all its Texas rivals but had become the third port in the nation for foreign exports, "being surpassed only by New York and Los Angeles."[181] As a public celebration of its success, "port officials invited the cruiser *Houston* to visit the city for Navy Day, October 27, 1930."[182] The City of Houston played a large role in getting a warship named for the city. Congress had determined to build "eight large cruisers to be named for various United States cities," and the City of Houston launched a massive campaign to secure one of them for Houston. Letters and telegrams poured in, including a massive campaign by schoolchildren and many civic groups until finally the secretary of the navy not only announced Houston as a winner but asked Mayor Holcombe to stop the letter-writing campaign.[183]

The cruiser *Houston* was built in Newport News, Virginia, and once it was completed, a delegation of Houstonians traveled there to watch the mayor's daughter, "Miss Elizabeth Holcombe christen the vessel with a bottle of Buffalo Bayou water," assisted by "Miss Charlotte Williams, a granddaughter of Sam Houston."[184] Later the USS *Houston* visited its namesake city, cruising up to the Turning Basin for a week of festivities and crowds of people lining up to view the warship. The citizens of Houston presented the ship's captain with a silver service designed with images of the Spanish missions in Texas as well as Sam Houston.[185] The port and city hosted a banquet at the Rice Hotel, and Senator Tom Connally "prophesied that within the next decade Houston would become the second port in the nation."[186]

The year 1930 was significant in the history of Houston and its port. The visit of the USS *Houston* "marked the end of one era and the beginning of another."[187] The locals rejoiced in their success of a deep-water port and massive domestic and international shipping. Business and political leaders looked ahead to greater growth and prosperity. But of course the stock market crash had already occurred the year before, and the effects of the

Great Depression were beginning to be felt around the country. It was subtle at first, and in fact "during the first half of the 1930s statistics showed that 30 percent more tonnage passed through the Port than in the same period for the previous year."[188] But then the drop-off began and continued through the following two years. However, for the Port of Houston, the Depression was less severe than for many parts of the nation. The year 1932 represents the severest drop in tonnage (12 percent below that of 1930), and after that the volume of cargo began to increase again, albeit slightly, until by 1939 the port had surpassed its cargo levels at the beginning of the decade. In 1939, Houston ranked as the number-three port in the nation behind only New York and Philadelphia.[189] That same year it was the number-one port in the nation for cotton.[190]

Grain began to be exported from the port again beginning in 1938, making use of a giant grain elevator that had sat unused for some years.[191] Trucking became increasingly important to the port, as greater numbers of trucks and more highways made onward shipment by road often as efficient as rail by the 1930s.[192] Interestingly, scrap iron became a "significant export cargo for the Port during the mid-thirties."[193] In one sixteen-month period of 1936–37, over 150,000 tons of scrap metal were shipped to Japan, which did not have sufficient raw material resources. The Americans of the Depression were glad to make a buck off of castaway junk, including discarded toys, sewing machines, and household tools, and did not think about what Japan might be using all the metal for at the time.[194]

In the 1930s, Houston also benefited from policies of the Roosevelt administration designed to stimulate demand for trade and to aid in a general recovery for the global economy, not just the US economy. One such foreign economic initiative was the Reciprocal Trade Agreements Act (RTAA) of 1934. Roosevelt declared to Congress "that a full and permanent economic recovery depends in part upon a revived and strengthened international trade" and sought from Congress the authority to negotiate trade agreements with other countries in which each would agree to reduce tariffs in a way to make the trade mutually beneficial. This "represented a fundamental shift in U.S. trade policy" since Congress, under the Constitution, has the right to regulate foreign commerce and establish tariff rates. But here, the president would now be able to negotiate, within wide latitude, temporary agreements of several years' duration without the formality of a treaty that required Senate ratification. Additionally, "U.S. tariff cuts negotiated under the RTAA would also be extended to all third countries to which the United States had accorded most favored nation status."[195]

The RTAA gave a great boost to international trade and allowed Houston to benefit from larger volumes of cargo shipping to and from overseas ports. The RTAA particularly focused on Latin American countries, and the Roosevelt administration had earlier targeted many of those countries with individually negotiated trade agreements. The Latin American trade favored the Port of Houston as the closest and most convenient port of entry to the United States. In addition, the General Agreement on Trade and Tariffs (GATT) undid much of the damage done by the Smoot-Hawley Tariff Act of 1930. That act had raised US tariffs on imported goods to record levels, making the movement of many goods economically impossible. Many economists believe Smoot-Hawley accelerated the Depression and made the global economic situation worse.[196] In the case of Houston, the volume of trade passing through the port did drop off in the latter half of 1930 just as the act took effect and recovered later as the act was undone by the RTAA.

Another boost for Houston's international trade in the Depression was the Merchant Marine Act of 1936. Its purpose was "to further the development and maintenance of an adequate and well-balanced American merchant marine, to promote the commerce of the United States, to aid in the national defense."[197] The merchant marine system had long been important to the United States, transporting passengers and cargoes in times of peace and acting as an auxiliary to the US Navy in time of war. However, by the mid-1930s, the merchant marine system was declining with fewer ships, inadequate personnel, abusive management, and poor quality. Congress rectified this situation with the 1936 act establishing quality controls, a merchant marine academy, uniform regulations, and personnel standards. For Houston, this meant a larger volume of more reliable ships coming with more valuable cargoes. And with the RTAA, it also meant trade in many more goods from many more countries than before.

In 1936, a further diversification of the Houston Ship Channel began with the establishment of "Champion Paper and Fibre Company . . . on the channel near Pasadena." This paper pulp mill was not only a new type of business for the channel, but it indicated renewed economic confidence in the region. "Thus, the coming of Champion marked an official end of the depression on the channel."[198]

Port of Houston in World War II

By the time the United States entered World War II, industries related to armaments had also begun to cluster on the Houston Ship Channel, including Dickson Gun Plant operated by Hughes Tool Company; Sheffield Steel

Corporation; Houston Shipbuilding Corporation (a subsidiary of Todd Shipbuilding of New York); and Brown Shipbuilding (under contract to the US Navy). The shipyards at Houston produced many EC2 cargo ships for the military, called Liberty ships, employing eleven thousand workers.[199] Brown mainly built subchasers and destroyer escorts.[200] Additionally, the US Army established a five-thousand-acre site with five miles of channel footage for an ordnance depot.[201]

During World War II, refineries on the ship channel "produced high-octane aviation gasoline and toluene (an ingredient for explosives.)"[202] In this way Houston played its role in making America the "Arsenal of Democracy."[203] Although some new industries boomed in the war effort, the overall volume of trade naturally declined during World War II as more goods were routed by truck and rail to East and West Coast facilities to be more easily moved to the European and Pacific theaters of war. Tonnage

Houston launched a massive campaign to ensure that one of eight new US battlecruisers was named for the city. Pictured is the USS *Houston*. Courtesy of the Cruiser Houston Collection, USS Houston & Military History Research Collection, University of Houston Libraries Special Collections.

shipped at the Port of Houston decreased from twenty-eight million in 1939 to twenty-five million in 1941 to only fifteen million in 1943. Houston's leaders worried about whether shipping would come back to the port after the war or whether merchants would have then settled into new patterns of commerce. They also worried about whether the new war-related industries built on the ship channel would remain in operation in some form or simply shut down.[204]

Fortunately, it did not take long for good answers to become apparent. By 1946, the tonnage had already reached a new high of over thirty-one million, which then jumped to almost thirty-nine million in 1948. More important, the value of cargo shipped through the port exceeded $1 billion in 1948 and doubled again to over $2 billion by 1952. By 1948, the Port of Houston was officially the second-ranking port in terms of tonnage in the nation.[205] After the war, Houston shipping millionaire R. P. Sanguily wrote of Houston's international role in rebuilding Europe: "Houston is the gateway for many shipments" of food and manufactured products flowing to Europe as part of the Marshall Plan and other aid programs that he credited as playing a role in the preservation of Western Europe. Sanguily also trumpeted the Rockefeller Foundation's formation of the International Basic Economy Corporation designed to promote trade ties to Venezuela and the Caribbean Rim from its base at Houston.[206]

Numerous writers and commentators emphasized the capacity of the port to make the economy of Houston and the region surge and to awe people with its size, technology, and grandeur over the years. One of the most memorable was the description by George Fuermann, who called the port the "First of the Seven Wonders of Houston" in his book *Houston: Land of the Big Rich*.[207] In 1947, Houston banker L. R. Bryan Jr. wrote about how Houston's banking industry was linked to its future in foreign trade: "Houston is a great port, [and] the banks of Houston are becoming aggressively aware [of the importance] of working with the foreign trade interests not only of our city but of our surrounding territory." Bryan went on to describe how local banks had become familiar with international trade transactions in order to facilitate Houston's commerce. He declared that Houston's future would be tied to the port and the international business it produced.[208]

Mayor Oscar Holcombe attended a conference in Geneva in 1949 and took promotional materials regarding the port for meetings with foreign export/import representatives.[209] Also in 1949, Houston sent a delegation to New York for the National Foreign Trade Convention composed mostly of port officials and representatives of the major shipping companies, refineries, and chemical plants on the ship channel.[210] They returned the following year and besides handing out printed materials showed a "Technicolor sound moving picture" of the Port of Houston to potential customers, using the Houston Room at the Waldorf-Astoria Hotel.[211]

In February 1950, the Duke and Duchess of Windsor, the former King Edward VIII and Wallis Simpson, visited Houston. The British Consulate advised the city that the duke wanted especially to see the ship channel he had heard so much about. Officials at the port arranged an excursion on board the touring boat *Sam Houston*, where the royal party could see the wharves and the industrial complex leading up to the San Jacinto Monument and battleground site, which they also toured. Sheffield Steel flew the Union Jack above its industrial complex. The contingent also visited the battleship USS *Texas*, where the duke found a photo taken during an earlier visit of himself and his father, King George V, on the wall in the trophy room. A representative of Governor Shivers presented a copy of an 1830s treaty between the Republic of Texas and the United Kingdom.[212] It was clear that the Port of Houston and the ship channel had become an important tourist attraction.

Port of Houston in the Post-World War II Boom

In 1957, Houston secured a bill in the Texas legislature that gave it authority to issue long-term revenue bonds to meet much larger financial obligations for future growth, maintenance, and technology.[213] Houston was then more directly in control of its future growth and means to finance it. Houston benefited from "postwar rebuilding in Europe and Asia [that] required raw materials."[214] These materials were supplied mainly by privately owned shipping lines that acquired vast new fleets of vessels from the US government, whose many "war-construction cargo vessels were surplus to military needs, and the US government disposed of them, selling them to shipping lines at bargain prices."[215] Such a windfall enabled an even greater amount of goods to move out of the Houston port.

One prominent example of such a shipping company was Lykes Lines, established by the Lykes family in Florida in 1900 to ship cattle and later other goods to Cuba in the immediate years following the Spanish-American War. The successful company expanded later to Galveston and then to Houston, which it made its corporate headquarters in 1923. The Lykes became prominent members of Houston society, joining the Houston Country Club, River Oaks Country Club, and Eagle Lake Rod and Gun Club and offered cruises on their ships between ports in Europe and the Americas.[216] The company's fleet was very large by the 1970s, after which through a series of reorganizations and mergers it eventually ceased as an independent company in 2005.[217]

Although the rapid increase of business in the post–World War II era was very welcome, it also "strained the port's capacity. Port facilities needed to be refurbished" due especially to deferred maintenance of the war years.[218] Even before the war ended, "Houston voters approved the issuing of bonds in December 1944 [allowing the] port authority [to] purchase all port facilities owned by the City of Houston."[219] In this way, the Port of Houston Authority had finally consolidated all authority and responsibility for the operation, maintenance, and future of the port.[220] Federal funds began to flow again after the war was over, allowing for the ship channel to be widened and, most important, allowing the depth to be increased to "36 feet over its entire length."[221]

Other improvements also came after the war, including the construction of "two highway tunnels under the Houston Ship Channel." Although the population of this once-open pastureland and swampy area had grown greatly, it was impossible to cross from one side of the channel to another without going into downtown Houston and using the bridge there or by using the ferry service farther downstream, which moved both passengers and vehicles. "The Washburn Tunnel, completed in 1950, linked Pasadena with Galena Park. The Baytown Tunnel, finished in 1953, connected La Porte with Baytown."[222] These communities were quite small at the time but now are large cities within the Houston metroplex.[223]

The news was not entirely rosy in the post–World War II years. The postwar reconstruction boom began to decline after a few years, and therefore the demand on the Port of Houston declined as well. Additionally, "the St. Lawrence Seaway opened in 1954, providing ocean access to the Midwest."[224] Cargoes of Midwestern products, especially cotton, grains, and other foodstuffs, could be shipped from Chicago instead. It still made sense to send goods by truck or rail to Houston if the cargo was destined for the Caribbean, Central America, and South America or was destined to traverse the Panama Canal. But if the goods were going to Europe, for example, they might just as well go out of Chicago through the St. Lawrence and then into the Atlantic. This factor, along with continued expansion of the old rival Port of New Orleans, kept Houston on its toes as time went on. Houston remained the second-busiest port behind New York until 1954 but "slipped to third place in 1955 when Philadelphia inched ahead of it"; in response, a "major expansion of port facilities was planned and funded in 1957, with more wharves and a bulk facility to be added."[225]

In the mid-1950s, the entire structure of international shipping began to change. American entrepreneur Malcolm McLean owned a large trucking company whose business model relied on being able to quickly and efficiently offload cargo at port terminals and then transport that overland to various inland destinations.[226] McLean developed the concept of "a detachable box" that could be stacked on board a ship, locked together, and then locked to the deck. These containers could then be offloaded to trucks with the container locked onto the "bed of a trailer" and driven away. There was no need to pack and unpack as with a traditional cargo ship, making the transfer from sea to land much easier. The early uses of this concept relied on a tanker modified to carry a load of stacked containers on the deck. One of the first, the *Ideal X*, entered the Port of Houston on April 23, 1956, and "its cargo would change the world, revolutionize shipping, and create today's global economy."[227] "McLean viewed the experiment as a success. In 1957, his Pan-Atlantic Steamship Company initiated sea-land service offering scheduled container service [and soon provided] two sailings weekly between Houston and New York."[228]

This new "containerization" of maritime shipping began to reshape the Port of Houston itself. Facilities specifically designed for containers were built, and by 1966 a special crane had been installed to unload multiple heavy containers at a time. By 1970, it was decided to construct a container-only facility and place it "outside the Turning Basin, building at Barbour's Cut at Morgan's Point. The terminal opened in 1977, the first port in Texas designed to handle standardized shipping containers."[229] This facility featured such specialized equipment as gantry cranes, called "Transtainers," that "would allow container ships to be loaded or unloaded in hours, rather than weeks," an almost unbelievable reduction of time.[230]

Simultaneously, the ships and containers themselves were redesigned and upgraded. McLean renamed his company Sea-Land, and instead of modifying tankers to make them cargo deck ships, he designed and ordered new ships designed specially for containers. Labor, time, and costs were all cut drastically by this new method. The cargo was packed once and never needed to be unpacked again until it reached its final destination. Meanwhile, the container could be loaded on or off one or more ships, transferred to a train, then a truck, another truck, and so forth.[231] Because the container was reinforced, the contents were protected against damage, weather, and theft. As customs officials grew confident in the security of the boxes, they could accept an inspection report made at origination without the need to reopen and reinspect each container. "McLean estimated that containerization cut shipping costs by over 97 percent. No shipper could ignore that bottom line. By 1980, the traditional break-bulk cargo ship was as obsolete as sailing-era clippers."[232] The concept of containerization, both the use of such containers and the design of ships and ports to accompany them, spread rapidly across the world. But Japan was especially early to embrace the revolutionary new idea, sending delegations to the Port of Houston to observe and train in order to retrofit their own ports.[233]

The Port of Houston and the Space Center

Nothing screamed "international place to be" like the selection of Houston as the site of a manned space center in 1961 with the prize facility and all its surrounding clusters of businesses built on the ship channel. The Port of Houston was a major factor in the city's selection for the space center. In fact, the requirements NASA promulgated for the manned space center specified that it must have "access to water transportation by large barges."[234] Houston easily met this requirement and dutifully constructed a necessary dock. However, unlike the Kennedy Space Center in Florida, which "needed port facilities to receive boosters [for its launch pads]," the cargo arriving for the Manned Space Center was much smaller in nature and usually just unloaded at the main Turning Basin docks and "trucked to the space center."[235] In fact, the barge dock at the Johnson Space Center "has only been used twice by NASA: once in the 1980s, when a Saturn V was moved to [the center] for display, and once in 2012, when a shuttle mock-up was transported to JSC."[236]

Houston fully realized the extent to which the success of the port, and of the city generally, had been dependent on international trade and business development. The new Manned Space Center only emphasized the international traffic to Houston. To better manage and accommodate foreign business visitors, Houston secured a twelve-story World Trade Center "designed to be the central point for international trade, international affairs, and international social life in the Houston area."[237] The World Trade Club, the Houston World Trade Association, and the Institute of International Education all located their offices in this new center along with consular offices and the many private businesses concerned with shipping, freight, and the administrative aspects of international trade.[238] The twelve-story building was dedicated by June Tellepsen, wife of the port chairman, who poured water from the port into the reflecting pool of the new complex representing the Seven Seas of the world. British Consul Allen Price spoke to the crowd about the importance of Houston in world trade, followed by entertainment from dancers in international costumes. In 1962, Houston also formed a World Trade Association, giving membership card no. 1 to former Undersecretary of State William Clayton and inviting him to speak at the inaugural event. His speech urged greater world trade and pointed to the European Common Market as an ideal political and economic arrangement. He urged the United States and Canada to join so that the Atlantic alliance would be so great that "Communist objectives in the cold war could not be realized."[239]

In 1964, the port celebrated its fiftieth anniversary. The best news for the golden anniversary was not an official celebration from the public authorities but an announcement by Humble Oil and Refining to construct Bayport, "a unique industrial project on Galveston Bay near the NASA Manned Space Center," featuring a seventy-five-hundred acre industrial site. To salute the port's anniversary and news of even greater expansion, Houston hosted a visit by the *Esso Houston*, the largest tanker ever built in the United States,[240] and then the British missile cruiser HMS *London*.[241] The visit by the British warship coincided with the Britain in Texas Festival, a business and cultural series of events organized by the Houston Chamber of Commerce. British Ambassador Lord Harlech came to Houston to receive the ship alongside Houston officials. Lord Harlech also opened the Sakowitz British Festival, featuring $1 million in British luxury consumer goods displayed at the Sakowitz stores in Houston.[242] Foreign trade for the year broke all records.[243]

The official celebration looked back to the original opening celebrations of 1914 as an example. At that time, President Wilson had pressed a button at the White House to fire a cannon in Houston to officially open the deep-water port. In 1964, it was arranged for President Johnson to speak, albeit remotely from his Western White House ranch in the Texas Hill Country, to a crowd gathered at the Turning Basin. Johnson said, "Back in the '30's, when I taught school in Houston, I remember that some people were still skeptical of the value of the ship channel, [but] it must be a good feeling today." President Johnson pressed a button on his desk "to send a cloud of bayou clay and sand skyward" and launch the port on its "second half century of progress." The 1914 christening was performed by Sue Campbell, the daughter of Mayor Ben Campbell, as she tossed a bouquet of roses into the water. In 1964, her granddaughter Susan Lee repeated her grandmother's words "I christen thee Port of Houston" as she too tossed flowers into the water. President Johnson addressed the crowd via speaker from a telephone connection: "I am proud to participate in this occasion both as the President of the United States and as a former resident

The design of the *Ideal X* changed the entire structure of international shipping. Courtesy of the American Merchant Marine Museum, King's Point, New York.

and longtime admirer of Houston. Houston's destiny and the nation's destiny are greatness."[244] That evening Houston celebrated in typically over-the-top style at the Shamrock Hotel, now the Shamrock Hilton Hotel, with Governor John Connally remarking that "the Port of Houston is an important key to the future of Texas and its existence is a lesson in advanced planning for growth and expansion."[245]

By the 1960s, the Port of Houston was particularly well regarded for its capacity to handle cargo items that might be very large, very heavy, very delicate, or a combination of factors.[246] Tonnage "exceeded 122,000 in 1979," and once again Houston deepened the channel, this time to "42 feet at Barbour's Cut."[247] Growth continued in the 1980s and 1990s with additional wharves and expansion of cargo-handling facilities. There were fewer actual workers as automation took over for the previous army of workers, yet more cargo was handled. The channel was deepened again, this time to 45 feet, "although the work was not completed until 1998."[248] The Port of Houston also expanded by acquiring private facilities, such as the Jacintoport (across the channel from the San Jacinto Monument) in 1987, the Woodhouse Terminal in 1993, and CARE Shipping Terminal in 1995. Cargo tonnage continued to grow in the 1980s, but it really boomed after 1990, hitting 148 million in 1996 and 175 million by 2000. "By tonnage, petroleum and petroleum products ranked first among imports and second among exports for the port during the 1980s and 1990s."[249] The Port of Houston reports that as of 2024, the port has handled over 293 million tons of cargo, worth $438 billion, and created over 1.5 million Texas jobs. The economic impact of the Port of Houston is almost 20 percent of the entire Texas gross domestic product.[250]

Houston used its early lead in containerization to the fullest, leading to another boom period of growth. "Shipping by container was so cheap that by 1990 it was being used for anything and everything."[251] Not only did overall tonnage of shipments increase, but a use of containers became more common and finally the standard. The diversity of shipments increased as well: "The first shipment of grocery supplies from Europe was in 1965; the

The *Ideal X* could be loaded with independent, detachable containers, making loading and unloading dramatically faster and easier. The independent containers on board could be unloaded to railcars or trucks for a nearly seamless shipping experience for bulk and heavy cargo. Courtesy of the American Merchant Marine Museum, King's Point, New York.

first shipment of Germany [*sic*] wine was in 1967."[252] Containerization not only improved the bulk of business at the Port of Houston but also allowed an internationalization that was more visible to consumers. Rather than bulk products of agricultural goods and raw materials, there could be more things available to put directly on the dinner table.

In 1988, the Port of Houston Authority established the Malcolm Baldrige Free Trade Zone. It was named for the late US secretary of commerce and designated an area where foreign goods could be handled in the form of processing, storage, and repackaging for shipment: "FTZ goods are not considered to be in the United States territory. They are not subject to customs duties or excise taxes unless distributed domestically."[253] In this way, goods could move through the Port of Houston as part of an international distribution without triggering US taxation. For example, a cargo ship of goods from Asia may come through the Panama Canal and into Houston for the ship to be serviced, and the goods may even be offloaded and divided into smaller lots for forwarding on other ships, but none of this will be subject to federal taxation. At the same time, Houston gains from fees assessed for a ship's usage of the port facilities, products sold to the ship, the employment of Houstonians working to service the ship and its goods, and other aspects of the international shipment.

The Houston Port and Ship Channel was a star for the 1990 G7 Summit. "The summit is Houston's chance to show the world this is an international city," said Jim Pugh, executive director of the Port of Houston Authority. "We are the No. 2 port in the nation and more than 4,600 vessels came here last year."[254] The Port of Houston is the second US port in terms of tonnage, with first place going to the Port of South Louisiana.[255] However, Houston is the undisputed leading US port for foreign tonnage with its traditional strong international trade ties. Houston continues to expand with a second dedicated container terminal, the Bayport Container Terminal, which opened in 2007, and a major refurbishment of the Turning Basin and its facilities in 2012.[256] The port continues to grow by constructing additional wharves, widening channels, building storage facilities, and making other infrastructure additions and improvements.

The slow-moving wilderness stream of Buffalo Bayou "had surpassed the wildest expectations of the dreamers. The Allen brothers could not have believed in 1836 that their paper city in the wilderness would one day rank as the greatest cotton port in the United States; Charles Morgan could not have envisioned the petroleum development of the 1920's, nor Ross S. Sterling the petrochemical industry of the 1950's. Nor could those who struggled with the shortages of the post-World War II period have envisioned the Port's role in man's probe into space."[257]

Many people and events shaped and guided the development of the port and the Houston Ship Channel to the modern wonder it became. However, the petroleum and petrochemical industry that clustered around the port, less than twenty years after the Spindletop discovery, was the most significant factor in shaping Houston to be both an international trade and energy center. The catalyst of these two major centers working in concert would raise Houston to new heights and raise its flag on a global level.

CHAPTER TWO

OIL AND GAS BOOM

1901

THE PORT OF Houston and the Houston Ship Channel are internationally acclaimed, and global shipping certainly ranks high when people consider the reasons for Houston's evolution as an international city. However, it is actually not international trade but oil and gas that first come to most people's minds when they think of Houston either in terms of an international center or just in general. Indeed, the term "Energy Capital of the World" is often used to describe Houston.[1] The role of the petroleum industry in Houston, and the quintessential image of the rich Texas oilman, is universally known and has been the subject of many articles, books, television shows, and movies. The image of the flamboyant, sometimes eccentric "Big Rich" has occasionally been used to ridicule Texans, but more often it is a point of pride for them and a very valuable marketing and publicity tool.

Oil itself is the center of Houston's energy history, but the magnitude of Houston's success as an energy center came about because of the city's capacity and ability to use oil production to fuel the "oldest, largest, and most diverse complex of oil—and natural gas related—activities in the world."[2] The oil industry may most often be associated with Texas, and with Houston in particular, but it did not start there. Early oil exploration occurred in the northern United States near those who invented uses for it and ways to obtain it, as well as the sources of capital to make it all happen. Only later was oil exploited in Texas once a proven world market had been established for its use. By the time that occurred, the Port of Houston and the Houston Ship Channel were well established, and Houston was seeking to become a deep-water port as well. Once the Texas oil boom began, its rapid expansion coincided with the dredging of the ship channel to accommodate large oceangoing vessels and construction of additional port facilities, ground transportation, and storage. In this way, Houston's international trade and its oil boom grew in an energizing reciprocal fashion.

The Discovery at Spindletop Field

The Spindletop oil well blew in on January 10, 1901, in Southeast Texas. The phenomenal well, and the massive reservoir it indicated, forever changed the destiny of Houston and the region. On that cold winter day, three men worked on a project already months in progress: seemingly endless drilling through "solid rock and quicksand in their search for oil."[3] On that morning as they lowered a new drill bit, they heard a hissing sound followed by a geyser of mud and four tons of drilling pipe shooting up out of the hole "that rained down around their heads." Only after they began to clean up the mess did the ground shake and a torrent of oil spew up from the earth.[4] The well blew a gusher of oil over one hundred feet high for over a week until it was finally capped. The flow was estimated at one hundred thousand barrels of oil per day, creating a lake around the well head.[5] A monument at Spindletop succinctly states the destiny-changing significance of the event: "On this spot on the tenth day of the twentieth century, a new era in civilization began."[6]

Geologists were not just guessing when they selected the Spindletop field for exploration. There were sulfur springs in the area, a geologic phenomenon associated with oil, as well as natural gas seepages near the surface that would ignite. The presence of gas was also normally associated with oil. Nevertheless, the geology of salt domes, and of petroleum reserves in general, was not a well-known science at the time.

Spindletop was a vast salt dome field in Jefferson County, south of the county seat, Beaumont. A group of investors, including George W. O'Brien, George W. Carroll, and Pattillo Higgins, formed the Gladys City Oil, Gas and Manufacturing Company to explore the Spindletop area.[7] Unfortunately, the exploration did not go well, and Gladys drilled a series of dry holes in 1893, 1895, and 1896. Investors naturally became wary and reluctant, or unable, to continue putting money into the venture. Higgins left the company to form a partnership with Anthony F. Lucas, a geologist and expert on salt dome formations.[8] They obtained rights from Gladys to continue exploration but also failed and ran out of money. Lucas finally got additional investors from Pittsburgh but had ceded all but one-eighth of the lease at that point, and Higgins had no capital shares left.[9] The well hit once it reached 1,139 feet, almost double the depth the drill had reached when Lucas ran out of money the first time.[10]

Nothing like Spindletop had ever been seen or imagined at the time. The size of the well, and the virtual certainty of more production in the region, set off a mad scramble for land, drilling rights, and new oil and supply companies. Land prices doubled and doubled again and just kept going as oil mania set in. The land immediately around Spindletop sold for $1 million an acre, up from $6 a few years before.[11] Investors and speculators rushed in, spending money with wild abandon, and others arrived en masse looking for jobs and opportunity in the discovery of black gold.

Although Spindletop was discovered south of Beaumont and almost ninety miles east of Houston, it is nevertheless associated with the city of Houston. The discovery electrified the whole of Southeast Texas, and investors soon focused geologists on an ever-expanding circle of land around the discovery field, finding vast new reservoirs in East Texas, North Texas, and all the way to the Permian Basin of West Texas.

The demand for oil predated the invention of the automobile. Although most people associate the growing oil industry with the invention and expansion of the automobile industry, it makes sense that the fuel would have to exist first to power the inventions that came later. And, indeed, there were many uses for petroleum products before the automobile.

Abraham Gesner, a Canadian inventor, geologist, and physician, is credited with inventing a process to distill kerosene in 1846. It was an improvement over whale oil and could be used for better lighting. Kerosene street lighting was first supplied in Halifax in the 1850s. However, Gesner later discovered a way to distill kerosene from petroleum in an easier manner. After that, the demand for petroleum took off because of its practical use in illumination.[12] The demand for petroleum for this purpose spread globally and was dominated early on by Russia, in particular, the Nobel Company of Azerbaijan.[13] The firm was established by the Nobel family in Baku and became one of the largest oil companies in the world by the late nineteenth century, well before the automobile age.[14]

Edwin Drake invented the drilling process in 1859, allowing oil to be extracted from deep underground. The new drilling technique was first used in Pennsylvania by firms including Standard Oil, founded by John D. Rockefeller.[15]

Oil was known to exist in Texas, and there was some extraction in the post–Civil War era for the purpose of distilling kerosene. However, much of the time oil was a nuisance to a state focused on agriculture and the water necessary to sustain it. One of the first oil wells in Texas was drilled near Nacogdoches in 1866. But it was not until the discovery of the Corsicana field in 1894 that a real economic impact was felt. The success of the Corsicana field and the growing international demand for kerosene and other derivatives of petroleum led to more exploration in various parts of Texas, eventually including the Spindletop field.[16]

Texas Oil Boom

The discovery of oil at Spindletop sparked a frantic rush of development and industrialization. This phenomenon is termed the "Texas oil boom" because the rate of wealth creation was so explosive in the region and eventually across the nation. Texas moved from a state economy focused on agriculture to one focused on oil and gas, as well as the industries related to and supporting energy. That new focus would remain in place for at least two generations.

It is relatively easy to see a new direction in Texas history occurring in 1901 with the Spindletop discovery. The Lone Star State began moving from an agriculture-centered to an industrial-based economy. The population grew along with the cultural and political importance of the state. The oil discovery occurred only four months after the Great Hurricane had struck Galveston, forever ending its role as the principal commercial and trading center of Texas. Houston, already gaining on Galveston, surpassed the island city. In the next few years, Houston would not only capitalize on a growing trade port and deeper ship channel but would also reap the massive benefits of an oil boom that rained down like the initial Spindletop blowout.

The watershed events for Houston over a few months of late 1900 to early 1901 paralleled national and international changes as well. Theodore Roosevelt was elected vice president on the ticket with William McKinley in the 1900 election and by the end of 1901 would himself be president. He carried out an aggressive populist agenda domestically while seeking to project the United States onto the world stage with its US Navy battleships known as the Great White Fleet and newfound role in international diplomacy following the 1898 Spanish-American War.[17]

Queen Victoria died at Osborne House on January 22, 1901, just twelve days after the discovery at Spindletop and shortly before the new McKinley-Roosevelt ticket was sworn in. Her death foreshadowed a coming decline in

British power and prestige as the United Kingdom was increasingly threatened by a rising Germany in Europe and a rising Japan in Asia. The British Empire was to grow increasingly dependent on a steady stream of oil to fuel the domestic economy and its worldwide military presence. This need for oil would draw British investors to Houston but also make them competitors of Houstonians abroad.

Oil was in demand in 1901 as a source for light and heat but only marginally for early combustion-engine-driven transportation. That was about to change dramatically in the coming years as oil became the driver of the world's great economies and the essential fuel of their armies, naval fleets, and new air forces. Houston was the center of it all as the central city of the Texas oil boom, the headquarters of a growing number of oil companies, the site for branches of European oil companies, and the refining and distribution center for oil and petroleum by-products.

At the beginning of the twentieth century, Houston was already a "city on the rise" and well positioned to exploit the many advantages that were soon to come with the oil boom. Although Spindletop was not in Houston, it was close, and attracted by the ship channel and the railroads, the center of the oil industry established itself at Houston.[18] Additionally, Houston already had national economic reach and connections as a commercial center for cotton and timber. Houston's law firms and banks were well connected with national centers in New York, New Orleans, Chicago, and elsewhere.[19] Other oil fields closer to Houston, including Goose Creek Oil Field, Blue Ridge and Pierce Junction, and then later Conroe, Eureka Heights, Mykawa, Tomball, and South Houston, further consolidated the oil industry center at Houston.[20]

By the time of Spindletop in 1901, Houston was already established as the principal commercial city of Texas; it was a road and rail center, and the work on transportation, such as deepening the ship channel, continued rapidly without regard to Spindletop. Before the discovery of oil, Houston was already moving ahead of Galveston in part because of an "aggressive civic/business elite and a habit of openness to ambitious outsiders that was not matched by [Galveston]."[21]

As population and wealth concentrated in Houston, it became natural for the newly rich of Beaumont and other parts of East Texas to want to move there for better homes, better schools, better clubs, and more upscale life in general. Beaumont was too small to exert the same national business reach that Houston enjoyed, and it was too small to exert the same business magnetism to pull in new population and capital. The greater wealth of

Spindletop is the most famous oil well ever drilled, and it changed the course of the Texas and US economies. Although the site was ninety miles from Houston, the city's established position as a shipping, manufacturing, and financial center quickly drew in the exploding Texas oil boom. Courtesy of the Fort Worth Star-Telegram Collection, University of Texas at Arlington Libraries.

Houstonians led to civic improvements not available in East and Southeast Texas, including parks, museums, music, and the birth of established, upscale neighborhoods.[22]

Before the oil boom, Houston's growth around its port and ship channel had proven a draw to "farmers and sharecroppers" in the region seeking to improve their lives and economic condition.[23] Houston was "politically

Pattillo Higgins was familiar with the Spindletop field years before the first oil well came in. He often took children on field trips to show them that gas would escape from the ground by just pushing a stick into it. Courtesy of the Texas Energy Museum.

stable" with the right amount of regulatory structure to maintain order and a fair business environment without stifling individual ambition and capitalist spirit. When the opportunities associated with oil came suddenly in 1901, it was Houston, not its neighbors, that "was ready and willing to open wide its doors."[24]

By 1918, the Houston Ship Channel was recognized as particularly well suited for the location of oil refineries. Petroleum Refinery, Sinclair Oil Company, Humble Oil and Refining Company, and Empire Oil and Gas were all built on the channel by the end of World War I. The refineries employed thousands of new workers, attracting investors and rapidly building the population base of Houston. The needs of new workers for housing, food, clothing, and other goods created a giant ripple effect in the region's economy. Houston had eight such major refineries by 1927. The oil boom produced chemical and fertilizer plants, enabling the Houston region to utilize all aspects of petroleum's potential and attracting even more workers and investors. When the Depression occurred in 1930, many farming families from "East Texas and western Louisiana fled depressed agricultural conditions in the interior and moved to the factories along the ship channel."[25] By the 1940s Houston was attracting large numbers of Mexicans and American Hispanics, as well as Cajuns from southern Louisiana, seeking industrial and manufacturing jobs. These successive waves of newcomers to Houston generally had mechanical skills from their previous work on farm equipment and early automobiles. What they needed was a steady paycheck, "paid vacations, health insurance, and the promise of upward mobility across generations," and Houston could provide this in abundance. The "optimistic tone" of Houston and the "collective impact" of so many jobs and investor dollars drove Houston to become a major American city and a global metropolis.[26]

Houston's position as the center of the oil industry, in terms of refineries, chemical plants, corporate offices, and pipelines, allowed it to weather short-term fluctuations in energy prices, as well as the boom-and-bust cycle of oil production, new discoveries, or the exhaustion of a field. Wherever the oil was being produced, and at whatever price, it still needed to be managed, financed, refined, and distributed from Houston. Not only did these

The frenzy that followed Spindletop exceeded that of any gold rush of the previous century. Everyone clamored for a piece of the action. Courtesy of the Texas Energy Museum.

Anthony Lucas was an Austrian military officer before immigrating to the United States. Undaunted by initial failures, his focus on science eventually brought in the most famous gusher of all time. Courtesy of the Texas Energy Museum.

Houston employers need a vast workforce, but also many outside workers were needed for the construction and maintenance of facilities. Moreover, a "growing body of professionals" was needed to consult and assist the energy industry in engineering, accounting, legal, and other technical aspects of the business. This meant an influx of both skilled and unskilled workers to Houston, furthering the international and polyglot nature of the city.[27]

The expansion of the ship channel, originally begun to make Houston a prosperous deep-water port for agricultural commodities and other goods, coincided nicely with the Texas oil boom. Houston's business and political leadership were able to see the bright opportunities for the city in the new century and to work robustly and in cooperation to bring the vision to reality. "Public-private cooperation in deepening the Houston Ship Channel demonstrated the willingness of the public sector to promote oil and economic development."[28]

In the 1920s oil surpassed cotton as the most important commodity in the Houston economy, as it was not only shipped through the port but increasingly was processed in the port into gasoline or other petroleum products. *Fortune* magazine stated that "without oil Houston would have been just another cotton town."[29]

Growing Demand for Gasoline

Kerosene was still the main petroleum product in 1901. Even with early cars in production, mostly in Europe at the time, gasoline was used in few automobiles. In fact, most early cars were electrically powered from batteries. It was only after such abundance of oil was discovered that expansive uses for petroleum, including gasoline, developed.[30]

The Spindletop field itself began to decline by 1903. Whereas it initially produced more oil than all the wells of Pennsylvania combined, that rate was not sustained. It was not just a matter of reserves in the particular Spindletop formation but also the number of wells drilled in close proximity. There was no concept of well spacing at the time, and new oil derricks were constructed within a few feet of each other. "By the spring of 1901 there were 138 producing oil wells . . . crammed on to a 15 acre site" immediately around the original well.[31] Due to the sudden glut, the price of oil fell from one dollar to just three cents a barrel.[32]

As car production ramped up, so did gasoline sales, so that by 1911 gasoline was a more common by-product of oil than kerosene.[33] Additionally, the spread of electricity was making kerosene less useful for lighting purposes, at least in urban areas. The glut of cheap oil may have disappointed some investors, but it also spurred new ways of using the abundance, which had the effect of driving the price back up again. Trains and barges, used for private and commercial transport, were fired by coal. In fact, "up until 1900, coal was used for 90 percent of the energy needs in the United States."[34] Rail lines found a way to modify their engines to run on oil instead of coal. Not only was it cheaper and more abundant, but it was local and did not have to be hauled from the East. The conversion for both rail and ships was relatively easy because they both ran on steam, so rather than replace the actual engine, only the boiler that produced the steam needed to be replaced. Fuel oil could be loaded onto a ship in hours instead of days, took up less space, and required less manpower to put it into the boiler. Running a ship at full steam meant grueling work for coal stokers until they were exhausted. With fuel oil, you simply turn on the tap and go until the reservoir runs out. "Three barrels of oil could generate as much heat as a ton of coal, and it burned cleaner."[35] More available space on the ships meant more commercial goods could be carried to greater profit in addition to lower fuel costs and lower manpower costs. Finally, the growing need for fuel oil meant a greater need for refineries and the infrastructure necessary to transport the petroleum to them and the resulting fuel oil shipped back out again.[36]

Once more, Houston was the natural center of the universe for this revolutionary new way that the commercial trade world now worked. Although the Spindletop fields declined quickly, the Texas oil boom had not only spurred exploration to find and develop new fields in the region, and around the state generally, but had also created an ongoing demand from business to find oil as a replacement for coal. This new dependence on oil drove further exploration and contributed to the expansion of automobiles and trucks.[37] Of course, when the Wright brothers first flew in 1908, the engine on that plane and every plane to follow would run on a petroleum product, not coal.

Whereas most cars that existed in 1901 did not use gasoline, by 1904 "there were more than 22,000 automobiles on the roads of America, and now a majority of them powered by gasoline."[38] Henry Ford took an early lead in the US car industry, especially with his Model T.[39] Ford's designs and assembly-line production methods made the automobile available to the wider middle class, not just a high-tech toy of the rich. Many other car manufacturers began production, and by 1914, there were 1.7 million cars on the road in the United States. The massive consumer demand caused an ever-larger market for petroleum and a surge in drilling companies, refineries, distribution companies, and retailers. Houston was at the center of it all.

World War I caused a further surge in demand for petroleum, first for the armies, navies, and nascent air forces of Europe and then for those of the United States.[40] Correspondingly, the end of World War I caused an abrupt and sharp decline in demand for oil by the militaries of the world, but the overall market demand actually surged even further as the automobile had become a necessity, not a luxury, and as the economy grew rapidly with big business in the 1920s.[41]

The end of World War I really opened a new chapter for Houston as the advantages of its port began to coalesce with the growing oil and gas industry in Texas and the southwest region. At the same time, World War I had "proved the usefulness of the internal-combustion engine thus creating a demand for petroleum."[42] Automobiles had existed in the consumer market since the 1890s, first in Europe with the Benz company of Germany.[43] However, these cars were intended for the affluent since the cost and maintenance were quite high at the time.

Henry Ford's first Model T came out in 1908. After that, assembly-line production grew with interchangeable parts and local service until middle-class Americans could afford to buy them. World War I ramped up production of vehicles, improving technology and mass-production techniques to more readily meet later consumer demand. And all these new cars needed gasoline refined from petroleum. Gasoline refineries were Houston's next big step.

Leading Texas Oil Companies and Executives

Standard Oil and the Rockefeller family held a monopoly on the petroleum industry in most of the United States at the beginning of the twentieth century. Although there was some resentment of such monopolies in general, the political atmosphere of Texas at the time was particularly populist and distrustful of such companies as Standard Oil. The State of Texas had enacted measures designed to curb unfair business practices and discourage companies like Standard Oil from operating in the state.[44] These state regulatory requirements sprang from a Texas brand of progressivism that dominated state politics at the time.

Joseph D. Sayers of Bastrop occupied the Governor's Mansion at the time of the Spindletop discovery. First elected in 1898, he was reelected in 1900 to a second term. Sayers was a leader in the progressive wing of the Democratic Party, which completely controlled Texas for over a century beginning at the end of the Republican era of Reconstruction after the Civil War. Sayers was aided by Colonel Edward M. House in his gubernatorial campaign, just as House had previously assisted James Hogg. Sayers favored populist policies associated with the ordinary citizen against big industry.[45] Texas in 1900 banned an oil-products marketing company associated with Standard Oil from doing business in the state, citing its "cutthroat sales practices."[46] Although the federal government was not yet so progressive, it would soon follow the Texas model under Theodore Roosevelt. Roosevelt was elected vice president on the ticket with William McKinley in 1900. The two men would take office in March 1901, two months after the Spindletop discovery. McKinley was assassinated in September 1901 and was succeeded by Vice President Roosevelt. Roosevelt would lead a major national progressive movement, including famously breaking up Standard Oil as part of his "trust-busting" campaign.

Standard Oil, or any other established company of the day, would find it difficult to enter the Texas market in order to benefit from Spindletop and the resulting Texas oil boom. The great distance from Texas to the existing centers of oil production in the East made it challenging for such companies to project into Texas.[47] At the same time, Standard was also focused on new production activities in "southern California and MidContinental fields."[48] Additionally, Standard simply "erred in evaluating the region's petroleum potential."[49] This lack of outside competition and the lavish opportunity at hand enabled new Texas companies to form and grow. It is well-known that the US Supreme Court ordered the breakup of Standard Oil in a 1911 decision that set a precedent for fair business practices and antimonopolistic behavior. However, the inability of Standard to break into, much less control, the early Texas oil boom had already "effectively destroyed its monopolistic position within the American petroleum industry."[50]

New oil companies formed in Houston and Texas, and the first of many energy-related companies formed to meet demands for "specialized equipment and services" for the new oil industry.[51] Although formed for local

The abundance of cheap oil helped fuel the rapid growth of the early automobile industry. Courtesy of the Library of Congress, Prints and Photographs Division.

and regional needs, some companies grew into international firms, such as Hughes Tools and Cameron Iron Works.[52]

It was Houston's capacity to build a base of businesses connected both vertically and economically with oil production that allowed it to maximize benefit from the oil boom and to maintain "permanent economic benefits" of the economic transformation of the region.[53] The new boom required drill bits of ever-increasing size and technical specificity, storage tanks, flow regulators, valve shut-offs, and tools to detect additional formations and sources. All of these needs required new technical and managerial expertise, so where better to locate the company and hire the workers than at the center of the oil boom? The need for pipelines and refineries required Houston to develop the "essential industrial base and infrastructure needed to support the operations of vertically integrated oil companies, as well as independent producing and refining companies."[54]

One of the early oil companies to come to Texas after Spindletop was Sun Oil of Pennsylvania, often marketed as Sunoco and owned and operated by the Pew family of Philadelphia. The Pews bought up large amounts of oil leases in Southeast Texas and then acquired storage facilities to ride out market fluctuations when the oil might be produced but not yet at a good price point for selling. The Pews developed pipelines for transport, and Sun Oil became a player in Texas for the long term.[55]

Joseph Stephen Cullinan is credited for establishing "Houston as the executive center of the petroleum industry" by noting in a letter the "requirements of oil refineries: deep water, abundant fresh water, large acreage, and protection from floods and tropical storms." Not only did Houston possess all these characteristics, but "refineries in these areas were assured of a long working life because of the abundant crude-oil supplies nearby and because additional supplies could easily be obtained from Mexico and Central and South America."[56]

Joseph Cullinan was born in Pennsylvania in 1860, almost at the beginning of the Pennsylvania oil rush, the nation's first oil boom that lasted until the 1870s and until Standard Oil had established a monopoly over the area. He was the grandson of immigrants escaping the Irish potato famine.[57] Cullinan had early experience in the oil fields in Pennsylvania and established himself as authoritative on proper management and production of a field. His move to Texas came rather unexpectedly.

In 1897, the city of Corsicana in central-east Texas dug a water well for municipal use and instead discovered a huge flow of oil. The city contacted Cullinan, "who agreed to interrupt a business trip to California" to visit

Corsicana and assess the situation.[58] Corsicana's city leaders met Cullinan in Dallas, arranged a tour of the Texas State Fair, set up a meeting with Governor Charles A. Culberson who was in town for the fair, and generally set out to be hospitable and impress Cullinan. Cullinan went by train from Dallas to Corsicana and wound up staying three weeks. He never made his planned trip to California but instead realized the great potential for himself and others in Texas.[59] Cullinan was a great asset to Corsicana in those early years, and because of his expertise and connections, he lured other "experienced oil talent" to Texas, first to Corsicana and then to Houston.[60]

Cullinan's role at Corsicana included the proper development and marketing of its petroleum and draw of national talent to the area. He also changed the way the oil business was structured. Before the turn of the twentieth century, Cullinan created both a producing company, Corsicana Petroleum, and a manufacturing company, Corsicana Refining, thereby launching the now-common "integrated operations" that came to define Texas and later international petroleum company corporate structure.[61]

With the discovery of Spindletop shortly thereafter, Cullinan relocated to Houston and formed a fuel company dealing primarily in kerosene production from petroleum. The start-up capital for his company was $50,000, half of which came from an investor group led by former Governor of Texas James Hogg.[62] The other major investor was Arnold Schlaet, a German businessman who worked in New York.[63] Schlaet successfully established a national distribution and sales network that made "Texaco less vulnerable to Standard's price-cutting."[64] Eventually Cullinan's Texas Fuel Company became Texaco, one of the world's leading energy companies.[65]

Texas Fuel had a competitive advantage from the outset in that Cullinan had arranged access to a very large storage tank in nearby Sabine. Cullinan was able to store oil to await a favorable contract price,[66] a practice that had not been used before. For a time, the Mellons considered a merger of their Gulf holdings with Texaco, but fears of a new Standard Oil–type trust raised the populist political fears in Texas and the legislature "came out against the merger."[67]

In order to compete with Guffey Petroleum, financed by the Mellons and expanding rapidly, Cullinan approached a business group called the Hogg-Swayne Syndicate. This partnership of former Governor Hogg and a group of lawyers originally did business with Guffey but eventually ran into trouble.[68] They sought help from Cullinan, who structured a new deal with Texas Fuel that gave his company a "wedge for expanded participation in Spindletop's development."[69]

Cullinan did not always have a confrontational relationship with the state government of Texas. In fact, it was in Corsicana that Cullinan realized the need for a good regulatory policy and structure to prevent waste and to protect public, as well as private, interests.[70] With Cullinan's support, the state representative from Corsicana (Navarro County) introduced a bill in 1899 "to regulate the drilling, operation, and abandonment of gas, oil, and mineral water wells and to prevent certain abuses connected therewith."[71] Cullinan himself went to Austin to testify, and the bill was eventually passed by both houses of the legislature and signed by Governor Joseph D. Sayers. In fact, the legislature considered the matter to be an emergency and suspended its own procedural rules to expedite passage of the bill and give it immediate effect upon passage and gubernatorial approval.[72]

Cullinan continued to support the state's role in regulating the petroleum industry. He favored additional regulatory measures and stiffer penalties, and Texas supported these same ideas over the next several years. Cullinan originally favored federal regulation as a way to bring national uniformity, but the success of the Texas Railroad Commission in finding the right balance of public-private interest caused him to change his mind. "State agencies that are staffed by expert personnel are probably better qualified to regulate the industry."[73] In this way, "the initial relationship in Texas between petroleum conservation and compulsory legislation was established" and would be important over the coming decades to ensure maximum opportunity and efficiency in the energy industry.[74]

Texaco was originally headquartered in Beaumont, but at the outset Cullinan said "that the time will come—perhaps in no distant day—when we will want our general office in Houston instead of Beaumont, as . . . Houston seems to me to be the coming center of the oil business."[75] Texaco was moved to Houston, although a New York office was established as well. Texaco also had a storage plant and marketing center in Antwerp, Belgium, before 1910.[76] Texaco "even had a tanker called *Texas* sailing across the Atlantic" to transport petroleum to Europe.[77] By 1914, Texaco had established its corporate offices in downtown Houston on the corner of San Jacinto and Rusk. Texaco expanded rapidly in the United States and by 1928 was selling its Texaco-branded gasoline at service stations in all forty-eight states.[78]

Cullinan created a corporate structure that emphasized the Texas nature and origin of his company. The Houston headquarters were decorated with the Texas star, which became universally associated with Texaco as a white star, the Texas Lone Star, in a red circle. Texaco ads emphasized this as well

Joseph Cullinan was instrumental in the development of the Houston Ship Channel and a generous supporter of the arts, but his greatest impact was to establish Houston as the center of the petroleum industry. Courtesy of the Joseph S. Cullinan Papers, Special Collection, University of Houston Libraries.

with advertising jingles: "You can trust your car to the man who wears the star" and the slogan "Star of the American Road."[79]

Cullinan was instrumental in the development of Houston, both in terms of business and the arts. But he was particularly influential with the Houston Ship Channel because it was so vital to his business and similar oil- and gas-related industries.[80] By the 1930s, "petroleum edged out cotton as the port's predominant commodity."[81]

Cullinan was politically interested and involved throughout his life. He considered himself a Democrat but was appalled by the Democratic Party's affiliation with groups he considered racist, xenophobic, and anti-Catholic (Cullinan himself was of Irish-Catholic heritage). At one point, he simply refused to back the Democrat candidate for US Senate, Earle B. Mayfield, who ran in 1922 backed by the Texas Ku Klux Klan.[82] Cullinan instead backed Republican George Peddy of Houston, although Mayfield won the election.[83] Cullinan was more supportive of national Democrats like Alfred Smith in 1928 and Franklin Roosevelt in 1932, despite a personal friendship with Herbert Hoover.[84] However, Cullinan turned on Roosevelt in his first term, considering the New Deal to be a form of socialism. He backed Republican Alf Landon in 1936 when Roosevelt was seeking a second term.

In the 1930s, the very visible and well-known chairman of Texaco was Torkild Rieber, a Norwegian born in Voss in 1882 who found work at sea as a teenager. He then worked on an oil tanker transporting petroleum from Houston to Europe and eventually became master of the ship. Texaco acquired his tanker in 1905, and Rieber began to rise in the corporate ranks and was assigned to headquarters. After Cullinan fell out with Schlaet, Rieber went with him to form a new oil company, American Republics, serving as vice president. However, in 1927, Rieber returned to Texaco to oversee exports and international shipping and became chairman by 1935. Rieber traveled the world seeking new opportunities for Texaco. Texaco also projected out from Houston to open offices in exotic locales in the world.[85]

A particular success was a project in the 1930s to drill wells in an oil concession purchased in Colombia and to then construct a pipeline across mountains and unexplored South American jungles and swamps to reach a coastal loading and shipping port that Texaco also constructed.[86] The oil concession, known as Barco, was located on the Petrolea Reserve on the border with Venezuela, and where Venezuela itself pumped much of its own oil production. The transport from there across northern Colombia to a port city was not only harsh, dense jungle, but the pipeline had to pass under rivers at several locations.

In 1936, Texaco launched a joint venture with Standard Oil of California (SoCal, which later became Chevron) called Caltex to focus on operations in Asia, East Africa, and Australasia. Through this venture, Texaco gained access to Arabian oil fields and a refinery in Bahrain. But the more important aspect of the arrangement was the formation of Aramco,[87] the Arabian-American Oil Company, formed from the joint investment of Texaco and SoCal. SoCal had originally gone into the Arabian Peninsula to see if it could replicate the success it had had drilling in Bahrain. To secure its initial concession, SoCal engaged St. John Philby as its lobbyist. Philby was a British Arabist and graduate of Cambridge. He converted to Islam in 1930 and was fluent in Arabic as well as several other Asian and Middle Eastern languages. He worked as a spy under Gertrude Bell before ending up in Palestine to work with T. E. Lawrence and the American spy Allen Dulles.[88] Eventually Philby was forced out of the intelligence service for various reasons, including anti-Semitic positions that conflicted with British policy. Philby became an adviser to King Abdulaziz of Saudi Arabia, guiding him in the ways of the world, including how to manage British hegemony in the region. It was Philby who invited geologists to Saudi Arabia to determine if there might be oil wealth there as in nearby Persia. However, SoCal did not have good luck originally in Arabia, making it open to a 50 percent split with Texaco to continue exploration. In 1938, SoCal struck oil at Dhahran, beginning decades of massive oil production in the region.

Torkild Rieber's swashbuckling style made him a "famous Houston figure." He had a "sailor's internationalism" in which "the world was a market with no barriers or taboos."[89] While such a personality made him popular in business and society circles and helped Houston's international reputation, it also sometimes got him and Texaco in serious trouble. Rieber was said to admire the fascist movements in Europe at the time, which seemed more efficient, enthusiastic, and focused to many business leaders.[90]

One such example was the Spanish Civil War, which began in 1936 and viciously pitted the elected, leftist Republican government of Spain against rebelling, rightist, and militaristic forces led by Francisco Franco. The Spanish government received support from the Soviet Union, while the Nationalists received support from the fascist governments of Italy and Germany. The major powers, including the United States, were officially neutral in the conflict. The US Neutrality Act of 1937 specifically disallowed credit for war materiel, including oil. However, Rieber met with Francisco Franco and agreed that Texaco would provide oil to him and his Nationalist fighters. Additionally, Rieber agreed to transport the oil to Spain. The oil tankers would leave Houston with a manifest showing petroleum heading to refineries in Belgium and the Netherlands. However, sealed instructions to be opened at sea would divert the tankers to Spanish ports controlled by Franco. The United States discovered and confronted Texaco about the shipments. Rieber was important enough that President Roosevelt met with him personally in 1937 to threaten serious action but to offer Rieber and Texaco a way out of the bind without a criminal proceeding. Rieber agreed to the terms and Texaco paid a fine; however, Rieber continued to ship oil to Franco with greater stealth.[91] Ultimately, Rieber steered 3.5 million tons of oil to Franco's Nationalist forces, while also using Texaco's Paris office to gather and funnel any discernible intelligence on the Republican forces and their activities and purchases. Years later, Franco bestowed on Torkild Rieber the Grand Cross of the Order of Isabella the Catholic.[92]

As the fascist movements progressed in Europe and the world moved toward war, Rieber built Texaco's ties with the Nazis and sought to give them business and trade. In one instance, he ordered several oil tankers to be constructed by a shipyard in Hamburg. These tankers would be paid for in kind with oil shipments from Texaco. However, one of the tankers was not yet ready before the outbreak of war in September 1939, and the

Germans refused to release it because it could be used in the aid of their enemies. Rieber personally flew to Berlin to negotiate a deal with the Nazis in which the tanker was released to transport oil to neutral countries. Rieber met with Herman Goering while on this trip,[93] and he also toured Nazi war factories.[94] All the while, Rieber ensured oil extracted by Texaco in Colombia made its way to Germany in defiance of the British blockade and American neutrality.[95]

Texaco managed to conduct its own version of foreign policy from Houston for years, but in 1940 Torkild Rieber's involvement with Nazi agent

Torkild Rieber led Texaco to global dominance in the oil industry, respecting no boundaries and essentially conducting his own foreign policy from Houston. Courtesy of the DeGolyer Library, Southern Methodist University.

Gerhard Westrick was his undoing. Westrick hosted a party in New York and invited numerous US business leaders from General Motors, Ford, Standard Oil, ITT, and of course, Texaco. In fact, Rieber had actually helped Westrick get established for such a role by arranging for offices, a home, and a car for him and his family. The pitch was essentially that the United Kingdom would soon be defeated and there would be many business opportunities in Europe for American companies. However, a British intelligence agent in New York found out about the meeting and disclosed it to the media. A public fury erupted over American businesses being linked to the Nazis and against the British. The Texaco board of directors forced Rieber to resign.[96]

Rieber was replaced by Star Rodgers, who continued to promote Texaco's international leadership. In 1943, Rodgers joined his counterpart at SoCal, Harry Collier, to visit Secretary of the Interior Harold Ickes, who was also in charge of petroleum for the war effort. The purpose of the meeting was to draw Ickes's attention to an oil concession in Saudi Arabia jointly owned by Texaco and SoCal. They told him not only how rich the oil resource was but also how fearful they were that the British could take it away with their diplomatic courtship of the monarch, Abdulaziz.[97] The mission worked, because President Roosevelt, only a few days later, authorized Lend-Lease aid, finding that "the defense of Saudi Arabia is vital to the defense of the United States."[98] This improved the American position in Saudi Arabia but did not ensure it. Throughout the war, Texaco continued to push for greater White House attention to the enemy threat to the kingdom and to the equally dangerous, from a business standpoint, threat from the British.

In July 1945, almost immediately after the war ended in Europe, SoCal and Texaco embarked on a new joint venture, the Trans-Arabian Pipeline Company, that would take oil from Saudi Arabia to Sidon, Lebanon, a distance of over seven hundred miles. Oil began to flow through the pipe in 1950, providing wealth to the investing companies as well as general economic development along the route.[99] For Texaco, the pipeline agreement followed by its construction was of great "diplomatic significance" since it provided reliable oil for the European market, and "it involved a commitment of U.S. foreign policy for over a quarter of a century [in the region]."[100]

The intertwining nature of American foreign policy and Texaco grew in importance after World War II accelerated by a growing need for oil but complicated by effects of Zionism in the region. American foreign policy priorities split between support for Israel and support for Saudi Arabia for completely different political, personal, and religious reasons. At the same time, Texaco had greater independence because it was "sitting on the biggest and cheapest source of oil in the world" and had its own diplomatic connections and influence in the kingdom and the world generally.[101]

To harness the ocean of oil in Saudi Arabia, Texaco established the Dhahran camp to house the many Houstonians and other Westerners needed to operate the field. Within the walls of the compound, rows of Western-style homes were built with green lawns, parks, and pools, "looking like a small town from Texas" but clearly separated from the "limitless desert" surrounding it.[102] The community, now part of Saudi Aramco, has grown over time and presently accommodates over eleven thousand residents with schools, media, entertainment, and everything needed for life far from home.

Another major oil company to form after the Spindletop discovery was Gulf Oil. George Lucas, the driller at Spindletop, sold his interests to J. M. Guffey and a group of investors who formed the Guffey Petroleum Company and the Gulf Refining Company of Texas (referring to the Gulf of Mexico). These companies later became Gulf Oil Corporation.[103] Even before World War I, Gulf was a major rival to Standard Oil "with much greater production than Exxon" and financed by the Mellon family of Pittsburgh.[104]

Gulf had pipelines from its production fields to the coast and was able to ship its product abroad on Gulf ships. Additionally, Gulf had a contract with Shell of the United Kingdom, which "guaranteed steady markets abroad."[105] Moreover, Gulf tapped new reservoirs of oil in Oklahoma, greatly expanding its resource base. Gulf's position was enhanced in 1932 when President Hoover named Andrew W. Mellon ambassador to London. At the time Gulf Oil, still 25 percent owned by the Mellon family, was seeking an oil concession in Kuwait. Although the British politically ruled Kuwait, the decision on mineral rights belonged to the emir, who was not sure he wanted to grant it to British Petroleum (BP). In the end, BP won the concession with pressure from the British and Gulf's position was compromised by Mellon's short tenure as ambassador.[106]

Gulf Oil became one of the best-known brands in the nation and was the first to have drive-in service stations and free road maps. Gulf built tankers to transport oil to its own refineries, marketed its famous Gulf No Nox Ethyl gasoline designed for the big-engine vehicles of the 1950s and 1960s, and entered into marketing arrangements with Holiday Inn designed to encourage Americans to tour the country in their cars, making the most of modern highways, frequent filling stations, and free maps.[107]

Another famous Texas oil company founded in this period was Humble Oil Company, now known as Exxon following its merger with Standard

Oil of New Jersey and later unification of brand names Enco and Esso into the name Exxon. Humble was founded in 1911 by Ross Sterling and his siblings, along with Walter William Fondren. Sterling later played a major role in reshaping the Port of Houston into a petrochemical and refining center after World War I and served as governor of Texas. Fondren become one of the great philanthropists of Texas history. Fondren was orphaned as a child and worked to support himself as a farm laborer until he got work in the Corsicana oil fields in 1897. He became an expert on drilling and operations and was an attractive business partner to Sterling.[108]

The company was called Humble Oil because it was originally established in the city of Humble, Texas; however, the headquarters moved to Houston to operate alongside the other major players in the energy industry. Humble Oil built the Baytown Refinery in 1919, the largest refining operation in Texas. Humble built a series of vast pipeline networks between its refineries in Baytown and Dallas, West Texas, and the Gulf Coast, making itself the largest crude oil transporter in the nation.

Royal Dutch Shell, an Anglo-Dutch company marketed as Shell, was the first international oil concern that was an equal competitor to Standard Oil. Shell made an attempt in 1910 to come to an arrangement for a cooperative approach to business with its main rival. When Standard rejected the offer and instead offered to acquire Shell, a price war broke out. As a result, Shell entered the American market in order to compete effectively with Standard.[109]

The East Texas area around Houston continued to be a magical ground for oil discoveries. One famous example was Columbus Joiner, known as "Dad" Joiner in oil history and later in his life.[110] Joiner hit a massive gusher well called the Daisy Bradford Number 3. Other wells followed until soon the East Texas field was called the Black Giant because it seemed like one massive reservoir of oil. Unfortunately, Joiner oversold interests in the area and wound up in legal and financial difficulties despite his amazing discovery. He sold his interests in late 1930 to H. L. Hunt, an independent oilman who had arrived to join the East Texas oil field frenzy.[111]

By the early 1930s, the problem in Houston was not a lack of petroleum, since new oil fields were continuously discovered and exhaustively produced. Instead, the problem was a surfeit of oil that collapsed prices. By the time President Roosevelt arrived at the White House, the situation had become dire to many Texans in the oil business. Field prices in East Texas were down to four cents a barrel. Harold Ickes was the new secretary of the interior, and barely two months into his new role he received a telegram from the new governor of Texas, Miriam A. "Ma" Ferguson, warning that "the situation is beyond the control of the state authorities."[112]

The Roosevelt administration made recovery of the oil industry an important part of the New Deal. Oil was addressed as part of the National Industry Recovery Act, but instead of placing control with the National Recovery Administration as with other industries, oil was placed specifically with Secretary Ickes at the Interior Department.[113] Harold Ickes was a curious political figure. He was a lifelong but not really an establishment Republican. He was aligned with Theodore Roosevelt but was also happy to bolt with him in 1912 to further the Bull Moose Party. Returning to the GOP later, he aligned himself with the Progressive wing of the party. Franklin Roosevelt sought him out for a cabinet-level position to show a bipartisan administration and to help secure needed Republican votes for his ambitious domestic agenda.[114] Ickes was not necessarily disposed to big business, but he recognized the special place oil held in the national economy. He once stated, "There is no doubt about our absolute and complete dependence upon oil," and "without oil, American civilization as we know it could not exist."[115]

Secretary Ickes focused on production as a means to stimulate price. Central to this effort was a plan to control "hot oil," the term used to describe bootleg oil that was produced without permit, smuggled across state lines, and sold for cash on a black market. The hot oil trickled into the legitimate market from numerous sources, resulting in a large total amount of oil, which suppressed prices. The federal government, using its power to regulate interstate commerce, sought to police the presence of hot oil in the marketplace. Roosevelt signed an executive order in July 1933 that specifically gave Secretary Ickes authority to enforce the federal hot-oil regulations.[116]

Federal investigators traveled throughout East Texas to examine records, "test oil gauges, inspect tanks," and find and prosecute any hot-oil violators. Ickes set monthly production quotas, which were welcome by the oil industry and the state's political leadership as a way to save the industry. The production controls had the desired effect without the need for actual price fixing by the federal government. Instead, the market continued to set prices. Additionally, the hot-oil regulations were seen as a positive state-federal partnership to resolve an important economic and public policy issue.[117]

By 1935, the US Supreme Court invalidated the provision of the National Industrial Recovery Act that Ickes relied on for federal enforcement authority. However, the political powers of Houston and Texas were by then so persuaded of the benefits of the system that new legislation was quickly passed, sponsored by Texas Senator Tom Connally,[118] to keep bootleg oil out of interstate commerce.[119] The regulatory structure provided by the federal government, with the cooperation of the state and the major oil companies, stabilized the market, allowed pricing to rise, and once again provided a boost to the state's economy and development. Through the rest of the 1930s, the price of oil "varied between $1.00–$1.18," the "dollar a barrel" sweet spot believed to be of maximum benefit, being neither too high nor too low.[120]

The Texas oil boom continued for decades as better technology allowed the discovery of additional pools of oil and the Houston Ship Channel allowed the import of crude oil from Mexico, South America, and beyond for refining. Houston dominated the refining and petrochemical business, as well as all the support jobs and infrastructure needed for the industry. These businesses included chemical, steel, and cement plants or any heavy industry that required abundant cheap energy, water, and good transportation. Houston was clearly the state's economic center by 1930. Although Houston was not immune to the effects of the Depression, it was so minimal by comparison that Houston was called "the city the Depression forgot."[121] By 1940, the value of oil and gas production in the state exceeded agricultural production for the first time, and much of this business was centered at Houston.[122] It was remarkable that in the same generation, Texas had gone from the discovery of oil to being the nation's leader.

It is not as though agriculture suffered, however, as the overall economy was growing. The energy boom centered at Houston boosted other industries throughout the state and region, including lumber for the construction of new commercial facilities and housing for the increasing population needed to operate them. The oil boom caused a corresponding boom in construction, banking, and insurance as each of those industries sought to serve and benefit from the increased oil production. An eventual, and perhaps unexpected, benefit was that the increasing population with increased purchasing power served to benefit the agricultural industry, even if agriculture was no longer the leading economic force in Houston or Texas.

The oil industry centered at Houston also had great political control in Austin as well as Washington and other world centers. By the late 1950s, there were "two Texans in key positions: Lyndon Johnson as Senate majority leader [and] Sam Rayburn as Speaker of the House," who were "steadfast in their support of the [oil industry and a favorable regulatory structure]."[123]

Access to sufficient rubber supplies was a particularly critical issue for the United States, which had been dependent on British and Dutch supplies before the war and was far behind in constructing any synthetic rubber production. Even before the United States entered the war, Jesse Jones, in an effort to build up the stockpile of rubber, had called on his old friend Lord Beaverbrook,[124] who was serving in Prime Minister Churchill's cabinet as minister of supply. Beaverbrook "put pressure on the [rubber] cartel" to help secure an agreement to supply the United States with over "430,000 tons of crude rubber."[125]

In the post–World War II era, the global demand for oil continued to expand as civilian fuel demands overtook the earlier military demands. Houston continued to be at the center of this international market but increasingly benefited from the related chemical and natural gas industries. World War II had driven the need for synthetic rubber and advanced aviation fuels. After the war, these needs expanded as technology found new uses for petroleum products. By 1950, "there were twenty-seven chemical plants along the Houston Ship Channel." The chemical plants were closely integrated with the many refineries of the area since the refineries were the source of the "feedstock used to make many of the new chemical products created in the postwar era." The chemical industry continued to grow in Houston until by the 1980s, the region "had more than half of the petrochemical capacity in the country."[126]

Related to the chemical industry was the postwar surge of natural gas use. Natural gas was a feedstock in the "production of basic chemicals."[127] For example, natural gas is used in the production of various plastics, fertilizers, antifreeze, and fabrics. It is used as a feedstock to make specialized fuels such as butane, ethane, and propane. In turn, these gases are used in the production of fertilizers and pharmaceutical products.[128]

Additionally, natural gas was increasingly used as a fuel to operate the refineries themselves as well as much of the region's industrial needs. One significant use for Houston was to fire power plants that supplied the electricity for a burgeoning population and to meet the electrical demands for a society growing accustomed to air-conditioning. Natural gas was inexpensive for many years, and its ready abundance and low cost attracted many new industries to Houston, where the lower operating costs added to the profit margin. "The availability of natural gas for domestic and industrial fuel gave the region an important competitive advantage over regions still dependent on coal and other fuels."[129]

Besides the use of natural gas as a feedstock for other products and to provide power for industrial use, Houston soon realized yet another lucrative use: sell it to other parts of the United States. In the early years, technology did not allow for long-distance transmission of natural gas. It had to be used at the source or at a nearby location. But as the ability to transport the natural gas over greater distances in a safe manner under the right pressure grew, Houston began to look for customers far afield, especially in the northeastern United States where there were "vast demands for fuel."[130]

To supply these new markets with natural gas required large gas reserves as well as an infrastructure to gather, hold, and transmit the product and a network of pipelines to carry the load. "Houston quickly emerged as the center of the nation's booming natural gas transmission industry."[131] The leading companies in this growing new field were headquartered in Houston, including "Tenneco, Transco, Texas Eastern, and Panhandle Eastern."[132]

Offshore production was another avenue of energy production and revenue expansion in Houston. Geologists knew the oil formations they so profitably tapped on land often extended farther offshore under the seabed. The only question was how to get to that oil and capture it in a safe and profitable manner. To that end, "firms such as Houston-based Brown and Root became prominent in the design and building of giant offshore platforms" that utilized new design and technology to house teams of workers for long periods of time in order to complete a drilling operation.[133]

By 1950, there were fifty million cars on the road in the United States, causing an ever-increasing demand for more oil. Demand for kerosene had fallen to a minuscule level with the advent of widespread electric lighting, even in rural areas because of the Rural Electrification Act and build-out programs in the years that followed. However, many more uses for petroleum besides gasoline evolved: plastics, polyester, nylon, medicines, cosmetics, and cleaning supplies. America found uses for as much oil as could be produced. The continuing and growing demand for oil was matched by increased production and new discoveries through the 1960s. However, by 1970, "the United States had to begin to import some of its oil from other countries."[134]

Houston was not the only energy world city in the post–World War II era. However, the layers of business built in Houston around "its oil-related core became thicker and more diverse, surpassing the concentration of similar activities in other energy capitals." This commercial and industrial base grew steadily over the years until "two large and unpredicted increases in oil prices, brought by the energy crises of 1973–74 and the Iranian Revolution of the late 1970s, drove [the] Houston skyline and its oil economy as a whole to new heights."[135]

Prosperity of Houston in a Turbulent Energy World

The 1970s was a period of turbulence in the world energy markets. In October 1973, an alliance of Egypt and Syria made a surprise attack on Israel in an effort to retake the Sinai Peninsula and the Golan Heights, which had been lost to Israel in the 1967 war. Although the Arab forces gained considerable ground in the early days of the conflict, Israel was able to reverse the trend and launched counterattacks with deep incursions into both Syria and Egypt. Of course, Israel's military capacity was greatly enhanced by a massive American resupply effort. Eventually a ceasefire took effect, but American support for Israel angered many Arab nations besides Syria and Egypt. OPEC decided to reduce oil production by 5 percent to pressure and punish the United States.[136] After President Nixon authorized additional military aid and supplies for Israel, Saudi Arabia declared an outright boycott, later joined by other oil producers. The result was the 1973 energy crisis. For the United States in general, this was a dark period economically. Consumer demand for gasoline and petroleum-related products had been driving upward in the post–World War II boom years but had accelerated in particular in the 1960s. Despite growing demand, prices remained cheap because of the abundance of oil imports from the Middle East, Africa, Indonesia, and other places. The OPEC oil embargo was a complete shock to American consumers, who not only saw gasoline prices increase dramatically but also had to wait in long lines at service stations across the country. The OPEC oil embargo contributed to the 1973–74 stock market crash and the loss of billions of dollars in American corporate value and stockholder equities. Americans soon had to deal with gasoline rationing, less demand for traditional large cars, more imports of small (usually Japanese) cars, reduced speed limits, and national campaigns to adjust thermostats and otherwise conserve energy. Houston, on the other hand, enjoyed a business surge.

The major American oil companies were alarmed by the prospect of embargo and went to Washington to court support and intervention. The State Department was dismissive of their worries, so they went to the White House to see General Brent Scowcroft. He sent them to the Pentagon to see Bill Clements,[137] the deputy secretary of defense, who was then the acting secretary. Clements knew the oil industry well, but "he made clear to his visitors that he had his own information and views about the Arabs: they would never unite, the companies' fears were unfounded, and King Faisal was dependent on America."[138]

One problem that had contributed to the energy crisis was greater dependence on overseas oil that could often be produced cheaply and in copious amounts. This arrangement had effectively reduced production in the United States given the inability of American companies to compete economically. However, the quadrupling of oil prices in less than a year made many known hydrocarbon fields suddenly profitable to harvest again. Additionally, many areas previously deemed too expensive to explore became attractive options for drillers. Houston was, of course, at the center of these activities and enjoyed both buoyed production and employment and increased values on businesses and equipment. In short, Houston made a killing off the 1973 oil embargo and economic crisis.

The continued profitability of Houston in the 1970s drove more people to move there and enabled Houston to increase its population by more than 30 percent over the decade.[139] The sustained economic growth and employment figures joined with greater business diversification and new technologies to produce a global city that was clearly the center of US energy but also a more broadly based global city. Oil prices remained high in the late 1970s to early 1980s, which made many Houstonians think the boom would never end, whereas much of the nation and world saw only economic problems from the same scenario.[140]

By 1990, world oil production stood at sixty million barrels per day with almost a third of that used by the North American market. Yet production in the United States could meet only half the market demand, requiring heavy imports from abroad. Most of the imports came from the Middle East. Dependence on Middle East oil made sense in a market analysis because two-thirds of the known reserves at the time were located in five Middle East nations. It was cheaper to import that oil than try to replace it with American finds. Searching for new reserves in the United States was very costly, and the easier, more shallow finds had already been exhausted. Heavy environmental regulations and expensive administrative overhead made it more cost-effective to import the oil. Houston benefited greatly from the policy of oil importation given its vast deep-water port facility, refinery capacity, and network of pipelines for distribution. As imports of petroleum expanded, Houston continued to expand its port facilities and dredge the channel to greater depths.

The United States sought to increase domestic oil production in a less costly manner by drilling offshore. The technology for offshore drilling, platform design and construction, and offload to tankers increased dramatically in the late twentieth century. Houston was the center of this technology.

Securing oil supplies overseas benefited Houston not only because of tanker traffic to its port and facilities from foreign production but also from the exploration work itself. US oil giants, usually based in Houston, searched worldwide to make new discoveries and expand production in known fields through deeper drilling, horizontal drilling, or other techniques. These companies sent colonizing armies of Houstonians to the Middle East to be sure, but also to Russia, Central Asia, China, South America, New Guinea, Brunei, and any other place that oil or natural gas might possibly be found. Petroleum engineers, geologists, computer scientists, all manner of technicians and the lawyers, businessmen, and accountants in support fanned across the globe. Many times they lived in communities built especially for them, as in Saudi Arabia, or melded into the local society, as in Norway. Many returned to Houston after several years posting abroad, and some maintained two homes, flying back and forth frequently.

Houston became regarded as the "Energy Capital of the World" because major oil companies were headquartered there but also because of the atmosphere of Houston: "It is in Texas, not New York, that the Exxon men feel more thoroughly at home: and it is the Exxon skyscraper in Houston, the headquarters of Exxon, USA which seems to house the soul of the company."[141] Oilmen from around the world liked to gather at the Houston Petroleum Club to negotiate deals or just to show off the view to visitors, much of which was made possible by oil.[142]

The Texas oil boom, and the growth of the energy industry in general, generated extraordinary wealth, which was distributed to individuals and public and private corporations in different locations. However, a great deal of the wealth stayed in the Houston region and helped transform the city and its inhabitants. Houston had matured into a "metropolitan area, complete with high culture, good restaurants, and major league sports."[143] Many of the leaders of the energy industry were also community leaders and used their personal and corporate wealth to support "major civic, cultural, and educational initiatives."[144]

One sector that benefited in particular from the philanthropic largesse of private energy wealth was higher education. Rice University was established before the Texas oil boom, but it benefited from many gifts over the years from oil companies such as Texaco and Humble Oil, as well as energy-related companies such as Brown and Root. Additionally, institutions like Rice developed curricula designed to train specialists for the energy industry in fields such as petroleum engineering. Students seeking "specialized technical degrees in great demand in the oil and petrochemical

The Swayne Moore field was located in Beaumont. Abuse and waste in the frenetic early days of the oil industry led to state regulation by the Texas Railroad Commission. The agency's balancing of public and private interests set an example to national and foreign regulators. Photograph by Edgerton Photography Studio, 1902.

industries" could likewise find what they needed at public university systems in the region, such as Texas Southern University, Sam Houston State University in Huntsville, and Lamar University in Beaumont. However, the University of Houston System, lavishly funded by "Houston independent oilman Hugh Roy Cullen and others from the oil and gas industries," was particularly adept at training a growing workforce of professionals.[145]

Oil and gas not only transformed the business and social structure of Houston but even the climate. Houston became known for high-quality and abundant air-conditioning such that even on a hot and humid day, "a Houstonian can spend his whole day inside strange-shaped structures with unchangingly equable weather: in a shopping arcade with a skating rink; in a Hyatt hotel built around its own bit of sky; or in the Astrodome, a vast concrete mushroom where he and 50,000 other Texans can watch the Houston Oilers playing air-conditioned football [because Houston] had triumphantly won the battle against the elements."[146]

The previously discussed importance of the oil and gas industry to Houston does not, standing alone, make Houston the global city that it is, nor does it explain Houston's influence on global affairs. A better way to illustrate this point is to examine an organization, World Energy Cities Partnership, whose membership includes the City of Houston. The partnership provides a structure for cities, which are principally identified with the

oil and gas industry, to work in a cooperative way on problems and policy issues common to the group. This includes economic growth, health and safety, environmental concerns, changing technology, commodity transport and storage, climate change, and other similar issues. The partnership hosts annual working group meetings and conferences for industry and political leaders that include high-profile speakers from member nations to speak on the state and future of oil and gas. Along with Houston, the membership includes seventeen other cities identified as significant global energy cities. Yet none of these cities would be regarded as especially important diplomatic players or influential in foreign policy on a broad scale. The ones that come closest to be regarded as major players in the foreign policy field are Doha and Kuala Lumpur. Even then the influence is mostly regional and is tied perhaps as much to those cities' roles as national capitals than to any other factor. Others on the list have little historical visibility and are in fact completely overshadowed by cities in their same nation-state that are quite visible in a current and historical way in the development and implementation of foreign policy. This is the case with Aberdeen (as opposed to London), Calgary (as opposed to Ottawa), Perth (as opposed so Sydney), Stavanger (as opposed to Oslo), and Dongying (as opposed to Beijing). Still others on the list are virtually invisible on the stage of foreign affairs, such as Esbjerg, Malabo, San Fernando, and Villahermosa. Yet each of those cities

In the post–World War II era, peace and growing prosperity enticed Americans to buy bigger, heavier, and fancier automobiles. Houston's surging energy industry ensured a plentiful supply of inexpensive gasoline. Courtesy of GM Media Archive, GM Heritage Center.

is a global center when it comes to oil and gas and is vitally important to the trillion-dollar global energy market.

Another prominent organization linking Houston and the international economy is the Offshore Technology Conference (OTC), "still the largest international conference on offshore technology, which has been held annually in Houston since 1969."[147] The OTC is the largest oil and gas trade show in the world, attracting more than two thousand companies and over fifty thousand attendees from over 120 countries. It is always among the top ten trade shows held in the United States each year. The OTC is sponsored by a group of industry associations who cooperate to showcase the latest technologies that can be harnessed to create wealth and jobs from offshore energy deposits. The attendees include not only energy executives and professional firms supporting the energy industry but also political leaders; ministers of energy, commerce, and trade; foreign secretaries; and European and Middle Eastern royalty. The weeklong conference includes breakfast programs, lunches, receptions, and dinners hosted by the leading oil and gas firms as well as the many consulates in Houston who represent nations heavily involved in the global energy market. The diplomatic representatives in Houston of the Netherlands, Russia, China, the United Kingdom, France, Sweden, Mexico, Saudi Arabia, Qatar, and others host lavish events, bring in their royal and political leaders, invite all the local business leaders and celebrities, and seek to place their nation and its energy companies in the most favorable light.

The difference between Houston and other cities on the list is its diversification of power and wealth. Houston is regarded as the global center in the oil and gas industry, one of the most significant even in such a group of star cities. But its global influence hinges on more than just that aspect. Houston has found a way, both intentionally and unintentionally, to incorporate its energy wealth and power into a larger package of attributes, including space exploration and technology, international trade (apart from energy), and medical research and treatment. These additional bases of wealth and power join together to create a city center that attracts global businesses and powerful individuals like a magnet.

As oil production has moved to other parts of the world, Houston has maintained its position by refining and processing oil and gas into high-end products for the international market. With the concentration of "administration, pipeline location, and technology," Houston will remain the center of the natural gas industry "no matter where the new gas is produced." For oil, Houston's ongoing advantage is that the world's "leading multinational oil and oil supply and service companies" are all strongly tied to the city.[148]

The wealth generated in Houston by the oil and gas industry greatly supplemented the wealth created earlier from trade. Additionally, the science, engineering, and technology employed in the energy and chemical industries helped steer the city in a new modern direction. By the end of World War II, Houston would discover a way to meet its health-care needs by combining the best scientific minds along with public monies and private fortunes to launch the world's largest medical complex, thereby establishing the third great pillar of Houston's global rise.

CHAPTER THREE

TEXAS MEDICAL CENTER

1941

THE TEXAS MEDICAL Center is truly one of the wonders of the world. In typical Texas fashion, it is "the largest medical complex in the world,"[1] hosting eight million patient visits per year. The complex contains fifty-four medicine-related institutions, including twenty-four hospitals, eight academic research institutions, four medical schools, six nursing schools, and schools of dentistry, pharmacy, and other specialties. All the institutions are not-for-profit.

The Texas Medical Center had the first and largest air ambulance service and the first inter-institutional transplant program. There are almost fourteen thousand heart surgeries per year in the center, by far the most in the world. It has both the largest children's hospital and the largest cancer hospital in the world. Over eight million people visit the center each year, including approximately twenty thousand foreign patients.[2]

Almost as amazing as the size and scope of the Texas Medical Center is the fact that it is so young. It was established in 1945 with initial funding from the MD Anderson Foundation created in 1936 by Monroe Dunaway Anderson. At $19 million the MD Anderson Foundation was the largest charitable fund ever created in Texas.[3] Before the Texas Medical Center was established, Houston was the "largest city in the nation without a medical college."[4]

Although it is true that the Texas Medical Center is young, its origins actually go deep into the history of Houston and Texas. By the time the center was formally established, there existed the fortunate coincidence of "philanthropy coming of age in Houston" along with a general growth of public attention to health issues.[5] The creation of the Texas Medical Center, and its size and capacity, is intertwined with Houston's own wealth, political power, and international reach.

Early Health Care in Houston

Physicians are often civic leaders in different societies both now and throughout history, and that is true for Houston and Texas as well. "When Texans formally declared independence from Mexico on March 2, 1836, at Washington-on-the-Brazos, eight of the fifty-nine signers of the Texas Declaration of Independence were doctors."[6] Prominent in this group was Lorenzo de Zavala, who became vice president of the Republic of Texas. Zavala had originally served in the government of Mexico, including a stint as ambassador to France, but he had a falling out with Santa Anna, who had seized dictatorial powers. Zavala owned land and built a home on Buffalo Bayou opposite San Jacinto where the decisive battle of Texas independence was fought. "In the aftermath of the climactic battle that took place there, his home served as a hospital for wounded Texans and Mexicans."[7]

Lorenzo de Zavala was a prominent leader in the Texas Revolution, later serving as vice president of the new republic. Not many people also know he offered his own home to serve as a hospital for soldiers injured in the Battle of San Jacinto. Courtesy of the Prints and Photographs Collection, Texas Library and Archives Foundation.

The early city of Houston suffered all the maladies one would expect of a fledgling town in a wet area without proper streets or sanitation. Disease outbreaks were common, whether caused by germs spreading in close quarters with lack of disinfectant or good hygiene or by vectors, such as mosquitoes, carrying malaria or dengue fever or rats carrying fleas with plague or typhus.[8]

Houston's civic authorities regularly stressed that citizens must take precautions, as best they were understood at the time, and there was even an early Medical and Surgical Society of Houston in 1838 that sought to unite health-care professionals to better the lives of local citizens.[9] Nonetheless, the city was hit with a series of disease outbreaks, especially yellow fever. One yellow fever outbreak in 1839 killed 10 percent of the population, followed by an epidemic almost as bad in 1843. These yellow fever outbreaks continued periodically into the late 1860s.[10]

In 1857, the Houston Medical Association was formed as a professional association of the city's doctors to "cultivate the science of medicine."[11] This group ended during the Civil War and was replaced in 1868 by the Harris County Medical Association. This countywide association drew in a larger swath of members from the rural communities then surrounding the city of Houston.[12]

The first hospital appeared in Houston as early as 1837 as a temporary facility to care for sick soldiers, but by 1839 there was a more general city hospital. Additional rural hospitals, including those sponsored by railroads, came and went in the area over the next several decades.[13] But in 1887, the Sisters of Charity of the Incarnate Word came up from Galveston to establish St. Joseph's Infirmary, a 40-bed hospital. This was expanded to a second building in 1889 before construction of a new building in 1893. Tragically, all the buildings were lost in a great fire in 1894. The citizens of Houston launched a fundraising campaign to help rebuild, and by 1896 a new 100-bed hospital was opened with an additional wing by 1905. This was further supplemented with an adjacent training school for nurses.

Other hospital facilities began to open in rapid succession, including a surgical hospital in 1907 as well as several private sanitariums. Baptist Hospital was established along with a school of nursing in 1904.[14] As Houston grew, additional general and specialty hospitals were opened to treat alcohol and drug addictions, mental illness, and nervous disorders. The city itself opened a 150-bed hospital in 1922 named for Jefferson Davis.[15]

Before the Texas Medical Center, the best hope for modern medical care in Houston lay with Hermann Hospital, which opened in 1925 with its own "electric light plant, ice plant and electric kitchen."[16] Hermann Hospital

Hermann Hospital was funded by the estate of George H. Hermann, an early Houston millionaire who wanted his city to have the best possible health care. Courtesy of the Texas Medical Center.

would later prove to be a cornerstone in Houston's health-care system. The hospital is named for George H. Hermann, who died in 1914 and left part of his fortune to establish a hospital. Hermann's vision for health care in Houston was excellent, especially for the time period, but it was an isolated facility not coordinated with any other health institution.

George Hermann was born in Houston in 1843 and was successful in both the lumber and cattle business, but oil made him a millionaire at the turn of the century. Although Houston's medical expertise would soon project into the world, initially Houstonians like George Hermann sought out the best technologies and practices and brought them back to Houston. Hermann traveled extensively in America and Europe to see hospitals and visit physicians and developed a great interest in health care and how it might be brought to his hometown.[17] Hermann Hospital was the first hospital on the site of what eventually grew to be the Texas Medical Center. Hermann was the first hospital in Texas to receive penicillin and was the hospital where the first cardiac catheterization was performed.[18]

The status of health care in Houston in the early twentieth century was at least on a par with that in similar cities and in many ways, as with Hermann Hospital, was very modern and ahead of most facilities of its era. But it was not until the post–World War II era that the global wonder of the Texas Medical Center was born, enabled by the MD Anderson Foundation bequest and the determination of city leaders. To understand how that circumstance came about, one must go back to the origins of Monroe Dunaway Anderson and understand both his success and his character, as well as the critical relationship between him and William L. Clayton.

The M. D. Anderson Story

Monroe D. Anderson was born in Jackson, Tennessee, in 1873, where his father was president of the local First National Bank. He was named for his maternal grandfather, William Monroe Dunaway, who was a Presbyterian minister, Masonic Grand Master of Tennessee, and one-time mayor of Jackson.[19] Monroe's older brother, Frank, married Burdine Clayton of Tupelo, Mississippi. Burdine's younger brother, William Clayton,[20] learned shorthand and typing in order to make his way in the business world. He landed a job with an executive of the American Cotton Company in St. Louis, which eventually led to a job with the same company in New York.[21] Over the years, Frank Anderson and Burdine Clayton Anderson prospered first in Texas and then in Oklahoma, where they saw an opportunity to open a cotton merchandising business of their own.

Frank first contacted his brother Monroe, who had saved enough money as a banker to be able to invest in a new enterprise. Frank then reached out to his brother-in-law, Will Clayton, in New York, who was ready to start his own venture. In 1904, the three young men formed Anderson, Clayton and Co. with their combined capital contributions and their combined expertise in cotton, banking, and finance. Ben Clayton joined as a partner the following year after he was laid off from his job in Houston with American Cotton Company.[22]

Although Anderson, Clayton was originally founded in Oklahoma City, it moved to Houston in 1916 to access the deep-water port for its large cotton shipments. Houston also offered good warehousing opportunities and railroad connections.[23] World War I was also an era in which the United States was transformed into a creditor nation, "a change that Will Clayton saw unfold first-hand as a member of the wartime cotton council."[24] Anderson, Clayton bought into a major British cotton firm but "started agencies of its own in the European cities of Le Havre, Bremen, and Milan; Osaka, Japan;

Monroe D. Anderson was an ambitious and successful banker who joined with others to form Anderson, Clayton and Co., soon to be the world's largest cotton merchandising company. RGE 0061-0006, Houston Public Library, Anderson, Clayton Company Records.

Shanghai, China; Bombay, India; and Mexico City." In the 1920s, the company was operating in Egypt as well as expanded European and Asian locations and was "the world's largest cotton firm." Not only did Anderson, Clayton use the Port of Houston as the "concentration point for cotton exports," but the company also forced the New York Cotton Exchange in 1928 to accept delivery of cotton at southern ports, rather than New York.[25]

The change in delivery location resulted in a greater shipping concentration at Houston and eliminated the unnecessary costs incurred from shipping cotton to a New York storage warehouse simply to satisfy a futures contract when the cotton could be stored in Houston at a lesser cost.[26] Moreover, it demonstrated that Houston had clout on the international commodity market. By the 1940s the company also operated in South America and expanded to service all stages of cotton production. By 1945, with 223 gins, 33 cottonseed oil plants, and 123 warehouses worldwide, *Fortune* magazine called Anderson, Clayton the largest buyer, seller, storer,

William L. Clayton was an extremely successful international businessman who later served as a top appointee of Presidents Roosevelt and Truman. Courtesy of the Museum of Fine Arts, Houston.

and shipper of raw cotton in the world.[27] The company became publicly traded under the symbol ACCO.[28] But there are many important side connections to this global company that also had a big impact on the city of Houston, especially for health care. One such important connection was the law firm Fulbright used by Anderson, Clayton as it began its global expansion. Monroe D. Anderson and Clarence Fulbright met through mutual banking friends. Coincidentally, Fulbright's family had also originated in Jackson, Tennessee, and this connection "likely helped to establish a rapport between the two men."[29]

The firm Fulbright and Jaworski originally formed in 1919, soon after Anderson, Clayton relocated to Houston, under the name Fulbright, Crooker, Freeman and Bates. Clarence Fulbright was a graduate of Baylor University and the University of Chicago Law School.[30] He first represented Anderson, Clayton in 1918 on rate matters pertaining to cotton shipments. John Henry Crooker read law independently and took the bar exam, as was allowed in those days without the necessity of law school. He was elected a justice of the peace in Harris County before becoming district attorney. He served as a Judge Advocate General's Corps (JAG) officer in World War I before returning to Houston and joining Clarence Fulbright to open a private practice.[31] John H. Freeman was also a graduate of the University of Chicago Law School. He brought legal experience in banking and real estate to the new firm when he joined in 1924. William Bartholomew Bates was a graduate of the University of Texas Law School and served as district attorney in Nacogdoches but was not reelected because of opposition by the Ku Klux Klan. Bates relocated to Houston and joined the firm in 1923.[32] "Throughout the 1920s and 1930s, both the Anderson, Clayton and the Fulbright & Crooker firms continued to grow."[33]

Over the years, "a level of trust and friendship" grew between the men of both firms, and when in "the mid-1930s, Anderson's health was in decline, he turned to his trusted attorneys and friends . . . to help him with his estate planning."[34] Monroe Anderson had never married and had no children, so there was concern about both what to do with his fortune and what the tax consequences would be.[35] Federal death taxes were not a concern in an earlier time when a wealthy individual like M. D. Anderson could have left his

Clarence Fulbright was a partner in what later became Fulbright and Jaworski and finally Norton Rose Fulbright. He and his early partners helped Monroe D. Anderson structure his estate to fund the MD Anderson Foundation. Courtesy of Norton Rose Fulbright, LLP.

The name Monroe D. Anderson was to later become famous as M. D. Anderson and associated with the most important and famous cancer treatment center in the world. RGE 0061-0005, Houston Public Library, Anderson, Clayton Company Records.

fortune to his family and business associates. But by the 1930s the tax situation was very different, and Anderson knew it. A nephew, Thomas Dunaway Anderson, recalled that his uncle had political motivations as well. "[He] disliked Franklin Roosevelt, and that is an understatement. He detested the fellow and all that he stood for." M. D. Anderson sought a way to preserve Anderson, Clayton and Co. and to prevent his fortune from going to the federal government.[36] Over time, Monroe Anderson and his lawyers at Fulbright and Crooker designed a "foundation that ultimately would change the face of Houston and have a lasting impact on health care in the United States."[37] M. D. Anderson established his foundation in 1936 for charitable and community services but without specifying a cancer hospital or medical center.

The foundation's initial disbursement was $150 to the Houston Junior League to help purchase eyeglasses for needy schoolchildren. Other small grants followed as Monroe D. Anderson began making more contributions to his new foundation.[38] On August 6, 1939, Anderson died, and Fulbright, Crooker and Freeman filed his will for probate.[39] Ultimately, his estate was valued at $20 million, of which he left $1 million to his heirs and $19 million to his foundation. For years it was the largest foundation in Texas.[40]

While the MD Anderson Foundation continued making a few small grants, once the probate and IRS review were complete, the trustees had to decide what specifically in the field of health care they should best target. How the MD Anderson Foundation came to focus on cancer, thus leading to a general medical complex, is a story rooted further back in Texas and US history.

Pre-World War II National Health-Care Policy and Houston Philanthropy

In general, Americans were increasingly aware of cancer in the late nineteenth and early twentieth centuries. Ulysses S. Grant publicly and famously died of throat cancer in 1885. Prominent New Yorkers, including John Jacob Astor III, helped form the New York Cancer Hospital that opened in 1887. In 1936, as the MD Anderson Foundation was established, John D. Rockefeller Jr. donated land for the new site of General Memorial Hospital for the Treatment of Cancer and Allied Diseases. And in 1940, "[Charles P.] Sloan and Charles F. Kettering, former executives of General Motors, established the Sloan-Kettering Institute" for the treatment of cancer.[41]

A parallel rise in interest in cancer arose in Texas at this time. In 1914, Texas became the second state in the nation to establish a committee on cancer, and in 1929, "the legislature authorized the creation of a cancer hospital in Dallas"; however, the idea was not funded and never materialized.[42] At the national level, two Texans, "Dudley Jackson, M.D., and his cousin Congressman Maury Maverick, played prominent roles in establishing the National Cancer Institute in 1937." Other Texans, Albert and Mary Lasker, living in New York became "powerful voices" in setting national health-care policy.[43] Before the twentieth century, there was not really such a thing as a "national health policy." Congress established the US Public Health Service in 1798, but the purpose was to provide medical care for sick or injured seamen, not to conduct research or engage in broad public health programs. In connection with the Public Health Service, Congress established a Hygienic Laboratory in 1887, but again the purpose was not to conduct research or engage in health policy. It was not until 1930 that the Hygienic Laboratory was replaced by the National Institute of Health based in Bethesda, Maryland. In 1938, Congress established the National Cancer Institute, focusing for the first time on a single disease and with the capacity to issue grants to other research laboratories.[44]

The World War II era provided abundant federal funding for research that had not previously been available. Vannevar Bush, a scientist at Harvard, ran the Office of Scientific Research and Development and successfully gained federal funding for research. Bush feared the end of the war would mean the end of federal dollars for research. Meanwhile, Albert and Mary Lasker, rich from the sale of his successful national advertising firm, established the Lasker Foundation to support medical research.[45] They lobbied a friend in the Roosevelt administration to continue federal funding of medical research after the war. President Roosevelt referred a memo to Bush on the subject from the Laskers.[46] Bush, who himself sought to change the normal thinking about funding, drafted a response to the Lasker memo in the form of a report: *Science: The Endless Frontier*. Bush's report was well received and became the basis for the National Science Foundation in 1950.[47] Congress added other institutes over the years, creating a plural National Institutes of Health.

Birth of the Texas Medical Center

In 1941, Arthur Cato, a state representative from Weatherford, introduced a bill to establish a state cancer hospital involving the University of Texas. Representative Cato had "lost both his parents and members of his wife's family to cancer."[48] Although Cato's bill came as a surprise to the University of Texas, the idea was not new since the Texas legislature had passed a similar bill in 1929 and again in 1931, but there was no funding appropriated to implement the bill. Additionally, the Depression prevented new legislation or funding throughout the 1930s.[49] However, Cato's bill passed the legislature and received an appropriation of $500,000.[50] Half the money was to be used for construction and half for operation. The bill provided for the University of Texas to administer the hospital and determine its location, although the presumption was that it would be in Galveston in conjunction with the university's medical school there. Governor W. Lee O'Daniel signed the bill on June 30, 1941, with a September effective date.[51] Dallas and San Antonio also lobbied for the hospital, but the UT Board of Regents ultimately chose Houston.[52] The selection was not done in a vacuum but was the result of a strategy launched in Houston and a successful lobby campaign of University of Texas officials by representatives of Houston, the MD Anderson Foundation in particular. Speaking to the Gulf Coast Historical Association meeting in 1956, W. B. Bates recounted the early days when a decision was made to lure the cancer hospital to Houston. The trustees of the MD Anderson Foundation had been dreaming of a medical center and how to build one. But after the Texas legislature decided the University of Texas should establish a cancer research hospital, Bates said, "It occurred to [us] that such an institution as a great cancer research hospital would make an ideal nucleus for the medical center [we] had been dreaming about." Bates goes on to recount how a meeting occurred on his back porch with other foundation trustees and John Spies, dean of the UT Medical School at Galveston, to plan a strategy.[53]

Bates's law partner, John Freeman, agreed with that assessment, stating that "we had nothing specific in mind at the start," and in fact it took some time for the trustees to even decide that health should be the area of focus.[54] Freeman recalled that the trustees talked about a "hospital for the white collar man" by which they apparently meant the middle class, since hospitals of the era seemed to be "either for the rich or for the poor" with nothing for "the man in the middle."[55] But once Representative Cato's bill passed and Governor O'Daniel signed it and the appropriation, Freeman said it "took our attention immediately and we moved over to that idea and away from what we had been thinking."[56]

The watershed moment came when leading "M. D. Anderson trustees William B. Bates, John H. Freeman and Horace M. Wilkins hosted a small luncheon at the Houston Club for University of Texas officials on December 13, 1941."[57] The guests from the University of Texas included President Homer P. Rainey and the dean of the UT Medical Branch in Galveston, John W. Spies. The lunch occurred only six days after the Japanese attack on Pearl Harbor when the nation's attention was riveted to immediate war in the Pacific and looming war in Europe as Nazi Germany joined its Axis ally Japan against the United States. The historical record does not reveal how far in advance the December 13 lunch had been planned, but it is likely that such men had very busy schedules, and with President Rainey needing to travel from Austin, the lunch may well have been planned weeks in advance or certainly more than six days. It is clear that the world events, as monumental as they were, did not deter the luncheon attendees from proceeding with a meeting on a topic very important to Houston and the state of Texas.

Negotiations soon began between the MD Anderson Foundation and the University of Texas guided by the lawyers of Fulbright, Crooker, Freeman and Bates with a result reached in 1942:[58] "The Foundation agreed that if the University of Texas would establish the cancer research hospital in Houston and call it the MD Anderson Hospital, we would furnish $500,000 to match the sum appropriated by the legislature, and we would provide twenty acres of ground at an appropriate place in Houston on which to build the hospital."[59] Administrative and managerial control would rest with the University of Texas. John Freeman records in his minutes of the luncheon meeting that the cancer hospital would be located "in the general neighborhood of the Hermann Hospital," thus indicating that from the very outset the plan was to co-locate facilities.[60]

The legislature had not specified where the cancer hospital would be located likely to avoid the political fight between Galveston, Houston, Dallas, and perhaps other cities. Since the hospital was to be run by the University of Texas, it was easy and politically convenient to pass the decision to the Board of Regents. It also made good management sense rather than deciding where the facility would go and then forcing the university to overcome any problems with the location. However, the passage of Representative Cato's bill and the appropriation of $500,000 toward a cancer hospital also occurred simultaneously with a political clash at the University of Texas. The root of the clash was political and philosophical differences between regents appointed by James V. Allred (a New Deal governor) and more conservative regents appointed by W. Lee O'Daniel and Coke R. Stevenson (both anti–New Dealers).[61]

Of course, it may be possible that an informal arrangement had already been made between key legislators and members of the Board of Regents by the time the session ended. The regents in August 1942, at the time the decision was made to place the cancer hospital in Houston, included a diverse array of powerful people well connected and experienced in business and politics, including Kenneth Aynesworth, who was a surgeon and graduate of UT's medical school. He had done postgraduate medical studies in Berlin in 1902 and at Johns Hopkins in 1909 before opening his own practice in Waco. Aynesworth was appointed a UT regent by Governor Miriam Ferguson in 1933 but continued to serve on the board until 1944 under the next three governors. In particular he served on the Medical Branch Committee.[62] Governor Coke Stevenson appointed John H. Bickett in March 1942 before the decision was made in August about where to place the hospital. Bickett was a lawyer who had served prominently on the Board of Law Examiners, as chief justice of the Fourth Court of Civil Appeals in San Antonio, and as general counsel of Southwestern Bell Telephone. He was elected president of the State Bar in 1945 and was a member of the Philosophical Society.[63]

Dan Harrison was on the board, appointed in 1941 by Governor O'Daniel. Harrison had made a fortune in oil with such gushers as the Old Ocean field in Brazoria County. He used some of his wealth to buy up ranchland that conferred further wealth.[64] W. Scott Schreiner, a Hill Country rancher, was appointed to the board in June 1942 by Governor Coke Stevenson. Governor Ferguson appointed Hilmar Weinert to the board in 1933. Weinert was a graduate of UT and UT Law School and served as mayor of Seguin as well as chairman of the Seguin State Bank. He made a fortune in oil and electric power development.[65] Three other regents, D. F. Strickland, Henry Jacob Lutcher Stark, and Orville Bullington, were notable for their clash with Homer Rainey, president of UT Austin, whom they fired in 1944 after a long battle over control of the flagship campus. Strickland was a lobbyist for the motion picture industry.[66] Stark was the heir to a lumber fortune in Orange and a graduate of UT. He had been on the board since 1919, appointed by Governor Hobby, and by the time he left in 1945, he had served twenty-four years, half of that as chairman.[67] Bullington is perhaps the most memorable of the group, appointed in 1941 by Governor O'Daniel. He was a graduate of UT Law School, opened a law practice in Wichita Falls, and was later partner in the first radio station in Waco, WACO. He joined the Republican Party in 1918 and was the GOP nominee for governor of Texas in 1932, losing to Miriam Ferguson. Bullington was fiercely anti-FDR and New Deal. He was a delegate to eight Republican conventions and served as state party chair. Bullington and some other board members sought to reduce UT funding, restrict certain lines of instruction at the university, and remove certain faculty with accusations of communism. Ultimately the regents fired Rainey in 1944 with only Marguerite Fairchild voting no. But in 1942, the regents, including Fairchild, were united on placing the cancer hospital in Houston. It is interesting to note that one of the issues of friction between Rainey and the regents was Rainey's effort to bring the UT Medical Branch at Galveston into the university proper—the regents rejected the idea.[68]

With success in hand, the MD Anderson Foundation began to look for a temporary home for the cancer hospital. By this time, the United States was fighting World War II, and materials needed for new construction were not available or were restricted. The perfect temporary choice turned out to be the Oaks, the large mansion and estate belonging to Captain James A. Baker, who had just died in 1941. Baker left his home to the Rice Institute, but Rice did not need it and sold it to the foundation to be used as the initial cancer hospital.[69] In this way the histories of William Marsh Rice and the Rice Institute, James A. Baker (and his grandson Secretary James Baker III and the Baker Institute at Rice University), the University of Texas, the MD Anderson Cancer Hospital, and the Texas Medical Center all became intertwined.

Meanwhile, the University of Texas tapped Ernst W. "Bill" Bertner, a Houston physician, as the first chief of the new cancer hospital. Bertner had medical experience in Houston as chief of staff at Jefferson Davis Hospital and then at Hermann Hospital. He had also served as president of the Texas Medical Association and was politically well connected in the state. In an interesting twist of fate, Bertner was working as a medical intern in New York when he was assigned to treat Jesse Jones, the Houston banker and builder, who had fallen ill on a trip to New York. Jones was so impressed with Bertner that he offered him the post of house physician in his new Rice Hotel in Houston.[70] Bertner moved there in 1913, lived at the hotel, and established a solid reputation with the city's elite that positioned him well when the thought of a cancer hospital and a medical center took off years later.

Bertner dreamed and talked of a cancer hospital for years to his neighbors and their guests and friends. One fortunate connection was Dudley Odom, a Houston physician and personal associate of Bertner. Odom was also friends with Searcy Bracewell and was able to bring the group together. Bracewell was a prominent lawyer and a member of the Texas legislature. One evening, Bracewell accompanied Odom to the Rice Hotel to visit Bertner's suite and hear his vision for the fledgling MD Anderson Hospital and how it might grow in the years ahead. Bracewell agreed "to sponsor a bill in the Legislature which would make it a part of the University of Texas." Bracewell also worked later with Frederick Elliott, dean of the Texas Dental College, to bring that institution into the UT System and to secure legislative funding for both the dental school (then a private institution) and the cancer hospital.[71] Bracewell would be a faithful ally of MD Anderson Cancer Hospital and the Texas Medical Center over the years, effectively playing the role of lobbyist to guide Houston medical officials around the Capitol and facilitate meetings with the governor, lieutenant governor, and other legislators.[72] Bracewell managed to be very effective for Houston even though urban legislators were far outnumbered by rural legislators in those days, who were much less concerned with large urban projects.[73]

Another crucial relationship Bertner formed was with attorney John Freeman, who also lived at the Rice Hotel during the World War II era and who discussed the idea of a medical center with Bertner even before the opportunity arose from both the Anderson Foundation and the Texas legislature.[74] With Bertner on board, the UT Board of Regents formally accepted "the Anderson Foundation's proposal placing the cancer hospital in Houston" and announced the name as the "M. D. Anderson Hospital for Cancer Research of the University of Texas."[75]

With the commitment between UT and the foundation formalized, the temporary hospital in place, and a chief physician onboard, the foundation then began exploring the idea of a broader medical center for Houston. "When we took the cancer hospital in hand, we then made up our minds that we would try to put a [medical] center in here [and although] we didn't envision anything like it is now, of course, but we wanted to put in a sizeable center," said John Freeman.[76]

As a first step in that direction, Frederick C. Elliott sought to integrate his dental school into the UT System and the new center planned for Houston. The Texas Dental College was a private, nonprofit institution, as was Baylor Dental College in Dallas; in fact, there were no public dental schools in Texas. Elliott proposed to donate the dental college facilities and property to the state to be operated by UT. In turn, "the M. D. Anderson Foundation agreed to provide land for a permanent home for the dental branch and also proposed a donation of $500,000 to help meet the cost of a permanent building." The legislature passed the enabling legislation in 1943.[77] It is interesting to note that while the dental school bill was being considered in the legislature, the Medical Branch at Galveston was recovering from the recent UT uproar and firing of its dean and the university president, so it stayed out of the matter. Additionally, Baylor University was fighting with Dallas over the College of Medicine, so it also was not involved in the dental school bill.[78] With the addition of the dental school to the cancer hospital, the vision of a medical center was beginning to take hold.

The charter of the Texas Medical Center was drafted in 1945, stating as its first purpose "to promote and provide for or assist in the establishment, support and maintenance of facilities for medical, dental and nursing education, and other phases of health and medical education, for hospitalization and treatment of the sick and afflicted, and for research in the field of health and science of medicine and dentistry."[79] The charter named original board members, including W. B. Bates, Ernst Bertner, Frederick Elliott, John Freeman, and Bishop Quin. It was filed and approved by Texas Secretary of State Claude Isbell on November 1, 1945.[80]

Rapid Growth of the Texas Medical Center

While events were moving so well and so rapidly in Austin and Houston, a drama was building in Dallas that would play nicely into the hands of the MD Anderson Foundation. Baylor University College of Medicine was created in Dallas in 1903 after it formed an alliance with the fledgling University of Dallas Medical School, which had been established in 1900.[81] Although the college enjoyed a good academic and professional reputation, it faced continuing financial problems, especially as the Depression lingered through the 1930s. A former dean of the Baylor College of Medicine, Edward Cary, formed the Southwestern Medical Foundation in 1939 with the idea that it could provide funding and facilities in a way to lure the medical school away from Baylor University and better serve the needs of the Dallas area. In 1942, a merger was tentatively announced with promises of land, construction, and capital. However, many viewed the agreement as more a "hostile takeover" than a true merger, and it was clear to many that a subplot existed to make the medical school sectarian and detach it from the Baptist Church.[82]

Even so, Baylor University was under financial pressure and faced the threat that its medical faculty might simply leave and go to Southwestern Medical Foundation anyway. The university trustees approved the agreement, and the General Baptist Convention of Texas and the Southern Baptist Convention subsequently approved it. However, three trustees of Baylor "voted against it, Carr P. Collins, D. K. Martin, and H. L. Kokernot [who] became increasingly more determined not to let the medical school fall under the control of the [Southwestern] foundation."[83] When the merger was approved despite their opposition, "Carr Collins resigned in protest," and he and the other two dissenting trustees headed to a ranch near San Antonio to rest and discuss the situation.[84]

The three Baylor loyalists determined that they could not stand for the Baylor College of Medicine to be secularized and absorbed into the Southwestern Foundation so decided to approach the MD Anderson Foundation about the possibility of a move to Houston. D. K. Martin and Clarence Fulbright had attended Baylor together, so Martin set off to Houston to see what possibilities existed. The discussions went well and expanded to include other Baylor representatives, including the Baylor president, former Governor Pat Neff.[85] The Baylor trustees generally felt that in fairness they should give the new merger some time to work, but as it happened, financial pressures on Southwestern, along with some bad political moves, resulted in annulment of the Baylor-Southwestern agreement in April 1943.[86]

The MD Anderson Foundation offered Baylor College of Medicine a twenty-acre site in Houston, $1 million for building, and $1 million over ten years for research.[87] Importantly, MD Anderson stipulated that it would exercise no management or policy-making function over Baylor but would leave Baylor to operate as it saw fit within the standard academic requirements of scholarship and qualification. Baylor accepted the offer in May 1943, and the deal was done.[88] Anderson Foundation trustee W. B. Bates later recalled that two Baylor trustees, W. K. Martin of San Antonio and Carr

The estate of Captain James A. Baker, the Oakes, was used by the MD Anderson Cancer Hospital as its initial cancer hospital until a new facility could be constructed after the war ended. Courtesy of MD Anderson Cancer Center.

Collins of Dallas, originally approached the Anderson trustees to inform them of their intent to leave Dallas and were looking for a new home for a teaching hospital. Governor Neff facilitated further meetings with other Baylor trustees.[89] John Freeman recalled that the Anderson trustees knew Baylor was planning to leave Dallas, and while they would not have deliberately sought to take Baylor away from Dallas, it became clear that Baylor would leave anyway, so it was proper to make Baylor an offer in Houston.[90]

In a short amount of time, Houston had assembled a cancer hospital, a dental school, and a college of medicine. Houston and the Anderson Foundation brought "the University of Texas and Baylor University, the only two institutions of higher education in Texas with experience in medical, dental and nursing education [together as] the cornerstones of a new medical center."[91] In an effort to emphasize that this new project was bigger than Houston, the name Texas Medical Center was chosen.[92] Although the MD Anderson Foundation was the financial driving force for the center, the only facility to actually have that name was the cancer hospital itself. Furthermore, the new president of the cancer hospital, Ernst Bertner, stated that the foundation has "nothing to do with the administration of the institutions financed by them. . . . They furnish the money without any strings."[93] Houston further made good on its promise to facilitate an easy transition by Baylor to its new home. It came up with several temporary homes for the medical school, and by June, barely a month after announcing the deal, Baylor moved "fifty van loads [of] equipment and furniture down from Dallas" and began summer "classes with 131 students."[94] The years ahead

Originally lured to Houston in 1913 by Jesse Jones, Ernst Bertner went on to become the first chief of the new cancer hospital. MS 070, R. Lee Clark Papers, OV087.Gaf-0019.

would show how mutually beneficial the move was for both Baylor and Houston. For Houston, Baylor represented a major part of their initial core medical center that functioned to draw in more players. For Baylor, already regarded as a very good regional medical school, the move to Houston and the infusion of public and private funds allowed it to become a nationally recognized medical school and attract pioneering physicians to its school and teaching hospital.[95]

By the end of 1943, the foundation had completed the purchase of a 134-acre tract from the City of Houston to begin building its permanent medical center.[96] The tract chosen was the same piece of land that Will Hogg had chosen in the 1920s for his earlier vision of a medical center for Houston. However, when his vision did not materialize, "Hogg sold the land at his cost to the city for parks."[97] Thomas Dunaway Anderson believes that Hogg was visionary in seeking a medical center for Houston, but his approach of buying the land and then simply inviting the UT Medical Branch at Galveston to move to Houston was not realistic. For one thing, the Sealy and Smith Foundation in Galveston produced income as an inducement for the medical school to stay there, so new land alone was not a sufficient lure. There had to be a bigger political and financial setup, a single medical center where "doctors from all over the city could be drawn together under one roof." It was this "concept of a medical center that appealed to the M. D. Anderson Foundation."[98] Once the land was purchased, Bertner and Herbert Kipp, an engineer and vice president of the River Oaks subdivision, went on a national tour to look at medical centers to determine how to design and build the best one for Houston.

By the beginning of 1944, the future looked bright for Houston and its dream of a medical center. The war still raged, but the tide had turned to the Allies and most people felt it was just a matter of time until peace was restored. Then the carefully laid plans for a medical center could be realized.[99] For Houston, the value of adding a college of medicine cannot be overstated. The whole approach to medicine had changed so that training requirements to be a doctor were much more rigorous. The Carnegie and Rockefeller Foundations, which had done so much on a national scale for medicine, put their weight behind medical school accreditation standards. The result was that "between 1910 and 1915 the number of [medical] schools nationwide declined from 131 to 95," and that number had dropped further by World War II to only 66.[100] Houston benefited just from having a medical school, but to have one integrated with a cancer hospital and the nucleus of a medical center was a huge boon.

Captain James A. Baker represented William Marsh Rice in many important legal matters. Baker was suspicious when Rice died suddenly, and he exposed Rice's valet as his murderer in conspiracy with a corrupt New York lawyer. Courtesy of the Woodson Research Center, Rice University, Fondren Library, Houston, Texas.

Throughout 1944, the new center did the best it could with wartime rations and building restrictions but managed to treat cancer patients at the old Baker mansion, train medical students, and plan aggressively for expansion in the postwar effort. The only hiccup occurred in July 1944 when UT President Homer Rainey proposed to the Board of Regents that all component parts of the university, including the Medical Branch in Galveston, be relocated to the main campus in Austin.[101] The matter was not well received by the board and was referred to the Medical Committee consisting of H. H. Weinert, Orville Bullington, and D. F. Strickland.[102] This committee reported back in September, rejecting Rainey's proposal, stating that it was best to leave the Medical Branch in Galveston and "that further agitation about removing the Medical School from Galveston should stop, as it is a detriment to the school."[103]

In hindsight, it is apparent that removal of the UT Medical Branch from nearby Galveston in the early stages of the Texas Medical Center in Houston would have been harmful or even fatal to the growth and success of the Houston plan. Instead, the dental school and the cancer hospital cooperating in a regional health-care plan "were fundamental building blocks" for the Texas Medical Center.[104]

In January 1945, Alan Gregg of the Rockefeller Center visited Houston at the invitation of the Texas Medical Center to assess the plans and see how the Rockefeller money might help. Gregg recorded that "the school has apparently an excellent site."[105] Gregg was favorable in his view of the plans but could not understand why the University of Texas insisted on keeping a medical school in Galveston while investing in Houston, referring to it in his notes as "pretty poor motives or out of stupidity."[106] Referring to the Monroe D. Anderson fortune, Gregg marveled in his diary that such a cotton fortune now "had an amazingly profound effect on the city of Houston and will have an important effect on the lives and health of generations to come." Gregg foresaw the international reach of the young medical center, writing that "the story of the Texas Medical Center of Houston has spread throughout the world."[107]

The Texas Medical Center held a dedicatory dinner at the Rice Hotel on February 28, 1946, attended by several hundred leading Houstonians. Although Houston's good health was the reason for the occasion, the menu focused on taste with such dishes as sherried fruit, rissole potatoes (sautéed in butter), smothered chicken on toast with butter sauce, and rolls with butter—lots of butter on the menu, followed by chocolate meringue ice cream.[108] Leland Anderson, nephew of M. D. Anderson, ceremonially handed over the deed to the Texas Medical Center land to Ernst Bertner, which of course had been financed with Anderson Foundation money. The first speaker was Raymond B. Allen, who had served in academic medical positions in Illinois and Washington but had also "been chief development officer at the Chicago Westside Medical Center." This was significant because Westside Center was "the kind of umbrella organization the Anderson Foundation envisioned for the Texas Medical Center."[109]

As dean of the Texas Dental College, Frederick C. Elliott sought to integrate his school into the new MD Anderson Cancer Hospital. This initial combination of medical treatment and teaching led to the charter of the Texas Medical Center in 1945. MS 071, Elliott Papers, McGovern Historical Center, Texas Medical Center Library.

In a visionary speech, Bertner laid out the international vision of the health-care complex: "Every generation or so in the life of a great city a chain of circumstances pulls wide the door of major opportunity for that city's advancement." He went on to compare the current opportunity with past life-shaping opportunities for Houston: "Such an opportunity brought to Houston its great seaport [and] it is not amiss to draw an analogy between the Houston Ship Channel and what the Texas Medical Center will be." Bertner stated, "One made Houston's place as a trade center [and] the other will make Houston's place as a health center. One brought great commerce; the other will bring great blessings to mankind, and perhaps—who knows—it will bring the answer to the cause, treatment and cure of cancer. The ship channel brought the captains of industry to our community; the Texas Medical Center will attract the great scientists of the world."[110]

Other community leaders quickly mobilized to ensure city support for the new endeavor. George A. Hill Jr., an attorney and oilman, wrote a letter to the president of the Houston Chamber of Commerce on March 11, 1946, emphasizing at length the importance of the medical center to Houston's future: "I cannot think of anything that would be more helpful,

Hugh Roy and Lillie Cullen provided the first major gift to the nascent Texas Medical Center. Their example of turning their wealth back into the community unleashed a rush by Houston's elite to participate in building the Texas Medical Center into the world's largest and most advanced health-care complex. Courtesy of Houston Methodist.

constructive and inspiring, in this utterly dispirited world . . . than for the Houston Chamber of Commerce . . . to boldly go out [and] champion this program of the University of Texas in the Texas Medical Center." He went on in his letter to call Houston the "most vital city in the most influential state in the greatest nation on earth" and called on others to "have the courage and strength and confidence to go ahead and demand the fullness of our rightful destiny."[111]

Other institutions quickly followed suit, seeking to build their own facilities in the new nucleus for modern health care that Houston had become: the University of Texas, Methodist Hospital, St. Luke's Episcopal Hospital, Shriners Hospital for Children, Hermann Hospital and more.[112] A major gift by Hugh Roy and Lillie Cullen provided the catalyst for a sudden rush to Houston. The Cullens were native Texans who initially made money in the cotton markets of both Texas and Oklahoma and then in Houston's commercial real estate market. But finally Cullen began drilling for oil on leased lands and made huge discoveries. The most famous was the Tom O'Connor #1 in Refugio County that eventually became 224 wells and made Cullen "one of Houston's wealthiest men."[113] In March 1945, the Cullens gave oil royalties to Memorial Baptist Hospital, Hermann Hospital, and Methodist Hospital. Although worth $1 million each at the time, they were calculated in terms of future production, so the values began going up immediately.

Episcopal Bishop of Texas Clinton Quin had been thinking about an Episcopal hospital for years and promptly asked the Cullens if he could also have a million dollars. They granted his request.[114] The first directors of St. Luke's Episcopal Hospital included John Crooker, Lottie Rice Farish, and Bishop John Hines. Construction began soon after, and St. Luke's opened in 1949 in the Texas Medical Center.[115]

Methodist Hospital at Houston was born in 1919 and was supported by prominent Houstonians, including James Elkins (cofounder of Vinson & Elkins law firm), James Marion West (leading rancher and oilman), William Clayton, Jesse Jones, and Ella and Walter Fondren.[116] The Fondren family was the most generous supporter of Methodist Hospital, freely sharing their oil wealth. Walter Fondren was an original partner of Humble Oil along with Ross Sterling. William Stamps Farish, Robert Lee Blaffer, and Harry Wiess later joined them. Fondren served on the board until he died and was replaced by his wife, Ella. The Fondrens supported the initiative to move Methodist Hospital into the Texas Medical Center with additional financial assistance from Hugh Cullen and the Anderson Foundation.[117] When the cornerstone for Methodist Hospital was laid on May 31, 1950, a large ceremony was held with many local dignitaries. But Hugh Cullen, who had given millions, did not focus on himself but praised other philanthropists present, calling them "great citizens," and said that "Houston is very fortunate in having such fine, civic-minded men."[118]

Like dominoes falling, the talk of a new medical center and new Baylor medical school, Methodist Hospital and Episcopal hospital caused Houston pediatric specialists to think about a children's hospital for the city. The main benefactor for this initiative was James Smither Abercrombie, a Houstonian who made a fortune as an independent oil driller and later through an oil field supply and tool company. Abercrombie worked throughout the Gulf region as well as South America, finding rich reserves and also perfecting tools that made the industry safer and more efficient. In 1947, Texas Children's Foundation was formed to explore the opportunity for a children's hospital, and Abercrombie guaranteed to Anderson Foundation that he would financially support it.[119] Children's Foundation leaders included Nina Cullinan, daughter of Texaco founder Joseph Cullinan, and Leopold Meyer, CEO of Foley's Department Stores.[120]

By 1946, the trustees of the Anderson Foundation recruited new members to help them establish the Texas Medical Center nonprofit corporation. This included Ernst Bertner, Frederick Elliott, Bishop Quin, Oveta Culp Hobby, Jesse Jones, and Hugh Roy Cullen.[121] Bertner and Elliott were already well known to the project, and Quin was becoming more involved given his dream of an Episcopal hospital for the new center. Jones and Cullen were wealthy and longtime benefactors of major civic projects in Houston. Oveta Culp Hobby was married to former Texas Governor William Hobby, owner of the *Houston Post*, and she took over as publisher.[122] Oveta's father served in the legislature, so she was accustomed to politics and public policy issues. She attended the University of Texas Law School after college but did not graduate. Instead, she served as parliamentarian of the Texas House of Representatives for the 1925 session. Afterward, she moved to Houston and worked for John Freeman in the Houston city attorney's office. With her marriage to Hobby and her political, legal, and journalism experience, she was a very attractive candidate for the board of the new medical center.[123]

A new president for the cancer hospital, Lieutenant Colonel R. Lee Clark, was hired to replace Bertner, who was moving up to be president of the broader Texas Medical Center. Clark was then stationed at Randolph Field at San Antonio and was recommended by the Mayo Clinic as one of the leading cancer surgeons of the nation.[124] He was a native of Hereford, Texas, and received a medical degree from the University of Virginia in 1932 followed by graduate medical studies at the University of Paris and University of Minnesota.[125]

When interviewed for the job, Clark "insisted that the cancer hospital be an independent entity, not a department of the medical school, and building program." He wanted broad authority and independence in running the cancer hospital. The board agreed, and the continuing pattern of independent institutions within the framework of the Texas Medical Center was established.[126] As a part of the structure of the Medical Center, an important arrangement was made in 1948 to provide for treatment and teaching to coexist in a good balance. The member hospitals agreed that "a minimum of 20% of their total beds" would be available for teaching purposes for the medical school and nursing schools also within the compound. This ensured that there "will always be sufficient clinical material for the education of doctors, dentists, nurses, public health workers and others receiving training in the Center."[127]

Bertner continued to voice an international vision for the burgeoning medical center, telling the Houston Chamber of Commerce in 1946 that "the combination of Houston's two major developments, the creation of the Texas Medical Center and the designation of this city as an international air gateway, holds promise of making Houston a leader in medicine for Latin American countries [whose] populations . . . are hungry for medical treatment and research and will look upon the services Houston will have to offer as America's gesture of sound good neighborliness."[128] Famed New Orleans surgeon Alton Ochsner lauded Bertner for his "far sighted planning" and stated that the Texas Medical Center is "the greatest thing that has been started in medicine in 50 years."[129]

The Texas Medical Center got good press out of its aggressive start. Paul de Kruif, a famous American microbiologist, said that "trustees of the Texas Medical Center should begin to seize their opportunity by importing as many personnel as possible to carry out the ambitious plans already outlined for the Center." Kruif was famous for his 1926 book *Microbe Hunters,* which appealed to a broad audience beyond the medical and technical. So his opinion carried weight when he added that a great medical center is more than buildings, but "it is the brains in the Center that make it great."[130] The *Milwaukee Journal,* much closer to the Mayo Clinic, wrote in 1946 that "Big Texas likes to do big things and the Texas Medical Center is no exception [and the planners] expect that the center will attract some of the nation's leading medical minds."[131]

The Cullens, already so generous with the Texas Medical Center, made a further announcement in 1947 of the formation of the Cullen Foundation. In a speech to the Texas Hospital Association meeting in Houston, Hugh Roy Cullen stated that he and his wife were conveying to their foundation properties that would produce thirty to forty million barrels of oil, which was estimated to be worth $80 million. Houstonians were amazed, but the next day the Cullens said they had underestimated the amount of oil reserves on the property, and it was closer to $160 million.[132]

In 1949, the French banker Edouard Escarra, president of Crédit Lyonnais, visited the Texas Medical Center with his wife and an aide. Escarra wanted to understand the concept of the Medical Center and how it had come to fruition. They toured the facilities and examined all the new equipment. After lunch, they contacted the center again and asked if they could see the cancer hospital as well. Escarra reported that the tour was the thing of greatest interest to them on their visit to Houston.[133]

Sadly, Bertner died in 1950 of cancer at age sixty-one. Before his death, he attended the dedication ceremony for the new Methodist Hospital along with his friend Jesse Jones, who had first brought him to Houston. Also before he died, Bertner agreed to an experimental injection of radioisotope to determine what effect it would have on an aggressive cancer. This approach of "treat to cure would eventually flower into an M. D. Anderson hallmark."[134]

After Bertner's death, Frederick Elliott, dean of the UT School of Dentistry, previously the private Texas Dental College, stepped in as temporary head of the Texas Medical Center and later was named the permanent director. Under his leadership until his retirement in 1962, he guided the center through an astonishing expansion. Elliott presided at the groundbreaking ceremony for the new MD Anderson Hospital for Cancer Research to replace the temporary housing in the old Baker estate. The occasion, on December 20, 1950, was attended by many city and state dignitaries, including "State Senator Searcy Bracewell, representing Governor Allan Shivers; Houston mayor Oscar Holcombe; oilman and philanthropist Hugh Roy Cullen; [and] UT Chancellor James P. Hart."[135]

The MD Anderson Foundation continued to provide seed and incentive money to encourage new health-care-related entities to locate in the Texas Medical Center, which included the UT School of Dentistry funded in 1951 by the Texas legislature, a new Texas Children's Hospital, the addition of a neuropsychiatric unit to the Veteran's Hospital, Houston Academy of Medicine Library, and Arabia Temple Shrine Crippled Children's Clinic.[136]

By 1954, the new MD Anderson Cancer Hospital was completed, and patients and equipment were transferred to it from the Baker estate. The dedication ceremony was held later that year when it was possible to gather many local dignitaries in addition to UT Board of Regents Chairman Tom Sealy, Representative Arthur Cato, Governor Allan Shivers, US Senator Price Daniel, and others. Messages were read from both President Eisenhower and US Secretary of Health, Education, and Welfare Oveta Culp Hobby, a Houstonian.[137] By 1955, the Texas Medical Center consisted of a medical college, a dental college, and five major hospitals with more projects already on the drawing board. The workload led to an expansion of the board to twenty-five members, with some being designated trustees for life and others elected. These new trustees included such leading Houstonians as Benjamin Clayton, Ben Taub, William P. Hobby Jr., Douglas Marshall, and Bernard Sakowitz. The board continued to use itself as the best way to reach the business, political, and philanthropic world of Houston.[138]

The vision of the Texas Medical Center was revolutionary, and the pace at which the project grew astounded everyone. But that is not to say that everything had become suddenly ideal in Houston's medical world, because the center was not free, and although the faith-based hospitals were non-profit entities, they had to take in patient fees to break even. This meant, of course, that the services were not available to poor people, who were often the black and segregated population. Houston struggled with desegregation pressures in the 1950s and, after several failed attempts, eventually passed a countywide hospital district with the power to tax and provide charity hospital services. Ben Taub, a successful Jewish real estate developer, was a leader of efforts to provide medical care for the poor citizens of Houston. His successful leadership, assisted by Leon Jaworski, resulted in a new charity hospital in 1963, named Ben Taub Hospital by a grateful county hospital board.[139]

The already cutting-edge Texas Medical Center took a very important futuristic step in 1958 when it "opened a helipad for air ambulance service" that would be able to bring emergency patients arriving by air into the Houston airport, who then needed to be transported as quickly as possible to the center, as well as to "transport accident victims quickly to the medical center's hospitals, saving precious time and lives." It was perhaps too soon for its time, since it was so unused that the service was closed until 1976 when helicopter ambulance service was reestablished, operating from Hermann Hospital under the direction of physician James "Red" Duke.[140]

In 1959, Leon Jaworski was appointed to chair a committee established to "develop a closer working relationship" between the Texas Medical Center and the Baylor University College of Medicine. The committee was successful and facilitated the construction of more facilities, including the Anderson Basic Research Center, the Jesse H. Jones Clinical Research Building, and the Jewish Institute for Medical Research. Jaworski contributed in a very significant way by arranging for the Texas Medical Center to apply for available federal funding that would benefit Baylor's expansion but allow the Baptist institution to avoid violating its policy of strict separation of church and state by directly taking federal funding.[141] The Baylor College of Medicine was further augmented over the years with the Michael E. DeBakey Center for Biomedical Education and Research and the Albert B. Alkek School of Biomedical Sciences.[142]

In 1959, the Texas Medical Center held a Report of Progress dinner, again at the Rice Hotel, to review its work since 1943 and to announce its future work. Again, the menu focused on taste, not health, with stuffed baked potatoes, beef tenderloin, and hollandaise sauce. But it was a great menu for an all-star lineup that included W. Leland Anderson, nephew of M. D. Anderson; John Freeman, one of the original attorneys; and William A. Kirkland, chairman of the First National Bank of Houston. The dinner remarks of both men recounted the remarkable progress from the original 142 acres of parkland in 1942. The Texas Medical Center, incorporated in 1945, had grown to include the Baylor College of Medicine, New Hermann Hospital, Methodist Hospital, Crippled Children's Hospital, MD Anderson Hospital, Texas Children's Hospital, St. Luke's Episcopal Hospital, UT Dental School, and the Texas Institute of Rehabilitation and Research. On the table for construction were Texas Women's University College of Nursing, Houston State Psychiatric Institute, New Charity Hospital, and various new research buildings.[143]

The Texas Medical Center acted as the "city hall" of a "city of health," providing an important headquarters to what are largely independent entities within.[144] One way in which the Medical Center provided for its component members was to establish the Thermal Energy Corporation to provide power throughout the complex and the Hospital Laundry Cooperative Association to provide sanitary laundry service without waste and duplication of services.[145] By 1968, "Houston Natural Gas Corporation built the Texas Medical Center's central heating and cooling plant" to provide climate control without duplication of services and to allow for "professional staff to run these climate control systems."[146]

The rapid growth of the Texas Medical Center coincided with big changes in national health policy. By the 1960s the National Institutes of Health, after successfully focusing on single-disease issues since World War II, had begun a more comprehensive approach with Medicare and Medicaid and "funds for medical, dental, and allied health education." Houston worked closely with native Texan Lyndon B. Johnson to bring about a new emphasis on health care. The Texas Medical Center had two particular stars at the time, Michael DeBakey of Baylor Hospital and Lee Clark of MD Anderson, who worked in national health policy issues. "DeBakey served on the Committee on Health Policy of the National Democratic Party Advisory Council in 1960, and frequently testified before Congressional committees."[147] Clark, the leader of the MD Anderson Cancer Center for over three decades, was the national pioneer of comprehensive cancer treatment, including surgery, radiation, and chemotherapy. He was "deeply involved in the politics of cancer" and would serve as an effective advocate for more financial and personnel resources for health care.[148]

In 1969, the Texas legislature further expanded the state's commitment to the Texas Medical Center by establishing the UT Medical School at Houston to supplement the UT Medical School long in existence at Galveston and to add to the presence of Baylor at Houston. More land and buildings would follow until the Board of Regents eventually "approved the creation of an umbrella organizational structure, the University of Texas Health Science Center at Houston, known today simply as UTHealth." In 1981, the Texas legislature established a new psychiatric center at Texas Medical Center, which constructed a new facility and merged into UTHealth in 1990.[149]

The early presidents of the Texas Medical Center were medical doctors. But the center deviated from that pattern in 1981 when Philip Hoffman was named president. Hoffman was not a medical doctor but had a PhD in history from Ohio State University. He had worked as a professor and dean at various institutions before moving to Houston in 1957 to serve as vice president of the University of Houston. By 1961, he was president and was able to convert the private institution to a state university in 1963 and spread the institution to three branch campuses. He retired as president of the University of Houston in 1977 to become the chancellor of the University of Houston System for two years and then fully retired. It turned out to be a short retirement, however, because Leon Jaworski, as chairman of the board of the Texas Medical System, asked him in 1981 to become president of the Texas Medical Center. Hoffman held this post for four years until 1984. Hoffman had already worked with the center when he established an agreement between the University of Houston School of Pharmacy and the Texas Medical Center and relocated it to a new building in the complex.[150]

The Texas Medical Center was not limited to UT and Baylor, for by 1986, "Texas A&M University established its Institute of Biosciences and Technology," becoming a part of the center and building its own facilities. Rice University had been involved with the Texas Medical Center since the inception, but "in 2003 it became a member institution." The last separation of Galveston from Houston in the medical field was completely erased by 2010 when University of Texas Medical Branch at Galveston (UTMB) announced it would be joining as a member institution of the Texas Medical Center at Houston.[151]

The Texas Medical Center continued to expand well outside its original site of 134 acres. In 1981, Mitchell Energy "offered $5.6 million and 150 acres of land in The Woodlands" as a site to construct a medical research park. The Woodlands was a massive planned community developed by George Mitchell to include schools, hotels, a conference center, parks, and new businesses so that residents did not necessarily have to commute into the traditional Houston business and industrial areas. The Mitchells believed medical research was a promising new field, and Baylor "was the first TMC institution" to move into the new campus when it established a Biomedical Nuclear Magnetic Center.[152]

New construction at Texas Medical Center grew at an increasingly faster pace with time. Construction at the site cost $750 million between 1943 and 1979. But in just the next five years, 1980–85, the center spent another $750 million on construction. Then in another five years, 1985–90, the amount was more than doubled to $1.6 billion. Even allowing for increasing costs of construction over time, the rate of growth is still very impressive.[153] The number of people working in Texas Medical Center also increased rapidly along with the pace of construction. By 1978, total employee count reached 26,000, but that doubled by 1991 to 52,000 and today stands at a staggering 106,000 employees.[154]

Texas Medical Center believed it had more land than it needed in the late 1940s with approximately 134 acres. However, with dozens of new institutions moving in; constant expansion of facilities; construction of utility buildings, parking lots, roads, and other infrastructure, by 2012 it had grown to "some 1,300 acres of land with 280 buildings providing 45.5 million square feet of space."[155] One expansion occurred in 1985 when the Shamrock Hotel was acquired with its more than 20 acres of land. The old building was torn down to add additional parking space. This decision was very controversial in Houston because of the hotel's fame and its important role in Houston's history. Holcombe Crosswell, chairman emeritus of the board of directors

Walter and Ella Fondren used their oil wealth to support Methodist Hospital and move it into the Texas Medical Center. Courtesy of Rice University.

of the Texas Medical Center, recalled a group that believed the Shamrock was an architectural monument and should be preserved. Crosswell believes it was in fact an ugly building, although the Texas Medical Center did consider using it for records storage. Unfortunately, the floors were not strong enough to support such great weight. Hilton Hotels was unwilling to try to preserve it as a hotel, hence their willingness to sell it. Crosswell said the board chairman at the time, David Underwood, was harassed and had windows shot out at his house. But in the end, the hotel had to go.[156] The Shamrock had been opened to international acclaim in 1946 about the same time as the Texas Medical Center, but the hotel proved to a temporary icon of Houston that gave way to a more permanent international center.[157] After the hotel was torn down in 1987, the Texas Medical Center replaced it with parking areas and a park including "30 foot tall water tower fountains" and other landscaping.[158] More important, the Institute of Biosciences and Technology was constructed as part of the Texas A&M Health Science Center.

The cancer hospital was expanded and improved many times over the years and in 1993 was supplemented with the "Jesse H. Jones Rotary House International, a specialty hotel for patients and families from out of town to stay during treatment visits."[159]

Famous Surgeons and Revolutionary New Medical Procedures

The growth of the Texas Medical Center into an international center for medical treatment, research, and education attracted high-profile physicians and other medical experts as well as celebrity patients. The concept of a medical center with a cluster of medical schools, dental schools, teaching hospitals, and training centers was an exciting prospect for many in the medical profession at the time. Leading physicians heaped praise on Houston and its grand vision. Edward D. Churchill, a professor of surgery at Harvard Medical School, came to see the new medical complex in late 1949 and delivered a lecture on "The Doctor and the Hospital." Churchill said, "The hospital belongs to society and society will in the long run determine how to use [it]." He congratulated Houston society on what they were building, and he encouraged doctors to be active in the vision and not just "a fire extinguisher on the wall."[160]

An early star of the new medical center was William Fields, who was born in Baltimore but is sometimes thought of as Canadian or British because of the fascinating life he had before arriving in Houston. Fields received both undergraduate and medical degrees from Harvard in 1934 and

1939, respectively. His medical internship was at Royal Victoria Hospital in Montreal, where he was first exposed to early neurological disorders and treatments. He joined the Royal Canadian Navy as a medical officer in World War II, as the United Kingdom had entered the war several years before the United States, and often served on board British warships "escorting convoys, which were favorite targets for German submarines." He received an MBE from King George VI for his service.[161] After the war, Fields taught neurology, as a Rockefeller Fellow, at the University of Washington before going to work for Baylor College of Medicine as an associate professor of neuropsychiatry. He was one of only three neurologists in the state of Texas at the time.[162]

Fields played a particularly interesting role in the Texas Medical Center because of his treatment of Jesse Jones. Early in the center's history, Jesse Jones was in Memorial Hospital being treated by Moise D. Levy, who called Fields in when he could not diagnose the problem. Fields determined that Jones had a collapsed lung and repaired it. Although Fields submitted an invoice, Jones did not think it was a sufficient amount and summoned the doctor to his office. Fields then proposed that if Jones wanted to spend more money, he could fund a medical library to properly organize and house the thousands of books of the Harris County Medical Society that were haphazardly gathered. Jones agreed, and the Jesse H. Jones Library Building was added to the Texas Medical Center.[163] Jesse Jones was among the Houston business and philanthropic leaders who believed that "he would prosper if his community thrived, so he was always nurturing that reciprocal relationship with the community."[164]

The Texas Medical Center began to draw in noted medical experts from around the nation and abroad to lecture students and medical professionals on new research and new treatments and protocols. In 1949, Rupert A. Willis, a noted British pathologist, delivered a lecture to doctors gathered from across Texas.[165] Willis was an early pioneer in the study of tumors and cancer and conducted experiments in 1959 on the effects of cigarette smoke on the lung tissue of rats.[166] Willis returned to the Texas Medical Center the following month to present a seminar on "Diagnostic Errors Caused by Metastatic Tumors" to an audience that included staff of MD Anderson Hospital for Cancer Research as well as other TMC staff and guests.[167] The center made it a point to be inclusive of the broader public to increase understanding of its mission and the high level at which it intended to operate. Another international cancer expert, Karl Kottmeier of Sweden, visited in June 1950 to lecture on cervical cancer. His Radium

Hemmet was regarded as the premier cervical carcinoma institute in the world at the time.[168]

The Texas Urological Society met at Texas Medical Center in November 1949, holding their evening presentations at the nearby Shamrock Hotel. Michael DeBakey, then new to the Texas Medical Center, spoke to the group on "Venous Obstructions."[169] At that time, the hotel was only two years old and the gathering place of oil tycoons, international celebrities, and Hollywood stars. The Shamrock Hotel also figured into community funding for the new MD Anderson Cancer Hospital. In December 1949, Houston oilman Glenn McCarthy, owner of the Shamrock Hotel, organized a Shamrock Bowl football game featuring the Cleveland Browns, champions of the All-America Football Conference (AAFC), against a selection of players from other teams in the AAFC. Hosted on Rice Field, the game was played to raise funds for cancer treatment and research as well as dazzle the public with "a parade of Hollywood stars."[170]

Some internationally famous doctors visited the Texas Medical Center for longer periods of time, including Naoki Toida of Japan, who stayed six months with the Baylor College of Medicine on a Rockefeller Fellowship in physiology, and Walter Boothby of the Mayo Clinic, who also was a research adviser in aviation medicine at Randolph Field. Boothby, while in Houston in 1952, received the Commander of the North Star decoration from King of Sweden Gustav VI Adolf, presented by Swedish Consul Gunnar Dryselius at the Kingdom of Sweden Consulate in Houston.[171]

The staff of MD Anderson Cancer Hospital not only attracted global experts to their facility but also traveled to represent Houston at international gatherings. In July 1950, two staff doctors traveled to Europe for the International Conference of Radiology in London and the International Cancer Conference in Paris. Another staff member in epidemiology lectured on cancer record registries in Paris and then in London on evaluation of cancer control methodologies in Texas.[172]

Programs at the Texas Medical Center sometimes mixed politics and policy with the latest medical news and techniques. In November 1950, it hosted a postgraduate medical conference that featured speakers and panels of medical experts as well as special addresses by former Texas Governor and US Senator W. Lee O'Daniel and Texas Congressman Martin Dies of the House Un-American Activities Committee.[173] A more startling example occurred in February 1951, when the Texas Medical Center hosted a two-day program at a Shamrock Hotel banquet featuring Charles W. Mayo of the Mayo Clinic (and son of Mayo Clinic cofounder Charles Horace Mayo) to

Community leader and skilled attorney Leon Jaworski helped thread the legal needle between Baylor College of Medicine and the Texas Medical Center to allow greater integration and leverage federal funding. Jaworski was part of a long line of Fulbright partners who facilitated the establishment and growth of the Texas Medical Center. Courtesy of Special Collections and Manuscripts Archivist in the Texas Collection, Baylor University.

"report on recent advances in research" and Glenn H. McCarthy to "talk on the fight against socialism."[174]

The Texas Medical Center was particularly famous for cardiovascular treatment. Both Michael DeBakey and Denton Cooley accomplished astounding, life-saving techniques that attracted international attention.[175] DeBakey brought much international acclaim to Houston and the Texas Medical Center over the years. He joined the faculty of the Baylor College of Medicine in 1948, eventually serving as chairman of the department of surgery, president of the medical school, and then chancellor. DeBakey invented a roller pump that allowed a continuous flow of blood during operations that greatly increased success and enabled open-heart surgery. He developed the ability to graft arteries in a way that can restore full blood flow and repair blood vessels. He is particularly famous for the first use of an artificial heart. DeBakey is also noted for playing a principal role in the development of the Mobile Army Surgical Hospital (MASH), which was first put into effect in the Korean War. DeBakey's theory was that survival rates are dramatically increased if treatment for a traumatic injury occurs within one hour.[176]

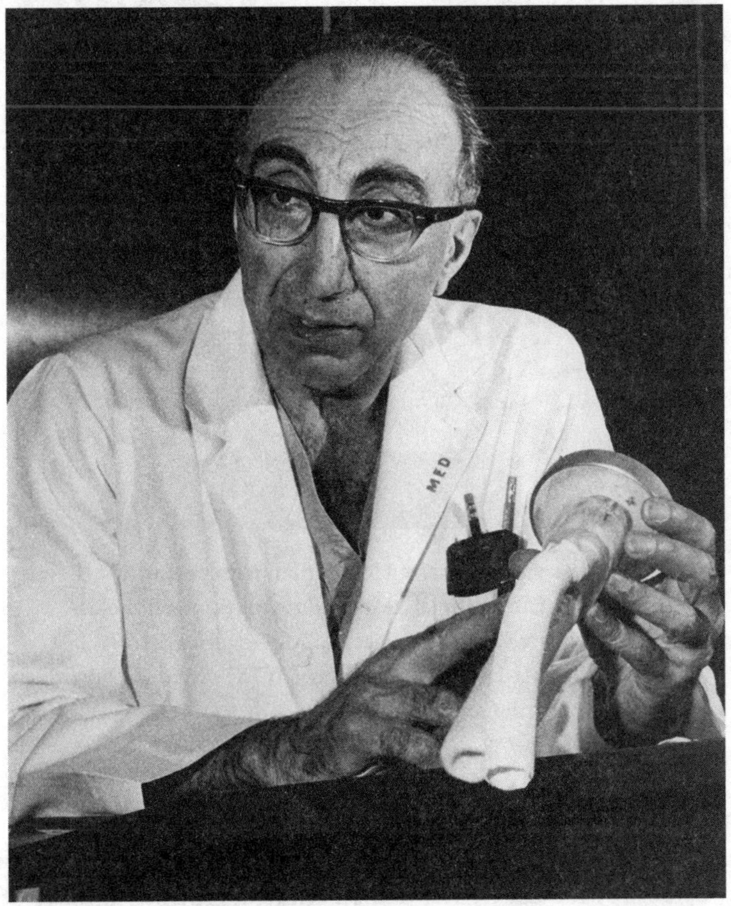

Perhaps the most famous of many leading physicians at the Texas Medical Center, Michael DeBakey pioneered miraculous heart procedures and even allowed cameras into the operating room. Courtesy of Special Collections, University of Houston Libraries Collection, University of Houston.

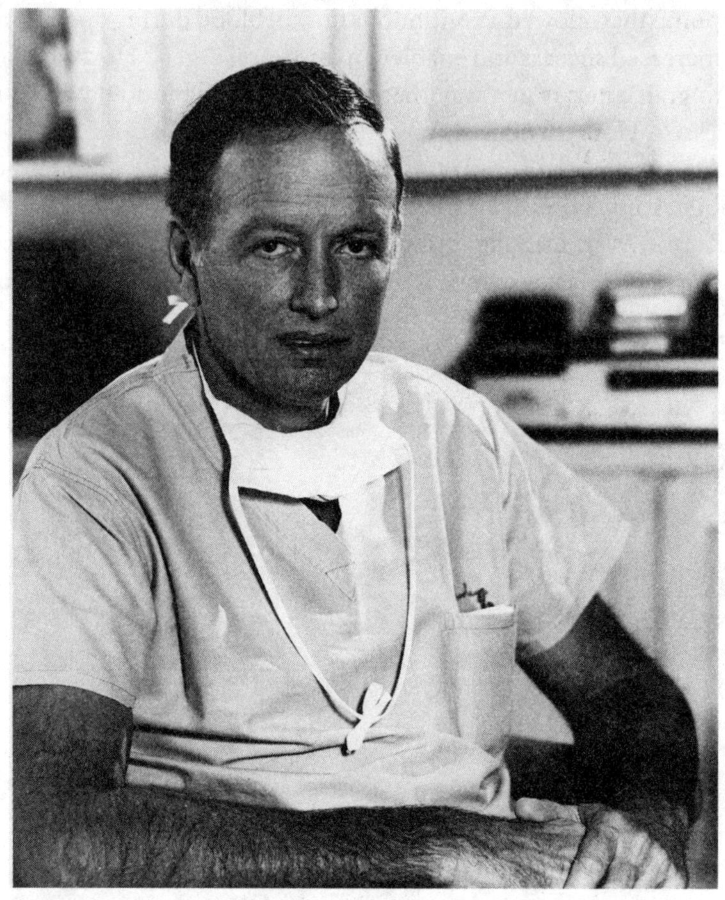

Denton Cooley was a native Houstonian who performed the first implant of an artificial heart and revolutionized the use of artificial heart valves. Courtesy of McGovern Historical Center, Texas Medical Center Library, IC 077 Medical World News Photograph Collection 229.32.

DeBakey was not camera shy and allowed surgeries to be filmed when such a thing was inconceivable. DeBakey's skill and the advanced medical care offered by Texas Medical Center helped attract a growing number of international celebrity clients.

Almost as famous as DeBakey is Denton Cooley, who performed the first implantation of an artificial heart. Cooley was a native Houstonian and graduate of both UT and UT Medical Branch. He joined the faculty of the Baylor College of Medicine and worked with DeBakey in new heart surgical procedures. On his own, Cooley revolutionized the use of artificial heart valves. Denton Cooley founded the Texas Heart Institute in 1962 but moved his patients to St. Luke's Episcopal Hospital after a professional dispute with DeBakey.

Cooley immediately began looking for sources of funding to construct a separate facility but was not successful until 1966 when Robert Herring, president of Houston Natural Gas Corporation, helped him reach the goal. Herring was also serving as chairman of the Ray C. Fish Foundation and pledged $5 million toward the Texas Heart Institute. These funds were supplemented with money from Ben Clayton and others.[177]

The Texas Heart Institute quickly became world famous and attracted both patients and heart doctors. Peter van der Schaar, a doctor from the Netherlands, worked frequently with Denton Cooley and used skills acquired in Houston to treat patients in Europe. However, in 1976, the institute began to airlift eight to ten patients at a time from Amsterdam to Houston to receive heart surgery. Eventually more than fifteen hundred such patients

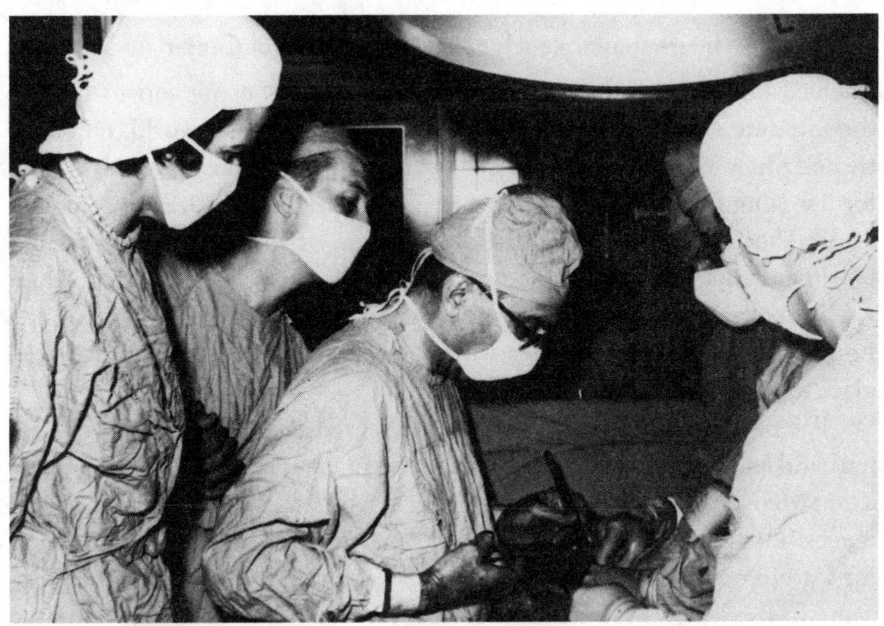

Princess Liliane of Belgium visited Houston in 1962 at the invitation of DeBakey to witness surgical procedures and learn about the health care afforded by the Texas Medical Center. DeBakey served as an adviser to the Princess Liliane Foundation for Cardiological Research. Courtesy of the Baylor College of Medicine Archives.

were flown from Europe, and the practice spread to other countries.[178] Cardiovascular treatment was so important to the Texas Medical Center because it is repeatedly ranked as the "#1 killer in the U.S." and "kills almost as many Americans as cancer, pneumonia, infections, accidents and all other causes of death including AIDS, combined."[179]

The Texas Medical Center not only attracted the bright minds and special patients of the world, but it also projected its skilled workforce abroad. One example is Cheves Smythe, who came to Houston to organize the UT Medical School in 1970. He was an internationally respected physician, which led to his selection as dean of the medical school at Aga Khan University in Karachi, Pakistan, from 1982 to 1985. Cheves was present for the dedication of the new medical school building in Karachi in 1985 at a ceremony led by the Aga Khan as chancellor of the school. It was hosted by President Zia-ul-Haq, and university President Shamsh Kassim-Lakha delivered an address.[180]

In 2000, George W. Bush asked Cooley to review Dick Cheney's medical records, especially his heart condition, to see whether he was up to the strain of a return to Washington.

International Reach of the Texas Medical Center

Michael DeBakey probably did more than any other person to project the intricate skills of the Texas Medical Center into the world. DeBakey treated Shah Mohammed Reza Pahlavi of Iran, the Duke of Windsor (the former King Edward VIII),[181] Turkish President Turgut Ozal, Nicaraguan leader Violetta Chamorro, and King Hussein of Jordan. He also treated US Presidents John F. Kennedy, Lyndon Johnson, and Richard Nixon. Additionally, he treated the sports and entertainment world, including Joe Louis, Marlene Dietrich, and Jerry Lewis, making Houston the international place to go for prestigious medical care.[182]

Princess Liliane of Belgium, who had served as queen consort until her husband King Leopold III abdicated in favor of his son, Baudouin, visited the Texas Medical Center in 1962 at the invitation of DeBakey. They met in social circles, and DeBakey served as an adviser to the Princess Liliane Foundation for Cardiological Research.[183] King Juan Carlos and Queen Sofia of Spain came to the Texas Medical Center in 1987. That same year, Indian Prime Minister Rajiv Gandhi visited to arrange "having medical and health short courses, seminars and patient information beamed by satellite from the Texas Medical Center to even the most remote Indian villages."[184] In 1988, King Carl XVI Gustav and Queen Silvia of Sweden came to the center, followed later in the year by King Osabarima and Queen Helena of Ghana,

The Duke and Duchess of Windsor arrived in Houston to see DeBakey in 1964. The duke suffered from an abdominal aneurysm that required the specialized skills and procedures available only at the Texas Medical Center. Courtesy of the Baylor College of Medicine Archives.

who wanted to view an open-heart surgery and meet the doctors performing the procedure.[185] The head of the World Health Organization (WHO) and a team of international health-care professionals visited the Texas Medical Center in 1988 to confirm it as an international patient center.[186]

Russian President Boris Yeltsin was perhaps the most famous of DeBakey's patients. In 1996, Yeltsin was running for reelection in Russia, but many feared he could not survive another term and maybe not even the election cycle. Yeltsin suffered a heart attack and desperately needed coronary bypass surgery, "but his Russian doctors said he could not survive such surgery."[187] Yeltsin asked DeBakey to come to Moscow to offer a second opinion. Besides the fact that DeBakey was famous as a cardiologist, he also had his own friends and contacts in Russian medical circles. DeBakey concluded that Yeltsin could survive the surgery if some related problems including a thyroid condition were managed first. The Russian doctor, Renat S. Akchurin, had trained under DeBakey in Houston, and DeBakey agreed to be present and to bring additional necessary equipment from Houston. DeBakey later reported that "Yeltsin's doctors were kidding me that the Communist Party did not like [my] report," a reference to the fact that if Yeltsin had been simply allowed to die, it might have been the end of the fledgling democracy in Russia that had existed only a few years. DeBakey was confident that Yeltsin would not live long without the surgery. Yeltsin later referred to DeBakey as "a magician of the heart."[188]

Houstonians talked up the Texas Medical Center and its various component institutions when traveling abroad. Some had themselves been former patients, and some just knew about its capacity and abilities. Ambassador Roy M. Huffington, a Houstonian, was himself a patient at MD Anderson in 1990 when he was successfully treated for prostate cancer. He later stated, "I have talked to a bunch of people in the Middle East about what's here. A lot of those people are coming in to this Medical Center. A lot of those [foreigners] come over here and get treated."[189]

Ben F. Love, a Houston banker, had his own story about the Texas Medical Center. "I [did] cadet training at Ellington Field near Houston [and after graduating from UT in 1947], I came to Houston [looking for opportunity]."[190] The center was barely established then, but Love recalls, "I rather quickly became aware of its presence." Love and his wife had three children, all born at Texas Medical Center, but in the mid-1950s, his wife was treated for skin cancer at MD Anderson by surgeon R. Lee Clark, the director of the cancer hospital. Love was very impressed and became a volunteer for the center.[191] Ben Love enjoyed telling the story of how he promoted the Texas Medical Center on his frequent international travels as chairman of Texas Commerce Banks, later Chase Banks of Texas. To sell an audience in London or Tokyo on his bank, first "I would sell them on Houston." He would tell them that "every day, 9,000 medical PhDs and MDs went to work" in the Texas Medical Center along with "another 50,000 people" working in various staffing positions. He concluded by stating that it was the largest accumulation of medical genius "assembled in one location daily anywhere else on this planet." Love noted that often someone in the audience would challenge him as a braggadocios Texan and perhaps it was only the biggest in the South or in the United States, but he would convince them that Houston had the biggest medical center and the biggest staff of doctors in the world.[192] The invitation to come to Houston has persisted over the years since the Texas Medical Center is such a source of pride to the city. Lynn Sakowitz Wyatt declared, "I always tell friends overseas that if you're ever sick with no matter what, come here to Houston—we have the best facilities and the best doctors in the world."[193]

The G7 Summit, hosted in Houston in 1990 by President George H. W. Bush, gave the Texas Medical Center an excellent opportunity to promote its international image. Fold-out color brochures depicted a color photo of the seven leaders of the major industrialized powers walking and talking, with the Houston skyline in the background. The caption read "Look Who's Talking About Houston."[194] Texas Medical Center put out its own press release reminding readers of its strategic location across from Rice University, the "principal site for the Summit meetings." The release also noted that it attracts "more than 15,000 foreign patients each year" as well as a "large number of foreign dignitaries who request that a tour of the Texas Medical Center be a part of their visit to the United States."[195]

Italian Prime Minister Giulio Andreotti particularly enjoyed his visit to MD Anderson Cancer Center, where he saw a new style of operating room that allows a patient to "receive radiation treatment while undergoing surgery for abdominal cancer, the only one of its kind in the U.S." Andreotti stated that "cancer is one of the main issues for all of us, and when I was in Houston, I didn't want to miss this."[196]

By the time of the G7 Summit in 1990, the Texas Medical Center had become one of the most popular tourist destinations in Houston with twenty-five thousand visitors a year. Vans took hour-long drives through the complex to show the "city in a city" and hear about surgeons on six continents simultaneously watching DeBakey perform heart surgery in Methodist Hospital. They learned that fifteen thousand babies are delivered each year at nearby Lyndon B. Johnson General Hospital and how "Red" Duke produces his medical telecast carried by seventy commercial US stations that are also beamed overseas.[197]

The year 1990 was also a time when Houston was recovering from a sharp downturn in the world energy market in the late 1980s. But the impact was not as severe as an earlier era, and significantly, Houston was "maximizing underused resources [including] the Texas Medical Center."[198] One writer noted that instead of a focus on Big Oil, the G7 leaders were "more apt to hear terms like 'recombinant DNA, megabits, superconductivity, or spiralveyor'" and to see labs "where researchers seek better ways to treat cancer, heart disease, AIDS and other disorders."[199] The Texas Medical Center was "all but untouched by Houston's recession," continuing to hire, build, and expand programs. Presumably in a recession, people still get sick and health care is not the area in which most people would economize. An important side benefit of growth at the Texas Medical Center is "nearly 60 private biotechnology companies in Houston [involved in a diverse range of activities, including] cancer diagnosis kits, artificial joints, tissue preparation and gene splicing techniques."[200] New advanced pharmaceutical companies were an important part of the economic diversification of Houston as well.[201]

Red Duke was a surgeon and professor at the Texas Medical Center for decades, introducing the Life Flight air ambulance service and bringing a Level 1 trauma center to Houston. Duke's syndicated television and radio spots were very popular with the public. Courtesy of UTHealth Houston and Memorial Hermann.

"In 1993 the M. D. Anderson Cancer Center began another era of construction that continued almost nonstop for the next twenty years."[202] One new construction was a specialty hotel connected to the cancer center by a sky bridge, making it easy for families to remain close to someone in treatment. Called the Jesse H. Jones Rotary House International, the building harkened back to a name instrumental in the early years of Houston and its medical center. The Baylor College of Medicine continued to expand, adding the Michael DeBakey Center for Biomedical Education and Research, the R. E. "Bob" and Vivian Smith Medical Research Building, and the Albert B. Alkek School of Biomedical Sciences. In 2001, Baylor in partnership with Methodist Hospital, lured the famous psychiatric hospital, Menninger Clinic, from Topeka to relocate in Houston.[203]

The Texas Medical Center continued to plow new ground medically at the same time that it was growing in size both physically and in terms of staffing. In 1983, the first in vitro fertilization birth in Texas took place there, which was only the third in the nation and relied on pioneering work of the UT Medical School.[204] The Children's Hospital famously hosted the "Bubble Boy," David Vetter, who suffered from a rare immune deficiency that required a sterile environment. Although Vetter died in 1984 at age twelve, the center made significant medical advances in its efforts to treat him and later established the David Center, "a research center dedicated to treating immunological deficiency diseases."[205]

The Texas Medical Center was able to create positive synergisms that were not only an asset for Houston and Texas but also for the world.[206] It was able to unite the leadership of Houston for a great cause, including many of the same people who were otherwise often divided in the business and political world. Jesse Jones and Hugh Cullen clashed several times over the years regarding zoning and port issues.[207] Cullen was very critical of Will Clayton and his work for President Truman to rebuild Europe after World War II and promote international free trade.[208] The Texas Medical Center today would be unrecognizable to the founders after World War II, but "the spirit that enabled it to achieve its present worldwide prominence continues to flourish." As member institutions have joined and expanded, the Texas Medical Center has continued its "city hall" function of coordinating and supporting the members and performing its role as "watchful guardian of the most unique medical complex in the world."[209] It had become an international institution attracting some of the best medical minds of the world as well as a continuous flow of international patient from all walks of life. Barbara Bush, a Houstonian and recipient of the center's professional services, said, "The Texas Medical Center is Houston's gift to the world."[210]

Because the founding of the Texas Medical Center is recent and the history of its phenomenal growth so fresh, many people today can give firsthand accounts of these events. The part of the story that is less clear is how such an internationally famous medical center sprouted in Houston and grew to such stature in a short amount of time. The answer follows along similar lines of why Houston developed as such an important international trading port or became the global energy capital or became home of the manned space program: It is a combination of circumstances and people that came together in remarkable ways with good timing that could not have been predicted or planned.

The success of Anderson, Clayton and Co. was not sufficient without the philanthropic generosity of Monroe Anderson, the legal skill of his advisers, and the wisdom of the foundation trustees. The desire of wealthy community leaders to give back to their cities is not uncommon, but "this altruism and beneficence seemed especially dominant in Houston." There was the feeling that "if you did not contribute to the cultural life of Houston, you were a poor citizen."[211]

Houston's community leadership sought to draw talented and upwardly mobile people into the Texas Medical Center as donors, board members, and advocates. Paul N. Howell served on the board of the Texas Medical Center, eventually rising to be vice chairman. Howell got involved with the center because George R. Brown and Herbert Frensley, chairman and president, respectively, of Brown and Root, sought him out. Frensley told him, "I want you to get involved in some of the things that are going on in Houston [and] one of the key institutions in this city is the Texas Medical Center."[212] Howell built his refining and chemical business into an international concern that was eventually acquired by Anadarko in 2002. His wife, Evelyn, reported that they had moved to Houston because "it was the heart of the petrochemical industry. [My husband] said he could do as much business over lunch in Houston as he could in two weeks at his desk in San Antonio."[213]

The timing of the MD Anderson Foundation was also very good. Although it began in the World War II era when wartime restrictions inhibited new construction, it was also the perfect time to bring people together, flesh out ideas, begin using temporary facilities, and perfect a long-term vision. When the war ended a short time later, Houston was in an economic boom that did not stop even with the end of federal war spending. Instead, the Port of Houston grew even more and the population expanded rapidly as oil and gas and energy-related industries exploded in growth. The surging population demanded greater medical services at the same time that cascading wealth looked for ways to showcase itself—including in the form of new buildings, academic chairs, programs, and schools. A beautiful cycle was thus established in Houston where the growing Texas Medical Center attracted the best medical facilities and health-care professionals, so that everyone could go there for treatment, and the grateful endowed the center with more funding for greater expansion. The economy and population of Houston grew and nurtured the Texas Medical Center, which in turn put Houston on the map for yet another reason—biggest medical center in the world and best treatment center for cancer, heart surgery, organ transplant, pediatric specialties, and many other areas. At the center of it all, of course, continues to be the MD Anderson Foundation, which started with $19 million but gave away over $276 million in its first seventy-five years.[214] W. B. Bates, an original Anderson Foundation trustee, said, "Mr. Anderson has done something extraordinary. His fortune has been permanently dedicated to the use and benefit of mankind."[215] One writer recalled the "epitaph in St. Paul's

The growth of the Texas Medical Center campus is unprecedented in the world. The political, professional, and philanthropic circles of Houston united in a spectacular way to assemble the world's greatest center of medical arts. Courtesy of Texas Medical Center.

Cathedral written for the renowned English architect Sir Christopher Wren as also being a fitting memorial for Monroe Dunaway Anderson: 'if you seek his monument, look around you.'"[216] Although the grant of the Anderson Foundation was the crucial catalyst in the formation of the Texas Medical Center, it is also true that many other wealthy Houstonians stepped up to fund the early initiatives and growth that was so important in attracting the critical mass of facilities and personnel. "Philanthropy then leveraged public funds" to create "a world class facility."[217]

The Texas Medical Center benefited Houston in a very significant way by simply recasting the city's image as one of high technology and as a city of the future. The medical miracles of the Texas Medical Center supplemented Houston's position as a global trade center and international energy headquarters. It also helped position Houston for one of the great achievements of a modern city: to be selected as the location of NASA's Manned Space Center. Houston would now have another moniker, "Space City."

CHAPTER FOUR

SPACE CENTER

1961

TEXANS LOVE TO remind the world that the first word spoken from the moon was "Houston," reflecting pride in their leading city and its universal fame. The story comes from the historic moon landing by NASA astronauts Neil Armstrong and Buzz Aldrin on July 20, 1969, when Armstrong says, "Houston, Tranquility Base here. The Eagle has landed."[1]

The Johnson Space Center in Houston played a large and defining role in the United States and the world, not just for its primary and obvious function in space exploration but also for its impact on technology development and deployment, defense, and military affairs, as well as political and societal developments. Born in a tense era of Cold War competition, the Johnson Space Center grew into a nucleus that spawned or nourished countless business expansions in the Houston region. Any city in the world would want to be the locale of such a massive endeavor as the US space program with the attendant population boom and economic expansion. Houston managed to achieve this distinction by leveraging its own natural attributes with such additional qualities that it could construct. Houston then harnessed this amalgam of qualifications to the rising political star of Lyndon Baines Johnson. The result was not only stunning success in the golden age of space exploration but a continuing association with all that is glamorous, inspiring, and profitable about cutting-edge science.

American astronaut Neil Armstrong was the first person to walk on the moon. The world watched him step onto the lunar surface on July 20, 1969, and communicate with the Manned Space Center at Houston. Courtesy of NASA.

The National Aeronautics and Space Administration (NASA) is composed of eleven different centers, including its headquarters in Washington, DC. Three of the centers are chiefly concerned with the flight of humans into space. The Kennedy Space Center in Florida focuses on launching missions. The Marshall Space Flight Center in Alabama is a research center focused on developing rockets and propulsion technology. The Johnson Space Center in Houston is responsible for the astronauts, including training, and for monitoring and directing space flight. In its role as Mission Control, the Johnson Space Center has been the "heart" of American space exploration and well-known as both the actual home of the astronauts and the "stage for the human drama of space exploration."[2]

Sputnik and the 1958 Space Act

In order to understand the impetus behind the massive US space program, it is first necessary to look at a key development in the Soviet Union during the early years of space exploration. On October 4, 1957, the Soviet Union launched Sputnik, the world's first artificial satellite. Sputnik was 22.8 inches in diameter, weighed 183.9 pounds, and took ninety-eight minutes for each orbit around Earth. But this single event "marked the start of the space age and the US-USSR space race."[3] In its low Earth orbit, Sputnik could be clearly seen around the world and its radio pulses heard by amateur radio operators. These signals continued over three weeks until its batteries finally wore out. The American Radio Relay League provided directions on how to tune in and hear the "beep, beep" sound Sputnik emitted as it made its way around the planet. Students at Columbia University recorded the sound and rebroadcast it to fascinated listeners.[4] The whole world was fixed on Sputnik with mixed feelings of wonder and fear.

The genesis of Sputnik began in 1952 "when the International Council of Scientific Unions decided to establish July 1, 1957 to December 31, 1958 as the International Geophysical Year (IGY) because the scientists knew that the cycles of solar activity would be at a high point then [and they called] for artificial satellites to be launched during the IGY to map the Earth's surface."[5] The Soviets began internal discussions soon thereafter to launch such a satellite and, in fact, wanted to make their launch before the IGY in order to outflank the United States.

President Eisenhower announced on July 29, 1955, that the United States would launch an artificial satellite during the IGY, thus beginning Project Vanguard.[6] The phrase "Dawn of the Space Age" was first used in 1955 when on "July 29 of that year, the White House and the National Academy of

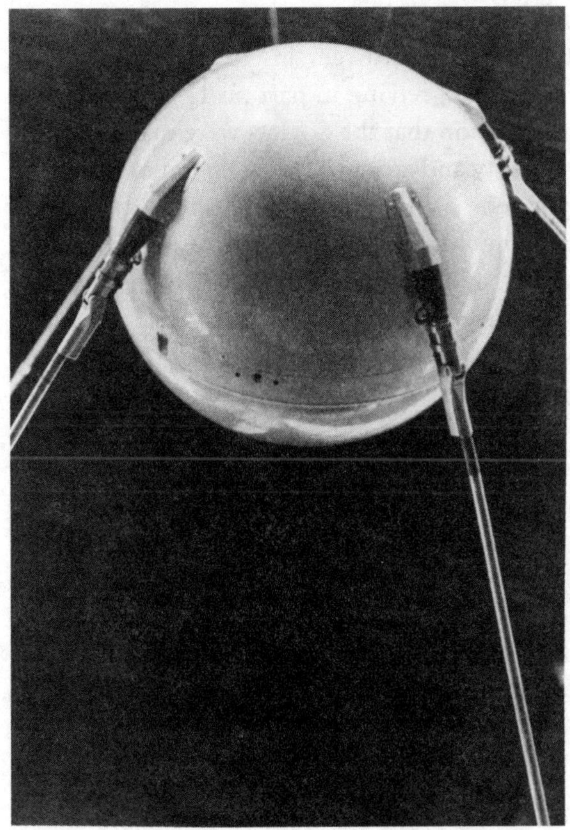

The launch of Sputnik by the Soviet Union in 1957 spurred the United States to rapidly ramp up its space program. Houston benefited enormously from prodigious federal spending and an influx of high-technology professionals. Courtesy of NASA.

Science with the National Science Foundation announced joint plans to study the utility of a vehicle revolving endlessly about the earth, high above the atmosphere, as an artificial satellite."[7] Despite these grand pronouncements, the American people were not really focused on space matters, nor could they appreciate the importance these topics would take after the launch of Sputnik. Like the nation as a whole, Houston did not then have any determined role in the Space Age and no vision of having one.

The Soviets were proud, but rather subdued, in their initial comments on the Sputnik launch. However, the world's stunned reaction caused further comments to take the form of hard-line propaganda. The success of Sputnik changed the view of the United States as the technological superpower and the Soviet Union as technologically undeveloped.[8] It had a severe psychological impact on the United States, and the West generally, but there was also the tangible worry that the Soviets would easily find a military application for artificial satellites, thereby putting all of American territory at risk.

The Eisenhower administration announced that it was "not surprised" about the launch of Sputnik and tried to remain "low key and almost dismissive."[9] In fact, US intelligence, relying in part on U-2 flyovers, had previously alerted the administration that the Soviets were making strong progress in missile launch capacity and accuracy. Even the following week, President Eisenhower responded to a reporter's question by stating that Sputnik "does not raise my apprehensions, not one iota [and I would] rather have one good Redstone nuclear-armed missile than a rocket that could hit the moon [since] we have no enemies on the moon."[10] However, the American public grew increasingly fearful, and their agitations were "inflamed by Democratic politicians and professional cold warriors which portrayed the United States as woefully behind."[11] Public agitation and fear culminated in the perception of a "missile gap," which was a dominant issue in the 1960 presidential campaign.[12] The threat to American security and the political opportunity afforded by such circumstance were not lost on Senate Majority Leader Lyndon Baines Johnson, who immediately recognized the issue and took steps to address it.

On the night that Sputnik was launched, Senator Johnson was relaxing at his ranch in the Texas Hill Country during a recess of Congress. He and his aide, Gerry Siegel, discussed how this development could impact the nation.[13] Johnson recalled, "When news of Sputnik flashed across the globe . . . simultaneously a new era of history dawned over the world."[14] Johnson telephoned Senator Richard B. Russell, who chaired the Senate Armed Services Committee, and over the course of the weekend they agreed to hold hearings on the matter through the Preparedness Investigating Subcommittee of the Armed Services Committee. Russell later said that "he had more or less turned this whole matter over to Senator Johnson."[15] Johnson, in addition to being majority leader, was the chairman of this particular subcommittee. Johnson himself was later to recall that he walked after dinner the night of October 4, 1957, looking up into the clear rural Texas sky, "straining to catch a glimpse of that alien object" while feeling "uneasy and apprehensive."[16]

George Reedy, who then served as director of the Democratic Policy Committee of Congress, was the most instrumental aide in helping Lyndon Johnson assemble the facts and emotions associated with Sputnik into a strategically useful political game plan. On October 17, 1957, Reedy wrote a lengthy memorandum to Johnson opining that Sputnik would "go far beyond a mere defense thing" and that it could be "one of the great dividing lines in American and world history."[17] Reedy says Johnson was cautious because he had so many other priorities at the time, but he agreed to receive briefings from the Pentagon to understand the impact of Sputnik and the progress of the United States along similar lines. Johnson emerged from those briefings determined to bring about a fundamental change in US policy and went before the Democratic Policy Committee to lay out his ideas. It was apparently a masterful performance, with Reedy later characterizing it as like "listening to an Old Testament prophet." Even then, President Eisenhower remained unpersuaded of the political or military urgency of the situation, commenting that "Lyndon Johnson can keep his head in the stars if he wants. I'm going to keep my feet on the ground."[18]

The Preparedness Subcommittee began to conduct hearings just a few weeks later on November 25.[19] In his opening remarks, Senator Johnson laid out the challenge of the space race and said it was a "call for Americans to respond with the best that is within them." He went on to more soberly state, "We do not have as much time as we had after Pearl Harbor."[20] Officially, these hearings were an "Inquiry Into Satellite and Missile Programs."[21] Staff members were added to assist the subcommittee, including Edward C. Welsh and William Houston, president of Rice University.[22] The hearings were conducted quickly, and the witness statements and commentaries promptly prepared and published. When Congress reconvened in January 1958, Senator Johnson presented "the key points that had been agreed to by the Subcommittee."[23] On February 5, Johnson received unanimous support for his resolution establishing a Special Committee on Space and Aeronautics "to frame legislation for a national program of space exploration and development, and to re-refer all bills regarding space to the special committee." Johnson, of course, became the chairman of this new committee and therefore was firmly in control of space policy.[24]

Johnson found himself as a national leader on an issue that had gripped the public's attention. Some historians have compared the psychological impact of Sputnik with the attack on Pearl Harbor sixteen years earlier. Many feared that the "United States had lost the lead in science and technology," threatening its political hegemony in the post–World War II order and even undermining the nation's own national security.[25] Walter Lippman wrote, "The Soviets have such a lead in the armaments business" and warned that if the United States faltered in scientific progress, it would inevitably decline.[26] The Soviets kept up the political and public relations pressure by moving quickly ahead with new projects. On November 3, 1957, just a few weeks after Sputnik, the Soviet Union launched another satellite with life on board, the famous dog Laika.[27]

With the new committee established, Senator Johnson quickly introduced, along with Senator Styles Bridges (R-NH), a bill to establish a civilian National Aeronautics and Space Council to coordinate the nation's space program. A final conference report of the House and Senate passed both houses on July 16, 1958, and President Eisenhower signed the measure on July 29.[28] It was a remarkable achievement in so short a time period. The "entire legislative process, from Sputnik to the end of 1958, was almost a textbook case of how law, spurred by technological advancement, should be made."[29]

The Space Act took center stage in the American effort to remain competitive with the Soviet Union. Lyndon Johnson was the ringleader of the entire show, and in fact, a grateful White House asked him to represent the United States in making a major address to the United Nations on November 17, 1958. President Eisenhower "sent a plane to Texas and LBJ flew with some staff to LaGuardia in New York where he was met by our UN Ambassador Henry Cabot Lodge" and escorted to the UN Headquarters.[30] Johnson delivered a well-received speech and "stressed the importance of conducting space activities for peaceful purposes."[31] Speaking later at the Southwest Research Institute in Texas, Senator Johnson said, "Now we have arrived at a new frontier [and] the space frontier is above all a perpetual frontier."[32]

During all this flurry of new initiatives, the United States was at pains to stress the peaceful nature of its space program. In the National Aeronautics and Space Act of 1958, Congress declared "that it is the policy of the United States that activities in space should be devoted to peaceful purposes for the benefit of all mankind." In that same vein, the crew of Apollo 11 would later leave a plaque on the moon stating "We came in peace for all mankind."[33]

The United States was actually not far behind the Soviet Union and continued working diligently on its own space initiatives. The United States launched its first successful satellite, Explorer, on January 31, 1958. On March 17, the Vanguard satellite TV-4 was successfully launched. By 1959, with the Sputnik panic over and the US space program working smoothly, the need for bipartisan cooperation between the White House and Lyndon Johnson seems to have faded. In fact, from 1958 to 1961, the "Space Council met only on rare occasions, without Eisenhower in attendance, and during that time had relatively little influence on national space or defense policies."[34]

Evolution of the Space Council

The Kennedy-Johnson ticket won a narrow victory on Election Day in 1960, and Lyndon Johnson, after twenty-four years in Congress, became the vice president of the United States. The Space Council remained on his priority list. On December 22, 1960, while Johnson was awaiting the inauguration, he received a memo titled "Possible Changes in the Space Law" from his aide, Ken BeLieu, staff director of the Senate Committee on Aeronautical and Space Sciences. BeLieu's memo describes how the Space Act could be amended to add the vice president to the list of council members and then to allow the president to delegate his presiding officer status in the event that "the President does not desire to actively serve on the Council and desires to delegate this authority to the Vice President." The memo cautions that the lawyers will need to draft the precise language, "but this [amendment] can be done quite simply if you approve this concept."[35]

On January 26, 1961 (six days after the inauguration), a memorandum circulated in the White House titled "Changes in Space Law," which was essentially a rewrite of BeLieu's memo from the previous month, and he may have drafted it. The memorandum set forth the precise language changes to the Space Act that would add the vice president to the council and allow the president to delegate to him. However, the memo also notes another option of simply substituting the title "vice president" for "president," thereby putting the vice president completely in charge of the council. A draft bill was attached to the memo. Also attached to this primary memo was another policy memo titled "Role of the National Aeronautics and Space Council in Coordinating US Space Activities." The six-page memo describes the structure of the Space Council and its duties and responsibilities before reaching the subheading "Failure to Use Space Council." In that section, the memo complains that "Eisenhower . . . never permitted the Space Council to function as a focus for executive branch coordination of key space policy matters, as contemplated by the Space Act [and that the president] never appointed an executive secretary or independent staff for the council." The memo further complains that "the Council only met eight times" with the last meeting over a year ago. The memo notes the criticism that the Space Council membership was "too high" and made it difficult for officials at such levels to attend its meeting. This criticism was rejected since "the same claim could be made regarding the National Security Council." The memo concluded by recommending the vice president be added to the council to direct it as the coordinating entity for US space policy.[36]

A few days later, on January 30, President Kennedy announced the appointment of James Edwin Webb as administrator of NASA.[37] The appointment of Webb had not been an easy task. Kennedy first focused on James Gavin, a retired lieutenant general who served with distinction in World War II.[38] The White House was divided on the policy question of whether to have a former military man head NASA and whether it would affect a choice to militarize the space program. In the end, it is not clear whether Gavin was excluded for this reason or declined the job.[39] President Kennedy asked his vice president to find a suitable candidate to run NASA, presumably relying on Johnson's solid familiarity with the space program. Before leaving the Senate, Lyndon Johnson installed his Senate ally Robert Kerr (D-OK) as chairman of the Space Committee.[40] Kerr was a former governor of Oklahoma who later served three terms in the US Senate. He and Johnson entered the Senate at the same time and had adjoining desks. As a liberal senator from Oklahoma, Kerr was often an ally of Johnson and indicated early support for Johnson as president.[41] Thus, when the new president asked the new vice president to find someone to head NASA, it was natural for Johnson to turn to Kerr, who was by now the chair of the Senate Space Committee.[42]

Senator Kerr first thought of his business partner at Kerr-McGee, James Webb, who previously served in the Truman administration as the budget director and then as undersecretary of state. He joined Kerr-McGee in 1952. Johnson agreed with Kerr's recommendation and submitted the name to the president. Webb tried to beg off first with Johnson and then with Clark Clifford, but when President Kennedy offered him the job in an Oval Office meeting, he accepted.[43]

At the same time, President Kennedy asked Johnson to make a study of the Space Council and report back on his findings and recommendations. Johnson answered in a letter to Kennedy on February 14, 1961, in which he concludes that the Space Council has a great coordinating responsibility and that "if it is your desire to remove the President as Chairman of the Council, it will be necessary to change the basic structure of the Council." Johnson goes on to recommend legislation be prepared to effect such change and be submitted to Congress.[44] This recommendation was apparently taken under advisement for a short while in order for White House legal and legislative advisers to determine their strategy. Meanwhile, the president met with NASA on March 22 to receive a briefing and funding estimates for "increasing the rate of closure on the USSR's lead in weight lifting capability [and] advancing manned exploration of space beyond Project Mercury."[45]

On April 4, President Kennedy sent his proposed legislation making changes to the Space Act to Congress with a six-page letter discussing the broader policy and philosophical underpinnings of the national space policy, and stating in particular, "In this Age of Space, we must often venture the unknown. We should never venture unknowingly. Our direction will be surer, our progress swifter, if our course is always a studied course. Space projects individually avail us little unless each is a part of a space program planned to avail us the most for our national efforts." The president then discussed the important role of NASA and the Space Council and explained why changes in law are needed to not only add the vice president and allow the president to delegate authority to him but also to add to the Space Council the responsibility to develop "a comprehensive program of aeronautical and space activities to be conducted by agencies of the United States."[46]

That same day, Kennedy drafted a letter to Johnson noting the proposed legislation and his message to Congress and stating his belief that "your long background and great experience in the field of space and defense matters equip you to give effective and meaningful direction to the Council." Further, "you will be undertaking a most responsible role and will play a very significant part in the development of a space program second to none."[47]

In less than forty-eight hours, the road map to pass the proposed legislation was clear according to an April 6 memo from Edward Welsh, the new executive secretary of the Space Council. Welsh's memo reported on his visits to members of Congress to help ensure passage of the proposed amendments to the Space Act. He reported that no one had expressed reservations and that the amendments would be considered in a hearing on April 11.[48] Without waiting for final passage, but assured of its success, President Kennedy sent a White House memorandum to Vice President Johnson on April 20, charging him as chairman of the Space Council to not just catch up with the Soviets but to get ahead of them somehow. Specifically, he asked, "Do we have a chance of beating the Soviets by putting a laboratory in space, or by a trip around the moon, or by a rocket to land on the moon, or by a rocket to go to the moon and back with a man? Is there any other space program which promises dramatic results in which we could win?" He continued, "Are we working 24 hours a day on existing programs—if not, why not?" and "Are we making maximum effort"? The president concluded by stating that he had directed "[NASA Administrator] Jim Webb, Secretary McNamara and other responsible officials to cooperate with you fully."[49] Lyndon Johnson now had a mandate from the president to make things happen, and quickly. President Kennedy publicly confirmed the urgency of his plans the next day, saying simply, "If we can get to the moon before the Russians, we should."[50]

Vice President Johnson, focused on space policy even before taking office, had already requested two noted space industry leaders to coordinate and prepare a report to suggest guidelines for the development of American policy. On April 24, this Interim Report on Space Policy was presented to the vice president and circulated around the White House and to the members of the Space Council.[51] The report first notes the ongoing struggle to keep up with Soviet space science advances and then explains the national security interest in focusing increased effort and funding on the US initiative. The report specifically cites the "great importance" of manned flight.[52] The next day after receiving this report, President Kennedy signed HR 6169 amending the Space Act and issued a statement: "It was a key step toward moving the United States into its proper place in the space race." He singled out Johnson for praise as the new leader of the Space Council, noting that "he was the author of the Space Resolution in the Congress, the Chairman of the Special Senate Committee which played such an important role in developing space legislation, and the Chairman of the Senate Preparedness Committee which as far back as 1958 urged immediate action for the development of a million pound rocket booster."[53] By this time, Johnson was fully vested with control of the Space Council, which now had broad and very visible authority. It was armed with reports and recommendations that the US space program was urgent and essential to the national security and specifically called for manned space flight as a critical component.

Within days, the new Space Council had something to crow about. On May 5, 1961, Alan Shepard became the first American in space on Mercury's *Freedom 7* spacecraft. Johnson wrote to NASA Administrator Webb: "I want to congratulate you again on the magnificent performance of today. It was a real success, and the country needed it."[54] Johnson and Webb would have a close working relationship both during this time and after Johnson became president. However, in his personal statements, Webb denies that President Kennedy had abdicated leadership of the space program. "It had a popular image, that the President in a sense had turned everything over to the Vice President, but this simply is not written into the law nor was it in fact true. On the other hand, he was happy for Mr. Johnson to take the lead . . . [and said] get it done."[55]

It may be that Houston first seriously thought about grabbing the Space Age brass ring in in March 1961 when US Air Force Colonel John P. Stapp spoke to an audience at the University of Houston. Stapp was then known for flying faster than any other man as a result of his experiments on the effects of acceleration and deceleration on people. He informed the audience, "Man is physically capable of space travel."[56]

Selection of Houston as the New Space City

A report from George Low, a mathematician and aeronautical engineer who headed a Manned Lunar Landing Task Group at NASA, unknowingly initiated Houston's prospects as the site of the Manned Space Center.[57] Low had been with NASA since its inception and had been part of the planning team for the proposed new agency before that. Low's task group reached the conclusion that the "manned spaceflight program should be separated from all NASA centers." By January 1961, the agency adopted the idea of a separate manned spaceflight center as policy, although officials still disagreed whether to simply place the new center at the Ames Research Center in California or find an entirely new location.[58]

Johnson reported to President Kennedy on May 8, 1961, that he was continuing his efforts to evaluate and coordinate the best way for "placing this country on the way toward leadership in space."[59] The same day, Johnson wrote to his friend Congressman Melvin Price (D-IL) to thank him for support on the space program and to ask for help in presenting practical solutions to the president "for accelerating our space efforts."[60] It seems likely that by the time Johnson sent these two communications, he had already set in motion the process that would result in the Houston Space Center. No doubt, as soon as an emphasis began on the need for manned space flight and possibly a lunar landing, there would have been attention to where physically and geographically to coordinate and manage such a program. Vice President Johnson had numerous staff and officials working on the issues but apparently had charged Administrator Webb in particular, who sent a memorandum to Johnson on May 23 as Johnson was returning to Washington from a long tour of Asian countries.[61]

Administrator Webb's memorandum first references President Kennedy's upcoming address to Congress on space policy and then talks specifically about locating a manned space center in Houston: "In preparing for the hearings [for the space program] before the House Appropriations Committee, and in other discussions with Congressman Thomas, he has made it very clear that he and George Brown were extremely interested in having Rice University make a real contribution to the effort, particularly in view of the fact that some research funds were now being spent at Rice, that the resources of Rice had increased substantially, and that some 3800 acres of land had been set aside by Rice for an important research installation."[62] The reference to Congressman Thomas in the context of the

Congressman Albert Thomas (D-Houston) was perhaps the most influential political figure in steering the Space Center to Houston. MSS0160-0168, Houston Public Library, John J. Herrera Papers.

House Appropriations Committee references Albert Thomas, the longtime congressman representing Houston. Thomas completed his undergraduate work at Rice before attending the University of Texas Law School. He was first elected to Congress in 1936 and formed a close alliance with Lyndon Johnson, who joined him a few months later after winning a special election held in the spring of 1937.

Webb's memo to Johnson continues: "I find that we are going to have to establish some place where we can do the technology related to the Apollo program, and this should be on the water where the vehicles can ultimately be barged to the launching site. Therefore, we have looked carefully at Rice, and at the possible locations near the Houston Ship Canal or other accessible waterways in that general area. George Brown has been extremely helpful in doing this."[63] George R. Brown, founder of Brown and Root Construction

Company, was a graduate of Rice and had been college roommates with Thomas.[64] By this time in 1961, Brown was also on the Board of Regents at Rice University and in a position to know what Rice had and could offer.[65] Besides mentioning the physical and geographic characteristics of Houston, Webb's memo to Johnson stated the "great importance to develop the intellectual and other resources of the Southwest in connection with the new programs which the Government is undertaking."[66]

President Kennedy stoked the fire on May 25 when he addressed Congress and declared that it "is the intent of the United States to take a clearly leading role in space achievement."[67] Vice President Johnson echoed that in a memo a few days later with a list of national goals, the first one being "earliest possible achievement of manned lunar exploration."[68] After President Kennedy accelerated the space program and Congress approved vast new funding, the idea of an "Apollo complex took the shape of a crescent moon running around the Gulf of Mexico from Texas to Florida. There were sound reasons for it: year-round warm weather, deep-water transport for the big rockets (imagine the Soviet difficulties in moving big rockets on rail beds across soft country), and contiguity."[69] Even in the Eisenhower administration, NASA was thinking that "a continuation and enlargement of the spaceflight program [would result in existing programs] being overwhelmed." Later, after the commitment to a manned spaceflight had been made, NASA quickly came to realize that "the manned spaceflight program should be separated from all other NASA centers."[70]

NASA generated specific site criteria in the early summer of 1961 and made this available to Congress and then to the general public. NASA stated that the location of the manned space center must possess "access to water transportation by large barges, a moderate climate, availability of all-weather commercial jet service, a well-established industrial complex with supporting technical facilities and labor, close proximity to a culturally attractive community in the vicinity of an institution of higher education, a strong electric utility and water supply, at least 1000 acres of land, and certain specified cost parameters."[71] In August 1961, Administrator Webb appointed a site selection team to be chaired by John F. Parsons. The team established a list of twenty-two cities that seemed to meet the criteria. Three Texas cities were on the list—Victoria, Corpus Christi, and Houston—although the Houston site was the San Jacinto Ordnance Depot.[72] Later, four sites were added, including the Rice University tract of land. The team visited twenty-three of the cities between August 21 and September 7, where they were greeted warmly and treated to all the local hospitality.

In the end, the site selection team selected MacDill Air Force Base in Tampa, Florida, with the Houston site offered by Rice University as alternate. MacDill had been slated to close, so it was believed that the manned space center would be a good use of the already available site. "Before a decision could be made, however, the Air Force decided not to close MacDill, omitting it from consideration."[73] Administrator Webb then informed President Kennedy on September 14 that the decision was made to locate the new space center in Houston. Webb informed the president of the criteria and procedures for the site selection and said, "Our decision is that this laboratory should be located in Houston, Texas, in close association with Rice University and the other educational institutions there and in that region."[74] The public announcement was made a few days later on September 19. John Parsons, of NASA's Ames Research Center, stated, "Houston more than meets the criteria."[75] President Kennedy apparently knew all along that there was some effort to steer the space center to Houston. Webb stated in a 1972 interview, "Kennedy called up [Congressman] Thomas one day and said 'I need your help on [some bills].' And Albert said, 'Now, Mr. President, I don't know about this.' And Kennedy said 'Now, you know Jim Webb is thinking about putting this center down in Houston' . . . and, he said, 'in that case, Mr. President—'"[76]

Houston was a good candidate on objective factors and easily matches the written site selection criteria published by NASA. However, the political process obviously began much earlier. Well before the site selection team had even been named, Abe Silverstein, the NASA director of space flight programs, asked, "I wonder where Albert Thomas' district is?"[77] Soon thereafter, Silverstein sent Philip Miller from Goddard Space Center and John Parsons from Ames Research Center to Houston to scout possibilities. They were "met at the airport in Houston on May 16 by George Brown, of the Houston-based Brown and Root construction company, who the previous month met with Johnson's Space Council. They [visited Rice University before touring] a large tract of land identified as the West Estate which had recently been donated to Rice University by Humble Oil Company. The tract included a 20,000 square foot mansion previously occupied by the West family that, although impressive, might not be useful in the space program."[78] However, the open expanse of land next to Houston was excellent, and the group noted that barge traffic would be able to reach the site through Clear Lake and the Houston Ship Channel.[79] "George Brown indicated Rice University would be favorably disposed to making the land available to the government for a research center installation."[80]

George R. Brown of Brown and Root had the political connections and business savvy to put together a coalition with a winning bid to bring the Space Center to Houston. Courtesy of Rice University.

It was Johnson, not Kennedy, who was knowledgeable about space exploration and had experience in the field when the two came to national office in 1961. But by 1962 in a speech in Houston at Rice University, President Kennedy had clearly embraced the vision when he asked rhetorically why the goal should be to reach the moon. He compared it to climbing a high mountain or flying across the Atlantic or Rice playing Texas in football. The president said it was good to "aspire, to strive" and that the frontier now lay in technology and, physically in outer space.[81]

President Kennedy's "Moon Speech" at Rice University in 1962 showed that the space program was a national priority and that Houston was the center of it all. Courtesy of NASA.

Houston was a strong candidate for the new space center as a city on the water with an especially large and well-developed ship channel and port system. Winters were mild, so there was no time of year when work could not proceed indoors or out. There was a security concern underlying the policy of not placing everything related to the space program in one locale, yet all aspects needed to be in logical connection to each other, hence the concept of a "crescent" of space program development around the Gulf of

Mexico. There was already a launch site at Cape Canaveral in Florida and a rocket construction complex in Alabama, so the politics leaned more toward locating the manned space center farther to the western side of the crescent, such as in Louisiana or Texas. In 1969, Administrator Webb said, "Here was a natural line of flow built around the Huntsville–Cape Kennedy axis with the New Orleans assembly plant and the Mississippi test facility in the middle. . . . [When thinking of the manned space center,] the very configuration of this axis concept led you to Houston." Additionally, that there was an assembly plant already at New Orleans helped eliminate that city as a rival to Houston for the manned space center. In the very hot nuclear climate of the time, government leaders thought in terms of survivability of facilities and operations. As Administrator Webb recalled, "You didn't want to put a second big installation in New Orleans." Nevertheless, Webb does acknowledge Johnson's strong interest in the location of the manned space center: "Mr. Johnson was always interested in Texas. A good deal of the time he was Vice President, he still sort of thought of himself as a Senator from Texas. He was interested in everything that went on in Texas."[82]

James Webb served as NASA administrator during the Kennedy and Johnson administrations, the nation's most crucial era of space exploration and a game changer for Houston's commercial development. Courtesy of Lyndon Baines Johnson Presidential Library.

Despite geography and politics favoring Houston, many other places tried to attract what promised to be the mother lode of federal spending and jobs creation. The governor of Ohio asked one of his constituents, former NASA Administrator T. Keith Glennan, to develop a proposal for locating the manned space center in Ohio. But Glennan could easily see how the politics and the natural candidacy of Houston had already fused together: "You know, I suppose that there are 25 states doing just this at the present time, and I'll lay you a year's salary that that Center is going to Houston."[83] Indeed, the site selection criteria published by NASA were written almost three months after NASA had already made a site visit to Houston and specifically to the Rice University tract in the company of George R. Brown.[84]

Brown, while acknowledging his own substantial involvement, credits the heavy lifting to Congressman Thomas. In a 1969 interview, Brown said, "Albert Thomas played a major part in [the selection of Houston for the manned space center]. He told me if we could get some 1,000 acres of land there we could put this Manned Space Center here. So, knowing about this big ranch the Humble Oil Company had, I went to the head of the Humble Company and he agreed to give a thousand acres. Albert asked me to get Rice University to do it because he wanted to get Rice involved. So the Humble Company promised to give it to Rice University if they'd use it for the Manned Space Center. They in turn gave it to the government."[85] Another indication that the political winds favored Houston was the speed at which the selection happened. William Reynolds stated in 1978 that "it seemed to happen rather quickly. Once they passed this, then all of a sudden the site was selected, and they started construction, and they started moving. I recall something about the appropriations, but it occurred so fast it just seemed to move right through Congress. [There was] a sense of urgency."[86]

One factor that favored Houston in particular was the mostly united front that the state presented. The other major city, Dallas, was not on the water, but it had found a way to benefit along with Houston. Webb noted this fact in his May 1961 memo to Johnson: "Texas offers an unusual opportunity at this time due to the fact that Mr. Lloyd Berkner, Chairman of the Space Science Board of the National Academy of Sciences, is establishing a Graduate Research Center in Dallas with the backing of [local leaders] estimated at about one hundred million dollars."[87] Webb goes on to lay out a scenario whereby the universities in the Dallas area could be united in the Berkner Research Center, while a strong engineering and technological center "could be established near the water near Houston and perhaps in conjunction with Rice University, these two strong centers would provide a great impetus to the intellectual and industrial base of this whole region."[88] Webb went on to describe how such a development could be a link in the chain of academic-technological centers around the country, including California, Chicago, and the Northeast. He believed this distribution would seem logical and would minimize political infighting in Congress.

The end analysis seems much like the first: Houston had many attributes that made it attractive as a site for a manned space center, and it was able to present its case through its own political lobby and to have such petition received by a well-placed political connection, Lyndon Johnson. Johnson, as powerful and experienced as he was, could not have forced the national space program to Houston against the will of NASA and the space science community, especially on such a fundamentally important aspect as manned spaceflight. It was necessary that Houston meet the objective criteria NASA promulgated for site selection, and it did. Of course, that is not to say that the criteria were not written with Houston in mind, but the requirements objectively made sense and drew no complaint from the scientific community. Importantly, the Houston Ship Channel "and its industrial complex were decisive factors in bringing to the area one of the most coveted of all governmental installations: the National Aeronautics and Space Administration."[89]

It is obvious from the sequence of events that NASA representatives had already visited Houston and that the Albert Thomas–George R. Brown local political machine was already engaged, even before the site selection criteria were published. However, none of the criteria listed seem created just to favor Houston, and in fact they reflect long-standing NASA considerations, for example, location on water near a major research university, large land tract availability, and adequate utilities. Congressman Thomas clearly had the most political stake in securing the manned space center for his district of Houston, and it is evident from the archival evidence that he worked diligently to bring the project about. Nothing less would be expected of a congressman in serving his district. Lyndon B. Johnson undoubtedly was pleased to have his home state selected. He no doubt encouraged it and would have been in a position to provide useful information and updates to advocates such as Congressman Thomas and George R. Brown. That said, the archival record does not indicate anything like a political overreach, especially given that Johnson's focus on the space program as a vital component of US national security extended back to the 1950s and well before he could have fathomed being vice president.

In sum, Houston was blessed with many natural and manufactured attributes that made it attractive to a facility like a manned space center.

Houston had very capable representation in Congress and elsewhere in Washington, all of whom were in a position to direct policy and funding in a favorable way. The escalation of the Cold War, the acceleration of the Space Race, and the evolution of technology all occurred at a time convenient to Houston's political moment. Lyndon Johnson as vice president and, more important, as chairman of the Space Council, made the circle complete in such a way that Houston could effectively step in when its particular qualifications were in great need by the nation. "But the truly deciding factor was not political pressure, concluded historian Stephen B. Oates in analyzing the reasons for NASA's choice. It was the winning combination of advantages which Houston itself had to offer. Chief among these was the excellent means of transporting bulky space vehicles to other NASA locations, especially to Cape Canaveral."[90]

Houston as the New Space City

The selection of Houston as the home of the Manned Spacecraft Center meant, of course, that a flood of scientists, engineers, and various technical specialties would be coming to the city. Houston already had a large scientific and technical population, but mostly it revolved around the oil and gas industry. Space exploration was entirely new, and a whole new demographic came to Houston. Of course, these newcomers were not coming on a short-term assignment for a special project—they were coming to stay and live in Houston, contributing to a great leap in the economic diversification of the city benefiting from "an influx of both scientists and related industries from throughout the world."[91] "The coming of NASA added a boom on top of a boom to the Greater Houston–Galveston Bay area."[92] This concentration of a wide base of scientific workers, coupled with oil wealth, would later help fuel a boom of computer and related high-tech industries in Houston.

Houston rolled out the red carpet to the new NASA arrivals just as it had for the selection team earlier. The site procurement chief, W. A. Parker, recalled that "we had police escort from meeting to meeting because everyone was interested in talking to us. . . . We had a constant audience."[93] Joske's department stores sent welcome letters and Stetson hats.[94] Hospitality teams were ready to greet the new Houstonians at the airport and ensure all their needs were met. Realtors provided tours of the city, including potential housing areas, and the Chamber of Commerce provided football tickets. NASA and Houston cooperated to produce promotional literature and slide shows to show NASA employees at Langley that the move to Houston was going to be a good one.[95] Finger Furniture Company offered furniture,[96] telephones were installed in the homes of new Space Center employees without charge or advance order, Joske's offered free draperies for the homes, and local car dealers offered free use of vehicles until the government cars were available.[97] Houston was enthused, excited, and anxious to make the newcomers feel welcome.

Not all the NASA space flight employees at Langley were excited to pack up and move to Houston. However, few if anyone regretted the decision later. Wesley L. Hjornevik, general manager of the Spacecraft Center, acknowledged that he had once opposed the selection of Houston but said, "I feel now it was a good decision. Certainly the community has welcomed us. And it is surprising how quickly one becomes a Texan."[98]

By July 1962, less than a year after Houston was selected as the home of the Manned Space Center, almost sixteen hundred employees moved to Houston. That number almost doubled by 1963. The federal government poured billions of dollars into the effort to land men on the moon with a great deal of money going specifically to Houston firms or universities.[99] NASA's budget in 1959 was $330.9 million; but in 1961, was $1,825 million; and in 1963, was $3,674 million.[100] Beyond direct federal appropriations, there were additional monies spent by state and local governments to facilitate the Space Center with roads, utilities, drainage, and other infrastructure and services. Additionally, the thousands of new Space Center employees bought homes and cars and engaged in the local economy. Houston began to develop a "space business complex" and a greater capacity to harness technology into the local economy beyond the already existing Texas Medical Center and refining and chemical industries. Even in future years when the oil boom subsided, the Space Center and all it supported continued to buoy Houston. And when federal spending on the Space Center declined, many of those highly educated personnel stayed and entered new oil boom fields, the medical complex, or the emerging computer industry.[101]

Houstonians began to speak in terms of "Vanguards, Explorers, Pioneers and other space vehicles" and compare them with "Sputniks, Luniks and Vostoks." Buildings were cleared and outfitted for NASA's use or simply torn down and rebuilt. Cattle were cleared from hundreds of acres of ranchland as massive construction projects launched. NASA closed the doors of its Manned Spacecraft Center at Langley, Virginia, on Friday, June 29, 1962, and opened on Monday morning, July 2, in Houston.[102]

To officially welcome the new Space Center, Houston held a big Texas bash for July 4, 1962. The celebration started with a parade in downtown

Houston featuring the "seven Project Mercury astronauts" along with Vice President Johnson, Governor Price Daniel, Senator Robert Kerr of Oklahoma, and Texas' two senators, John Tower and Ralph Yarborough. The parade concluded at the Sam Houston Coliseum, site of a huge Texas barbecue with all the trimmings.[103] The president of the Houston Chamber of Commerce, George T. Morse, told the new Houstonians that "we are delighted that you will make your homes in our community, that you will be our friends and neighbors."[104]

Houston enjoyed continuing world attention as each mission into space was controlled from its city. For example, in June 1965, Gemini 4 orbited the earth with astronaut voices carried on radio and television. "Command Pilot James A. McDivitt exclaimed to Capsule Communicator Gus Grissom, 'We're right over Houston. . . . That's Galveston Bay right there.'" Later in the summer, another astronaut was outside the space capsule on tether and said, "We're looking right down on Houston. . . . I'll get a picture."[105] Of course, Houston was now home for these astronauts, and they expressed hometown pride when looking down from outer space.

The Manned Space Center had its own public affairs department and drafted its own press releases, although they were transmitted to NASA headquarters in Washington. Houston implemented "very strong public affairs programs including exhibits" and speaking forums for NASA personnel, including the astronauts. Houstonians vied for opportunities to host astronauts and NASA officials in their homes and at parties and galas. "We knew them all," said Lynn Wyatt, "and we loved to entertain them and make them love Houston as we did."[106]

One strong reason for selecting Houston in the first place was its local education institutions, Rice University and the University of Houston, as well as other respected institutions of higher education nearby. However, once there, the Manned Space Center was a catalyst to greater expansion of academic programs. The University of Houston accepted grants from the Space Center that funded graduate fellowships in space and technology fields. In 1969, the University of Houston established a branch campus at Clear Lake near the Space Center, which eventually grew into the University of Houston–Clear Lake.[107]

The new image of Space City permeated Houston's society and culture and tapped into a national and international fascination with outer space and with culture and taste that reflected that new obsession. One example is fashion of the 1960s that was often portrayed as more minimalist and sleek, with the incorporation of modern materials like plastic, vinyl, and metals. In

Houston relished its new role as Space City. The world's fascination with the Space Age carried over to high fashion, including the designer André Courrèges, who launched a new fashion line inspired by space. Lynn Wyatt noted the new Space Age miniskirts offered by André Courrèges in Paris. She connected Courrèges with her brother, Robert Sakowitz, the CEO of Sakowitz department stores. Courtesy of Jacqueline Barrière Courrèges.

1964, the French fashion designer André Courrèges presented, to international acclaim, his "Space Age" collection with shorter skirts, go-go boots, modern fabrics, and "a palette of astronaut-friendly white and silver."[108] In January 1965, Courrèges presented the miniskirt as part of his spring collection, with minimalist skirts set four inches above the knee.[109]

In 1965, Houstonian Lynn Wyatt was in Paris for the Courrèges spring fashion show and met the designer at a dinner party through mutual friends. She was dazzled by his spectacular designs and completely new take on women's fashion. She told him that "he should bring his mini-skirts and futuristic clothes to Houston because it was the Space City and the best launch site for such innovative new designs."[110] She then called her brother in Houston, Robert Sakowitz, the buyer for Sakowitz department stores, the most upscale retailer in the city. Lynn had grown up the daughter and granddaughter of Houston's luxury retailers Tobias and Bernard Sakowitz, and she obviously knew a good opportunity when she saw it. Robert flew over and

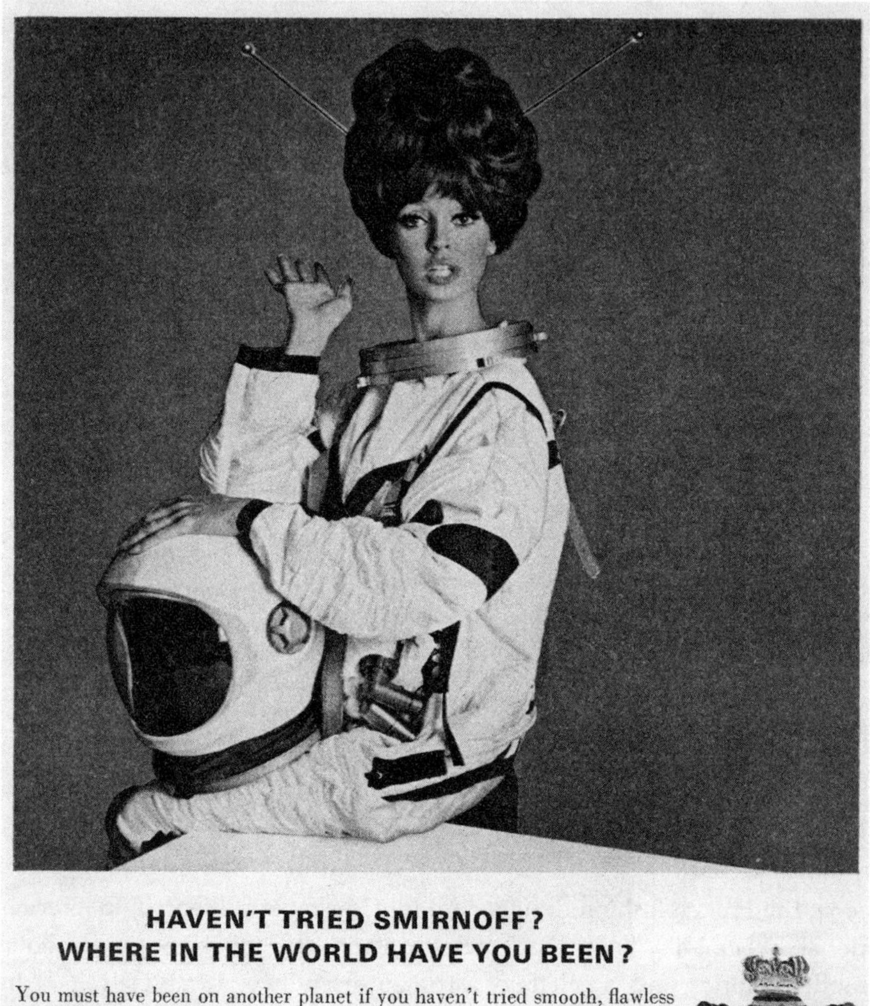

HAVEN'T TRIED SMIRNOFF?
WHERE IN THE WORLD HAVE YOU BEEN?

You must have been on another planet if you haven't tried smooth, flawless Smirnoff. Smirnoff is *not* like other vodkas. The unique filtration process (through 9,000 pounds of charcoal), makes Smirnoff crystal clear, remarkably free of taste or odour. Nothing less will do for your party. Smirnoff shows you *know*. Smirnoff says you *care*.

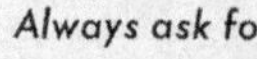

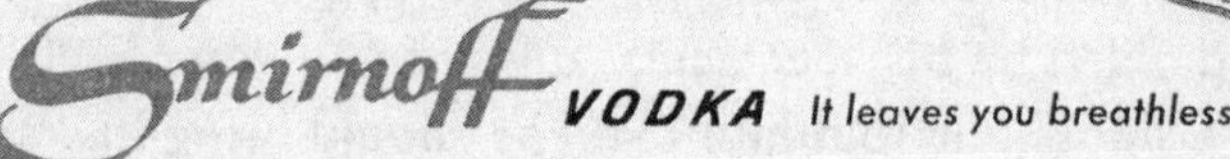

75

The Space Age image projected by Houston carried over into fashion, music, design, food, drink, and culture. Association with the Space Age symbolized success. © 1965 Diageo North America, Inc. All rights reserved. Used by permission.

made his pitch to Courrèges, who was intrigued at the possibility of a fashion launch in Houston and through the hands of people he knew.[111] Moreover, Sakowitz proposed that instead of being paid only for the original couture, which would be copied by someone else, Courrèges would be paid for the design and then also produce it in his own shop to the sizing specifications of Sakowitz. Courrèges agreed, thereby starting a new trend among other designers to produce their own fashion lines and market them, not simply sell the original design. Sakowitz took out half-page ads in *The New York Times,* both in New York and its Palm Beach editions, in addition to heavy advertising in Houston about the new fashion coming to Space City for the spring 1966 season.

The business coup by the Houston retailer and the "salt in the wound" of the advertising campaign aroused the resentment of retailing competitors. New York's Bonwit Teller went to Paris and offered to buy three times as much product as Sakowitz if it could have the exclusive. Robert Sakowitz

Sakowitz was the most upscale retailer in Houston and was already projecting itself as a sleek, modern store when André Courrèges debuted the miniskirt in 1965. Suddenly Houston became a fashion mecca. MSS 0019-1570, Houston Public Library, Alfred C. Finn.

Tobias Sakowitz founded the family's luxury goods business. Management later passed to his son Bernard Sakowitz and then to grandson Robert Sakowitz. Courtesy of Robert Sakowitz.

returned to Paris to speak with Courrèges and urge him to keep the deal. In the end, Courrèges agreed to give Sakowitz a two-week head start. *The New York Times* sent a reporter to Sakowitz to cover the launch, and history was made: ready-to-wear fashion directly from a top European designer's own production shop to a Houston retailer.[112] Sakowitz very successfully marketed the new Space Age clothing lines to the residents of Space City, playing into the city's attitude of modernity and on such popular culture themes as the TV show *Star Trek*, which debuted in September 1966.

"The placement of the Manned Space Center was a huge plum for the city. It positioned Houston as a forward-looking city, one that built the first domed sports stadium," said James Baker, native Houston lawyer and former US secretary of state.[113] Baker's reference to the sports stadium is the Astrodome, the first fully enclosed and air-conditioned sports stadium in the world. Houston voters approved bonds for the Astrodome in 1958 and 1961 even before the Space Center was announced.[114] The Astrodome's first event was a baseball game pitting the Houston Astros against the visiting New York Yankees on April 9, 1965. By 1968, the Houston Oilers were using the Astrodome for professional football as well. After conquering its climate with the Astrodome, Houston conquered its turf problem by inventing an outdoor carpeting appropriately called Astroturf. The Astrodome and Astroturf were copied all over the world for sports and special events centers.[115]

The Manned Space Center at Houston was renamed the Lyndon B. Johnson Space Center on February 19, 1973, in honor of the former president shortly after he died on January 22. A ceremony to formally dedicate the new name was held on August 27, attended by Lady Bird Johnson along with members of the Johnson family, Governor Dolph Briscoe, US Senator John Tower, former NASA Administrator James Webb, and many local officials. President Nixon did not attend personally but sent a statement to be read: "Few men in our time have better understood the value of space exploration than Lyndon Johnson [who] drew America up closer to the stars, and before he died he saw us reach the Moon—the first great plateau along the way."[116] Lady Bird Johnson spoke at the event and remembered Congressman Albert Thomas in particular, "who was most responsible for transforming this Texas pasture into the command post for humankind's greatest adventure."[117]

By the 1980s, the Manned Space Center had moved on to its new role as lead for the Space Shuttle program. The first orbital tests occurred in 1981, and the program expanded throughout the 1980s and 1990s. The Space Shuttle program was connected to Europe's Spacelab and to the US-Russian Space Station.

After Houstonian George H. W. Bush was elected president in 1988, he "resurrected the National Space Council which had fallen into disuse during previous administrations."[118] Bush was personally interested in the Space Center and what the space program meant for Houston and the nation. Bush nominated a new NASA administrator, Richard H. Truly, a former navy fighter pilot and astronaut. Truly was the first astronaut to head NASA.

George Fuermann opined that the "[space] center gave [Houston] a bond with the old ports of western Europe that played leading roles in the great exploration voyages of . . . centuries before."[119] Writing these words in 1971, Fuermann was right of course—Houston would be a global center of technology in the future, as it already had become in energy and international trade. Houston would continue to "colonize" the world with its oil and gas personnel. Just as the imperial capitals of Europe had drawn the wealthy and powerful to them, Houston would now draw the best and brightest in a new world of exploration. Space was the new frontier, just as Houston itself had been a new frontier in Texas, and as Texas had been a new frontier in the United States, and as the American West had been a frontier in general for American society. Space was now a frontier for humankind in general, and Houston was literally the control center for the American effort. As London had been the center for British exploration of the New World (and Paris for French exploration, and Madrid for Spanish, and so forth), Houston would be the command center for the American efforts in outer space. This high responsibility was made all the more strategically critical because of the accelerating Cold War and the fierce competition with the Soviet Union for primacy in space. As the 1960s progressed, the phrase "space: the final frontier" became culturally common because of the enduring popularity of the television show *Star Trek*.[120]

Houston's reinvention of itself into Space City is truly remarkable. The Texas Medical Center did much to reinvent the city's image after World War II into one of advanced technology, education, and skill. But the center was not even twenty years old when Houston was chosen for the new space center. In many ways, the accomplishments of the Space Center promoted the Medical Center, and vice versa. "Many Houstonians considered their city to be a Disney-esque city of the future, where anything was possible," says James Baker. "If we can send men to the moon and bring them back, certainly we can solve other challenges, like finding cures for cancer, as they are at M. D. Anderson."[121] Houston had also used its geography on the water, enhanced as it was by over a century of dredging and digging. To this was added a carefully choreographed joint effort of business, political, and education leaders to implement a sound strategy. And of course, all these efforts were backed by the promise of more to come. Houston seems like the perfect Space City to contemporary eyes, but it was truly an unlikely scenario even five years before it happened.

CHAPTER FIVE

BUSINESS, POLITICAL, AND SOCIAL LEADERS

Houston has produced many interesting characters over its long history since 1836. Like any large city, Houston has had generations of community leaders in business, politics, society, and the arts. Houston's famous names are often nationally and internationally famous names as well. The best-known include some from established families, such as the Hoggs or the Bakers. But the aggressive and daring personality of Houston has also produced a large number of "rags to riches" type of celebrities. It is perhaps the nature of Houston, which rose initially on its position as a nineteenth-century trading port, to produce the type of determined personality who sees opportunity and squeezes every possible drop of benefit from it. Even more so, the oil and gas industry drew the particularly daring and bold from other parts of the state or nation to search for the next big gusher. Before technology better illuminated the hidden wealth deep underground, and even afterward, it required a certain personality with confidence and calm nerves to put time and capital into the frightening uncertainty of oil and gas exploration.

By the time Houston spent its first hundred years building itself into a major trade port and energy center, it was ready to embrace a new wave of gutsy entrepreneurs in technology. First came the individual philanthropists and ambitious medical leaders that created the Texas Medical Center. Then came community philanthropy and political strategists to harness the

Manned Space Center into Houston. Both endeavors successfully launched Houston into new international realms beyond its well-recognized bases of trade and energy.

At each stage of Houston's development into an international city, there have been colorful men and women of extraordinary skill or leadership, or both, to guide, enable, or sometimes shove the city forward. Some of these leaders set out with specific agendas for Houston and fought and strove tenaciously to ensure the success of their ambitions for the city. Others contributed more indirectly or only when asked, but their actions were critical for the future of Houston.

The lives and careers of some of these Houstonians are intertwined specifically with a certain industry or a certain philanthropic project or cause. But many of them transcend any particular label and, instead, lent critical aid to Houston across several decades in a variety of projects. Internationally prominent Houstonian James A. Baker III says Houston's "can-do spirit [that it's always had] remains alive" and continues to push the city forward in extraordinary ways.[1] Whether it was to create a massive deep-water port and ship channel miles inland, build the world's biggest medical complex, or land the largest space exploration center at the height of the Cold War, Houston's leadership was on the task in a thorough, even overwhelming way, lest anything stop them from achieving the goal.

The scope of Houston's growth from a rough, fledgling town plat into a major trade port in only one generation is remarkable in itself. Additionally, the rapid emergence of the city as the world energy capital, manned space exploration headquarters, and home to the world's largest medical center involves individually amazing stories and, collectively, is simply phenomenal. However, it is important to note that alongside the remarkable growth of the city's population, wealth, and technology, there were succeeding generations of leading Houstonians who believed that "aggressive economic expansion and innovative cultural achievement can march together." These cultural leaders built "an urban landscape destined to achieve world-class status [and make Houston] a laboratory of cultural experiment where generous patrons have created a climate essential to the flowering of genius."[2]

Indeed, the city's commercial rise and its cultural ascendancy were really parallel movements that had great interdependency, especially in the early years. The eastern United States and more especially Europe were the cultural centers of the world. As Houstonians became more wealthy and worldly, they undertook more frequent international travel. These journeys

Both President Bush and Secretary of State James Baker were Houstonians and served in Washington at a time when Houston had become a truly global city, leading in shipping, energy, medicine, space, and manufacturing. Courtesy of George H. W. Bush Presidential Library and Museum.

included the art museums of London, Paris, and Rome, as well as the operas and music festivals of Italy, Germany, and Austria. These sights and experiences "trained the eyes and ears of these travelers" and created an intense desire and energy to see such cultural sights and sounds in their own city of Houston. These ambitions coincided with Progressive Era thought in which "clean sewers, paved streets" along with "forest parks, museums [and] civic orchestras" were all a part of the ideal world city.[3]

William Marsh Rice

One of the earliest builders of modern Houston was William Marsh Rice, who was born in Massachusetts in 1816.[4] He moved to Houston in 1837 when it was still a city of tents with a provisional capitol building still under construction.[5] Rice acquired land around Houston, adding to it over the years as he built up his business interests to include shipping, railroads, and insurance. By 1860, Rice was reportedly the richest man in Houston and the second-richest man in Texas.[6]

William Marsh Rice was the richest man in Houston in the late nineteenth century. His wealth funded educational programs for young people, including the Rice Institute, now Rice University. Courtesy of Rice University.

William Marsh Rice became acquainted with Cesar Lombardi, a Houston businessman originally from Switzerland, who was serving as president of the Houston School Board in the late 1880s. Lombardi impressed upon Rice the notion that his wealth could be used to benefit the children of Houston through education. Rice established the Rice Institute in 1891 to serve both boys and girls and then wrote a will giving the bulk of his estate to fund the institute.[7] The lawyer who prepared the will was James A. Baker Sr., the son of James Addison Baker, the first of five generations of Bakers who served as lawyers in the Baker Botts law firm of Houston.[8] William Marsh Rice moved to New York but continued to use James Baker's services for his business interests in Houston while using Albert Patrick to handle his legal affairs in New York. In late June 1900, James Baker received a telegram from New York advising that Rice, age eighty-four, had passed away. At about the same time, a check drawn by Rice for $25,000 was presented for payment at his bank. The bank was suspicious of the amount, the signature, and the endorsement and declined to honor the check.

Baker, perhaps alerted by the bank, went to New York to look into the affairs of his late client and learned that Albert Patrick had prepared a new will, written only three months earlier, that essentially left nothing for the Rice Institute but left plenty of money for Patrick. An autopsy of Rice revealed that he had been poisoned. The subsequent investigation and legal proceedings proved that Patrick, in conspiracy with Rice's valet, Charles Jones, had poisoned Rice over time with mercury and forged a new will. At the end, the valet finished the sickly Rice off with a cloth soaked in chloroform. Patrick was sentenced to death, but the sentence was later commuted to life before he was released altogether in 1912.[9] The happier side of the story is that Rice University, an internationally recognized research university with particular renown in the sciences, came into being because of the initial funding of William Marsh Rice and the legal skill and alert responses of his lawyer James A. Baker Sr.

Rice Institute, now known as Rice University, was officially established in 1904. Its first president was Edgar Odell Lovett, who headed the Department of Mathematics and Astronomy at Princeton before coming to Houston. The Rice trustees hired Lovett in 1907 on the recommendation of Princeton's president, Woodrow Wilson.[10] Lovett guided Rice through the planning stages, even spending several years touring the top universities of the world for ideas and inspiration. Lovett helped structure the best curriculum and teaching methodologies, drawing on the best national and international examples for Houston's new institution of higher education. Finally by 1912, Rice admitted its first class of students, both male and female. Lovett remained president until 1947 by which time Rice was firmly established as a prestigious institution. William Marsh Rice's wealth and generosity, coupled with the skill of his lawyers at Baker Botts, enabled the birth of one of the great universities with all the advantages and distinction that it would bring to Houston over the years.[11]

Jesse Jones

Jesse Jones may be the single most influential leader of Houston in terms of his diverse and substantial impact. He was not a politician, but he commanded the respect and admiration of local, state, national, and international leaders for decades. He was a superb businessman who lent his skill to combat the Depression of the 1930s. He was a civic leader, promoter of the arts, and a great philanthropist. His story of success is remarkably intertwined with Houston's own rise on the national and international stage. He was widely regarded in both business and political circles, with President Franklin Roosevelt calling him Jesus Jones, and *Time* magazine reassured its readers: "To many a U.S. citizen great or small, if Jesse Jones says O.K., O.K."[12]

Jesse Holman Jones was born in Tennessee in 1874 to a prosperous family. In 1898, Jesse's uncle, Martin Jones of Houston, died unexpectedly. Jesse was named one of the executors of the estate and decided the time was right to move to Houston to take over management of one of his late uncle's lumberyards.[13] A few years later, Jones opened his own lumber company, South Texas Lumber, and managed to secure timber concessions in East Texas. Using the profits from lumber, he began buying real estate and undeveloped land. In 1908, he acquired a 50 percent portion of the *Houston Chronicle* and would eventually own all of it. He was an early investor in the Humble Oil and Gas Company, later to become Exxon, and he became president of the National Bank of Commerce in 1912, later to become Texas Commerce Bank.[14]

Jesse Jones is particularly noted for commercial construction, and he excelled at hotels early on. His early affluence and his love of international travel and culture made him different from many young Texas builders of the day, even the wealthy ones. He traveled extensively, even seeing "the coronation of King Edward VII" in 1901 while with family on a European vacation. He was worldly and had an international vision for Houston that fit his own enjoyments of travel, "opera, theater, symphonies and lectures in the world's major cities; he wanted the same for Houston."[15]

Jesse Jones believed that a great city needed a great hotel, and he would build several of them during his career. His first experience with a hotel was in 1906 when he bought the Bristol Hotel and launched an ambitious plan to upgrade it. He renovated it extensively and built a luxury addition. "He wanted Houston to have a first-rate hotel like those he had enjoyed in New York and Europe."[16] By 1913, Jones was ready to launch another hotel, which he named the Rice Hotel. Its site was already historic and well-known by the time Jesse Jones came along. The site had originally been the location of the first Capitol Building of the Republic of Texas, where "Sam Houston, first President of Texas, received the diplomatic representatives of European nations, as well as envoys of Presidents Andrew Jackson and Martin van Buren, from Washington."[17] However, Houston did not remain the state capital, and when the government left, the building was run as the Capitol Hotel.[18]

William Marsh Rice bought the hotel as an investment, but after he died, the property was transferred to the Rice Institute and the hotel was renamed the Rice Hotel. The Rice Institute's board of trustees was headed by James A. Baker Sr., who made a deal with Jesse Jones to improve the property. Jones demolished the building and replaced it with a seventeen-story hotel that became the showplace of Houston.[19] In this way, Jesse Jones, even before World War I, was able to introduce a substantial level of international elegance and culture to his adopted home city.[20]

By timing the Rice Hotel as he did, Jones was able to have a world-class hotel ready for new business flowing from the Houston Ship Channel, which opened in 1914. Jones made money, but his investments also provided jobs and made money for the City of Houston. Houston and Jesse Jones enjoyed a mutually beneficial relationship for decades. Long "before most of Houston was aware of Jones, he had firmly fixed in his mind that Houston's prospects were better than any other Southern city and by 1908 he was prepared to help it reach that destiny."[21]

Jesse Jones was also responsible for the Lamar Hotel, a sixteen-story hotel built downtown in 1927 primarily because Jones wanted a downtown residence. He and his wife enjoyed foreign travel and filled their penthouse with furnishings from Europe and Asia. While away, it was easier to have a suite cared for by hotel staff than a stand-alone home.[22] The Lamar Hotel was not only convenient for Jones but was a good business move as well. Houston had a rapidly increasing need to accommodate business travelers and even some tourism.

Jesse Jones's construction was not limited to hotels. He also built the Texas Company Building (Texaco) and the Houston Chronicle Building, using some of the profits to purchase his one-half interest in the newspaper. With the city on its way to becoming a deep-water port, and with the burgeoning oil and gas business bringing in new residents and travelers, Jones bet heavily that his new constructions would be used and his investment rewarded.

Through the 1920s, Jones continued his development vision inspired by international sites and themes. In 1926, Jones opened the Metropolitan Theatre designed in classical ancient Egyptian style to showcase silent and later Hollywood talking motion pictures.[23] Next to the Metropolitan, Jones built the Loew's State Theatre in heavy French style.[24] It was during this time that Jones was inducted into Allegro, an elite social club for leading Houstonians who "are unwilling for Houston to be longer criticised for lagging behind the other cities of the State in the matter of large and generous social entertainment."[25]

Jesse Jones was also a successful banker, and Houston benefited from that expertise. Like other cities, Houston was affected by the Depression, and bank failures were an early and devastating consequence. As business loans failed, personal loans likewise began to fail. The failure of some early banks led to withdrawals by panicked depositors, thereby leading to more bank failures in a vicious cycle fueled by fear as much as actual economic decline.

Jesse Jones called a meeting of other bankers and directors at his office on a weekend in the fall of 1931. In an all-night session, Jones cobbled together an agreement for cash infusions to save the two imminently failing banks. Amazingly, no banks failed in Houston, "even in 1932 and 1933, when thousands of banks all over the country failed. Furthermore, there was no Reconstruction Finance Corporation when the Houston situation arose. . . . Houston had taken care of its own troubles, under the leadership of Jones."[26] Former Texas Secretary of State George Strake Jr. occupies the office in the J. P. Morgan Chase Building on Main Street where Jesse Jones once worked, even using Jones's office furniture. Strake tells a story he heard repeatedly from his father who was around at the time and a prominent oilman in Houston. "Jesse Jones had gathered all the big bankers together one weekend right where we are sitting now," says Strake. "One banker was so distraught that he said he'd be better off to jump out the window, which was standing open, than to throw good money after bad, and Jones called his bluff and said 'go on, there's the window.'" Strake said, "Actually there is a balcony-wide ledge just below so the guy would not have fallen far."[27]

At the same time that Jones was meeting financial success in his new hometown, the city was honoring him in public ways. In 1902, less than four years after moving to Houston and the same year he opened South Texas Lumber, Jones was crowned King Nottoc of the Notsuoh (sometimes spelled No-Tsu-Oh) Festival, the highest honor of one of the most prestigious of Houston events. The name came from spelling backward "Cotton" and "Houston" from King Cotton of the Houston Festival.[28]

At this time, with his personal fortune, business reputation, and community prestige established, Jesse Jones began to be involved in national politics. In 1912, the Democratic National Convention in Baltimore chose Woodrow Wilson as the nominee, but only after a protracted fight and a total of forty-six ballots.[29] Playing a major role in the convention was Colonel Edward Mandell House of Texas. Colonel House was an adviser to Woodrow Wilson and was able to deliver the Texas delegation votes and secure sufficient endorsements to eventually swing the nomination to Wilson. Importantly, he "also brought Jones to Wilson's attention."[30]

Edward Mandell House was called Colonel House not because of military service but because the courtesy title was bestowed on him by Texas Governor Steven Hogg, who benefited from House's political skill and advocacy.[31] Hogg was first elected governor of Texas in 1890 and reelected to a second term in 1892. Hogg was always grateful to House and facilitated House's connections in Washington where possible.[32] House's stature with Governor Hogg and the three governors who followed him who also benefited from House's political advice, Charles Culberson, Joseph Sayers, and Samuel Lanham, also made him a respected figure in business and social circles.

Jesse Jones saw in Wilson a president who was willing to use the levers of governmental power to stimulate the economy and to lift people in society. The use of government funds in the Houston Ship Channel was just one example of the public sector leveraging the private sector into greater prosperity for the benefit of society as a whole.[33]

Colonel House continued to advise and counsel President Wilson after he was elected. He recommended his fellow Houstonian Jesse Jones for a senior position—in fact, for a series of positions trying to find something attractive for him. "Treasury Secretary William McAdoo asked Jones to be his undersecretary,[34] and he declined. He was then offered ambassadorships to Argentina and Belgium, but declined both. Finally Wilson, through Colonel House, asked Jones to become Secretary of Commerce, giving him until February 1913 to decide, but he turned the job down." Jones remained focused on his business and civic interests—the "Houston Ship Channel was almost finished and Mayor Campbell appointed Jones as the Houston Harbor Board's first chairman."[35]

Principally because of the lobbying efforts of Colonel House, the name Jesse Jones was kept before President Wilson. Wilson also heard good reports on Jones from Stockton Axson, a professor who was President Wilson's brother-in-law from his first wife, Ellen Axson Wilson. The two were close until Wilson's death, including the years after Ellen Wilson's death

Colonel Ed House of Texas with President Wilson, Secretary of State Lansing, and other members of the American delegation in Paris following the armistice with Germany in 1918. From *Illinois in the World War: An Illustrated Record Prepared with the Coöperation and Under the Direction of the Leaders in the State's Military and Civilian Organizations* (Chicago: States Publication Society, 1920), 44.

and the president's remarriage to Edith Bolling Galt.[36] Stockton Axson moved to Houston in 1914 to become chair of the English Department at Rice University and became, at the same time, very involved in the Houston community. Colonel House was one of the most prominent members of Houston society at the time, and the two men shared a mutual connection and admiration for President Wilson. Additionally, they both shared an admiration for Jesse Jones, and it was only natural that the two should become informal lobbyists for the promotion of Jones onto the national stage. Although Jones had declined several prominent posts in the first term, President Wilson's second term and the US entry into World War I created a different kind of opportunity.

President Wilson appointed Henry P. Davison of J. P. Morgan and Co. to chair the American Red Cross. Davison reached out to Jesse Jones to assist with a fundraising campaign. After Jones far exceeded his assigned amount, he received a telegram from President Wilson asking him to come to Washington and serve full-time in the Red Cross. Finally, this was a request for national service that Jones did not try to avoid.

Jones's outstanding performance and President Wilson's political suspicions of most of the Republican leadership of the Red Cross meant that "Jones' ability to get the ear of Wilson was very valuable to Davison and the Red Cross War Council."[37] It was this remarkable connection between Jesse Jones and Woodrow Wilson that enabled the Red Cross to have such an international impact. The Red Cross planned a parade up Fifth Avenue in New York to bring attention to its immense fundraising efforts. President Wilson refused to attend the event because he considered many of the Red Cross leaders to be political enemies. Jones, however, convinced Wilson not only to attend the parade but to walk next to Jones in the lead.[38] At Jones's urging, Wilson spoke publicly on the Red Cross with the famous line, "If you give until it hurts, then your heart blood goes into it." The Red Cross then adopted "Give till it hurts" as a slogan and went on to exceed the $100 million fundraising goal.[39]

Jesse Jones returned to Houston in 1919 after two years in Washington and traveling the world to serve Red Cross and country. "Jesse Jones came back to Houston a cosmopolite," reported the *Houston Post* in an editorial in 1919.[40] Looking back at Jones's life to that date, he really was already rather cosmopolitan, well traveled, politically well connected, and socially prominent. Jones was active in many clubs and organizations for the elite of Houston and beyond. He was a member of Glenwood Country Club, the Houston Club, the Fort Worth Club, River Oaks Country Club, and the Manhattan Club and Lotos Club of New York, and many others.[41] Jones was also a participant in the Bohemian Grove.[42]

The Houston that Jesse Jones returned to after his service for President Wilson and the Red Cross was a prosperous city in many ways. However, it was not politically influential because it suffered from being a Southern city in the post–Civil War era. No major party conventions were held in Texas, or anywhere in the South, from after the Civil War into the 1920s. For over sixty years, or about three generations of voters, the Republican and Democratic conventions were held in the North, the West, or the Midwest. The South was avoided like a political plague.[43] It was Jesse Jones of Houston who brought the South's long political convention exile to an end.

The path to the 1928 Democratic National Convention in Houston began in 1924 in New York. Jones and his fellow Texan John Nance Garner "were delegates from Texas to the Democratic National Convention which met in Madison Square Garden in New York City on June 24, 1924."[44] Texas supported former Treasury Secretary William Gibbs McAdoo, whose chief rival was New York Governor Alfred E. Smith. Eventually, after almost two weeks of balloting, the convention chose former Congressman and Ambassador John W. Davis of West Virginia. Davis asked Jones to serve his presidential campaign as finance chairman, although it was a difficult year to raise funds. However, this proved to be a chance for Jones to get to know Franklin D. Roosevelt better, who worked with him in the campaign office. On election night, Roosevelt said to Jones and others in the room, "I believe the party is defeated, [but] there are men in this room tonight who will live to see the Democratic party in power again."[45] Importantly for Jones and for Houston, the work of the 1924 Democratic National Convention and presidential campaign laid the groundwork, established the national connections, and created the experience needed for a renewed effort in 1928.[46]

Although the Democrats were not successful and President Coolidge was reelected, Jesse Jones definitely made a name for himself at the 1924 Democratic National Convention. By 1928, he wanted to bring the convention to his hometown. The Democratic National Committee met in Washington on January 12, 1928, for the purpose of hearing presentations from interested cities. Jones was present in his continuing capacity as finance director and hosted the relatively small group "in the parlor of his suite at the Mayflower Hotel." The cities of Cleveland, Detroit, Chicago, and San Francisco had already submitted offers, including cash payments to the party to offset expenses to the Democratic National Committee.[47]

Jones first sat and listened to the presentations by the other cities before pitching Houston as host city. As a particular inducement, he offered his personal check for $200,000 to offset expenses and promised that Houston would build a new convention center to accommodate twenty-five thousand people. Jones sought to overcome Houston's political isolation as a city in the South. Additionally, he realized the economic benefit of bringing so many people to Houston and familiarizing them and the national media with Houston's role as an international trade and energy center. As a newspaper owner, Jones understood the value of publicity and would have also known the increased power of radio in the 1920s to reach millions of Americans. Jones the businessman knew the investment would pay off.[48]

Houston was obviously taken by surprise at the news that it had been selected as the host city of the 1928 Democratic National Convention, and the mayor telephoned Jones in New York to inquire what the city's obligations would be.[49] However, it appears it was only surprise and not irritation because Houston, and indeed all of Texas, was excited with this new honor. Leading Houstonians joined in to help make the convention a success and, in the process, make Houston look good. Will Hogg sent a lengthy telegram to Jesse Jones on January 16 while he was still at the Waldorf-Astoria Hotel in New York with suggestions for the new convention hall.[50] Two days after he telegraphed Jones, Hogg sent a letter to Ross Sterling proposing a finance committee to raise funds for the host committee and to make the convention arrangements in Houston. Hogg proposed sponsorship units sold to raise a total of $500,000 to be borne by himself, Jesse Jones, Ross Sterling, Kirby Interests, James A. Baker, T. P. Lee, Farish-Humble, Joseph Cullinan, Hughes Tool Co., and Sakowitz Brothers, with smaller units to be purchased by others, including James A. Elkins and William P. Hobby. Hogg copied Jesse Jones on this letter as well as Mayor Oscar Holcombe.[51] Ultimately, the Executive Committee of the 1928 Host Committee was chaired by Mayor Holcombe but included Will Hogg, Jesse Jones, William Hobby, and Ross Sterling.[52] The tickets to the 1928 Democratic National Convention proudly showed the new Coliseum building on the one side and, on the reverse, images of past Democrat Presidents Jefferson, Jackson, Cleveland, and Wilson.[53]

The convention met in Houston in the newly completed building and ultimately chose former New York Governor Alfred E. Smith, who sent an envoy to ask if Jones would be willing to serve as the vice presidential nominee, thus putting a Northerner and Southerner on the ticket.[54] However, Jones declined.[55] Franklin Roosevelt made the nomination of Governor Smith at the Houston convention, but that year nothing could overcome the widespread popularity of incumbent President Coolidge and the man nominated to succeed him, Herbert Hoover.[56]

Although the 1928 convention in Houston was not politically successful, it was a success for the city and its leaders just as Jesse Jones had planned it to be. Attendees praised Houston's efforts and the city's friendliness and hospitality. H. B. Duval of the *St. Louis Globe-Democrat* wrote to Will Hogg to congratulate him on a successful convention and to thank him for "the liquids which were dispensed under your patronage," especially "stein after stein of foaming suds."[57] William Hogg's hospitality is the more amazing since Prohibition was in effect at this time.[58]

J. Fred Essary, president of the National Press Club, pronounced the convention hall in Houston as "amazing" and noted that it was completed in just a few months after the groundbreaking, which he had personally attended. Essary said that "the hall is superior to Madison Square Garden."[59] Franklin Roosevelt himself would remember the convention years later, remarking to Jesse Jones in a 1934 letter that "the visit to Houston in 1928 was in every way a pleasant one."[60] The 1920s was not a time of national political success for Jesse Jones, but it did enable him to form a friendship with Franklin Roosevelt, who invited Jones to attend his January 1929 inauguration as governor of New York. Jones was unable to attend, but he did send the Roosevelts a box of Texas grapefruit for Christmas.[61]

The Depression of the 1930s presented a new opportunity for Jesse Jones to use his business experience and political skills to the benefit of Houston. The city certainly had troubles during the Depression in terms of employment, public funding, and tax collection. But "the traditional view that the Depression struck Houston a soft blow in comparison to other cities in the nation seems correct."[62] The flow of federal money was crucial to Houston as the Depression wore on, and in that regard the city was in good hands with local son Jesse Jones heading the Reconstruction Finance Corporation (RFC) and later the Federal Loan Department. Ultimately Jones became US secretary of commerce, and throughout this time, he was very accessible to Houston's business and political leaders for funding and regulatory issues.[63]

Jones was actually appointed to the RFC by Republican President Herbert Hoover,[64] but he continued in the role under Democrat Franklin Roosevelt, elected in 1932.[65] Jones's oversight responsibilities at the RFC included many subsidiary agencies, such as the Export-Import Bank. Through this agency, Jones made many foreign loans and sought to stabilize global economic conditions while drawing on his knowledge of international trade, having seen the importance of the Port of Houston to his city's development. For example, one loan was to the Franco government of Spain after the end of the Spanish Civil War, enabling Spain to purchase American cotton. Jones also loaned money to the Chiang Kai-shek government in China, who serviced the note through tin and tung oil. Jones loaned money for electrical projects in Brazil, Chile, and Colombia and for roads and railroads in Chile, Brazil, and Paraguay.[66] Jones's performance was excellent, and President Roosevelt not only retained him at the RFC but elevated him to chairman.[67]

Jones often traveled to meet with foreign officials and assess prospects for himself, such as a fact-finding mission to France in 1938 coordinated in part by Ambassador William Bullitt.[68] Jones continued his international lending and was crucial to President Roosevelt's ambition to "create a two-billion-dollar cartel for trading with Central and South America."[69]

President Roosevelt was very pleased with Jesse Jones's performance at the RFC and penned a poem to him in the late 1930s, which begins, "Shiver me timbers, over the stones, I too have a tale 'bout Jesse Jones," and goes on

Jesse Jones and Franklin Roosevelt enjoyed a close political and personal relationship for many years before it soured in early 1945. Jones later moved in Republican circles. Jess Gibson/© Houston Chronicle. Used with permission.

to recount how Jones somewhat cautiously hands out money to keep the nation rising above the Depression.[70]

In 1939, Roosevelt appointed Jones to the post of federal loan administrator to further use his considerable banking and business skills on a national level, while also continuing his RFC duties.[71] The president was careful to caution Jones that he needed to accomplish the spending objectives while keeping the agency within the overhead guidelines set by Congress, no easy task for Jones with essentially two masters of spend and save.[72] The Federal Loan Agency had jurisdiction over foreign loans as well, and Jones used that new authority to make loans good for American business and national security. In March 1940, he recommended the president approve loans to Denmark, Sweden, and Finland to enable them to buy exports of US farm products. He further recommended financing the sale of US cotton to French mills, all actions incidentally helpful to Texas and sought by a fresh young congressman, Lyndon Johnson.[73] President Roosevelt followed Jones's advice on foreign loans, even suggesting some additional ones. When approving the loans to the Nordic nations, Roosevelt sent back a handwritten note asking Jones about making a loan to China at the same time.[74]

During the 1940 Democratic National Convention Jones himself was widely supported as the vice presidential nominee. In fact, the President's son, Elliott Roosevelt, openly supported Jones and wanted to second the nomination.[75] However, after Wallace was chosen as the vice presidential nominee and the Roosevelt–Wallace ticket was elected in 1940, the president offered the cabinet post of secretary of commerce to Jones. Jesse Jones accepted with the stipulation that he would also continue as chair of the RFC. This required special enabling legislation from Congress, which granted it in Jones's name only so no one else would ever be able to hold the joint roles.[76]

As both chair of the RFC and secretary of commerce, Jones was able to utilize his international contacts built while in Houston as well as draw on the skills of other Houstonians in meeting the huge, and often desperate, material and production requirements of the war effort. Jones created the Metals Reserve Company and the Rubber Reserve Company to accumulate stockpiles of raw materials.[77] Jones, while at the RFC and later at the Commerce Department, carefully inventoried what critical war raw materials were available, where more could be obtained, whether synthetic rubber was reliable, and how to gather, produce, and stockpile products like copper, tungsten, mercury, industrial diamonds, nickel, beryl, and chrome ore. Jones regularly updated the president on his efforts.[78]

Jesse Jones was frequently invited to Washington parties at the elegant embassies operated by the many foreign powers represented in the United States. Invitations to dinners and balls came in from Brazil, Cuba, the United Kingdom, the USSR, Denmark, Greece, Germany, the Netherlands, China, and others. Interestingly, Jones declined a party at the Japanese embassy in the spring of 1939 to celebrate the emperor's birthday.[79]

Nazi Germany's sweep through Europe had included the capture of the world's largest tin smelter in the Netherlands. This created an urgent crisis for Jesse Jones, since the United States was the largest customer for tin even before the war. Jones worked out an arrangement with a British-Dutch-controlled tin company to build and operate a new tin smelter. He determined this was best located in the Houston area to allow for import of ore by ship, availability of manpower and energy, and the easy transport of product. The company was organized by Billiton and set up in Texas City, part of the Houston metropolitan area on the southwestern shoreline of Galveston Bay.[80] Jones also established a new petrochemical plant at Texas City and contracted with Monsanto Corporation to run it. This important industrial complex continued a vast expansion after the war ended.

As secretary of commerce, Jesse Jones met with foreign leaders and proposed loans and subsidies to President Roosevelt. In August 1943, Jones sent a memo to the president discussing the postwar needs of the Netherlands and reporting on his meeting with Finance Minister van den Broek. Jones proposed a loan of $300 million using Dutch gold deposited in the United States as collateral. Jones reminded Roosevelt that the Dutch needed to rebuild not only their homeland but also their Pacific territorial possessions (mainly Indonesia, rich in resources) and help to the Netherlands now would allow them to help others as well.[81]

Jesse Jones, as a senior American official, was also in an excellent position to be an advocate for Houston in the administration. One important example was the issue of flooding, which sometimes occurred in the heavy downpours of semitropical Houston, causing widespread damage and even disrupting the operations of the Port of Houston and the ship channel with swells of water and submerged docks and berths. Jones was instrumental in first coordinating political support among County Judge Roy Hofheinz, US Senators Tom Connally and Morris Sheppard, and Congressman Albert Thomas of Houston. He then lobbied for voter approval of $3 million to help pay for a main dam, two smaller dams, and a drainage canal. Despite all this work, the request to the federal government for matching funds was rejected on advice of Secretary of War Henry Stimson, who opined that it was not critical to the war effort because ships could reach Texas through another port on a temporary basis in the event of flooding. Jesse Jones personally intervened with President Roosevelt, pointing out the irrelevance of whether ships could enter another port in Texas—everything that was important to the war effort, the refineries and chemical plants, were in Houston. His logic and persuasion carried the day, and Houston got its funding.[82]

Had the president been dissuaded from nominating Henry Wallace as vice president by either the Democratic convention or his own family, the Jones nomination might have carried forward. Jones had long enjoyed strong support within the party structure but, in addition, had broad bipartisan and business support that would have proved useful in a general election. With Roosevelt's unexpected death in 1945, it could have been Jones becoming president instead of Truman, who had replaced the unpopular and controversial Wallace as Roosevelt's running mate in the next election. Roosevelt was reelected to a fourth term in 1944. On November 29, he wrote to Jesse Jones in his capacity as publisher of the *Houston Chronicle* to thank him for the newspaper's editorial support as well as its news coverage of the campaign. He ended the letter by saying, "Let us keep up the good work together."[83]

As it turned out, Jones was ousted as secretary of commerce in January 1945 by President Roosevelt only so he could make room for Henry Wallace. On January 20, President Roosevelt wrote to Jesse Jones, recounting their long friendship and Jones's "splendid service" with "many difficult tasks." However, he goes on to say that Henry Wallace has also been loyal and deserves to have a suitable place in the administration since his post as vice president was about to expire. Since Wallace had asked for the secretary of commerce position, Roosevelt wanted to give it to him and would instead give Jones an ambassadorship or any other post he would like to have.[84] Jones replied the same day, refusing any other post and states plainly that the decision to give his office to Wallace is a mistake.[85] Roosevelt invited Jones to the White House the next day to discuss the situation further, but Jones was unmoved by any entreaty. Jones refused the ambassadorships to either Italy or France, saying he thought it was a mistake for the United States to spend so much to rebuild those nations. He further refused to chair the Federal Reserve Board. Jones stayed on only until Wallace was confirmed by the Senate as the new secretary on March 1, 1945.[86]

Jones was obviously embittered by his treatment at the hands of Roosevelt and may have felt that Harry Truman wound up in the job he could have had for himself.[87] Not only had Jones served Roosevelt so ably in a public capacity, but he once came to the rescue of his son Elliott by arranging to bail him out of financial trouble with his chain of Texas radio stations.[88] Once back in Houston, Jones and his wife withdrew from the Roosevelts and instead developed a very good friendship with Dwight and Mamie Eisenhower, hosting them in Houston and exchanging notes and social invitations for years until Jones's death in 1956.[89]

Jones spent his remaining years tending the Houston Endowment, a foundation he and his wife established in 1937 as a gift to Houston. The Joneses not only made substantial gifts to the fund during their lives, but their wills directed the bulk of their fortune to the fund as well. The Houston Endowment is one of the largest private charity funds in the United States and has disbursed the staggering sum of almost $1 billion in grants over the years.[90]

The Jesse Jones Center for the Performing Arts, commonly called Jones Hall, is a grand memorial to its namesake. The music center opened in 1966 and is the permanent home of the Houston Symphony Orchestra. In a black-tie gala opening, the hall was named for Jesse Jones, referred to in promotional literature then as "Mr. Houston," and his legacy was lauded by Houstonians.[91]

Jesse Jones's impact on Houston was felt throughout his life and continues today. The Houston Endowment, which he was too modest to name the Jones Foundation, is a constant reminder. But the impact is more for his vision of Houston as a great city, a city deserving of its place in the world. Jones successfully sought to bring fine hotels, arts, health care, parks, libraries, and education to his community. To further this, Jones sought to build businesses, harness the port and ship channel, construct offices, bring important people and events to Houston, and travel the nation and world talking about Houston.

William Clayton

In a similar fashion to Jesse Jones, William Clayton achieved great business success in Houston before going to Washington with the Roosevelt administration. He rose in the ranks to be called, in the words of Dean Acheson, "the architect of the Marshall Plan."[92] Clayton, with family members, was a founder and president of Anderson, Clayton and Co., a Houston cotton business. His career exposed him to the international market and gave him broad contacts and experience in global trade and finance. During his tenure with Anderson, Clayton, the company opened offices in numerous European cities as well as China and Japan, becoming the largest cotton merchant in the world.[93] Although Clayton lived in and ran his business from Houston, he traveled frequently overseas, seeking to maintain and expand the company's global economic empire. Clayton liked to remind people that cotton, so identified with Texas and the South, was not even native to the Americas, noting that "some of Alexander the Great's generals got to India [and brought back] samples of cotton," which soon became a necessity in the West. Clayton realized the importance of good public relations with local populations when operating abroad, even when that meant donating goods or services unrelated to the primary business just to help the local standard of living and create a positive atmosphere.[94] He would apply these principles later at the State Department in the formulation of US foreign policy.

Clayton became assistant secretary of commerce and deputy federal loan administrator under Jesse Jones and "was quickly put in charge of the overseas procurement activities on Defense Supplies, Rubber Development Corporation, Metals Reserve Company, and eventually the United States Commercial Company."[95] Clayton had known Jones for many years in Houston, and Anderson, Clayton had availed itself of Jones's power at the RFC to increase its foreign business to new markets, including the Soviet Union.[96]

At the Commerce Department, Clayton's principal duties were to facilitate the "importation of strategic and critical materials for the war."[97] Clayton bought practically anything that could be produced in Latin America and then be transported to the United States for immediate use or to stockpile in the event of war.[98] In 1942, Clayton sent a note to Harry Hopkins in the White House suggesting Averill Harriman for a job with the agency since Harriman's role in Lend-Lease was, in Clayton's view, "considerably diminished."[99] However, Harriman was instead named ambassador to the Soviet Union in 1943.

Although Clayton performed well at the Commerce Department, by the end of 1944 the importance of that role was declining as people looked ahead to the work to be done by the State Department in the postwar era. In November 1944, Roosevelt sent a telegram practically begging Clayton to become assistant secretary of state for economic affairs and enlisting Edward Stettinius, who was about to become secretary of state, to help persuade him.[100] Clayton accepted the next day.[101]

Clayton would later work for Secretary of War Henry L. Stimson and Vice President Henry Wallace before finally becoming an adviser to President Truman and served as Truman's chief economic adviser at the Potsdam Conference in 1945. Clayton was appointed the first undersecretary of state for economic affairs and was a major figure in the development of the Marshall Plan. Clayton represented the United States in numerous postwar international negotiations, especially opposite Lord Keynes as the United States and United Kingdom settled into the Bretton Woods system of international finance and trade.[102] Clayton consulted with Treasury Secretary Henry Morgenthau on the Bretton Woods conference but declined to go with him because of his other priorities at the State Department.[103] After the Potsdam Conference in Germany, Truman asked Clayton to go on to London rather than return with him to Washington. The British needed a loan as the war wrapped up, and Truman wanted Clayton to meet with Lord Keynes and other officials and develop a plan. Clayton did so and arranged for a British delegation to arrive in Washington in September.[104]

In April 1945, even before the war in Europe was quite over, Clayton prepared a paper on Saudi Arabia and predicted that the kingdom would soon have budget deficit problems once wartime Lend-Lease assistance ended. He suggested a loan to Saudi Arabia to be secured by future oil royalties to replace Lend-Lease funding and to fill the gap he believed would exist as the

United Kingdom contracted its global responsibilities to focus on Asia and Europe. Clayton believed that such a measure would preserve Saudi oil for American national security interests both directly and by reducing European demand for American oil.[105] Clayton was also advocating a position very advantageous to Houston oil companies, although he does not state that in his recommendation.

Clayton led State Department economic decisions regarding the occupation of Germany, especially the potentially lucrative Rhineland and Westphalia regions.[106] Clayton also advocated trade and financial assistance to China, then falling back into a communist versus nationalist civil war circumstance.[107]

William Clayton played a prominent role in the General Agreement on Trade and Tariffs, and Truman dispatched him to London and then to Geneva for the international negotiations. Clayton reported regularly to the State Department and the White House through the establishment conference held in Havana in 1947.[108] Even after Clayton resigned as undersecretary of state, he continued for another year as a special assistant to Secretary George C. Marshall. Clayton was asked to remain in Washington as president of the World Bank, but he declined partly from his own age and exhaustion from years of service but also because of his wife's declining health.[109]

The only time Clayton's business ties in Houston caused a political problem for him in Washington was with regard to his own cotton interests. Clayton had to defend himself before the Senate Committee on Foreign Relations before his confirmation when questioned about Anderson, Clayton's dealings with Germany and Japan. Clayton testified that business with Germany stopped in 1939 and with Japan well before Pearl Harbor.[110] For the rest of his life, Clayton remained a firm advocate of free trade as a way to foster better international relations.

Ima Hogg

While men like Jones and Clayton brought Houston international recognition in business and politics, there were other leaders who sought to bring world-class arts and culture to the city. Ima Hogg, daughter of a Texas governor; heiress to an oil fortune; benefactor of the arts, music, and education; and the leading grande dame of Houston for decades is the leading star of Houston's reinvention of itself as a center of international culture.

Ima Hogg was born in 1882 in Mineola, a small town in East Texas.[111] She was a young child when her father became attorney general, so she began school in Austin.[112] In 1890, Jim Hogg was elected governor and was the first governor of Texas who had actually been born in the state.[113] Ima attended the inaugural ceremony and ball in January 1891 at the age of eight. She later described it as a "great event" and said that "prominent society people and political leaders from all over the state attended."[114]

It was during these years in the Governor's Mansion that Ima appears to have developed the interests that would be so identified with her in later life. First of all, she thought the Governor's Mansion was in "dreadful disrepair" and "shabby," and her parents believed that it had to be redone before the family could even live there. Ima took a keen interest in the projects of repainting, cleaning, acquiring new draperies and furniture, refinishing, and making the mansion look grand again. She also took up gardening and wrote admiringly of the flower gardens, vegetables, fruit trees, and croquet lawn.[115]

For part of her childhood in the Governor's Mansion, the family engaged a German woman who taught the language to Ima. She used her German-language skills later as a music student in Vienna and Berlin and on her many trips to Europe over her lifetime. Ima took an interest in clothing and was particularly taken with the ball gowns created by an Alsatian seamstress in Austin. She enjoyed the visitors her father received and was especially appreciative of the Chinese minister who called on her father, completely charmed young Ima, and then sent her a gift box with Chinese dolls and wooden eggs that came apart as puzzles. Most of all, Ima grew to love music, including the traveling operas and other musical shows that came through Austin. Importantly, she also began receiving piano lessons from Edmund Ludwig of Russia who had settled with relatives in Austin. Ima would carry these language and music skills to Europe, using them in collecting antiques, art, and friends and bringing it all back to Houston.[116]

Ima began to travel with her father when he went on business trips or semiofficial trips as a former governor still well connected with Texas and US government leaders. She enjoyed New York, finding some of it grand, such as her Fifth Avenue hotel and the luxury steakhouse Delmonico's. However, she compared other parts of New York to Austin and found them lacking: "Broadway was not as wide as Congress Avenue," and "Macy's was not as stylish as Hatzfeld's."[117] She also traveled with her father in 1898, at age sixteen, to Hawaii for the ceremony of raising the American flag over the Hawaiian Islands as a US territory. She met the deposed Queen Liliuokalani at the event.[118] On the way, they stopped in Los Angeles to visit some of her father's business contacts. Already focused on decoration and design, she notes their Palace Hotel is "one of the finest and prettiest buildings I ever saw" and admired the Spanish-style architecture and Moorish reception

Ima Hogg was a beautiful, refined, and wealthy young woman of the world. Her years studying music in Vienna and Berlin instilled in her a notion of how Houston's culture should look and feel. Courtesy of the Museum of Fine Arts, Houston.

room, which she compared favorably with the Moorish Room of the Waldorf Hotel in New York.[119]

Ima went to Europe in 1907 with her brother Will. After several months, Ima's brother returned to Houston, but Ima was so smitten with European culture that she chose to remain there, studying first under a pianist of the Austrian Imperial Court at Vienna and then later in Berlin with another prominent musician. Decades later, Ima would recall to Houston friends that "Kaiser Wilhelm used to ride his horse through the park."[120] Ima kept an occasional journal during her stay in Berlin and noted her music lessons and favorite pieces. She attended the Bayreuth Festival, the high holy of German opera, for the first time in 1907, writing in her diary her assessments of different performers in terms of music, acting, and dance.[121] Her German instructor wanted to present Ima at a Berlin performance; Ima declined for reasons unknown.

In 1909, Ima returned to Houston after two years abroad, with a notion of how culture should look and feel in a city and with a determination to remake the cultural scene in Houston to reflect what she had experienced in Vienna and Berlin. In Europe, as in New York earlier, she lamented that "Houston had no orchestra, no schools of music, no museums, and no art galleries. . . . Instead of accepting this situation, however, Miss Ima turned it into an opportunity."[122]

In 1913, Ima Hogg organized the first performance of a symphony in Houston, gathering the best orchestral musicians she could find in in the city. Satisfied with the results, she formed the Houston Symphony the following year and served as its president for most of the rest of her life. She knew music, and she knew how it was presented in the great cities of the world. She worked diligently over the decades to design programs, raise funds, attract musicians, and build the Houston Symphony into a world-class symphony orchestra. She served in various offices over the years, sometimes taking the lead role for herself and sometimes seeking out someone else to be the front of the organization for a while. She struggled through the years of World War I when German music became controversial, and indeed the symphony suspended performances for some time.[123] The creation and growth of the Houston Symphony seem improbable for its early years. But for the work and vision of Ima Hogg and culturally aware Houstonians at the time, it might never have happened. But one observer of Houston culture remarked that "the city itself is an unlikely occurrence and does the improbable naturally."[124]

By 1930, Houston determined that its global economic prominence made it worthy "for recognition as one of the nation's elite cultural centers." Houston secured a spot as the only Southern city to be on the tour of the German Grand Opera's visit to America. *Der Ring des Nibelungen* was presented with Ima Hogg providing organizing and underwriting support.[125] She was a devotee of Wagner and especially loved the Ring Cycle at Bayreuth.[126]

Although Ima focused on the Houston Symphony, she loved opera as well. She attended the Chicago World's Fair in 1933, and while there, she clipped a newspaper article speaking admiringly of the Houston Civic Opera in town to perform *Aida* as a climax to Texas Day at the Century of Progress Show. The newspaper headline says "Cowboy State to Show the World It's Opera Minded at Fair in Chicago," and the article goes on to state that the "Lone Star State intends to show the world it can produce grand opera on the grandest scale ever attempted."[127]

Ima Hogg was always heavily involved, if not controlling, in the selection of conductors for the Houston Symphony.[128] In 1931, she arranged for Italian opera specialist Uriel Nespoli to take over as conductor. Nespoli had been a colleague of Giacomo Puccini and was the third conductor in the world to conduct the famed opera *La Bohème.*[129] He was replaced by Frank St. Leger, who had studied at the Royal Academy of Music in London and went on to prestigious positions in the classical music world, including the American Opera Company and the Royal Opera at Covent Garden. In 1936, Ima led the symphony to choose Ernst Hoffmann, a graduate of Harvard. He had further studied and performed in Berlin before becoming conductor of the Breslau Opera for years until, in 1934, he was found to be unacceptable by the new regime of Hitler.

The Houston Symphony began its annual gala fundraising in 1939 with a "Viennese ball at the Houston Country Club."[130] During the war years, Ima Hogg reached out to leaders such as Hugh Roy Cullen to assist with fundraising and provide financial security for the symphony. Cullen did so and contributed very generously for many years from his own wealth made in Houston's oil and gas industry.

After World War II, Ima Hogg surveyed the continued rapid growth of Houston's population and economy and determined that the timing was right for her to push forward with her dream of making Houston a truly international center for music.[131] Ima took on the role of president and then recruited Gus Wortham as chairman of the board to further ensure financial stability.[132] Efrem Kurtz emerged as the next choice for permanent conductor. Kurtz was born in tsarist Russia and studied and performed there and throughout Europe. For several years he conducted music to accompany the ballet star Anna Pavlova. He served as conductor of the Ballet Russe de Monte Carlo before coming to Houston.[133] The announcement was as pleasing to the city of Houston as it was to the symphony board. Kurtz and his elegant German wife, Katherine, were both regarded as a "darling of the new society known as the International Set,[134] which had sprung up since the end of the war." They were widely known in the upper echelons of society in New York and Europe and regularly appeared on the party circuit and in society columns.[135] This was very pleasing to Ima Hogg and other leading

Ima Hogg was the undisputed force behind the Houston Symphony, making it into one of the great symphonies of the world. She brought the best talent to Houston and pushed the city into the forefront of performing arts excellence. Courtesy of the Museum of Fine Arts, Houston.

Houstonians because it legitimized Houston's place in the world by showing that someone as internationally sophisticated as Efrem Kurtz would want to be in Houston and that Houston was a city that attracted such individuals and their talents. The Kurtzes ensconced themselves in a suite at the newly opened, luxurious, and internationally acclaimed Shamrock Hotel. In 1951, even the *Dallas Morning News* conceded that Houston had moved ahead of the Dallas Symphony in performance and visibility.[136]

When Ima Hogg finally retired from the Houston Symphony board, letters of praise for her and regret for her leaving poured in. The British conductor Sir Thomas Beecham wrote that she had performed a great service for Houston over a long period of time.[137] Leopold Stokowski wrote that "we all owe you an immense debt of gratitude for the great things you have done for the Houston Orchestra, and for your vision of its growth and future."[138] Van Cliburn was her houseguest during this time and wrote a thank-you letter describing her "dynamic personality" as the "single force" behind the Houston Symphony.[139]

Ima would return to the board of the Houston Symphony again after a few years and remained in some capacity the rest of her life. She was particularly engaged with Maurice Hirsch during the long term that he served as president of the Houston Symphony from 1956 to 1970. Hirsch was native to Houston and had a law degree from Harvard. He served in World War II, attaining the rank of brigadier general. He very much wanted Houston to be broadly integrated in the world and was the founder of the Japan American Society in Houston.[140] Maurice Hirsch and Ima Hogg bonded over their mutual commitment to music and promoting Houston abroad. From cities and ports around the world, Hirsch kept up a steady stream of courtly correspondence with Ima Hogg, usually signing his notes with "much, much love" and praising her constant and lifelong patronage of the symphony. Ima did likewise and kept him updated on her continuing efforts for their favorite arts organization. In May 1964, Ima wrote to Hirsch from Washington, DC, telling him about the Houston Symphony's performance there and sitting in the presidential box with Lyndon and Lady Bird Johnson.[141]

With music, Ima sought to bring the very best Europe had to offer and showcase it in Texas. But her passion for art and antiques went the other way, and she sought instead to promote Texas and American antiques to the world. In a visit to Philadelphia in 1923, Ima was enchanted by a shop dealing in Early American glass and ceramics. Her interest was boosted by her brother Will, who was himself already a prodigious buyer of antiques and art. He supplied her with antique reference books, and soon it was Ima who said to her brother, "We have a rare opportunity—to collect American antiques for a museum in Texas. It's never been done before."[142]

The Hogg family's plunge into collecting art and antiques, like Ima's passion for rich music, flowed in significant part from a vision they had for the city of Houston. "The Hoggs believed that if Houston were to be a great city, its leaders must collect and display examples of humankind's

Ima Hogg and her brothers built Bayou Bend, the most famous residence of the gilded River Oaks neighborhood developed by Will Hogg. Ima used the mansion to showcase Houston and its stars for decades. Bayou Bend with its world-class collection of art and antiques is now the jewel of the Houston Museum of Art. Photograph by Rick Gardner, courtesy of the Museum of Fine Arts, Houston.

creativity."[143] The collections of American art and antiques that Ima and Will both amassed came to be housed together at their home, Bayou Bend. They built the mansion in Will Hogg's own famous land development, the prestigious River Oaks neighborhood. It was designed to be a haven for the affluent with large homes, high costs, lush landscaping, wide boulevards, homeowner regulations, underground utilities, and for Caucasian residents only.[144] In promotional literature, River Oaks was described as a place where the neighbors are of "good taste and refinement" and "your kind of people." The atmosphere had clean country air away from the city traffic. The promoters further explained that they had visited the top residential enclaves in the United States and Europe in order to come up with the finest development for Houston.[145]

People paid top dollar for the lots and set about building some fifteen hundred of the finest homes found in any neighborhood in the world. The first home built was on Inwood Drive for W. L. Clayton, of Anderson,

Clayton.[146] Other names appearing on the 1926 homeowners association list include Tom Ball, Robert Farish, William Hobby, Thomas House Jr., John Marshall, and the principal architect himself, John Staub.[147]

The Hogg family themselves built the showpiece of River Oaks in Bayou Bend, a twenty-two room pink mansion set in vast, elaborately landscaped gardens. The rooms of the mansion have varying themes along the lines of American furnishings and styles of Americana. The Murphy Room showcases pieces from the earliest period of American colonial history, 1620–1730, with simpler, more practical furniture as well as early crockery and pewter items. In contrast, the Queen Anne Suite is more baroque and reflects the later period of 1730–55 with graceful and intricate wood carvings and a famous and stunning piece of chinoiserie of elaborately ornamented lacquer work. The straw-gold drawing room reflects the Georgian architectural style of railings, carvings, and framing with rococo furnishings popular in the 1755–90 time period. Artworks by Gilbert Stuart and John Singleton Copley give the room a Mount Vernon feel. Other rooms reflect neoclassical, Federal, and rococo revival, while the Folk Art Room is dedicated to painted and often whimsical pieces. Of particular importance to Ima Hogg was the Texas Room furnished with a style of Biedermeier furniture brought by German immigrants to Texas in the 1840s to 1850s. It was popular with leading families of the early republic and state of Texas and came to be identified as Texian. The room also has ceramics made by the Staffordshire china company commemorating the Texas War of Independence in 1835–36 and the Mexican-American War of 1846–48.[148]

Bayou Bend, in the heart of River Oaks, remains a jewel of the Houston Museum of Fine Arts and the anchor of its world-class collections.[149] The estate demonstrates the keen sense of art and design that Ima Hogg developed from her time and studies in New York and Europe, which she later channeled into building a collection in Houston. When Ima noticed and appreciated the beauty of Early American furnishings, she was one of the very few in the United States and apparently the only serious such collector in Texas. Everyone seemed to be focused on Europe and to a lesser extent on Asia. She sought out the best curators and antique experts and made it a discipline to travel, look, and learn. Ima kept her own notes about pieces she was looking for and recorded what she had seen with descriptions and pricing.[150]

When NASA announced Houston as the site of the new Space Center in 1961, she became involved in that endeavor as well, touring the site and hosting "astronauts in her box at the symphony" so they could see a cosmopolitan Houston.[151] Annette La Freniere, in her introduction to Gwendolyn

Cone Neeley's book, *Miss Ima and the Hogg Family,* stated that "much as a parent raises a child, Miss Ima 'raised' Texas up to share her interests and develop its talents. She honored the state of her birth many times over by making it into the place she wanted it to be, and Texans are proud to call Ima Hogg their own."[152] While this statement refers to Texas and Texans as a whole, it seems clear that Ima Hogg's efforts were focused on Houston in particular and that she desired foremost for Houston to be the cultural center of Texas and thereby a city globally recognized as a center for the arts and society.[153]

Oveta Culp Hobby

Oveta Culp Hobby was a different type of leading Houstonian than Ima Hogg. Both were widely recognized women and socially prominent, but Oveta was also more business and politically inclined. She was born in the central Texas town of Killeen in 1905. Her father served in the Texas legislature, and she grew up surrounded by lawyers, politicians, and journalists. She was almost grown by the time women were first able to vote in a presidential election in 1920. She became the parliamentarian of the Texas House of Representatives at the age of twenty-one, and in 1928 she helped organize the Democratic National Convention brought to Houston by Jesse Jones. She remained in Houston to work on some local political races and even ran unsuccessfully for the legislature herself. The following year she married William Hobby, a widower twenty-eight years her senior who had previously served as governor of Texas. William Hobby was the president of the *Houston Post,* which he would later own.

Oveta was very active in community activities, including the Houston Symphony with Ima Hogg. She wrote and edited books and worked with her husband to grow the newspaper while also adding a radio station. She worked on women's issues for the War Department before Pearl Harbor, but afterward she became director of the Women's Army Auxiliary Corps, eventually becoming a colonel and receiving the Distinguished Service Medal.

Her activities in World War II won the admiration of Dwight Eisenhower, who named her director of the Federal Security Agency and included her in many high-level White House meetings, even cabinet meetings. Oveta Hobby was no stranger to Washington and traveled there frequently, if not for political reasons, then for the *Houston Post* covering politics. She represented the newspaper covering the NATO signing agreement in Washington on April 4, 1949.[154] She established a friendship with George C. Marshall, a former army general and US secretary of state, that would last beyond his

By the time she joined President Eisenhower's cabinet in 1953, Oveta Culp Hobby was already a national figure in journalism, business, and politics. Courtesy of Rice University.

tenure in Washington.[155] However, her fellow Houstonian and rival newspaper publisher Jesse Jones may also deserve some credit for her appointments in Washington.

After the election in 1952, Jesse Jones wrote to President-elect Eisenhower, urging him to appoint Oveta Hobby as secretary of either interior or health, education, and welfare. Jones advised Eisenhower that women were an important part of the vote and that Oveta was an especially brilliant and capable executive.[156] Within months, President Eisenhower named her secretary of health, education, and welfare.[157] She was the only female in his cabinet and only the second woman ever to serve at the cabinet level following Franklin Roosevelt's appointment of Frances Perkins as secretary of labor in 1933.

Secretary Hobby was a national sensation and made the cover of *Time* magazine on May 4, 1953.[158] Certainly some of this was due to her being a female in the cabinet but also because she already possessed such a thick résumé of public service independent of her husband. She worked on issues important to ordinary Americans in their daily lives, such as welfare of "the nation's disabled and needy, orphans and old folks," and on such diverse topics as tapeworms, cancer research, and fluoride. Her agency was the largest of any cabinet portfolio save defense and treasury. Lyndon Johnson, as the sponsoring senator for her nomination, walked her around the Capitol to meet people and ensure a quick confirmation hearing.[159] Her admirers included Madame Chiang Kai-shek, who sent her a gift of tea with congratulations on her federal appointment.[160]

Oveta Hobby had to leave the cabinet in 1955 because of her husband's poor health, but she remained close to Eisenhower, who even encouraged her to run for president in 1960. She also had strong ties with Democratic Party officials, including Sargent Shriver Jr., who sought her advice in 1961 on the Peace Corps.[161] She was likely a genuine bipartisan official and one who brought much credit to Houston.

The Age of the Socialite

Ima Hogg brought the world to Houston, and vice versa, through music and the arts. Oveta Culp Hobby showcased business and political skills at the highest levels. But the modern era in Houston later gave rise to a different type of woman, often referred to in popular media as a "socialite." These women promoted Houston, raised charitable and political funds, and garnered attention in a new way to both the city of Houston and themselves. With global, high-level contacts, two women in particular, Joanne Herring and Lynn Wyatt, became closely identified with Houston. At the same time, they were very visible in the world working in social, political, business, and charity circles.

Lynn Sakowitz Wyatt, born in 1935, is the granddaughter of the founder of the Sakowitz department store chain. Her grandfather and his brother were Jewish immigrants from Ukraine who first opened a Sakowitz store in Galveston in 1902. The Sakowitz stores became increasingly more expensive, moving into luxury goods. In 1910, the young brothers made the shrewdest business decision of their lives by borrowing money to buy out a store in what was then the center of downtown Houston. In the years after the catastrophic 1900 hurricane, it had dawned on some Galveston investors that Houston might well turn out to be the coming city, and the Sakowitz brothers were determined to go where the public was going to be. "By 1912, the Houston location had doubled in size and outstripped the ten-year-old parent store." After a hurricane once again struck Galveston in 1915, the brothers closed the Galveston shop, and in 1917 they moved into three floors of the Kiam Building at Main and Preston.[162]

Sakowitz continued to grow until by 1929 the store occupied five floors of the impressive new art deco–styled Gulf Building constructed by Jesse Jones.[163] With the continued growth of the retailing operation, by 1951, Sakowitz opened its own five-story building in downtown Houston in a white marble and classical Greek design. The brothers also opened a boutique in Glenn McCarthy's "splashy new Shamrock Hotel."[164] From there, Sakowitz made a move to the suburbs and in 1959 opened "a large store at the intersection of Westheimer and Post Oak that not only cemented the family's commitment to the suburbs, but also was a prescient move."[165] The Galleria, near the tony areas of River Oaks, Memorial, and Tanglewood, grew to and remains one of the richest and most prestigious shopping and dining areas of Texas.

Lynn Sakowitz did not participate in running the family luxury goods business. She married Oscar Wyatt, a Houston oil executive, in 1963. Although Lynn came from a notable background, Oscar came from a childhood of poverty. Oscar typified the ambitious approach of earlier Houston businessmen. A 1991 *Texas Monthly* cover story pronounced him "mean as a junkyard dog."[166]

"By 1980 the company Wyatt had started from scratch in 1955 was a multinational conglomerate whose $5 billion in annual sales made it the third largest Houston-based company, behind Shell and Tenneco."[167] Lynn acquired a home for them on River Oaks Boulevard, an area not available to Jewish people in an earlier time, and made it one of the most impressive homes in an already posh neighborhood. Using the mansion as a base of operations, Lynn Wyatt threw charitable fundraisers and hosted international political leaders, rock stars, and royalty. Newspapers and magazines reported on guests at the "Wyatt Hyatt," including Princess Grace, Princess Margaret, the Duchess of York, Mick Jagger, Sir Elton John, Queen Noor, and King Hussein and a long list of the beautiful people, including Dominick Dunne and Carolina Herrera.

Lynn Wyatt (seated, center) was dubbed "Socialite of the Century" and made Houston a destination for the international jet set. John Van Beekum/© Houston Chronicle. Used with permission.

"In 1978, the Wyatts made international society page headlines by throwing a gala party for the soon-to-be-wed Princess Caroline of Monaco at Maxim's in Paris." Lynn Wyatt summered at a home she acquired in Cap Ferrat on the French Riviera but was reliably back in Houston by September for the round of parties, galas, and balls that ran from fall until late spring. She was named to the International Best Dressed List and made the news in

New York, Los Angeles, London, and Paris so many times that *Texas Monthly* proclaimed her "Socialite of the Century" in 2000.[168]

Importantly, Lynn Wyatt made Houston a familiar city outside the oil and gas industry, the technology sector, or even the political realm. She made it familiar to the international jet set: the style arbiters and trend setters, the readers *of Vanity Fair, Women's Wear Daily, Tattler*, and *Society*. The predictable result was the global elite's greater fascination with Houston. Lynn Wyatt moved in international circles, but she never pretended to be anything but a Houstonian. Her accent was Texan, and maybe even emphasized at times. Carolina Herrera once quoted Princess Margaret saying that only Lynn Wyatt could make "hello" sound like a six-syllable word.[169]

Lynn Wyatt's brother, Robert Tobias Sakowitz, is a celebrity figure in his own right.[170] His line of work was the fashion and accessories of the family's high-end retailing business. For many years, Robert Sakowitz did as much as or more than his sister to promote the image of Texas, and especially Houston, onto the global stage in a glamorous way. "Robert even dressed the part, packaging himself in cowboy hat and boots for the biannual Paris fashion shows."[171] After graduating from Harvard, Robert gained retail experience at Galeries Lafayette in Paris and then with Macy's in New York. Returning to the family store, Robert kicked off a more international feel for the retailer with Yves Saint Laurent and André Courrèges ready-to-wear lines—no one else in Texas, including Neiman Marcus, had these lines.[172]

After Robert took over management of the store from his father, he rapidly ratcheted up the international glamour factor with buying trips to the fashion shows in Paris and Milan. He launched massive marketing campaigns promoting Sakowitz and its Houston base as futuristic and luxurious. He personally arranged for President Valery Giscard d'Estaing to attend a Sakowitz fashion festival and once "helicoptered dramatically into the Post Oak parking lot in time to play host to a group of British peers." Eventually, Robert bet too big, and the Houston economy, still very energy sensitive, reeled under the recession of the early 1980s. Although Robert and his sister were both international celebrities, they were not on the same trajectory for long. While Sakowitz went into Chapter 11 bankruptcy reorganization, Lynn Wyatt held her widely publicized "Indian-theme birthday party in the south of France with such guests as Henry Ford II, the Begum Aga Khan and Estee Lauder."[173]

The rise of Lynn Sakowitz Wyatt to the heights of both Houston and international society is a reflection of the changing nature of Houston itself. The city has grown to international prominence and gathered a critical nucleus of art museums, parks, universities, performing arts centers, leading

Glenn McCarthy opened the Shamrock Hotel in Houston in 1949 with a huge party attended by business and political leaders and a trainload of Hollywood stars. HPost staff/© Houston Chronicle. Used with permission.

restaurants, and luxury goods stores. The demographics of Houston, reflecting a diverse workforce and class mobility, allowed a woman like Lynn to progress socially even though not married to a man of inherited wealth or aristocratic background. In Houston, there was a modern respect for the self-made man or woman, someone who could achieve great wealth with a bold approach. It was not unlike Glenn McCarthy of an earlier generation with his oil wealth and Shamrock Hotel, except that some of established Houston society at that time avoided McCarthy, believing him to be low class, albeit rich, and even shunned his family for years. By the late twentieth century, those attitudes were gone, and many Houstonians embraced Lynn

Joanne Herring used her beauty, intelligence, and social position to advocate for national and international policy goals. She was portrayed by Julia Roberts in the film *Charlie Wilson's War* (2007). Photo by Ron Galella/Ron Galella Collection/Getty Images.

Wyatt for her beauty and style, and they loved the way she helped make the image of Houston glamorous.[174]

The socialite that best personifies Houston's modern coming of age as an international city is Joanne King Herring. She set high bars in terms of political influence, work capacity, and international visibility. For seven decades she has been famous well beyond the city limits of Houston long before

Hollywood discovered her story. But the movie *Charlie Wilson's War*, with Julia Roberts playing the part of Joanne and Tom Hanks playing the part of her lover and international partner in adventure, Charlie Wilson, made her a general household name and made her story internationally famous.[175]

The year 1979 was a bad ending to what had already been a turbulent decade that included Watergate, the 1973 Arab-Israeli War, the OPEC oil embargo and energy crisis, and a recession. During the Carter presidency, additional events had troubled many Americans, especially Republicans like Joanne. In 1979, militants overran the US embassy in Tehran and took hostages, thus starting a long period of American angst.[176] Many American political conservatives were upset with Carter's decision to return the Panama Canal to Panamanian sovereignty. They were further upset with what they viewed as an overemphasis on human rights issues and insufficient attention to security issues like Soviet military capacity and growing militancy. So in December 1979, when the Soviet Union invaded Afghanistan to impose a Marxist regime friendly to Moscow, the anti-Carter coalitions of conservatives, Republicans, and Southern Democrats began to coalesce into a political force.[177]

Joanne Herring had long identified as a Republican, but Houston, like most of Texas, had been mostly a one-party Democrat-voting city since the end of Reconstruction in 1877. Things began to change somewhat in the 1950s when World War II hero Dwight Eisenhower was elected and then reelected as president. The GOP formed county parties in some of the major urban areas, including Houston. One early participant was George H. W. Bush, who was elected Harris County Republican chair in 1963. As an oilman and half-owner of Zapata Oil Company, Bush sought to reposition from Midland to Houston to take advantage of the city's dominant position as the center of the American oil and gas industry.[178] Bush was the son of a former US senator, Prescott Bush, of Connecticut. Once in Houston, George sought to remake the local politics into the traditional Republican politics he knew in the East. The conservative and moneyed interests of Houston, especially in the tony Rivers Oaks and Tanglewood areas, were responsive to this new political alternative.[179]

Joanne King Herring was born Joanne Johnson in 1929. Her father was a successful businessman in Houston who parlayed his wealth into a genteel lifestyle that included a full-scale replica of Mount Vernon.[180] Joanne claims she was an ugly duckling as a girl but suddenly became popular as a teenager. Joanne's parents initially sent her to kindergarten in River Oaks, where she met a young James Baker III. The two of them would encounter each other many times over the years both in River Oaks social circles and in international gatherings. Joanne later attended college at the University of Texas but was not much interested in pursuing a degree. She was smart and she liked to read books, especially history and biographies, but she was disinclined to academic discipline and the way it infringed on one's social life.[181]

When the Soviets invaded Afghanistan in 1979, Joanne Herring recalls she was frightened but also angry. She was angry at Soviet aggression in spreading the communist system that she hated, but she also believed it was an affront to mainstream, urbane, and educated Muslims in Kabul, the type of worldly Sunnis she had known in Riyadh, Muscat, Amman, and Brunei, as well as ones she knew in Washington, New York, London, and Houston. For Joanne, it was a mockery of the United States, a threat to national security, and a threat to the life she believed was crucial for the proper development of individuals and societies. For Joanne, the Soviets had crossed an inviolable line that had to be reversed, not only for the benefit of the Afghan people but also for the security of Pakistan, South Asia, and the free world in general.

At the time of the Soviet invasion of Afghanistan, Zia ul-Haq was president of Pakistan.[182] Zia first met Joanne in the early 1970s at a dinner party. They kept in touch, and when Joanne and her husband, Robert Herring, traveled to Pakistan in 1980, President Zia hosted a banquet for them in Islamabad.[183] The event cemented the relationship between Joanne and Zia, and they kept in more frequent contact over the coming years. As Joanne later stated, "During our first dinner, something clicked between Zia and me."[184] Robert Herring died of cancer the following year, and Joanne began making trips to Pakistan on her own to confer with Zia and to discuss ways to bolster his diplomatic and military positions against the Soviet Union.[185]

In time, Joanne came to help Texas Congressman Charlie Wilson in very significant ways in support of Afghanistan and against the Soviet Union.[186] But first, it is fair and important to note that Charlie Wilson was keenly anti-Soviet and angry over the Afghanistan invasion even before he joined forces with Joanne Herring.[187] In 1983, Joanne took Congressman Wilson to Islamabad and introduced him to President Zia ul-Haq. She made sure Wilson knew of Zia's commitment to stopping the Soviet advance and of his friendship with the United States. She made sure Zia knew of Wilson's sincerity, his capacity to secure funding for needed military weapons and supplies, and, importantly, of her personal commitment to facilitate the whole arrangement. On this same trip, she took Wilson to an Afghan refugee camp to show him the atrocities of the war. In particular, there were children who had been killed or permanently maimed by Soviet explosive devices disguised to look like toys and dropped from planes. Wilson later claimed that the trip shocked his conscience at Soviet brutality and galvanized his determination to bring about greater funding and efforts to aid Afghanistan to independence.

Over the years, Congressman Wilson was able to secure greater funding and more-sophisticated weaponry to enable the Afghan resistance to inflict increasingly harsh reprisals on the Soviet occupation. Coupled with diplomatic pressure and a general escalation of the arms race with the West, the Soviet Union eventually announced its withdrawal from Afghanistan in 1988. Throughout this geopolitical chess game, Joanne Herring alternately pressed Congressman Wilson, consulted with President Zia, reached out to federal officials,[188] and sought to maintain a forward momentum of aid to the Afghans and Pakistanis to create pressure on the Soviet Union. Joanne Herring threw parties in Houston and Washington, carefully planning the right mix of business, political, and society leaders and then strategically determining the seating arrangements.

The movie *Charlie Wilson's War* shows Joanne's deft engagement of the levers of power to achieve the political result she wanted. Like any movie, it is a product of Hollywood and does not purport to be a documentary, much less a precise historical account.[189] However, an important point of the movie is simply to express Houston's place in the modern, globally interconnected world because of leading citizens like Joanne. The Cold War was the defining scenario of the last half of the twentieth century. That all-encompassing power struggle between the United States and the Soviet Union defined the course of the post–World War II era. At the apex of the struggle, with the Soviet Union finally so overextended that it was vulnerable, a group of Houstonians in positions of federal power and another Houstonian, Joanne Herring, not in an official position but wielding enormous influence, set in motion the downfall of a superpower and the end of the Cold War.[190]

At a River Oaks Country Club reception in 2008 in honor of Joanne Herring, former US Secretary of State James Baker paid homage to her, stating that she had been a great patriot and had been of enormous influence in promoting US foreign policy and helping secure a peaceful end to the Cold War.[191] Houston society had much to be proud of that evening. First they were gathered in the River Oaks Country Club, set on the banks of Buffalo Bayou near the very landing where the Allen brothers had first conceived the idea of a city 172 years earlier. The River Oaks neighborhood where they stood, in the most posh neighborhood of the city, had been organized by William and Michael Hogg, sons of one of Texas' most famous governors, Jim Hogg, and brothers of the legendary Ima Hogg, whose own home, nearby Bayou Bend, was the cornerstone of the affluent community. Second, they were discussing world events in which the United States had been successfully led by a president from Houston, a secretary of state from Houston, and a beautiful Houston socialite who had just been recognized in Hollywood.

The city of Houston had made its influence felt over the years through its wealth built on international trade, oil and gas, and medical and space technology. This reservoir of great and diverse wealth and talent had created the platform from which political power could be projected and sustained and an environment in which society leaders could move with freedom to launch good causes and create good results, both at home and abroad.[192] Some observers have been skeptical, even critical, of according any serious weight to any prominent society leader, whether it is Joanne Herring or anyone else, when it comes to serious business matters or political developments. Even the former Pakistani ambassador to the United States, Husain Haqqani, said Herring was "known more for glamour than for political wisdom" and complained that "she knew little of the country."[193] Of course, Ambassador Haqqani's views are contradicted by other US and Pakistani officials, but they also somewhat miss the mark in terms of influence. Someone like Joanne Herring could succeed in thwarting Soviet policy in South Asia, not because she was an academic or because she had an official position but because she exercised real influence over the people who had such credentials.[194]

Zia ul-Haq pursued Western, especially American, support against Soviet expansion because Joanne Herring convinced him it was crucial and because she would help him obtain the practical help needed. She could deliver on that promise because she was close to Charlie Wilson and other American officials with control of foreign policy, appropriations, defense, and intelligence matters. Even Ambassador Haqqani conceded her capabilities when he said that "Zia showered her with hospitality to use her connections."[195] Obviously, Zia would not have wasted his time if he thought she could not provide help to him and his country.

Yaqub Khan, former foreign minister of Pakistan, was also critical of Herring, noting in his memoirs that "she absolutely had his [Zia ul-Haq's] ear, it was terrible."[196] Factually, he admitted the truth of the matter, which was that Herring had access to and influence over the president of Pakistan. Khan also viewed that circumstance as terrible, perhaps because he belongs to the school of thought that such society people should not have influence over official policy, because she was a devout and outspoken Christian and it offended his Muslim sensibilities, because she was a woman in a society where such influence over men was not always well received, or because he was of the school of thought that believed there was an inappropriate relationship between Herring and Zia. Yaqub Khan is not specific in his reasoning behind his opinion of whether Herring's influence was proper or beneficial. But it only matters that he admits her influence was real and that it affected governmental policy.

Joanne Herring believed Soviet aggression should not be appeased. She believed then, as she does now, that the Soviets had designs on Pakistan in order to expand their sphere of influence and, importantly, to eliminate Pakistani assistance to Afghan resistance and to eliminate refugee camps and other spots where the truth of their occupation techniques could reach a wider world. She was, perhaps, in the right place at the right time. But she also knew what to do and how to do it.[197]

Many people believe that Becca Cason Thrash has now assumed the role of Houston's international society hostess. Her prolific fundraising has garnered close to $20 million for the Louvre Museum in Paris for a series of Liaisons au Louvre galas in Houston, Paris, Los Angeles, and Palm Beach. The French government was so impressed they awarded her the Legion of Honor for service to the nation.

However, Becca spent years raising funds for Houston charities before she ventured to help foreign institutions as well. One memorable party required a gondola to be lowered by crane to a massive indoor pool, after sufficient glass ceiling tiles were removed. The River Oaks mansion she shares with energy executive John Thrash is a modern palace with the couple's renowned art collection and has been the setting for many fancy-dress galas with celebrity guest lists over the years. Many say the magic of Becca's hospitality is not just over-the-top decor, lighting, and food and drink but her ability to draw the most varied crowd of old society, newcomers, flashy celebrities, academics, and professionals. The magic for Houston can be seen in her drive to make Houston known in the world and to make the world want to come to Houston. Taking a cue from Lynn Wyatt, Becca takes planeloads of Houstonians on the road for elegant galas in foreign locales and does not change the nature of the affair—it is still a Houston party, but in Paris or wherever. Likewise, her out-of-town celebrity guests, who have included Prince Albert of Monaco, Anna Wintour, and John Taylor (Duran Duran), see the side of Houston and Houstonians that people like Becca

Becca Cason Thrash is noted for superlative destination parties that raise prodigious sums for charity. Photo © David Brabyn. Courtesy Dabid Brabyn Archive.

have thoughtfully wrought: a big, tough city that sprang from the dreams of its early leaders and evolved into a beautiful and cosmopolitan metropolis that is famously generous to all.

There are many other Houstonians whose social standing and civic and charitable involvement helped project Houston's international image in the modern era. It would be difficult, and maybe risky, to list them all; however, a few of the most colorful characters should be noted.

When Sarah Campbell, daughter of a Texaco founder, married Robert E. Lee Blaffer, an Humble Oil founder, it united two of the great oil families of Texas. The wedding in Lampasas in 1909 was attended by Governor Jim Hogg and his daughter, Ima, the future queen of Houston arts and music. Courtesy of the Museum of Fine Arts, Houston.

Sarah Blaffer, born in 1885, was the daughter of William Thomas Campbell, one of the founders of Texaco. In 1909, she married Robert E. Lee Blaffer, one of the founders of Humble Oil, later Exxon, thus uniting two of the great oil families of Houston and Texas. Ima Hogg served as maid of honor for the ceremony held in Lampasas. The newlyweds honeymooned in Europe, and Sarah was enthralled by the art she saw at the Louvre. Back in Houston, she began a lifelong collection of paintings from fourteenth-century religious art to modern impressionist and expressionist works. She donated heavily from her collection to the Houston Museum of Fine Arts (HMFA) and established the Sarah Campbell Blaffer Foundation. The foundation continues to maintain the Blaffer Collection at the HMFA and arranges traveling exhibits to share the collection outside of Houston. The University of Houston art museum was named for Blaffer when it opened in 1973.

The Blaffers had four children, and two of the daughters continued their mother's example of dedication to Houston. Jane Blaffer (Owen) grew up in Houston and attended the first class of the Kinkaid School. After college at Bryn Mawr, she married and initially turned her attention to the preservation

Sarah and Robert Blaffer's daughter Cecil went by "Titi." In 1975 she married Prince Tassilo von Furstenberg and was highly visible in the arts, music, and opera in Houston and throughout Europe for decades. Steve Campbell/© Houston Chronicle. Used with permission.

and renovation of New Harmony, Indiana, the utopian society founded in 1824 by Robert Owen, an ancestor of her new husband. She later returned to Houston and generously supported local charities, especially the Blaffer Art Museum and the Gerald Hines College of Architecture at the University of Houston. She founded the English Speaking Union of the United States and brought many British luminaries to Houston. She was made a commander in the Order of the British Empire by Queen Elizabeth II. Jane Blaffer Owen died in Houston in 2010.

A younger Blaffer daughter was Cecil Blaffer, who went by "Titi." She divorced her first husband, Edward Joseph Hudson, and was represented by Percy Foreman in a trial that generated wide publicity at the time. She married and divorced a second time before marrying Prince Tassilo von Furstenberg of Austria in 1975 in Paris. The wedding was attended by Princess Grace of Monaco, whose husband, Prince Rainier, was related to the groom.[198] The House of Furstenberg originates with princes of the Holy Roman Empire. Titi von Furstenberg was fluent in four languages and was a lifelong student of European history and art. She supported the Wagner Opera Festival in Bayreuth, reminiscent of Ima Hogg a generation earlier. She supported the American Cathedral in Paris and her mother's art foundation in Houston,

Carolyn Farb was the first Houston hostess to hit the million-dollar mark for charitable funds raised at a single evening event. Michael Paulsen/© Houston Chronicle. Used with permission.

Margaret Alkek Williams is one of the most-seen women on the modern Houston social scene. She gives and raises great wealth for the visual and performing arts, theater, and health care. Photo by Gittings. Courtesy of Margaret Alkek Williams.

the Sarah Campbell Blaffer Foundation. She further supported the Houston Symphony and Houston Grand Opera and introduced her European friends to the city she loved.

Other prominent society women have played a similar role, using a glamorous public profile, personal charm, wealth, and plain hard work to accomplish great feats for civic and charitable causes in Houston. Carolyn Farb was the first to reach the magic level of $1 million raised in a single evening when she chaired a gala for the Stehlin Foundation for Cancer Research in 1983.[199] Margaret Alkek Williams has been a ubiquitous presence on the gala scene in Houston for decades. However, she spends less time raising funds and more time simply donating them from her personal wealth and from the Alkek Foundation established by her parents. No one gives so generously across the board to the visual arts, the performing arts, the theater, and health-care charities. While she does not focus on international events like some, her lavish promotion of Houston and its image is deserving of praise.[200]

Houston has many edifices to commemorate its famous adopted architect son Gerald Hines. Hines was native to Indiana but came to Houston after college in 1948. He was successful in the booming city, but his first big commercial project was the design of the One Shell Plaza in downtown Houston in 1967. It was the tallest building west of the Mississippi River when it opened. He also designed Pennzoil Place and Bank of America Center in Houston. In 2007, the architecture school at the University of Houston was renamed the Gerald D. Hines College of Architecture and Design. His architectural designs are seen in twenty-five countries, including the Lipstick Building in New York, the DZ Bank in Berlin, and the Porta Nuova Building in Milan.

Finally, no discussion of leading international personalities of Houston would be complete without a mention of Ricky and Sandy di Portanova—the Baron and Baroness di Portanova, that is. Ricky was a grandson of Hugh Roy Cullen, a legendary oilman who found the Tom O'Connor field near Victoria that has gushed oil for many decades. Hugh Roy Cullen's daughter, Lillie, married the Italian Baron Paolo di Portanova in 1932, hence the noble title that passed to her firstborn son, Ricardo. After much wrangling, Ricardo wound up with substantial assets from the Cullen Trusts and married Houston girl Sandy Hovas. The baron and baroness divided their time between Houston and Rome as well as an immense villa in Acapulco called Arabesque, where they entertained the jet set of the day. The villa was used in the James Bond film *License to Kill*. In Houston, they threw star-studded

Baron di Portanova was the son of an Italian nobleman and the grandson of legendary oilman Hugh Roy Cullen. Besides their mansions in Houston and Rome, the di Portanovas entertained the jet set at their Acapulco villa Arabesque. Photo © Norman Parkinson Ltd. Courtesy Norman Parkinson Archive.

parties at their twenty-one-thousand-square-foot mansion on River Oaks Boulevard complete with an enclosed and air-conditioned backyard. The di Portanovas were not noted for charitable fundraising, but they certainly put an international spotlight on Houston for many years. In 2000, the couple died within a few weeks of each other, both from cancer.

More International Houstonians

John and Dominique de Menil were both French born, he a baron from a family ennobled since Napoleon and she an heiress to the Schlumberger oil fortune. They settled in Houston after World War II and made a lasting artistic influence on the city. First, they built a modern international-style home in River Oaks in 1949, a departure from the traditional Southern plantation design that was so prevalent. They promoted modern art, collected art, and encouraged the academic study of art. They established the Institute for the Arts at Rice University and founded the Art Department at the University of St. Thomas. After John died in 1973, Dominique moved forward with

The French-born Menils made Houston their home and gave lavishly to the arts. Their fortune built the Menil Collection as well as substantially funded the adjacent Rothko Chapel. Photo by Hickey-Robertson, Houston. Courtesy Menil Archives, the Menil Collection, Houston.

their plans to build a museum to house their immense personal collection of art. The ambition came to fruition in 1987 with the opening of the Menil Collection. Thousands of visitors come from around the world to visit the Menil Collection as well as the adjacent, and Menil-supported, Cy Twombly Pavilion, Byzantine Fresco Chapel, and Rothko Chapel. The *Broken Obelisk* by Barnett Newman stands outside the Rothko Chapel and is dedicated to Martin Luther King Jr. Houston has benefited from so many generous patrons of the arts, but the Menils were extraordinary in adding major international components of modern, contemporary, pop, minimalist, abstract, and other fields not previously represented in the city in any substantial way. Dominique de Menil received the National Medal of Arts from President Reagan in 1986. She died in Houston in 1997.

Fayez Sarofim was a fund manager and investor with a net worth estimated at $2 billion. He was born into an aristocratic Egyptian Coptic family that held large cotton estates in the Middle East. Sarofim graduated from the University of California at Berkeley and the Harvard Business School. He came to Houston to work for Anderson, Clayton, an international cotton company. He soon founded his own investment firm, which has been an international success story. He gave millions to the Houston Ballet, the Houston Museum of Fine Arts, the Houston Grand Opera, and the Hobby Center for the Performing Arts. He also gave generously to Texas Children's Hospital and the UT Health Science Center at Houston, including funding for the Sarofim Research Building. Later, he endowed the Sarofim Visual and Dramatic Arts Building at Rice University. In 2004, he married another billionaire, Susan Krohn, whose daughter Lori was previously married to Sarofim's son Phillip. Fayez Sarofim died in 2022.

Hushang Ansary served as an ambassador and minister in the government of the shah of Iran for almost twenty years before the Iranian Revolution in 1979. He came to the United States, eventually settling in Houston and becoming an American citizen. He has owned several successful businesses in Houston and has been a benefactor to numerous charities, often educational projects associated with politics. He generously supported the creation of the James Baker Institute at Rice University and funded the Ansary Gallery of American History at the George Bush Presidential Library.

Houston's growing place in the world has also been fueled by larger demographic changes in its population. The civil rights movement, the Immigration and Naturalization Act, and general shifts in American social thought have made Houston society more reflective of its diverse citizens. It is hard to imagine now that Houston had very few Asian Americans at the time the Texas Medical Center began or even when the Space Center opened. The surge began after the Immigration and Nationality Act of 1965. This federal legislation abolished previous immigration formulas that favored Western Europeans and opened the doors more widely to Southern and Eastern Europeans and Asians. The new policy allowed immigration based on family relations and favored skills in math, science, engineering, and technology. Major energy, medical, space, and technology companies, many based in Houston, would conduct campus interviews looking for the top students in the fields, who often were Asian citizens studying in the United States on a student visa. Once hired by a Houston firm, the student would apply for citizenship and settle permanently. Such new Houstonians would then be an immigration "anchor" for their parents, siblings, or other relatives to apply to come the United States. The new laws also allowed immigration based on investments, so Houston could attract people with money to come in and buy property, launch new businesses, or invest in local businesses. Waves of highly skilled, often wealthy, foreigners began to pour into the city so that now, more than one in every four residents of Houston was born outside the United States.

Additionally, the Indochina Migration and Refugee Assistance Act was passed in 1975 to respond to the fall of Saigon and the masses of desperate refugees. Houston was designated as an official resettlement site and, as many joked, had the same climate as Vietnam. Thousands of refugees poured into Houston and began building homes and businesses, including restaurants, that catered to a cosmopolitan Houston. The Vietnamese invested heavily in the Midtown area of Houston during the 1980s oil bust and then rebuilt it as the market recovered. Today there is an official Little Saigon area, as well as Vietnamese-language newspapers and magazines and a Vietnamese-language radio station, KREH, that is commonly called Radio Saigon Houston.

The Iranian Revolution of 1979 also sparked a wave of Iranian refugees to Houston where many already had business connections through the oil or shipping industries. Although it was a much smaller influx than the Vietnamese, the Iranian contingent was almost all wealthy and came immediately ready to pour money into the local economy.

Houston has what is now referred to as "Old Chinatown" near the George R. Brown Convention Center and was once the central community of the small Chinese population that existed up until the 1980s. By that time, many Chinese Americans began to resettle in Southwest Houston, eventually creating what is now regarded as Houston's Chinatown. However, that name has been controversial among many residents who feel that it is really more "Asia Town" given the heavy numbers of Vietnamese, Korean, Taiwanese, and other Asian groups. But street signs in the area are in Chinese as well as English, and several mainland Chinese banks operate along a stretch of Bellaire Boulevard through the heart of Chinatown.

The People's Republic of China made Houston a priority after the normalization of relations during the Nixon administration. Deng Xiaoping made his first official visit to the United States in 1979. After official ceremonies in Washington, Deng flew to Houston with a local congressman, Mickey Leland, on board.[201] While in Houston, he toured the Johnson

Space Center and attended a rodeo, where he received and wore a Stetson hat. Deng believed Houston was his greatest priority in the United States, and it was the first city in which China opened a consulate.

The Chinese Consulate on Montrose Boulevard is a large, imposing edifice and has been the site of some controversy over the years. In 1981, the Chinese ballet dancer Li Cunxin was in Houston as part of a program between the Beijing Dance Academy and the Houston Ballet. He had intended to defect but was lured to the consulate on a pretext. His new American wife alerted his local attorney, Charles Foster, who was able to quickly escalate the matter in Washington with the office of Vice President George H. W. Bush. The federal government negotiated his release. Li stayed with the Houston Ballet for sixteen years and won numerous international ballet competitions. The drama with a happy ending is told in Li's 2003 autobiography, *Mao's Last Dancer*, which was made into a movie of the same title in 2009.[202]

The Asia Society was established in New York by John D. Rockefeller III in 1956. Its purpose was to promote Asian culture in the United States and foster understanding by focusing on art, business, culture, and education. The Asia Society grew rapidly and began to establish branch societies in major international cities. The Texas Asia Society branch was formed in 1979 by Barbara Bush and Ambassador Roy Huffington.[203] The Texas Asia Society operates from a strikingly beautiful building in the Museum District designed by Yoshio Taniguchi. The society displays art and hosts educational events, family programs, and speaker events all designed to enhance Houston's ties with Asia. The leadership includes James A. Baker III, Hushang Ansary, Margaret Alkek Williams, Nancy Allen, Albert Chao, Charles Foster, Gordon Quan, Neil Bush, Chase Untermeyer, and other Houstonians well versed in diplomacy, international business, and culture.

Another important demographic change to note in Houston's modern composition is the extraordinary influx and influence of the Muslim community, which is, in fact, the largest Muslim population in the South, comprising Shia and Sunni Muslims, with various sects in the two main branches of Islam. One especially visible group are the forty thousand Shia Ismailis who first began coming to Houston in the 1960s as skilled workers and health professionals at the Texas Medical Center. The community grew rapidly and is noted for being especially focused on education and entrepreneurship. In 2002, the Ismaili community's spiritual leader, the Aga Khan, accompanied by Texas Governor Rick Perry, broke ground for a new $10 million Ismaili Jamatkhana and Center. There are now five jamatkhanas in Greater

Houston, and a grand Ismaili Center for the general public is under construction on eleven acres of prime real estate on Allen Parkway. This center will be the first of its kind in the United States and is expected to open by the end of 2025.

One prominent member of Houston's Ismaili community is Ambassador Sada Cumber, who is native to Pakistan but was able to immigrate to the United States in 1978 as part of the new immigration focus on skilled workers and investors. Like the classic American Dream story, Sada and his wife, Mumtaz, succeeded in a series of successful business start-ups while also being involved in community and charity work. He was appointed to several state government posts before President George W. Bush appointed him ambassador to the Organization of the Islamic Conference (OIC), composed of fifty-seven member nations of majority Muslim populations.

Immigrants from India have also become prominent in Houston society. Renu Khator is the chancellor of the University of Houston System with seventy thousand students. Sean Mehta, entrepreneur in fashion and beauty, was instrumental in his family's endowment of the Mehta Arts of India Gallery at the Houston Museum of Fine Arts. Jugal Malani, international importer and distributor, is trustee of India House, a nonprofit serving the needs of Houston Indian Americans. The Indian American community of Houston opened the Eternal Gandhi Museum in 2023 located in the Brays Oaks area. The only museum of Gandhi in the United States, it preserves Mahatma Gandhi's legacy through exhibits, programs, lectures, and youth activities.

The Consular Ball

Houston's international activities were often conducted through civic organizations instead of individuals. In the post–World War II era, young Houstonians conceived of the idea of a diplomatic ball. By the 1950s there was a sufficient nucleus of consulates and a growing realization of Houston's international role to give rise to the first ball, called the Consular Ball, organized and run by the Houston Junior Chamber of Commerce (Jaycees). The Jaycees formed in Houston in 1930 and were originally called the Young Men's Division of the Chamber of Commerce, becoming the Junior Chamber of Commerce in 1940.[204] This event was first held in 1952. The diplomatic ball centered on the many nations who had official representatives at consulates located in Houston. France and the United Kingdom both had consulates in Houston soon after the Great Hurricane of 1900 destroyed their facilities in Galveston and made improbable the continued viability of Galveston

The Houston Consular Ball, always a white-tie affair, was long the hallmark of the Houston social season. In 2001, the ball honored the United Kingdom with Princess Alexandra representing the British Crown. Author's collection.

as the leading commercial city of Texas. However, over the years more and more countries opened official consulates in Texas or at least opened honorary consulates with similar duties and with official sanction from the US Department of State.

Even before commencing annual diplomatic balls, the Houston Jaycees were already committed to promoting Houston's international ties. In 1948, the Jaycees organized a welcome for President Romulo Gallegos of Venezuela, who arrived in the city to meet with both trade and oil leaders. The Jaycees were part of the airport welcoming committee and then organized a private yacht to take the visiting president on a cruise down the Houston Ship Channel. They provided Spanish-speaking guides and passed out Spanish-language literature explaining the Port of Houston and the many attributes of moving goods through the Houston Ship Channel.[205]

In 1949, the Jaycees began participating in Houston's annual World Trade Week programs. The Jaycees launched an essay contest, with prizes awarded, directed at junior high and high school students who were encouraged to write essays on "Why World Trade Brings Goods and Good Business to

Houston." The Jaycees furnished information reference kits from the Port of Houston and offered tours of facilities.[206]

The Jaycees of Houston at that time included Andre Crispin, a Belgian American businessman. Crispin was born in Brussels and, as a young man, joined the Belgian underground resistance movement against the Nazi occupation of his homeland.[207] He became a member of the Belgian Army and was assigned as liaison and interpreter to Allied Forces, including the US Army, during the liberation of Belgium. He subsequently moved to Houston and established the Crispin Company, a steel trading firm that operated internationally.[208] Crispin joined the Houston Jaycees and was an active and popular member, and in 1953, he was elected the statewide vice president.[209] Crispin also kept close ties to his homeland, and the government of Belgium named him as its honorary consul in Houston. He served on the International Reception Committee of the Houston Livestock Show and was active in the Houston Symphony Society.[210]

The first Houston Consular Ball honored the consular corps of Houston as a group. The stated purpose was to "celebrate the distinguished consular corps and the diplomatic and trade ties they provide between Houston and the rest of the world."[211] The 1953 Consular Ball again honored all the diplomats posted in Houston, with Jaycees President Jack Rynd and Mayor Hofheinz heading up a receiving line welcoming the honored guests, led by Swedish Consul General Gunnar Dryselius.[212] By 1957, there were twenty-nine consulates in Houston to honor at the annual ball, which was held that year at the River Oaks Country Club. The Jaycees' organizing committee that year included journalist Marvin Zindler.[213]

In the early 1950s, the Houston Jaycees also formed a specific International Committee to stimulate interest in international relations, especially with regard to the Port of Houston. As a part of this program, the Jaycees formed a Foreign Visitor Hospitality Project in which one or more Jaycees would be assigned to escort foreign visitors around Houston to entertain them and to point out the ship channel, business district, refineries, leading hotels, and other points of interest in an effort to promote the city in international business circles.[214]

The Port of Houston and the ship channel were major draws for international visitors, and the Jaycees went beyond merely showing it off as a tourist attraction to visitors. Instead, they took it upon themselves as businessmen to promote the port, including an organized campaign for approval of a $7 million bond package for port improvements in 1957. To "stimulate interest in the proposed bond issue," the Jaycees received the donation of a new 1957 Mercury, which they offered as the prize for an essay contest on the importance of the bonds for Houston. There were more than six thousand entries, and the winner was Herman Tschumy, who then "drove his new car to the polls to vote 'for' the bond issue."[215] The bond package was indeed approved by Houston's voters. The Jaycees also organized talks at their meetings and luncheons by port officials, including one by Jake Aston, Houston port chairman, to speak about the importance of foreign affairs to the city.[216]

The 1960 Houston Consular Ball was held at the Shamrock Hilton Hotel on September 9, much earlier than usual, in order to coincide with the opening day of the International Trade and Travel Fair, also to be held at the Shamrock.[217] Houston Mayor Lewis Cutrer led the receiving line, assisted by Honorary Ball Chairman W. Bedford Sharp, chairman of Mission Manufacturing Company. The tickets were priced at $30 per couple, including champagne, dancing to the music of a classical orchestra, and a midnight breakfast buffet.[218] Foley's Department Stores presented a fashion show of unique French designs using synthetic fibers made from petroleum created by DuPont. In this way, Houstonians could show European-designed fashions, created by an American company, using a product Houston famously produced. The gowns had previously been shown in New York and Miami, but it was their first exhibition in Houston. Juliana Larsen, an "internationally known chanteuse," sang for the ball guests in what was described as the "entertainment highlight of the evening, and very probably of the entire social season." The Jaycees noted that Larsen had previously entertained guests at well-heeled functions in New York, London, Paris, Miami, and Palm Beach.[219]

The 1961 Consular Ball had to contend with Hurricane Carla, which made landfall at Port O'Connor just two days after the ball. However, for several days in advance the Houston area experienced wind and strong, rolling rainstorms. But the Jaycees actually reported the highest number of attendees ever and claimed that "Carla did not come any sooner because she did not want to intrude [on the] beautiful and festive affair."[220] The ball featured Natasha Rawson, a singer who performed in seven languages along with dancers performing ethnic dances.[221]

Late in 1961, the Jaycees launched a business education project in which they would "bring foreign economics and business students to Houston for short term industrial traineeships." For each foreign student that came to work at a Houston firm, a student at Rice University or the University of Houston would work on a reciprocal basis with a foreign company. The

Jaycees organized a board of prominent businessmen to advise the program and raised funds to support travel costs.[222]

The Jaycees' Foreign Visitor program later morphed to include contacts abroad made by Houston Jaycees who were otherwise traveling for their own business or personal reasons. For example, one member, Howard Personage, called on Jaycees throughout a long trip through Mexico and Central America and promoted Houston, including making them honorary Houston Jaycees.[223]

In 1961, the Jaycees launched a new program, Operation Maiden Voyage, again to promote the Port of Houston and stress the importance of international trade. In this new program, the port would identify for the Jaycees any new ships "coming to Houston on their maiden voyage." The Jaycees would then present plaques to the captains of the ships at a welcoming ceremony that included port officials and the local consular official from whose country the ship arrived. The Jaycees said it was necessary to "make a small hole in the dike of misunderstanding that can exist between our citizens and those of many foreign lands."[224] Other projects in 1961 included adoption of two foreign orphans and placing them with suitable Houston families, bringing foreign movies to Houston for free screening, and organizing a business trip to Monterrey, Mexico.[225] By the end of 1961, the International Committee of the Houston Jaycees had become the largest of the organization's committees and declared itself to be committed to generating international goodwill for Houston.[226]

Over the years the Jaycees developed three objectives: "First, it offers an opportunity for Houston to celebrate its truly distinguished consular corps (the 3rd largest diplomatic corps of any American city); second, the Consular Forum (a business symposium held the day before the ball) is designed to help promote opportunities for international trade with the featured country; and finally, because understanding of and respect for international differences are essential prerequisites for successful international commerce, the Consular Forum's concluding banquet is a fundraiser for the Houston Junior Chamber of Commerce Foundation, which uses the proceeds to support international educational programs, scholarships and internships."[227]

The system of having the ball honor all the diplomats accredited to Houston continued for the first eleven years. Not until 1964 was the ball dedicated specifically to Spain and France jointly. At that same ball, the idea of having a "patrons chair" began. This person would be in charge of gathering corporate sponsors to underwrite the expenses with enough left over for charitable purposes. That first patrons chair in 1964 was Joanne King (later Herring). Later patrons chairs included Lynn Wyatt and Barbara Bush.

In 1961, the ball organizers began the practice of naming a specific honored guest as a part of the ball. These honored guests were locally prominent citizens, such as George R. Brown in 1965 in the ball honoring Italy, George Strake in 1968 for Japan, George H. W. Bush in 1978 for the Netherlands, James A. Baker III in 1981 for the United Kingdom, Jack Blanton in 1983 for Denmark, Ben Love in 1984 for Australia, Barbara Bush in 1990 for Switzerland, Chase Untermeyer in 2008 for Qatar, and Eduardo Aguirre in 2009 for Spain.[228] In many cases, the honored country would send a representative in addition to its local consular official. In some cases, this was their ambassador in Washington, and in other cases it was a high-ranking guest from the home country, such as Princess Alexandra for the United Kingdom in 2001.[229]

As Houston grew, the ball grew more exclusive and became an invitation-only event. Moreover, the dress code was always white tie and decorations, not merely black tie. Rather than a tuxedo, gentlemen wear jackets with black tails and a white waistcoat and white bow tie. Of course, most Houstonians did not have any decorations to wear, but their honored diplomatic guests did, and the Houston hosts began wearing official sashes that honored the country whose table they were hosting.[230]

The corporate sponsors for these events naturally followed the pattern of the honored country. Royal Dutch Shell underwrote the costs of the ball to host the Netherlands as the honored country in 1978 and again in 2003.[231] When Qatar was honored in 2008, and even Russia in 2005, there was stiff competition among the major oil companies to determine who would be privileged to spend the most money to host the white-tie gala.

By the 1970s, the Consular Ball became an extended event starting with an announcement reception held in the official residence of an honored diplomat or in a corporate sponsor's office to announce the nation to be honored and present a program of events. Following that, a trade mission would always be organized to go to the honored country. Houston would send a delegation of business, political, and society leaders to impress the targeted nation with information about Houston, to present all the opportunities of greater business ties, and, of course, to emphasize the significance of being honored as the hosted country. A patron's dinner then followed in Houston for all the corporate sponsors to gather along with representatives of the honored country before the actual day of the ball itself. Not only does the ball, and all its antecedent events, promote the city of Houston, but the profits raised in the endeavor are used to provide scholarships for endowed programs at the University of Houston, Rice University, and the University of St. Thomas, as well as UNESCO gifts directed to the country being specifically honored. In this way, the event became simultaneously an international event, an opportunity to promote Houston, and the chance to benefit a worthy charitable cause at the same time.

Besides the Consular Ball, there are many other high-profile galas such as the Houston Opera Ball, Houston Ballet Ball, Tiger Ball, Annual Symphony Ball, and Bayou Bend Garden Party. In all these spectacular events, Houston's leading members of society have the opportunity to showcase the accomplishments of Houston while raising millions for nonprofits.

The four main pillars of Houston's rise as an international city—trade, energy, medical treatment, and space technology—have created the platform upon which individuals can become globally recognized leaders and public figures. In the modern era, such international Houstonians now come from every race, religion, and cultural heritage.

CONCLUSION

Houston's rise as an international city enacted a new model of political-economic development. It made Houston a global magnet and leader, if still sometimes ignored by traditional coastal elites. The history of Houston's rise illustrates important concepts about how such a city may attain a position of global prominence despite significant obstacles and competition. Houston's trajectory demonstrates the important balance required between local, state, and national governments. It also reveals how such a balance helps foster an environment at the local level in which business, political, and social leaders may productively join together to build a successful metropolis.

Houston was born and evolved in a governmental structure that had a loose, decentralized national government corresponding to a centralized local government. Houston was established in 1836 when the Republic of Texas was only a few months old and had no real control over the new city. Instead, the national government of Texas was expected to provide only for the defense of the new nation while it also began to establish some minimal administrative controls. Houston served for a time as the capital of the Republic of Texas, which status further aided its early development without ceding urban independence.

In the early years, the founders and first investors of Houston sought to populate the city and build infrastructure through trade. These opportunities were advertised in New York and elsewhere, promoting the business opportunities for new residents. Thus, Houstonians were utterly in control of their own destiny from the outset because there was virtually no support from the national government and only competition from other cities, most of which were older and more established.

An early priority of the Texian government was to establish diplomatic relations with as many foreign governments as possible. This was necessary to provide diplomatic support against Mexico and to promote business ties and trade. Texas' foreign policy worked to Houston's advantage, as the national government was responsible for conducting foreign affairs and the expense and staffing of foreign offices. That left the leaders of Houston free to focus on business and local improvements and to build foreign trade relationships wherever Texas had established an embassy.

In 1845, the Republic of Texas was annexed by the United States and became the twenty-eighth state. However, the pattern of decentralized national government remained unchanged, as the federal government in Washington was similarly disengaged from the same daily regulatory functions already performed by Houston at the local level. Washington's responsibility was primarily to provide for the common defense against Mexico or any other foreign threat that might arise. There was a greater body of US law that replaced some Texas laws, but the federal system allowed Houston to remain highly independent.

The decentralized national government and the strong local government meant that Houston was responsible for its own police, schools, sanitation, and other issues of urban and localized concern. The business community looked to the local political leaders to provide urban law and order that made economic development productive. The political community depended on the business community for tax revenue sufficient to support only the costs of local government. The social leaders came from the same two groups, and in many cases they overlapped.

The Port of Houston and the Houston Ship Channel benefited from a supportive, but not controlling, federal presence. The federal government was responsible for the very important but more detached responsibility of military protection of the port and the protection of commercial and passenger vessels that used it. The federal government provided substantial funds to dredge the channel and create a deep-water port. With those improvements, Washington designated Houston as an official port of entry. The federal government constructed the Intracoastal Waterway to better link Houston domestically and also dug the Panama Canal, further connecting

Houston internationally. The latter two projects were performed entirely at the expense of the federal government, and the dredging required only a 10 percent contribution from Houston. The port and ship channel belonged to Houston and brought the city great benefit, but the local and national government structure created the atmosphere in which this fundamental element of Houston could be developed.

The oil industry made Houston internationally famous as the "Energy Capital of the World" and created the fortunes that flowed to other successes for the city. This industry also first operated with no local or national control. However, the state and federal governments did eventually establish some minimal spacing and production controls to stabilize the market, support minimal prices (and therefore profits), and prevent waste. These changes were not only supported by the business and political community but were actually initiated at their request to maintain a good business climate.

The Texas Medical Center was completely a local initiative in concept and initial funding. The center grew tremendously over time at local direction and control. The federal government did not control the center, but the center benefited from evolving federal policies that provided grants from the National Institutes of Health, as well as later funding from federal Great Society programs such as Medicare and Medicaid that vastly increased the paying patient-customer base using the Medical Center's facilities and services. The federal government cooperated by facilitating the visits of thousands of foreign, cash-paying clients who needed the high-end specialized cardiac, cancer, and organ transplant capabilities.

Finally, the Space Center was initiated by the City of Houston with a grant of land provided by a local donor. However, the billions of dollars spent for the program over the years flowed from the federal government for construction, employees, and third-party contracts in Houston. The city continues to benefit from the improved roads and other infrastructure needed to support the program, but it does not pay for that nor have the responsibility of determining the policies and programs of NASA. Houston simply benefits from the direct federal expenditures, as well as the local economic impact, including tourism.

The decentralized federal government coupled with a strong local government produced another helpful dynamic of three distinct local power-wielding classes: political, business, and social. A single individual may be in more than one of the groups at a time and may be in all of the groups at various points over the course of a lifetime or career. But each group, or a member in it, has historically exercised power to advance Houston and has used this power alone or in coordination with members of other groups.

Ima Hogg was a leading matriarch of the social group for many decades, although she might also be regarded as a transitional member of the political group for the time she was the daughter of a sitting governor and perhaps even afterward, given the prominence and popularity of the name Hogg in Houston and Texas.[1] As a social leader, she founded the Houston Symphony and was instrumental in bringing other performing arts to the city. She built up one of the greatest collections of Texan and American antiques and then donated them and her mansion to the city as a museum. She and others like her sought to build up the image and culture of Houston to world-class standards.

Jesse Jones was a leading member of the business class with commercial building projects that fundamentally changed Houston. However, as an influential member of this group he also organized banks in 1931 to ensure no Houston bank failed in the recession. He compelled support for a bond package to match federal dollars for the ship channel. He brought the Democratic National Convention to Houston in 1928 and helped organize business support to pay for it. He served in prominent political positions under three US presidents and was thus better able to aid Houston, help it survive the Depression, and then position itself for the next growth spurt.

Tom Ball was a member of the political group, serving as a member of Congress who successfully brought funding to Houston to dredge, enlarge, and improve the port and ship channel. He managed this accomplishment despite political obstacles. Ball helped others in Washington see and appreciate Houston in a new light as an important American trading port and a city worthy to be an official port of entry.

Each of these groups could flourish because they were relieved of big-picture issues like defense, foreign affairs, federal judiciary, taxation, monetary policy, banking structure, and stock market and other national-level functions. Instead, secure in the knowledge that these basic governmental functions were fulfilled, the three local groups could focus their time and resources in a targeted and efficient way to advance local priorities. They were able to carry out their plans for success and improvement within the roomy, but secure, bubble provided by a decentralized national government.

The Allen brothers' first advertisements of Houston focused attention on trade and the advantages of Houston's water link to Galveston and beyond. As Houston grew, every generation of businessmen and political leaders has focused on the port and the ship channel and how they may be enlarged and improved. Houston business and political leaders have joined forces in the past to form a city harbor board and then a county navigation board to manage the port. Later when it was considered expedient, the same groups merged the two governing authorities into one Port of Houston Commission. These groups successfully lobbied Austin and Washington for funding, bond approval, federal customs houses, state and federal police assistance, and other programs that would further the local purposes.

The business class established the oil industry in Houston and then cooperated with the political class to impose regulations that served its own best long-term purposes. Houston's business and political leaders successfully lobbied Washington to support their efforts to expand overseas and to protect their interests and employees in the Middle East and elsewhere. After the 1973 energy crisis, these same groups secured federal approval for regulatory support to carry out new exploration initiatives and to open new areas, such as Alaska, for oil drilling.

The close cooperation of business and political leaders established the Texas Medical Center. Both these groups cooperated over time to enhance the center through lobby and funding programs. Later, an organized group of social leaders joined the effort, intent on charity galas, endowments, and other efforts to enhance the center.

Finally, the Space Center was obtained with the cooperation of business and political leaders, but again, the social leaders adopted the Space Center to promote it and to use it to enhance the image of Houston. Sakowitz promoted a line of minimalist Space Age fashions, and Ima Hogg invited astronauts to sit in her box at the Houston Symphony.

In this analytical framework, Houston is seen to arise as a great world city and international player because a decentralized national framework provided both security and funding without any negative interference. The strong centralized local structure facilitated precise, efficient, and effective actions that propelled Houston forward in a generally planned and conscientious manner. In this way, Houston could make a series of decisions that continually elevated it economically and politically to the position of major state, then regional, then national and international city. Houston made these choices not as simply the city of Houston, although in some cases the city government may have made or supported a particular decision in the chain of events. Instead, Houston made these choices as a community of political, business, and social leaders who agreed on a course of action and took the steps, through the appropriate component group, to obtain the desired result. The "Houston" making these decisions and taking these actions is a composite entity that is geographically Houston but is actually larger than the political entity "City of Houston," just as it is also bigger than the Houston School Board, River Oaks Homeowners Association, Space City Parks Board, Texas Medical Center Volunteers Auxiliary, or other single legal entity. It is the greater composite entity of Houston that has established itself as an international city.

The composite structure of Houston's three major groups operating within the decentralized national but centralized local governmental system is an important construct, and it illuminates both the environment and method of Houston's successful rise as an international city. However, the paradigm is important for another reason: global urbanization.

American society is predominantly urban and has been for at least two generations. Houston itself is a great example of the process of urbanization. The port and ship channel required an increasingly large workforce to load and unload, operate equipment and grain elevators, and pilot ships. As the oil industry grew, Houston required workers for tankers, refineries, and chemical plants. More people left the farms and ranches around Houston and moved into the city for jobs, better living conditions, and better educational opportunities.

These same patterns occurred across the United States, in varying degrees, and they occurred elsewhere in the industrialized world as societies shifted from urban to rural. The growing concentration of wealth and population created greater political power in cities and allowed more urban representatives to rise to leadership positions in state legislatures and the US Congress. In 1898, when Houston first sought federal funding for the ship channel, the US Congress was still tilted toward rural interests, and that factor worked against Houston's lone congressman's efforts to obtain funding. The same was true in the mid-1940s when Houston sought funding for the Texas Medical Center from the Texas legislature, which was still dominated by rural interests at the time. It took particular effort by Houston's political and business representatives to secure even modest funding or bond authorizations. However, by 1961 when Houston sought the Manned Space Center, the chairman of the House Appropriations Committee in Washington, Albert Thomas, was a Houstonian and in a much better position to secure the federal approval and funding required for the city's ambitious space program.

In the contemporary era, urbanization is a global phenomenon and not limited to the developed world. Currently, 90 percent of urbanization occurs in the developing world.[2] Whether the rapid urbanization of a given city transforms it into an international city may depend on whether the city has the Houston model of a strong local government functioning under a decentralized national government. In this analysis, it would be difficult for a city like Tianjin to project itself in the same way because the Chinese national government is very strong and the Tianjin municipal government is weak. Additionally, the Chinese system does not really allow for the distinct three classes of political, business, and social leaders. Even though Tianjin has a surging population, a very successful modern port, and an advanced manufacturing base, it is not in control of its own destiny in a pattern like Houston's. It also has no real class of social leaders to promote the city's individual culture.

The city of Dubai offers a good example of a city that could become an international city on the Houston paradigm. It is a strong city with its own royal family and local municipal control, although it is also within the United Arab Emirates, a decentralized federal government possessing only powers that are delegated to it by the independent emirates. Dubai has a strong political and business class, but its social class is not a distinctly separate group, and the city faces religious and cultural barriers that may ultimately inhibit its rise.

The Houston model seems more akin to that of Chicago and the way it developed as a strong urban center within the same decentralized federal system. Like Houston, Chicago has historically strong business, political, and social classes. Both cities emerged and grew into major urban areas within relatively short time periods. Both cities relied on trade as their initial economic base, both of which involved a level of international trade. Both cities harnessed the environment around them and were, in turn, shaped by that same environment. As their wealth and populations grew, both cities exercised great political power, acting not so much as city hall but as composites of the metropolitan political, business, and social leaders.

Houston's international rise is instructive of an important model of political-economic development that may be repeated in another location, within the United States or not, that replicates the structure of a strong local government in a decentralized national system along with cooperative groups of community leaders. Such a formula creates incentives for international growth in a free, yet orderly, structure of business and political systems. It also incentivizes individuals by linking their personal success to the broader success of the community. Individual political, business, or social leaders may promote their own interests in a symbiotic relationship with the city's growth and success. The result is the truly remarkable global city of Houston.

Afterword

The written history of anything has to stop at some point, and this is certainly true for a city as big, complex, and dynamic as Houston. The more current the events are in a historical record, the more difficult it is to gain perspective. Historical writing is not to be confused with journalism, which reports current events and may be incomplete or biased because of the inability to gain sufficient vantage to properly view and understand events and circumstances. With that in mind, I could not trace the story of Houston's global position too close to the present, and I recognize the limitations of examining even relatively close history as I have tried to do in this book.

I chose to end the main thrust of my book with the 1990 G7 Economic Summit because I considered it to be the crowning event of Houston's superb rise as a global city. The G7 Summit focused the world's attention on the international reach of the city's wealth, political power, technology, and culture. I extended some individual chapters for a longer period of time to more fully express the thrust of a particular area of the city's international rise, that is, one of the pillars that I use to categorize and explain Houston's evolution.

Nevertheless, it seems an incomplete story to not append some closing remarks on the city's more recent history to both demonstrate the continued upward trajectory of the city's success and point out its remarkable resistance to some serious setbacks, even disasters.

The population of Houston continues its rapid rise. At the time of the G7 Summit in 1990, the decennial census was approximately 1.6 million. By 2020, it has increased by 44 percent to 2.3 million.

The Port of Houston remains the top US port in terms of foreign tonnage, surpassing two hundred million tons in 2019. It is also ranked as the top

US port for petroleum, steel, and building materials cargo. Its phenomenal economic impact is calculated to be approximately 20 percent of the entire GDP of the state of Texas.

Houston continues unchallenged as the "Energy Capital of the World," not just because of prodigious oil and gas production in Texas but also because it has positioned itself as the business and intellectual center for every segment of the energy industry, including exploration, production, transmission, marketing, supply, and technology. Houston is the home to over forty-six hundred energy-related companies, including behemoths ConocoPhillips, Halliburton, Baker Hughes, Schlumberger, Exxon, Shell, and Chevron.

The Texas Medical Center remains the world's largest medical center, encountering over ten million patients each year with 180,000 annual surgeries, including over 13,000 heart surgeries, and delivers a baby every twenty minutes (approximately 26,000 per year). The Texas Medical Center continues to astonish the world with new firsts since the G7 Summit: having the first patient to leave with a portable, battery-operated heart pump (1991); producing a way to grow blood vessels and capillaries (2011); and delivering the first surviving sextuplets (2012). The MD Anderson Cancer Hospital remains the leader in cancer treatment with the world's leading technology to pinpoint each patient's unique cancer and tailor treatment. In 2011, MD Anderson received $150 million, the largest single gift ever, from the royal family of the United Arab Emirates to accelerate the pace of pancreatic cancer research in particular. The gift symbolized not only Houston's preeminence in global health but also its high regard in the eyes of the world's elite.

The Johnson Space Center employs over three thousand people and remains NASA's center for spaceflight research, training, and mission control. Additionally, the Johnson Space Center leads the operations and missions of the International Space Station, coordinating five space programs and fifteen countries. Houston is the center for NASA's development of Orion spacecraft to launch humans into deep-space travel and the Gateway program to install an outpost orbiting the moon as part of a renewed presence on the moon, as well as to support future missions to Mars and beyond.

However, not all news is good, and Houston has suffered notable setbacks over recent decades. The collapse of Enron in 2001, the largest bankruptcy in history at the time, was a blow to Houston economically since the firm employed almost thirty thousand people and claimed revenues of over $100 billion annually. But the exposure of fraud and corruption was also demoralizing to many, and Enron's name was stripped from the professional baseball field that is now known as Daikin Park, the home of the Houston Astros.

Houston has always had issues with weather, especially flooding. While less exposed than its one-time shipping rival, Galveston, Houston has had serious weather impacts in the last few decades. The Great Flood of 1994 was fueled by Hurricane Rosa, a Pacific hurricane that came ashore in southwestern Mexico, triggering over thirty inches of rain in Houston, killing twenty-two people, and rupturing oil pipelines. Houston endured Tropical Storm Frances in 1998, Tropical Storm Allison in 2001, Hurricane Ike in 2008, the Memorial Day Flood of 2015, and Houston Tax Day Flood of 2016. However, nothing compared to the impact of Hurricane Harvey in 2017 with over fifty inches of rain from a Category 4 storm that killed fourteen people and destroyed thousands of buildings, cars, and homes.

In 2003, the Space Shuttle *Columbia*, directed by Mission Control in Houston, broke up as it reentered the earth's atmosphere, killing all seven astronauts and strewing debris across a wide swath of Texas and Louisiana. Thousands gathered at the Space Center for a memorial service led by President George W. Bush. In 2011, the United States closed its Space Shuttle program altogether.

More recently, Houston has found itself a hotspot in the COVID-19 global pandemic. While 49 percent of workers nationwide were impacted by the pandemic, the figure was a much stouter 64 percent in Houston. The pandemic infected over one hundred thousand Houstonians and had killed almost two thousand by September 2020. Additionally, for a city with a global reach, a pandemic destroys the international human interaction that has been at the crux of its growth.

But if Houston's history shows anything, it is the resilience of the city and its people. Maybe the difficult climate and hardscrabble nature of the early years created a type of psychological herd immunity, an inner determination to move forward no matter what. And certainly, Houston's ups and downs have been decidedly more up than otherwise. The city continually adds new features and more innovative ways of creating wealth. The city continually expands and revises its long-standing economic assets to make them more competitive and attractive.

Houston's most valuable assets are citizens who are entrepreneurial, ambitious, hardworking, compassionate, and energetic. That particular well of talent has never run dry for Houston. In the years since the G7 Summit, the city has produced an amazing crop of new leaders in all fields, including singer Beyoncé, directors Richard Linklater and Wes Anderson, actor and dancer Patrick Swayze,[1] designer Amir Taghi, designer Choe Dao, and actress Renée Zellweger. New business stars include billionaire restaurateur, hotelier, and Houston Rockets owner Tilman Fertitta;[2] billionaire chemicals manufacturer and Taiwan native Albert Chao; and energy billionaire Richard Kinder. New political leaders from Houston include US Senator Ted Cruz and Lieutenant Governor Dan Patrick. And in the general cool category Houston has chef and author Sylvia Casares, boxer and entrepreneur George Foreman, and author and televangelist Joel Osteen.

In sports since 1990, Houston has cheered the Astros to a 2017 World Series win that was especially welcome in the aftermath of Hurricane Harvey. The Houston Rockets won the NBA Championship in 1994 and 1995 in what some call the Hakeem Olajuwon era. The Houston Texans have won eight AFC South division championships. Houston also has professional soccer (Houston Dynamos), professional women's soccer (Houston Dash), and professional rugby (Houston SabreCats), and RodeoHouston is an official Professional Rodeo Cowboys Association (PRCA) event. All these sports combined with many parks, world-class museums, and premier performing arts show that Houston knows how play hard as well as work hard.

Houston has focused on its core strengths and has fully utilized every resource and advantage that Providence has provided. The city has driven forward in spite of serious setbacks and stiff competition. Houstonians have united time and again whenever there was a new brass ring to grab or a ditch to climb out of. The city is not perfect and certainly has made mistakes along the way like any entity run by humans with all their frailties. But there is a distinctive mystique about Houston and a certain quality of its people that is as positive, energetic, and hopeful as any community the world has known. If the past is a lesson, then Houston will continue to create its own bright future.

Acknowledgments

Every historian needs help from others to find sources, sift ideas, chase down leads, and organize his thoughts. This is even more true for a first-time author like myself trying to find his way through intimidating research libraries and historical collections. And this is before the labor of distilling down information to a coherent theme of a draft.

This book evolved from my PhD dissertation at the University of Texas at Austin in 2016. I thank my all-star committee of H. W. Brands, Jeremi Suri, Mark Lawrence, and William Inboden for their kind encouragement and excellent guidance.

In writing this book, I was informed by the work of many previous authors listed in the bibliography, especially those writers who told the fascinating stories of the Houston Port and Ship Channel, the Texas oil boom, the Texas Medical Center, and the Manned Space Center and those who wrote biographies of some of the amazing personalities of Houston's history.

I am very grateful for the knowledge, kindness, and patience of the research librarian staffs of the Woodson Research Center at Rice University, the Houston and Texas Research Collection of the University of Houston, the LBJ Presidential Library, the George H. W. Bush Presidential Library, the McGovern Research Center at the Texas Medical Center, the Briscoe Center at the University of Texas, the NASA Johnson Space Center History Collection, and the Document Library of the Port of Houston.

Conducting interviews was important both to gain firsthand knowledge of leading Houstonians and to clarify some information learned from archival research. I am especially grateful for the remarkable insights and knowledge provided by former US Secretary of State James A. Baker III, Joanne

King Herring, Ambassador Chase Untermeyer, former Texas Secretary of State George Strake, Lynn Wyatt, historian Kate Sayen Kirkland, Margaret Scarbrough Wilson, Carolyn Farb, Don Hartsell, and Charles Foster. Many others have contributed to my work with ideas or memories that led me in search of more records, and they have my sincere gratitude.

I am thankful to Erik Eriksson, general counsel of the Port of Houston, who personally showed me around the Historical Documents rooms and ensured I could access the records I needed. Thanks also to Bonnie Campbell, curator of Bayou Bend, who gave me a private tour of Bayou Bend, Ima Hogg's River Oaks Estate, helping me see so much that I had only read of in the archives.

I am grateful to Charles Carver for help with citations and technology challenges, and to Taylor Brigance, who proofed the citations again. Margaret Johnson did yeoman's work to find needed photos from both public archives and private collections. In some cases, she had to just search out my hunch that a certain photo probably existed, and I am very grateful. And my thanks for additional research help from Janice Harrison, Brandon Janes, Cammy Jones, and Marta Greytok.

Finally, I am very appreciative of Cynthia Lindlof for her detailed copyediting work, which saved me from numerous errors. And I am especially grateful to Shannon Davies, former director of Texas A&M University Press, who encouraged me in my initial manuscript submission and subsequently buoyed me through the long slog of the publishing process.

With final thanks to everyone named, and with earnest apologies to anyone I failed to name, I wish you happy reading.

Notes

INTRODUCTION

1. Ken Lay was chairman of Enron (formerly Houston Natural Gas) and a former federal energy regulator. George Strake Jr. came from an old Houston oil family and had served as Texas secretary of state under Governor William P. Clements Jr. from 1979 to 1982.
2. Bush, *A Memoir*, 346.
3. Bush, *A Memoir*, 347–48.
4. Fuermann, *Houston: The Feast Years*, 36.
5. Bush, *A Memoir*, 346.
6. Bush, *A Memoir*, 346.
7. Don Hartsell, former president of Solex Environmental Systems, contractor for G7 Summit, interview by author, June 20, 2015.
8. Fuermann, *Houston: The Feast Years*, 3.
9. Platell, "How Margaret Thatcher Taught Me Powerful Women Never Wear Trousers."
10. Hartsell, interview, June 20, 2015.
11. Bush, *A Memoir*, 348.
12. Hartsell, interview, June 20, 2015.
13. Johnston, *Houston, the Unknown City*, 11.
14. Marguerite Johnston served as Washington bureau chief of the *London Daily Mirror*. She covered UN events for the *Houston Post* before going to work for the *Post* as a columnist and then as assistant editor for foreign affairs.
15. Marie Phelps McAshan attended the Kinkaid boarding school in Houston and then the Rice Institute before going to Columbia University. Her grandfather was Texas Attorney General George Clark, who lost the 1892 governor's race to Jim Hogg.
16. Burrows and Wallace, *Gotham*, 1236.
17. Gregg Cantrell, Erma and Ralph Lowe Chair in Texas History at Texas Christian University, quoted in J. N. Lomax, "Is Texas Southern?"
18. Cummins, "History, Memory and Rebranding," 37.
19. Cummins, "History, Memory and Rebranding," 39.
20. Cummins, "History, Memory and Rebranding," 39.

21. Cummins, "History, Memory and Rebranding," 41.
22. Cummins, "History, Memory and Rebranding," 42.
23. Cummins, "History, Memory and Rebranding," 43. *Texas Rangers* was later made into a Hollywood film of the same name and released in 1936 to coincide with the Centennial celebration.
24. Cummins, "History, Memory and Rebranding," 43. Other intellectuals of the period contributed to the westernization of Texas through their advocacy of "regionalism" as an academic way to explain different areas of the United States. They "advocated a reverence of the past, the values of tradition, and a sense of place amid the homogenizing aspects of modernization" (42).
25. Cummins, "History, Memory and Rebranding," 42, quoting Kevin Edward Mooney, "Texas Centennial Music and Identity" (PhD diss., University of Texas at Austin, 1998), 14–15. A striking example is the foundation of the *Southwest Review*, "a scholarly journal that proved to be an eloquent voice for Texas regionalism during the 1920's and 1930's" (42).
26. Painters favored western landscapes, and "Tom Lea almost single-handedly legitimized the Trans-Pecos west as part of the Texas artistic heritage." Cummins, "History, Memory and Rebranding," 44.
27. Pompeo Coppini was selected to sculpt a cenotaph at the Hall of State at Fair Park in Dallas. He presented the "heroes of the Alamo as western frontiersmen in appearance, instead of southerners." Cummins, "History, Memory and Rebranding," 44.
28. The rise of country and western music spread across North America and beyond, reflected especially by Texan Gene Autry. Cummins, "History, Memory and Rebranding," 44.
29. Barnstone, "Staub, John Fanz."
30. Cummins, "History, Memory and Rebranding," 46.
31. J. N. Lomax, "Is Texas Southern?"
32. K. Kirkland, *The Hogg Family*, xvi.
33. Cummins, "History, Memory and Rebranding," 49.
34. Foik was a Canadian who came to the United States for college at Notre Dame followed by seminary studies at Holy Cross and then a PhD in history from Catholic University. He came to Austin to serve as librarian at St. Edwards University and was a prolific researcher and writer on Texas history, especially regarding the history of the Catholic Church in the region.
35. Cummins, "History, Memory and Rebranding," 49.
36. Herring, interview.

CHAPTER 1

1. Sibley, *The Port of Houston*, 12.
2. Cabeza de Vaca later returned to the New World in 1540 as governor of the colony of Argentina, Paraguay, and Uruguay. Chipman, "In Search of Cabeza De Vaca's Route Across Texas," 127.
3. Sibley, *The Port of Houston*, 13; see also Muir, *Texas in 1837*, 5.
4. Ramsdell, "Why Lafitte Became a Pirate," 465.
5. Sibley, *The Port of Houston*, 14.
6. Sibley, *The Port of Houston*, 15, citing Prichard, "George Graham's Mission to Galveston in 1818," see generally 619–50.

7. Sibley, *The Port of Houston*, 15. Stephen F. Austin was later a leader in the Texas independence movement and was referred to as the "Father of Texas." He served as Texas' first secretary of state.
8. Sibley, *The Port of Houston*, 18–19.
9. Sibley, *The Port of Houston*, 21.
10. Sibley, *The Port of Houston*, 21–22. The *Cayuga* also ferried David Burnet and Lorenzo de Zavala to safety from Harrisburg before Santa Anna destroyed it in April 1836.
11. "The Famous San Jacinto Battleground," 29.
12. The Congress of the Republic of Texas declared independence from Mexico on March 2, 1836. The Alamo would fall to Mexican General Antonio López de Santa Anna on March 6, but Santa Anna would himself be defeated at the Battle of San Jacinto on April 21, 1836, by General Sam Houston.
13. John Kirby Allen, Marker 10594, Texas Historical Survey Committee, Founders Memorial Park Cemetery, Houston, 1968. The land the Allen brothers purchased came from the Galveston Bay and Texas Land Company, which had in turn received the titles from prominent Texans, including David G. Burnet and Lorenzo de Zavala. These early Texans had received the land titles in an 1826 grant from the government of Coahuila y Texas.
14. K. Kirkland, *The Hogg Family*, 1.
15. Mexico declared independence in 1810, but this independence was not consummated until 1821 and still not officially recognized until 1836.
16. Archeological and historical evidence indicates that some Indians were present in the Harris County region earlier and survived by fishing and gathering. However, the area was not conducive to such a lifestyle, and by the 1820s all had migrated to more suitable areas. Houghton, *Houston's Forgotten Heritage*, 2.
17. Johnston, *Houston, the Unknown City*, 4.
18. Johnston, *Houston, the Unknown City*, 4.
19. Johnston, *Houston, the Unknown City*, 9. The Allens invited General Houston to dinner at their home in Nacogdoches during which Charlotte Allen asked for permission to name the city for him. Naturally, the guest of honor could not refuse his hostess.
20. Siegel and Moretta, *A Chronicle of the Bayou City*, 19.
21. The Battle of the Alamo and the advances of the Mexican army panicked the civilian population of Texas, who fled in an often chaotic manner. This mass exodus came to be called the "Runaway Scrape."
22. After the surrender of Santa Anna at San Jacinto, some Mexican soldiers were detained as prisoners of war and forced to clean up and repair damage the army had done. Repairs and rebuilding of the Harris family home was one of the tasks assigned. Houghton, *Houston's Forgotten Heritage*, 5.
23. Success was not so good for the Allen brothers. John Kirby contracted a fever or pneumonia, or both, and passed away August 15, 1838, at the age of twenty-eight. Augustus Chapman eventually fell into dispute with his wife about financial matters, separated, and finally signed over to her all his property in Harris County before leaving for Mexico. He served there as US consul, slowly rebuilding his investments before passing away from pneumonia in 1864. Both brothers are remembered in

Houston through sites named for them, including Allen Parkway and Allens Landing. See Williams, "Allen, Augustus Chapman."

24. Young, *Thumb-Nail History of the City of Houston*, 7.
25. Johnston, *Houston, the Unknown City*, 4.
26. Later historians would be critical of the lack of attention paid to Native Americans, slaves, or later freed black slaves, women, and other groups. Turner did not accord time to these groups in developing his thesis but focused instead on the broad swath of American society and its actions.
27. Ironically, the first railroad in Texas was chartered in 1850 as the Buffalo Bayou, Brazos, and Colorado Railway, which included service to the city of Harrisburg. The railroad did not make Harrisburg a significant city but did contribute to the growth of Houston on the main line between New Orleans and Los Angeles.
28. Cartwright, *Galveston*, 75.
29. E. King, *The Great South*, 111.
30. Johnston, *Houston, the Unknown City*, 9. It is interesting to note that Gail Borden was the inventor who created a process for condensed milk, famously marketed as Eagle Brand Condensed Milk, as well as other dairy products under the Borden name. The Texas county of Borden and its county seat of Gail are named for him. Crowley, "The Man Who Invented Elsie." His distant cousin Robert Borden was prime minister of Canada in the World War I era. His cousin Lizzie Borden was the famed defendant in the Fall River murders of her father and stepmother in 1892.
31. Fuermann, *Houston: The Once and Future City*, 19–21.
32. Sibley, *The Port of Houston*, 31.
33. Sibley, *The Port of Houston*, 32.
34. Sibley, *The Port of Houston*, 34.
35. Vela and Edward, *Reaching for the Sea*, 15.
36. Vela and Edward, *Reaching for the Sea*, 16.
37. Sibley, *The Port of Houston*, 34.
38. Sibley, *The Port of Houston*, 56.
39. Sibley, *The Port of Houston*, 56.
40. Sibley, *The Port of Houston*, 57.
41. Harrisburg is no longer a city but a community area in eastern Houston south of where Buffalo Bayou meets Brays Bayou. Harrisburg got a fresh start in 1853 as the starting point of the Buffalo Bayou, Brazos, and Colorado Railway, the first functioning railroad line in the state. However, the railyards were destroyed by fire in 1870 and rebuilt in Houston. What was finally left was simply annexed by Houston in 1926. McComb, *Houston, the Bayou City*, 35, 97.
42. McComb, *Houston, the Bayou City*, 58.
43. McComb, *Houston, the Bayou City*, 58.
44. Sibley, *The Port of Houston*, 38. Lubbock recorded in a letter that the "city" of Houston was not really much to notice, and they first went past it before coming back and then noticed stakes and footprints.
45. Sibley, *The Port of Houston*, 37.
46. Lardas, *Port of Houston*, 25.
47. Vela and Edward, *Reaching for the Sea*, 17.
48. Johnston, *Houston, the Unknown City*, 28.
49. Johnston, *Houston, the Unknown City*, 28.

50. Cartwright, *Galveston*, 82.
51. Sibley, *The Port of Houston*, 39.
52. Lardas, *Port of Houston*, 25–26.
53. Lardas, *Port of Houston*, 26.
54. Vela and Edward, *Reaching for the Sea*, 20.
55. Lardas, *Port of Houston*, 26.
56. Lardas, *Port of Houston*, 26.
57. Sibley, *The Port of Houston*, 57.
58. Sibley, *The Port of Houston*, 57–58.
59. Sibley, *The Port of Houston*, 58–59.
60. Sibley, *The Port of Houston*, 59.
61. Sibley, *The Port of Houston*, 67; *Port of Houston Magazine*, June 1924, 10.
62. Sibley, *The Port of Houston*, 61, quoting Chester Newell, *History of the Revolution in Texas* (New York: Wiley and Putnam, 1838), 35.
63. Roemer and Mueller, *Texas*, 70.
64. Roemer and Mueller, *Texas*, 61–62.
65. Roemer and Mueller, *Texas*, 72.
66. Roemer and Mueller, *Texas*, 72.
67. Roemer and Mueller, *Texas*, 72.
68. Lardas, *Port of Houston*, 26.
69. Sibley, *The Port of Houston*, 73. Francis Richard Lubbock was an early settler of Houston and, subsequent to this state tour on railroad planning, was elected lieutenant governor of Texas, then served as governor of Texas during part of the Civil War. Thomas William House was a leading cotton merchant who later served as mayor of Houston; his son, Colonel Edward House, would play an even greater role in Houston and the world; William Marsh Rice would leave his fortune to found Rice Institute (later, Rice University).
70. Sibley, *The Port of Houston*, 73.
71. Sibley, *The Port of Houston*, 74.
72. Sibley, *The Port of Houston*, 75.
73. Sibley, *The Port of Houston*, 79–80. His son, Colonel Edward Mandell House, would serve as a top adviser to President Wilson and become the most prominent Houstonian in world affairs until the George H. W. Bush administration.
74. Sibley, *The Port of Houston*, 80.
75. Confederate heavy artillery had already been withdrawn in fear of a Union attack and with the belief the island might be indefensible against sufficient Union force.
76. Sibley, *The Port of Houston*, 81, quoting Thomas North, *Five Years in Texas*, (Cincinnati: Elm Street Publishing, 1871), 102.
77. Marguerite Johnston's Notes on Dr. E. N. Gray, Subject Files 1830–1991, Box 11, Folder 1, Marguerite Johnston Barnes Collection, Research Materials for Houston, Woodson Research Center, Rice University (hereafter cited as Barnes Collection).
78. Lardas, *Port of Houston*, 26.
79. Lardas, *Port of Houston*, 26.
80. Johnston Notes, Box 11, Folder 1, Barnes Collection.
81. Lardas, *Port of Houston*, 26.
82. Horace Greely, New York journalist, 1871, quoted in Vela and Edward, *Reaching for the Sea*, 9.

83. Fisher, "Deep Water Houston," 3.
84. Sibley, *The Port of Houston*, 84.
85. Baughman, *Charles Morgan*, 25.
86. Baughman, *Charles Morgan*, 25.
87. Sibley, *The Port of Houston*, 88.
88. Lardas, *Port of Houston*, 26.
89. Lardas, *Port of Houston*, 26.
90. Sibley, *The Port of Houston*, 85.
91. Baughman, *Charles Morgan*, 200.
92. Johnston, *Houston, the Unknown City*, 73. The company, which would be owned by Charles Morgan by 1873, moved millions of bales of cotton down the bayou. See Reed, "Houston Direct Navigation Company."
93. Sibley, *The Port of Houston*, 103.
94. Sibley, *The Port of Houston*, 105.
95. Sibley, *The Port of Houston*, 106.
96. Sibley, *The Port of Houston*, 106.
97. Sibley, *The Port of Houston*, 107–8.
98. Lardas, *Port of Houston*, 39.
99. Morgan died in 1878, only two years after completing the water connection between Buffalo Bayou and the main waterway to Galveston Bay.
100. Jetties are artificial structures projecting out into the sea to both regulate water in a harbor and provide safety and guidance for ships.
101. Sibley, *The Port of Houston*, 114.
102. Sibley, *The Port of Houston*, 114.
103. Sibley, *The Port of Houston*, 115. President Wilson appointed Hutcheson's son, Joseph C. Hutcheson Jr., to the federal bench, and President Hoover elevated him to the Fifth Circuit. His grandson, Thad Hutcheson, would be a Republican candidate for US Senate in a 1957 special election.
104. Sibley, *The Port of Houston*, 115. Things could have gone the other way for Houston, for in the months preceding the visit of the committee, a prolonged and unusual drought occurred in the Houston area—"Buffalo Bayou had dwindled to a trickle." But a huge downpour occurred after the official delegation was en route from Washington, and "the bayou rose in its banks and then overflowed" (116). See Johnston, *Houston, the Unknown City*, 112.
105. Sibley, *The Port of Houston*, 118. Colonel Robert was already famous for having authored *Robert's Rules of Order*.
106. Sibley, *The Port of Houston*, 121–22.
107. Sibley, *The Port of Houston*, 123.
108. Sibley, *The Port of Houston*, 124.
109. Vela and Edward, *Reaching for the Sea*, 37.
110. Vela and Edward, *Reaching for the Sea*, 38.
111. McAshan, "A Houston Legacy," 137–42.
112. Burrough, *The Big Rich*, 128.
113. The prestigious Kirby Drive through the heart of River Oaks is named for John Henry Kirby.
114. See Blake and Gibney, *Most Intense United States Tropical Cyclones*.
115. Sibley, *The Port of Houston*, 133.

116. Sibley, *The Port of Houston*, 133. Horace Baldwin Rice was a nephew of William Marsh Rice.
117. Sibley, *The Port of Houston*, 134.
118. Sibley, *The Port of Houston*, 135.
119. Sibley, *The Port of Houston*, 136. Congressman Ball was quoted in the *Daily Post* on December 19, 1909, as saying that "prior to Houston's offer, no substantial contribution had ever been made by local interests to secure the adoption of their projects, and no project has since been adopted by the national government without promise of local contributions and assurances that the waterfront would not be privately controlled."
120. "The Port of Houston," November 1924, 5.
121. Jesse H. Jones was a banker, publisher, and real estate developer who would serve in Washington for President Wilson and President Roosevelt.
122. Sibley, *The Port of Houston*, 137.
123. Sibley, *The Port of Houston*, 138. Dillingham and Sterling were both prominent bankers, with Sterling later becoming governor of Texas. Dillingham was originally a Union Army officer but obviously well integrated into the southern city of Houston. Dillingham's home on Austin Street in Houston is now the headquarters of the Child Guidance Center. Biographical Note, 1858–1958, Dillingham Family Papers, Woodson Research Center, Rice University.

    Pillot was a founding partner of the Henke and Pillot supermarket chain, eventually acquired by Kroger. The Pillot family home, a mid-Victorian mansion, operates as a historic site in Sam Houston Park. It originally stood where the George R. Brown Convention Center is now located in downtown Houston.
124. Sibley, *The Port of Houston*, 138–39.
125. Texas Department of Transportation, *2005 Gulf Intercoastal Waterway*.
126. Sibley, *The Port of Houston*, 141.
127. The discovery of oil at Spindletop provided a major impetus to development of the Gulf Intracoastal Waterway.
128. "The Intracoastal Canal and What It Means to Houston," *Port Houston*, June 1925, 79.
129. Sibley, *The Port of Houston*, 141.
130. Sibley, *The Port of Houston*, 141.
131. Sibley, *The Port of Houston*, 144.
132. Sibley, *The Port of Houston*, 144.
133. Sibley, *The Port of Houston*, 144.
134. Vela and Edward, *Reaching for the Sea*, 47.
135. Sibley, *The Port of Houston*, 146. King Retaw, in the then popular fashion of spelling backward, was King Water, referring to the local society gala juxtaposed against the dark war of the great powers in Europe.
136. Sibley, *The Port of Houston*, 146–47.
137. Sibley, *The Port of Houston*, 147.
138. Sibley, *The Port of Houston*, 148.
139. Sibley, *The Port of Houston*, 148–49.
140. Lanoy, "Southern Steamship Company," 43–45.
141. Sibley, *The Port of Houston*, 149.
142. Cartwright, *Galveston*, 194; "Upper Texas Coast Tropical Cyclones in the 1910s."
143. Sibley, *The Port of Houston*, 150.

144. Sibley, *The Port of Houston*, 150.
145. Sibley, *The Port of Houston*, 151.
146. Sibley, *The Port of Houston*, 152–53.
147. Ross Sterling was president of Humble Oil, which developed into Exxon. He also developed real estate, owned two newspapers, and served on the state Highway Commission. He was elected governor in 1930 but was defeated after one term by Miriam Ferguson.
148. Sibley, *The Port of Houston*, 153.
149. Sibley, *The Port of Houston*, 153–54.
150. Sibley, *The Port of Houston*, 155.
151. Johnston, *Houston, the Unknown City*, 216.
152. Vela and Edward, *Reaching for the Sea*, 55.
153. Peden, "A Brief Survey," 31. (Peden was then chairman of the Houston Port Commission; Sterling was vice chairman.) The first issue of the *Port Magazine*'s cover read, "Where 17 Trunk Lines Meet the Sea," a reference to the very significant link of rail to port constructed at Houston.
154. Peden, "A Brief Survey," 31.
155. "A Record Breaking Cargo," *Port Houston*, June 1924, 19.
156. "A Record Breaking Cargo," 21.
157. "Chicago Cotton Market Recognizes the Port of Houston," *Port Houston*, May 1925, 27.
158. Sibley, *The Port of Houston*, 153.
159. McAshan, *A Houston Legacy*, 180–81.
160. The actual quote was "on a wave of oil." Yergin, *The Prize*, 183.
161. "A Record Breaking Cargo," 14.
162. Peden, "A Brief Survey," 1.
163. "Annual Cruise from Port Houston to West Indies," *Port Houston*, May 1925, 31.
164. Sibley, *The Port of Houston*, 158.
165. "The Port at Present," *Port Houston*, November 1923, 11.
166. "The Port at Present," 11.
167. "Houston Gets Texas' Largest Cold Storage Warehouse," *Houston Port and City*, November 1926, 55.
168. "Privately Owned Terminal and Industrial Facilities."
169. "Privately Owned Terminal and Industrial Facilities," 17–19.
170. "Fifth Annual Report," *Port Houston*, November 1925, 42.
171. Statement by Ernest L. Tutt, US Department of Commerce, published in "Houston's Foreign Trade," *Port Houston*, June 1927, 39.
172. "Passenger Service Through Port of Houston Developed," *Port Houston*, June 1924, 39.
173. Sibley, *The Port of Houston*, 159, 161.
174. Sibley, *The Port of Houston*, 161.
175. Sibley, *The Port of Houston*, 162.
176. Sibley, *The Port of Houston*, 164. There were unfortunate clashes between Houston and Galveston in the 1930s, including a time when Galveston papers refused to carry any news about Houston's No-Tsu-Oh water carnival or when delegations from the two cities literally came to blows in a Washington hotel lobby (165–66).
177. Vela and Edward, *Reaching for the Sea*, 41.

178. Sibley, *The Port of Houston*, 166–67.
179. Sibley, *The Port of Houston*, 167.
180. Sibley, *The Port of Houston*, 168.
181. Sibley, *The Port of Houston*, 168.
182. Sibley, *The Port of Houston*, 169.
183. Sibley, *The Port of Houston*, 169. Oscar Holcombe served twenty-two years as mayor of Houston in nonconsecutive terms spread across the 1920s–50s. He famously won a challenge by the Ku Klux Klan when he refused to fire Catholics from his administration. Holcombe Boulevard is named for him.
184. Sibley, *The Port of Houston*, 169.
185. "The Houston Port Bureau: Its Purposes and Accomplishments," *Houston Port and City*, June 1930, 25–26.
186. "The Houston Port Bureau," 25–26. Tom Connally would serve Texas in Congress from 1917 to 1953, first as a member of the House and later the Senate, where he would serve as chairman of the Senate Foreign Relations Committee during the time of both FDR and Truman. He was responsible for the US commitment to NATO. Biographical Note, 1924, 1931–52, Tom Connally Papers, Dolph Briscoe Center for American History, University of Texas at Austin (hereafter cited as Connally Papers).
187. Sibley, *The Port of Houston*, 171.
188. Sibley, *The Port of Houston*, 174.
189. "Development of Port Houston," *Houston Port Book*, November 1939, 36.
190. "Development of Port Houston," 52.
191. Sibley, *The Port of Houston*, 175.
192. Sibley, *The Port of Houston*, 180.
193. Sibley, *The Port of Houston*, 187.
194. "Scrap Iron and Steel," *Houston Port Book*, May 1937, 17.
195. "New Deal Trade Policy," US Department of State, Office of the Historian, accessed April 17, 2025, https://history.state.gov/milestones/1921-1936/export-import-bank.
196. Ben Bernanke said, "Economists still agree that Smoot-Hawley and the ensuing tariff wars were highly counterproductive and contributed to the depth and length of the global Depression." Bernanke, "Monetary Policy and the Global Economy."
197. Morse, "Study of American Merchant Marine Legislation," 57–81.
198. Sibley, *The Port of Houston*, 186.
199. "Building 'Liberty Ships' at Houston," *Houston Port Book*, November 1942, 38.
200. Its most famous ship built was the *Samuel B. Roberts*, which fought Japan's main battle fleet at the Battle of Leyte Gulf. Lardas, *Port of Houston*, 66.
201. Sibley, *The Port of Houston*, 190.
202. Lardas, *Port of Houston*, 66.
203. Lardas, *Port of Houston*, 73.
204. Sibley, *The Port of Houston*, 194.
205. "Port's 1947 Commerce Hits New All-Time High," *Houston Port Book*, May 1948, 45.
206. Sanguily, "International Houston," 43.
207. Fuermann, *Houston: Land of the Big Rich*, 142.
208. Bryan, "Development of Houston's Foreign Trade," 29.
209. "A Detailed Description of the Port," *Houston Port Book*, November 1949, 42.
210. *Houston Port Book*, November 1949, 62.

211. “World Trade Is a Two-Way Street,” *Houston Port Book,* November 1950, 32.
212. “Port of Houston Honored by Visit of the Duke and the Duchess of Windsor,” *Houston Port Book,* May 1950, 46.
213. Sibley, *The Port of Houston,* 204.
214. Lardas, *Port of Houston,* 77.
215. Lardas, *Port of Houston,* 77.
216. Johnston, *Houston, the Unknown City,* 229. The “shipping company” is referred to in the Tom Clancy novel *Red Storm Rising.* The Soviet LASH ship *Julius Fucik* is disguised as the *Doctor Lykes* for the attack on Iceland in the opening phases of the Soviet battle plan.
217. “Lykes,” advertisement, *Houston Port Book,* November 1949, 64.
218. Lardas, *Port of Houston,* 77.
219. Lardas, *Port of Houston,* 77.
220. Lardas, *Port of Houston,* 77.
221. Lardas, *Port of Houston,* 77.
222. Lardas, *Port of Houston,* 77–78.
223. Pasadena had grown from approximately 3,500 in 1940 to 22,500 in 1950 and to 151,950 in 2020. Galena Park was only 1,500 in 1940, but 7,000 in 1950 and 10,740 in 2020. La Porte was approximately 3,000 in 1940, 4,500 in 1950, and 35,124 in 2020. Baytown did not exist in 1940, but by 1950 an amalgamation of three small towns had formed Baytown with an approximate population of 23,000, which grew to 87,301 by 2020. Of course, today there is really no countryside as you move from one part of this region of Greater Houston to another—each city flows into the other in a constant landscape of urbanity. “Texas Almanac.”
224. Lardas, *Port of Houston,* 78.
225. Lardas, *Port of Houston,* 78.
226. McLean started his trucking company with a used truck, which he drove himself to haul empty tobacco barrels during the Depression. He developed a successful trucking company before selling it and buying a shipping company. McLean and a hundred invited dignitaries were on the dock when the *Ideal-X* left to sail from Newark to Houston carrying fifty-eight containers and a load of liquid cargo. He then flew to Houston to welcome its arrival later. “Malcolm McLean.”
227. *Houston Port Book,* Spring 1956, 33.
228. Lardas, *Port of Houston,* 91.
229. Lardas, *Port of Houston,* 92.
230. Lardas, *Port of Houston,* 100.
231. Railways had always been important to the Houston Ship Channel, but “trains have had an even greater role since the introduction of the standard shipping container,” as the rails can carry heavy loads, sometimes stacked two deep with containers, and connect across the nation and continent. Lardas, *Port of Houston,* 114.
232. Lardas, *Port of Houston,* 92. “The container revolution created its own language. Traffic was measured in TEUs, or twenty-foot equivalent units. The TEU represented the volume of a standard 20-foot long shipping container” (92).
233. Lardas, *Port of Houston,* 96.
234. Dethloff, *Suddenly, Tomorrow Came,* 38.
235. Lardas, *Port of Houston,* 91–92.
236. Lardas, *Port of Houston,* 98.

237. Sibley, *The Port of Houston*, 205.
238. Sibley, *The Port of Houston*, 205.
239. Clayton, "Clayton Urges More Trade," 12. Belgian Consul Andre Crispin was the first president of the club.
240. *Esso Houston* had a capacity of over 582,000 barrels of oil. "*Esso Houston*."
241. The HMS *London* had been commissioned only the year before in 1963. The United Kingdom used the ship as part of a fleet of missile cruisers and other battleships for deterrence against China in Asia, and in Hong Kong specifically, and as part of regular Mediterranean and Atlantic patrols. The HMS *London* represented the United Kingdom in New York in July 1976 for the Bicentennial celebrations in conjunction with the queen's official visit. The ship was sold to Pakistan in 1982 and later decommissioned in 1993.
242. "Britain in Texas Festival to Start Here in September," *Port of Houston Magazine*, September 1964, 17.
243. Sibley, *The Port of Houston*, 211.
244. "President Johnson Breaks Ground for 3 Docks on Port's 50th Anniversary," *Port of Houston Magazine*, December 1964, 8.
245. "President Johnson Breaks Ground," 8.
246. Lardas, *Port of Houston*, 98.
247. Lardas, *Port of Houston*, 92.
248. Lardas, *Port of Houston*, 104.
249. Lardas, *Port of Houston*, 111.
250. "Economic Impact of the Houston Ship Channel," Port Houston, 2025, https://porthouston.com/about/our-port/statistics/.
251. Lardas, *Port of Houston*, 104.
252. Lardas, *Port of Houston*, 92.
253. Vela and Edward, *Reaching for the Sea*, 84.
254. "1990 Economic Summit: Houston in the Spotlight," *Houston Port Magazine*, July 1990, 4–5.
255. Lardas, *Port of Houston*, 115. In fairness to Houston, it should be noted that the Port of South Louisiana is the former Port of New Orleans now combined with the whole of the shipping enterprise on the Mississippi River between New Orleans and Baton Rouge. Additionally, "its tonnage benefits from Mississippi barges loading oceangoing ships, allowing it to count the same tonnage twice" (115).
256. Lardas, *Port of Houston*, 116. The Port of Houston has major challenges ahead. Foremost is the current expansion of the Panama Canal, which will triple its cargo capacity and deepen its draft to sixty feet, much more than Houston's current depth of forty-five feet, and more cargo than Houston's current facilities can manage. Houston is looking at different ways to deepen its current waterways and add additional facilities to ensure that the valuable international trade coming through the Panama Canal still comes to Houston and not to another port (116).
257. Sibley, *The Port of Houston*, 208.

CHAPTER 2

1. Pratt et al., *Energy Capitals*, 30.
2. Pratt et al., *Energy Capitals*, 30.
3. Bredeson, *The Spindletop Gusher*, 7.

4. Bredeson, *The Spindletop Gusher*, 7–8.
5. A barrel of oil is forty-two gallons.
6. Pratt et al., *Energy Capitals*, 33.
7. The name "Gladys" came from Gladys Bingham, a young woman in a Sunday school class taught by Pattillo Higgins. Higgins sometimes took the class to the Spindletop area on field trips. One trick he enjoyed was to push a stick into the ground and then light the escaping gas. Bredeson, *The Spindletop Gusher*, 14.
8. Lucas had been born Anthony Luchich in modern-day Croatia. He served as an officer in the Austrian Imperial Navy before coming to the United States to visit an uncle in Michigan. Eventually, he became a naturalized citizen and married an American. By the time he met Higgins, Lucas had experience in mining both in Colorado and Louisiana. Olien and Olien, *Oil in Texas*, 28. See also Yergin, *The Prize*, 88.
9. The investors from Pittsburgh were brothers Andrew and Richard Mellon from a family already wealthy from banking. The brothers later sent their nephew William Mellon to Texas to check investments, and he determined that management of Guffey Petroleum and Gulf Oil had to be wrested from James Guffey. Yergin, *The Prize*, 88–89.
10. Lucas had stopped at 575 feet when there was no money to continue before obtaining the backing of some Pittsburgh investors. He kept drilling deeper, sure that the oil would be there in the salt dome formation. The gusher he later hit was named the Lucas Gusher. Olien and Olien, *Oil in Texas*, 29.
11. Bredeson, *The Spindletop Gusher*, 29–30.
12. Yergin, *The Prize*, 23.
13. Yergen, *The Prize*, 59.
14. Yergin, *The Prize*, 237–38. Nobel was nationalized in 1920 after the Bolsheviks seized power in the Caspian region. The Nobel family sold many of their shares to Standard Oil in the United States. The Rockefellers were expecting the Bolsheviks to be only a temporary setback.
15. Yergin, *The Prize*, 26–28.
16. Yergin, *The Prize*, 83–84.
17. The "Great White Fleet" was the nickname for a group of sixteen US Navy battleships sent on a round-the-world voyage to demonstrate growing US military power while making friendly visits. The hulls of the ships were painted white, a peacetime color.
18. Vela and Edward, *Reaching for the Sea*, 49.
19. Pratt et al., *Energy Capitals*, 34–35.
20. Vela and Edward, *Reaching for the Sea*, 50.
21. Pratt et al., *Energy Capitals*, 35.
22. Both Houston and the entire state more broadly benefited directly from the Texas oil boom from the state oil production tax first levied in 1905. This provided a lucrative income for many decades, financing state infrastructure and services without the need for a state income tax as was more common elsewhere. The absence of a state income tax was a significant incentive to attract entrepreneurs to Texas. Hamrick et al., "Relief from Severance Taxes."
23. Pratt et al., *Energy Capitals*, 35.
24. Pratt et al., *Energy Capitals*, 35.
25. Pratt et al., *Energy Capitals*, 38.

26. Pratt et al., *Energy Capitals*, 39.
27. Pratt et al., *Energy Capitals*, 39.
28. Pratt et al., *Energy Capitals*, 37.
29. Pratt et al., *Energy Capitals*, 37.
30. Bredeson, *The Spindletop Gusher*, 43.
31. Bredeson, *The Spindletop Gusher*, 27.
32. Bredeson, *The Spindletop Gusher*, 33. Spindletop continued to decline until the site was nearly abandoned in 1924. But the Younts Oil Company introduced a new drilling method in 1925 that hit another large reservoir and created a second Spindletop oil boom. This too declined after a few years. However, the Younts-Lee Oil Company was successful long term. It was sold in 1935 at great profit to Stanolind Oil, and its assets were eventually acquired by Amoco. Two of the Younts founders, brothers Thomas Peter Lee and William Ellsworth Lee, were remarkable in many ways. Thomas was an active Republican who declined the gubernatorial nomination in 1924. He built a stunning mansion in Houston, Lee House, which is now the centerpiece of the University of St. Thomas (Klein, "T. P. Lee"). William, besides his success in oil, was also prominent in banking and civic affairs. His daughter, Faustine, married Glenn McCarthy, the famous wildcatter who built the Shamrock Hotel in 1947 and inspired the character Jett Rink in Edna Ferber's *Giant*. William's son, William Howard, was first married to movie star Hedy Lamarr and then to Gene Tierney (Oscar-nominated actress who had first been married to Oleg Cassini), who returned with him to live in River Oaks (Tierney and Herskowitz, *Self-Portrait*, 217; Joanne Herring, interview).
33. Yergin, *The Prize*, 95.
34. Bredeson, *The Spindletop Gusher*, 36.
35. Bredeson, *The Spindletop Gusher*, 37.
36. Bredeson, *The Spindletop Gusher*, 37.
37. Bredeson, *The Spindletop Gusher*, 43.
38. Bredeson, *The Spindletop Gusher*, 43.
39. Henry Ford first produced an automobile in 1896, essentially a four-wheeled bicycle powered by a small engine (Bredeson, *The Spindletop Gusher*, 43). Ford would eventually sell fifteen million of his Model T's (45).
40. Bredeson, *The Spindletop Gusher*, 45.
41. Bredeson, *The Spindletop Gusher*, 45.
42. Sibley, *The Port of Houston*, 151–52.
43. Karl Benz, a German engineer, was the first to patent a gasoline-powered engine in 1879. By 1885, he had built the first gasoline automobile. His company, the Benz Company, later merged to become Daimler-Benz, although the cars were called Mercedes-Benz, beginning in 1901, for Mercedes Jellinek, daughter of Austrian engineer Emil Jellinek. Krebs, "Her Name Still Rings a Bell."
44. At one time, Standard Oil was barred from Texas and its assets placed into receivership for sale. The sale occurred at the Driskill Hotel in Austin, but the buyers turned out to be agents for Standard Oil. Yergin, *The Prize*, 97.
45. After leaving office, Sayers served as a regent of the University of Texas and supported the school in its struggle with Governor James A. Ferguson. He also chaired the Industrial Accident Board, later the Texas Workers Compensation Commission, now merged into the Texas Department of Insurance.

46. Chernow, *Titan*, 431.
47. Pratt et al., *Energy Capitals*, 36.
48. J. King, *Joseph Stephen Cullinan*, 93.
49. J. King, *Joseph Stephen Cullinan*, 93.
50. J. King, *Joseph Stephen Cullinan*, 94.
51. Pratt et al., *Energy Capitals*, 36.
52. Pratt et al., *Energy Capitals*, 36. "So many people rode trains to Houston seeking work at Hughes Tool that conductors would at times simply call out 'Hughes Tool' instead of 'Houston' at the main railroad station in the city" (36).
53. Pratt et al., *Energy Capitals*, 36–37.
54. Pratt et al., *Energy Capitals*, 37.
55. Yergin, *The Prize*, 92. Sun became, and remains, a publicly traded corporation and expanded to international operations. It moved its headquarters from Philadelphia to Dallas in 2016. The Pew family established the Pew Charitable Trusts, which distributes millions in grants each year from an endowment of over $5 billion.
56. Sibley, *The Port of Houston*, 152.
57. Sampson, *The Seven Sisters*, 40.
58. J. King, *Joseph Stephen Cullinan*, 4.
59. J. King, *Joseph Stephen Cullinan*, 4.
60. J. King, *Joseph Stephen Cullinan*, 64.
61. J. King, *Joseph Stephen Cullinan*, 66–67.
62. Sampson, *The Seven Sisters*, 40.
63. Eventually Cullinan and Schlaet would have disagreements over management of the company, and finally "in 1913 a whole contingent of stockholders came down from New York to Houston in a special railroad car" and ousted Cullinan. The board then recruited a new leader from the East Coast, Elgood Lufkin. Sampson, *The Seven Sisters*, 40.
64. Sampson, *The Seven Sisters*, 40.
65. One of Cullinan's prominent business partners was Will Hogg, son of a former governor and a major land developer in Houston, especially of River Oaks. J. A. Lomax, *Will Hogg, Texan*, 9.
66. J. King, *Joseph Stephen Cullinan*, 96.
67. Yergin, *The Prize*, 94.
68. Williamson and Daum, *The American Petroleum Industry*, 83–84.
69. J. King, *Joseph Stephen Cullinan*, 100–102.
70. J. King, *Joseph Stephen Cullinan*, 68.
71. J. King, *Joseph Stephen Cullinan*, 69.
72. J. King, *Joseph Stephen Cullinan*, 70.
73. J. King, *Joseph Stephen Cullinan*, 211.
74. J. King, *Joseph Stephen Cullinan*, 72.
75. Yergin, *The Prize*, 94.
76. J. King, *Joseph Stephen Cullinan*, 183.
77. Sampson, *The Seven Sisters*, 41.
78. *Texaco Star* 50, no. 2 (1963).
79. *Texaco Star* 50, no. 2 (1963).

80. J. King, *Joseph Stephen Cullinan*, 213. He also served in the Food Administration in World War I as a special adviser to Herbert Hoover. In the 1920s, he served on the Mount Rushmore Committee as that national monument was being designed and constructed.
81. Vela and Edward, *Reaching for the Sea*, 50.
82. J. King, *Joseph Stephen Cullinan*, 211.
83. J. King, *Joseph Stephen Cullinan*, 211–12. Earle Mayfield won the Democratic primary for governor of Texas in 1922; however, a group of prominent Democrats were so offended by his affiliation with the KKK that they drafted George Peddy, a Houston lawyer later with Vinson and Elkins, to run. Peddy had to run as a write-in because it was too late for Republican Party officials to put his name on the ballot (no Republican primary for governor had occurred that year). Mayfield won the election by an almost 2-to-1 margin; however, he served only one term before Tom Connally defeated him in the 1928 Democratic primary. Fleming, "Peddy, George Edwin Bailey"; Smyrl, "Mayfield, Earle Bradford."
84. J. King, *Joseph Stephen Cullinan*, 212.
85. James, *The Texaco Story*, 67–68.
86. Hochschild, *Spain in Our Hearts*, 168.
87. Exxon and Mobil later bought into Aramco. After the 1973 Arab-Israeli War the Saudi government bought a stake in Aramco, adding to it over time until they owned all of it by 1980. In 1988, they renamed the company Saudi Aramco; it was the world's largest company by 2005 with a market value of $781 billion. Yergin, *The Prize*, 410.
88. Philby recommended his son, Kim Philby, to MI-6, who engaged him as an agent. The young Philby rose to high rank in the Secret Intelligence Service before seeking asylum in Moscow in 1963 and being exposed as a Soviet agent. Yergin, *The Prize*, 290–91.
89. Sampson, *The Seven Sisters*, 81.
90. Hochschild, *Spain in Our Hearts*, 170.
91. Sampson, *The Seven Sisters*, 81. US Attorney General Homer Cummings had threatened publicly to indict Rieber after first discussing the matter with President Roosevelt.
92. Hochschild, "The Untold Story."
93. Goering committed suicide by swallowing cyanide while awaiting execution by hanging after his conviction at Nuremberg in 1946.
94. Hochschild, *Spain in Our Hearts*, 357; Hochschild, "The Untold Story."
95. Hochschild, "The Untold Story." Rieber met with Goering again in 1940 and took a message from Hitler to Roosevelt asking for support for a united Europe led by Germany.
96. Sampson, *The Seven Sisters*, 82–83. It is also interesting to note that after Rieber was forced to resign, part of Texaco's response to public outrage was to begin, just a few months later, to sponsor the radio broadcast of the Metropolitan Opera in New York. This arrangement continued for sixty-three years until Texaco merged with Chevron in 2003 and discontinued the sponsorship.
97. Sampson, *The Seven Sisters*, 94–95.
98. Sampson, *The Seven Sisters*, 95.

99. The pipeline is no longer used due to political and military issues over the years and the greater availability of oil tankers for transport.
100. Sampson, *The Seven Sisters*, 99.
101. Sampson, *The Seven Sisters*, 100.
102. Sampson, *The Seven Sisters*, 104.
103. Sampson, *The Seven Sisters*, 38–40. Gulf would eventually be acquired by Chevron. Yergin, *The Prize*, 738–39.
104. Sampson, *The Seven Sisters*, 40.
105. Sampson, *The Seven Sisters*, 39.
106. Sampson, *The Seven Sisters*, 92. Mellon previously served as secretary of the treasury in the Hoover administration. However, he was forced to resign and was given London as a consolation prize. So intense was FDR's dislike of Mellon that in 1933, the president replaced him and sought to have him indicted.
107. The Gulf brand was replaced by Chevron in 1986 but was revitalized in 2010. "Company History."
108. Ross Sterling, as governor of Texas, would prove crucial to the Texas oil industry and global petroleum prices. He called a special session of the Texas legislature in 1932 to pass a bill giving the Texas Railroad Commission authority to issue prorationing orders to maintain price stability and prevent "chaotic production." Yergin, *The Prize*, 251.
109. Yergin, *The Prize*, 128.
110. Joiner was called "Dad" because he was considered the "daddy" of the East Texas oil boom. Yergin, *The Prize*, 244.
111. Yergin, *The Prize*, 246–48. H. L. Hunt would bring in many more wells in the area and form the Hunt Oil Company.
112. Yergin, *The Prize*, 254. Miriam A. Ferguson became governor of Texas on January 13, 1933, for a two-year term, having already served a term during 1925–27. She replaced Governor Ross Sterling, who had improved regulation of oil production but could not, in the face of legal and political obstacles, do enough to control pricing.
113. Yergin, *The Prize*, 254.
114. White and Maze, *Harold Ickes of the New Deal*, 87, 98.
115. Yergin, *The Prize*, 254.
116. Yergin, *The Prize*, 255.
117. Yergin, *The Prize*, 256.
118. Tom Connally was a powerful Texas senator for fourteen years, serving previously in Congress for twelve years. He chaired the Senate Foreign Relations Committee for ten years and was instrumental in the formation of NATO. Senator Connally and his family were important to Houston not just in energy but also in the Port of Houston and expansion of the Houston Ship Channel. Biographical Note, 1924, 1931–52, Connally Papers.
119. The act was known as the Connally Hot Oil Act.
120. Yergin, *The Prize*, 259.
121. Kraemer and Newell, *Texas Politics*.
122. Olien and Olien, *Oil in Texas*, 220.
123. Sampson, *The Seven Sisters*, 144–45.
124. Lord Beaverbrook was born a commoner, Max Aitken, in Canada and became rich at an early age in business and newspapers both in Canada and the United

Kingdom. He became involved in British politics and was created a baron in 1917. "Lord Beaverbrook."

125. Timmons, *Jesse H. Jones*, 304.
126. Pratt et al., *Energy Capitals*, 40.
127. Pratt et al., *Energy Capitals*, 40.
128. "Uses in Industry." Ethane is used to produce ethylene, which in turn has many uses in the global economy as diverse as plastics production or in agriculture to speed the ripening of fruits. Butane is used in gasoline production and as a stand-alone fuel for lighters. It is used in cartridges for cordless hair irons and as a propellant in aerosol sprays. Propane is often used as a heating or cooking fuel and is especially common for portable stoves or barbecues or for travel trailer heating and cooking.
129. Pratt et al., *Energy Capitals*, 40.
130. Pratt et al., *Energy Capitals*, 40.
131. Pratt et al., *Energy Capitals*, 40.
132. Pratt et al., *Energy Capitals*, 40–41.
133. Pratt et al., *Energy Capitals*, 41.
134. Bredeson, *The Spindletop Gusher*, 48.
135. Pratt et al., *Energy Capitals*, 41.
136. OPEC was established in 1960 in Baghdad by Saudi Arabia, Iran, Iraq, Kuwait, and Venezuela. It is headquartered in Vienna and has grown to thirteen nations with the addition of Algeria, Angola, Equatorial Guinea, Gabon, Libya, Nigeria, the Republic of the Congo, and the United Arab Emirates. Ecuador, Indonesia, and Qatar are former members.
137. William P. Clements Jr. would later serve as governor of Texas during 1979–83 and 1987–91.
138. Sampson, *The Seven Sisters*, 246.
139. "Historical Population: 1900 to 2017, City of Houston," 2017, https://www.houstontx.gov/planning/Demographics/docs_pdfs/Cy/hist_pop_1900_2017.pdf.
140. Pratt et al., *Energy Capitals*, 42.
141. Sampson, *The Seven Sisters*, 10.
142. Sampson, *The Seven Sisters*, 12–13.
143. Pratt et al., *Energy Capitals*, 41–42.
144. Pratt et al., *Energy Capitals*, 41.
145. Pratt et al., *Energy Capitals*, 51.
146. Sampson, *The Seven Sisters*, 184. The Houston Oilers moved to Tennessee in 1997 and were the Tennessee Oilers for two seasons before becoming the Tennessee Titans in 1999.
147. Pratt et al., *Energy Capitals*, 41.
148. Pratt et al., *Energy Capitals*, 57.

CHAPTER 3

1. "Facts and Figures—Texas Medical Center."
2. "Facts and Figures—Texas Medical Center."
3. Macon, *Monroe Dunaway Anderson*, 72.
4. Tinsley Narrative, Box 35, Folder 2, 1, Texas Medical Center, McGovern Historical Collections and Research Center (hereafter cited as Tinsley Narrative).
5. Tinsley Narrative, Box 35, Folder 2, 1.

6. Kellar, *Enduring Legacy*, 3.
7. Kellar, *Enduring Legacy*, 3. Another famous surgeon of early Texas is Anson Jones, who served as a physician to the troops of General Sam Houston at the Battle of San Jacinto. He served the new Republic of Texas as ambassador to Washington and later as president of the republic from 1844 to 1846 when Texas joined the United States (3).
8. An "Anti-Rat Society [was formed in 1839] with the goal of destroying [a particularly bad] infestation." Kellar, *Enduring Legacy*, 4.
9. Kellar, *Enduring Legacy*, 4.
10. Kellar, *Enduring Legacy*, 5. Yellow fever is an acute viral infection spread by mosquitoes. It causes fever, chills, nausea, and muscle aches. In some people, the infection enters a second phase where liver damage causes jaundiced skin and bleeding, which can be fatal. "Yellow Fever Virus."
11. Kellar, *Enduring Legacy*, 13–14.
12. Kellar, *Enduring Legacy*, 13–14.
13. Kellar, *Enduring Legacy*, 14–15.
14. Boutwell, "George Hermann and His Hospital."
15. Kellar, *Enduring Legacy*, 18. The city hospital was constructed over a Confederate soldier burial ground, and in an effort to placate a public uproar, Houston Mayor Oscar Holcombe named "the hospital after Jefferson Davis, the president of the Confederacy" (18).
16. Kellar, *Enduring Legacy*, 18.
17. Boutwell, "George Hermann and His Hospital."
18. Kellar, *Enduring Legacy*, 18; Boutwell, "George Hermann and His Hospital."
19. Macon, *Monroe Dunaway Anderson*, 1–2.
20. Will Clayton would serve as an appointee of Presidents Roosevelt and Truman, ultimately becoming undersecretary of state and a "principal architect of the Marshall Plan." Tinsley Narrative, Box 35, Folder 1, 11. Will Clayton also initiated the Clayton Center for International Economic Affairs at Tufts University (12).
21. Macon, *Monroe Dunaway Anderson*, 10–12.
22. Macon, *Monroe Dunaway Anderson*, 27.
23. Kellar, *Enduring Legacy*, 49–50.
24. Tinsley Narrative, Box 35, Folder 1, 5.
25. Tinsley Narrative, Box 35, Folder 1, 6.
26. Garwood, *Will Clayton*, 100.
27. M. D. Anderson Plaza Act, Pub. L. No. 112-85, 125 Stat. 1872 (2012).
28. Anderson, Clayton and Co. The company diversified into other businesses, including the food lines Chiffon margarine and Seven Seas salad dressings, as well as coffee, cocoa, and soybeans. It maintained cotton firms in over forty countries, launched subsidiary businesses in insurance, and acquired Igloo, itself a Katy-based Houston global company and producer of ice chests. Quaker Oats acquired Anderson, Clayton in 1986 and closed the Houston headquarters. M. D. Anderson Plaza Act, Pub. L. No. 112-85, 125 Stat. 1872 (2012).
29. Kellar, *Enduring Legacy*, 50.
30. Kellar, *Enduring Legacy*, 49.
31. Crooker "crusaded against the Ku Klux Klan in the twenties and played a key role in the legal maneuvers that preserved Lyndon B. Johnson's election to the United

States Senate in 1948" (Gresham and Tinsley, "Crooker, John Henry"). Before leaving his post as district attorney, one of his last acts was to file suit to remove the executors of George Hermann, who had left his fortune to build a hospital. But there was widespread dissatisfaction that those wishes had still not been carried out years after Hermann's death. The successor district attorney, James A. Elkins, got new trustees appointed, including Ross Sterling. Elkins was a founding partner of what grew to be the international firm of Vinson & Elkins based in Houston. Elkins was a regular attendee of the Suite 8F group.

32. Macon, *South from Flower Mountain*. Bates had also interviewed with Vinson & Elkins, but while waiting to hear back from them, he got a job offer from Fulbright and Crooker (Kellar, *Enduring Legacy*, 62–63). Bates also represented Texas oilman Glenn McCarthy, who was referred to as "King of the Wildcatters" and the builder of the legendary Shamrock Hotel (Davis, *Corduroy Road*, 245–56).
33. Kellar, *Enduring Legacy*, 62.
34. Kellar, *Enduring Legacy*, 65.
35. Tinsley Narrative, Box 35, Folder 1, 8.
36. Thomas Dunaway Anderson, Oral History, Box 15, Folder 1, 8, Texas Medical Center, McGovern Historical Collections and Research Center (hereafter cited as Anderson, Oral History).
37. Anderson, Oral History, Box 15, Folder 1, 9.
38. Kellar, *Enduring Legacy*, 70.
39. Kellar, *Enduring Legacy*, 73–74.
40. Tinsley Narrative, Box 35, Folder 1, 9.
41. Kellar, *Enduring Legacy*, 77.
42. Kellar, *Enduring Legacy*, 77.
43. Tinsley Narrative, Box 35, Folder 1, 1.
44. Tinsley Narrative, Box 35, Folder 1, 1–2.
45. With his advertising experience, Albert Lasker famously advised Margaret Sanger to change the name of Birth Control Federation into something positive like Planned Parenthood. Tinsley Narrative, Box 35, Folder 1, 4.
46. Tinsley Narrative, Box 35, Folder 1, 3–4.
47. Tinsley Narrative, Box 35, Folder 1, 2–3.
48. Kellar, *Enduring Legacy*, 76.
49. Tinsley Narrative, Box 35, Folder 1, Chapter 2, 3.
50. Kellar, *Enduring Legacy*, 78.
51. Tinsley Narrative, Box 35, Folder 1, Chapter 1, 1.
52. Kellar, *Enduring Legacy*, 78–79.
53. W. B. Bates, "History and Development of the Texas Medical Center" (November 20, 1956), Texas Medical Center, McGovern Historical Collections, Box 36, Folder 2.
54. Draft, "John H. Freeman and Friends," Texas Medical Center, McGovern Historical Collections, Box 22, Folder 7.
55. Draft, "John H. Freeman and Friends," 9–10.
56. Draft, "John H. Freeman and Friends," 11.
57. Tinsley Narrative, Box 35, Folder 1, 1.
58. Bates became a partner in 1940 and had been particularly involved with Monroe D. Anderson in the establishment of the foundation. Kellar, *Enduring Legacy*, 62, 80.

59. Kellar, *Enduring Legacy*, 81. Galveston had continued to press for the cancer hospital but was undermined by the dean of the UT Medical School, John Spies, who plotted to move the school to Houston. A struggle ensued between the dean and the regents, and in the end, the UT regents placed the hospital in Houston but also fired Spies. The American Medical Association by 1942 had placed the Galveston school on probation. Spies may have been a poor manager, but he had excellent medical credentials, including a degree from Harvard and experience teaching at Yale and in Peking. He was serving as director of Tata Memorial Hospital in Bombay when he was recruited to be dean of UT Medical Branch. Tinsley Narrative, Box 35, Folder 1, Chapter 2, 1.
60. Tinsley Narrative, Box 35, Folder 1, Chapter 1, 1.
61. Tinsley Narrative, Box 35, Folder 1, Chapter 1, 4.
62. Wygant, "Aynesworth, Kenneth Hazen." He was also instrumental in the acquisition of important new collections for UT on Latin American and Texas history. He donated his large collection of Texan and American Indian artifacts to Baylor, his undergraduate alma mater.
63. John H. Bickett Jr. Papers, 1916–70, Dolph Briscoe Center for American History, University of Texas at Austin.
64. His grandson Daniel III and brother are billionaires with large Texas landholdings and a famous Quarter Horse breeding operation. "Daniel Harrison, III."
65. Gesick, "Weinert, Hilmar Herman."
66. Keith, *Eckhardt*, 94.
67. His collection of western art, crystal, porcelain, and rare botanical books and prints is in the Stark Museum in Orange as well as in his restored mansion, Stark House. Maxwell and Baker, *Sawdust Empire*.
68. Homer Price Rainey Papers, 1861, 1938–46, 1961–74, 1985, 1991, Dolph Briscoe Center for American History, University of Texas at Austin.
69. Kellar, *Enduring Legacy*, 84; Tinsley Narrative, Box 35, Folder 1, Chapter 2, 6–9.
70. Steven Fenberg, Oral Histories, Texas Medical Center, McGovern Historical Collections, Box 15, 4 (hereafter cited as Fenberg, Oral Histories).
71. Searcy Bracewell, Oral Histories, Texas Medical Center, McGovern Historical Collections, Box 15, 7 (hereafter cited as Bracewell, Oral Histories).
72. Bracewell, Oral Histories, Box 15, 8, 10–11.
73. Bracewell, Oral Histories, Box 15, 19.
74. Tinsley Narrative, Box 35, Folder 1, Chapter 2, 8.
75. Tinsley Narrative, Box 35, Folder 1, Chapter 2, 9.
76. Draft, "John H. Freeman and Friends," Box 22, Folder 7, 13; see also Kellar, *Enduring Legacy*, 93. The Freemans and the Bertners lived on the same floor of the Rice Hotel and had opportunities to discuss a broader vision for Houston.
77. Kellar, *Enduring Legacy*, 95–96.
78. Tinsley Narrative, Box 35, Folder 1, Chapter 2, 1.
79. Charter of Texas Medical Center, McGovern Historical Collections, Box 36, Folder 2, 1.
80. Charter of Texas Medical Center, Box 36, Folder 2, 6; see also Charter of Texas Medical Center, Box 37, Folder 2.
81. Kellar, *Enduring Legacy*, 98. The name was an invention since at the time there was no University of Dallas.

82. Kellar, *Enduring Legacy*, 99.
83. Carr Collins was the son of Vinson Allen Collins, who had served in the Texas Senate and carried the legislation that established the Texas Industrial Accident Board, the Texas workers compensation system, and the eight-hour work day. He ran unsuccessfully against Martin Dies for Congress and then against Miriam Ferguson for governor. His son, Carr, became the first secretary of the Industrial Accident Board in 1913 after his father's enabling legislation.

    D. K. Martin was a graduate of Baylor. In 1954, the men's dormitory D. K. Martin Hall was opened and named in his honor.

    Kokernot came from a distinguished Texas ranching family. His grandfather David Kokernot was a Dutch immigrant who served as a scout for Sam Houston. The family acquired ranchland in West Texas, eventually amounting to one-half million acres with one of the state's leading Hereford herds. Besides serving as a trustee of Baylor University, Herbert Lee Kokernot was president of the Cattle Raisers Association, a regent of Texas A&M, president of the board of the San Marcos Baptist Academy, and chairman of the board of the Texas Baptist Foundation.
84. Kellar, *Enduring Legacy*, 102.
85. Kellar, *Enduring Legacy*, 102–5.
86. Kellar, *Enduring Legacy*, 105–6. The Southwestern trustees told the city and county governments of Dallas "that they actually had control of Baylor College of Medicine, despite their insistence to Baylor during the merger talks that this was not their intention." They went as far as to sign a contract with Dallas that Parkland Hospital would "be used only by a medical college that was not part of any denominational institution," meaning that Baylor College of Medicine would be forced to admit that it was not controlled by Baylor University or its personnel would be excluded from Parkland Hospital. The Baylor trustees were dismayed and voted to annul the agreement (105–6).
87. Tinsley Narrative, Box 35, Folder 1, Chapter 2, 16–17.
88. Kellar, *Enduring Legacy*, 107–8.
89. W. B. Bates, "History and Development of the Texas Medical Center," Box 36, Folder 2.
90. Draft, "John H. Freeman and Friends," Box 22, Folder 7, 20.
91. Tinsley Narrative, Box 35, Folder 1, Chapter 2, 24.
92. Kellar, *Enduring Legacy*, 109.
93. Kellar, *Enduring Legacy*, 109–11.
94. Kellar, *Enduring Legacy*, 112–13.
95. Jack S. Blanton, Oral Histories, McGovern Historical Collections, Box 15, 8. Blanton's father served as general manager of the Houston Chamber of Commerce from 1929 until the early 1950s (2).
96. Kellar, *Enduring Legacy*, 114–15. The Baylor College of Medicine opened in 1948 after having received an additional $800,000 of funding from Roy and Lillie Cullen, using their oil fortune from Houston's energy boom to fund another boom for the city: health care. The Baylor building was named the Cullen Building and was the first air-conditioned building erected in postwar Houston (129–30).
97. Tinsley Narrative, Box 35, Folder 1, Chapter 3, 1.
98. Anderson, Oral History, Box 15, 13–15.
99. There was briefly a Naval Hospital in Houston located in the same complex that helped establish the concept of "a variety of medical facilities within close proximity

to each other," but it closed a few years after World War II. Tinsley Narrative, Box 35, Folder 1, Chapter 3, 3.

100. Tinsley Narrative, Box 35, Folder 1, Chapter 2, 12.
101. Kellar, *Enduring Legacy*, 119–20. This despite an earlier assurance by Rainey to Baylor and MD Anderson Foundation that he had no objection to the relocation of the Baylor College of Medicine to Houston and the formation of the medical center there (105).
102. Kellar, *Enduring Legacy*, 120.
103. Kellar, *Enduring Legacy*, 120–21. In response, Rainey publicly listed his areas of disagreement with the regents at a faculty meeting in October after which the board fired him on November 1, 1944, while meeting at the Rice Hotel in Houston.
104. Kellar, *Enduring Legacy*, 121.
105. Fenberg, Oral Histories, Box 15, 4; Charter of Texas Medical Center, Alan Gregg Diaries, McGovern Historical Collections, Box 37, 1.
106. Charter of Texas Medical Center, Alan Gregg Diaries, Box 37, 5.
107. Charter of Texas Medical Center, Alan Gregg Diaries, Box 37, 6.
108. Texas Medical Center Dedicatory Dinner, "Dinner Program," Mary Schiflett Papers, Box 5, Folder 1, Texas Medical Center, John P. McGovern Historical Collections and Research Center (hereafter cited as Schiflett Papers).
109. Tinsley Narrative, Box 35, Folder 1, Chapter 3, 20.
110. Charter of Texas Medical Center, "The Future of the Medical Center," McGovern Historical Collections, Box 37.
111. Charter of Texas Medical Center, Board of Trustees, Letter from George A. Hill to Paul J. Heff, McGovern Historical Collections, Box 37, Folder 3.
112. Kellar, *Enduring Legacy*, 125.
113. Tinsley Narrative, Box 35, Folder 1, Chapter 3, 10. The Cullens had five children, one boy and four girls. Daughter Margaret would marry Douglas Marshall, who famously lobbied President Johnson on behalf of Lebanon. Daughter Wilhemina married Corbin Robertson, a successful oilman whose son Corbin Jr. captained the UT Longhorns to a Cotton Bowl victory in 1969 and then made a new fortune in coal. The Cullens are also famous for their philanthropy to the University of Houston that began in the tragic circumstance of their only son's death in 1936 in an oil field accident. The Cullens donated the first building on the UH campus as a memorial to Roy Jr.
114. The Cullens later gave another $1 million to Memorial Baptist for a nursing school and $1 million to the Catholic Infirmary for a Cullen Family Children's Building. They became major players in Houston's new role in health care. Tinsley Narrative, Box 35, Folder 1, Chapter 3, 8.
115. Tinsley Narrative, Box 35, Folder 1, Chapter 5, 16–17.
116. Tinsley Narrative, Box 35, Folder 1, Chapter 5, 7.
117. Tinsley Narrative, Box 35, Folder 1, Chapter 5, 9. The Fondrens' grandson, David Underwood, served for decades on the board of the Texas Medical Center. David M. Underwood, Oral Histories, McGovern Historical Collections, Box 16, 7.
118. *Texas Medical News*, June 1950, McGovern Historical Collections, Box 15, Folder 1.
119. Tinsley Narrative, Box 35, Folder 1, Chapter 5, 22–23.
120. Tinsley Narrative, Box 35, Folder 1, Chapter 5, 23. The Lutherans were latecomers to the churches involved at Texas Medical Center. They did not build a separate

hospital, but using initial funding from Marshall and Lillie Johnson, they constructed a Lutheran Pavilion as a new wing of MD Anderson for outpatient services and coupled it with a chaplaincy service. The new addition was opened in 1976 with Betty Ford and Lady Bird Johnson present for the ceremony. Tinsley Narrative, Box 35, Folder 1, Chapter 7, 5–15.

121. Tinsley Narrative, Box 35, Folder 1, Chapter 3, 13.
122. Oveta Culp Hobby would later serve as secretary of health, education, and welfare in the Eisenhower administration and is noted as the federal official who approved the Salk polio vaccine.
123. Tinsley Narrative, Box 35, Folder 1, Chapter 3, 14.
124. Kellar, *Enduring Legacy*, 126; Tinsley Narrative, Box 35, Folder 1, Chapter 3, 23.
125. Saxon, "Lee Clark." Clark helped shape the National Cancer Act of 1971, which designated MD Anderson as one of the three comprehensive cancer centers in the nation. Clark served as senior scientist on the President's Cancer Panel under Nixon, Ford, and Carter. He served as president of the American Cancer Society and was a frequent international speaker. See also Tinsley Narrative, Box 35, Folder 1, Chapter 3, 24–25.
126. Kellar, *Enduring Legacy*, 127.
127. Publicity Materials 1948, McGovern Historical Collections, Box 37, Folder 3.
128. Kellar, *Enduring Legacy*, 128–29.
129. Tinsley Narrative, Box 35, Folder 1, Chapter 3, 27.
130. Publicity Materials 1948, "Can Houston Become a Top Medical Center?," March 4, 1948, Box 37, Folder 3. Paul de Kruif served in General Pershing's expedition into Mexico in pursuit of Pancho Villa and later served in World War I, where he worked with French biologists. He worked as a doctor, medical professor, and then a writer, producing many books and articles involving science and medicine.
131. Publicity Materials 1946, *Milwaukee Journal*, September 22, 1946, McGovern Historical Collections, Box 37, Folder 3.
132. Publicity Materials 1949, Memorandum, December 10, 1949, McGovern Historical Collections, Box 43, Folder 2, 4.
133. Publicity Materials 1949, Memorandum, December 10, 1949, McGovern Historical Collections, Box 37.
134. Kellar, *Enduring Legacy*, 133.
135. Kellar, *Enduring Legacy*, 137–38.
136. Kellar, *Enduring Legacy*, 139–41.
137. Kellar, *Enduring Legacy*, 148.
138. Tinsley Narrative, Box 35, Folder 1, Chapter 6, 1–2.
139. There is also a Ben Taub Research Center in the Baylor College of Medicine and a Ben Taub General Hospital operated by the county.
140. Kellar, *Enduring Legacy*, 153; Tinsley Narrative, Box 35, Folder 1, Chapter 6, 14.
141. Kellar, *Enduring Legacy*, 154.
142. Albert B. Alkek (1909–95) was a Houston oilman and philanthropist whose fortune during his lifetime was directed primarily to institutions of the Texas Medical Center, including Baylor College of Medicine and Alkek Hospital at the MD Anderson Center. He and his wife, Margaret, also funded the Alkek Institute of Biosciences and Technology at Texas A&M University. His daughter, Margaret

Alkek Williams, chairs the Alkek Foundation, which continues to donate millions to charity each year.

143. Events, A Report of Progress Dinner, McGovern Historical Collections, Box 51, Folder 3.
144. Kellar, *Enduring Legacy*, 161.
145. Kellar, *Enduring Legacy*, 163.
146. Kellar, *Enduring Legacy*, 163–64.
147. Tinsley Narrative, Box 35, Folder 1, Chapter 8, 1.
148. Tinsley Narrative, Box 35, Folder 1, Chapter 8, 1–2.
149. Kellar, *Enduring Legacy*, 171, 172.
150. Philip Hoffman, Oral Histories, McGovern Historical Collections, Box 15, 2–6. Philip Hoffman was born in Japan and spent his childhood there as the son of missionaries. His wife, Mary Hoffman, is the niece of President Warren G. Harding. Philip Hoffman obituary, *Houston Chronicle*, November 1, 2008.
151. Kellar, *Enduring Legacy*, 174, 175.
152. Tinsley Narrative, Box 35, Folder 1, Chapter 9, 19.
153. Tinsley Narrative, Box 35, Folder 1, Chapter 9, 22.
154. Texas Medical Center Dedicatory Dinner, Statement by Mary Schiflett, Schiflett Papers, Box 5, Folder 5. The number had reached 61,041 in 2000 when the statement was issued.
155. Kellar, *Enduring Legacy*, 162.
156. Holcombe Crosswell, Oral Histories, McGovern Historical Collections, Box 15, 5–6.
157. Kellar, *Enduring Legacy*, 162.
158. "Futuristic Park Soon Will Occupy Site of Historic Shamrock Hotel," *Houston Post*, April 17, 1990, McGovern Historical Collections, Box 23, Folder 1.
159. Kellar, *Enduring Legacy*, 169.
160. *Texas Medical Center News*, December 1949, McGovern Historical Collections, Box 36, Folder 1.
161. Abram, "Deaths: William Fields."
162. *Texas Medical Center News*, October 1949, McGovern Historical Collections, Box 36, Folder 1.
163. Anderson, Oral History, Box 15, 29–31. See also Fenberg, Oral Histories, Box 15, 14–15.
164. Fenberg, Oral Histories, Box 15, 4–5.
165. Fenberg, Oral Histories, Box 15, 4–5.
166. Although referred to as British, Willis was actually born in Australia and remained an Australian passport holder all his life, although his career certainly centered on the United Kingdom. Howie-Willis, "Willis, Rupert Allan (1898–1980)."
167. *Texas Medical Center News*, November 1949, McGovern Historical Collections, Box 36, Folder 1, Vol. 2.
168. *Texas Medical Center News*, June 1950, McGovern Historical Collections, Box 5.
169. *Texas Medical Center News*, November 1949, McGovern Historical Collections, Box 36, Folder 1, Vol. 2.
170. *Texas Medical Center News*, December 1949, McGovern Historical Collections, Box 36. The AAFC competed with the NFL at the time.
171. *Texas Medical Center News*, February 1952, McGovern Historical Collections, Box 5.

172. *Texas Medical Center News*, July–August 1950, McGovern Historical Collections, Box 5.
173. *Texas Medical Center News*, October 1950, McGovern Historical Collections, Box 5.
174. *Texas Medical Center News*, December 1950, McGovern Historical Collections, Box 5.
175. Jack S. Blanton, Oral Histories, McGovern Historical Collections, Box 15, 18.
176. Chronologies, McGovern Historical Collections, Box 22, Folder 20.
177. Tinsley Narrative, Box 35, Folder 1, Chapter 8, 18. Houston Natural Gas Corporation would later become Enron. A few years later, Herring married Joanne King. He died of cancer in 1981 at MD Anderson.
178. Tinsley Narrative, Box 35, Folder 1, Chapter 8, 23; see also Cooley, "Brief History of the Texas Heart Institute," 235–39.
179. Chronologies, McGovern Historical Collections, Box 22, Folder 20.
180. Aga Khan University, dedication program, Cheves Smythe Collection, Box 22, Folder 22. Shamsh Kassim-Lakha came to Texas in 2002 with the Aga Khan for the opening of the Shia Muslim Jamatkhana in Sugarland and helped arrange the Muslim Cultures program with the University of Texas at Austin in 2010.
181. The Duke and Duchess of Windsor arrived in Houston in 1964 for Dr. DeBakey to remove an abdominal aneurysm. The visit helped focus international attention on the facilities and medical skill available at the Texas Medical Center. Macon, *Monroe Dunaway Anderson*, 159.
182. Altman, "Michael DeBakey."
183. Macon, *Monroe Dunaway Anderson*, 157.
184. Macon, *Monroe Dunaway Anderson*, 200.
185. Macon, *Monroe Dunaway Anderson*, 202–3.
186. Macon, *Monroe Dunaway Anderson*, 203.
187. Altman, "In Moscow in 1996."
188. Altman, "In Moscow in 1996." At a medical conference in Mexico City in the 1950s, DeBakey befriended some Soviet doctors and invited them to Houston. They accepted and watched him operate on a patient. Soon afterward, DeBakey was invited to speak at a medical conference in the USSR and made many more trips over the years. Altman, "In Moscow in 1996."
189. Roy M. Huffington, Oral Histories, McGovern Historical Collections, Box 15, 40. Roy Huffington was native to Tomball and received a PhD in geology from Harvard. He served in the navy before going to work for Exxon, eventually opening his own oil and gas company to explore and develop energy reserves overseas. He was especially successful in Indonesia and chaired the Asia Society in New York. He was appointed ambassador to Austria by President George H. W. Bush in 1990. His son Michael served as a California congressman and was married to Arianna Huffington, founder of the *Huffington Post*. Martin, "Roy M. Huffington."
190. Ben F. Love, Oral Histories, McGovern Historical Collections, Box 16, 3.
191. Ben F. Love, Oral Histories, Box 16, 3–4.
192. Ben F. Love, Oral Histories, Box 16, 7. Love was CEO of Texas Commerce Bank from 1972 to 1989 during which time it went from "one bank with $1 billion in assets to 80 banks and 7 foreign offices with over $20 billion in assets." He served as chairman of the MD Anderson Cancer Center. "Ben Love, Obituary."
193. Lynn Wyatt, interview.

194. *Texas Medical Center News*, Outside News Items 1990, McGovern Historical Collections, Box 23, Folder 1.
195. *Texas Medical Center News*, News Release by Mary Schiflett, McGovern Historical Collections, Box 23, Folder 3.
196. *Texas Medical Center News*, Outside News Items 1990, "Andreotti Drop in at M. D. Anderson," July 12, 1990, Box 23.
197. *Texas Medical Center News*, Outside News Items 1990, "A Healing Place," July 1990, Box 23, Folder 2.
198. *Texas Medical Center News*, Outside News Items 1990, "Houston's Measured Steps Along the Comeback Trail," June 18, 1990, Box 23, Folder 2.
199. *Texas Medical Center News*, Outside News Items 1990, SBC Update, "Houston Has the Right Stuff," Box 23, Folder 1.
200. *Texas Medical Center News*, Outside News Items 1990, SBC Update, "Houston Has the Right Stuff," Box 23, Folder 1, 5.
201. Texas Medical Center News, Outside News Items 1990, SBC Update, "Houston Has the Right Stuff," Box 23, Folder 1, 5–6.
202. Kellar, *Enduring Legacy*, 169.
203. Kellar, *Enduring Legacy*, 170, 10. Menninger had moved to Houston by 2003 and by 2012 had opened a newly built facility in mental health designed to function on an "international basis" (171).
204. Macon, *Monroe Dunaway Anderson*, 188.
205. Macon, *Monroe Dunaway Anderson*, 190.
206. Kellar, *Enduring Legacy*, 183.
207. Kilman and Wright, *Hugh Roy Cullen*, 109–11.
208. Tinsley Narrative, Box 35, Folder 1, Chapter 3, 21.
209. Kellar, *Enduring Legacy*, 183.
210. Kellar, *Enduring Legacy*, 185.
211. Kellar, *Enduring Legacy*, 187.
212. Paul N. Howell, Oral Histories, McGovern Historical Collections, Box 15, 8–9. Howell survived the attack on Pearl Harbor as a young navy officer and later survived the sinking of his ship in the Battle of the Coral Sea. He raised funds for Richard Nixon's 1960 campaign and moved to Texas when he acquired a refinery, which he later built into Howell Corporation, a petrochemical giant based in Houston.
213. Lezon, "Arts Patron Paul N. Howell Dies at 82."
214. Kellar, *Enduring Legacy*, 196.
215. W. B. Bates, "History and Development of the Texas Medical Center," McGovern Historical Collections, Box 36, Folder 2.
216. Kellar, *Enduring Legacy*, 199.
217. Tinsley Narrative, Box 35, Folder 1, 6–7.

CHAPTER 4

1. Despite decades of repetition by Texas politicians and citizens, the story is not quite right. There was actually a brief preceding exchange along technical lines with such words as "contact light, engine stop, engine arm is off, and so forth." But after a few seconds came the line beginning "Houston." It might be fair and accurate to say that the first nontechnical word spoken from the moon was "Houston."
2. Dethloff, *Suddenly, Tomorrow Came*, ix.

3. Launius, "Sputnik and the Origins of the Space Age."
4. Hamilton, "The Launch of Sputnik."
5. Launius, "Sputnik and the Origins of the Space Age."
6. *NASA's Origins and the Dawn of the Space Age.*
7. Hurley, *Decisive Years for Houston*, 142.
8. Hamilton, "The Launch of Sputnik."
9. Divine, *The Sputnik Challenge*, xiv.
10. Caro, *Master of the Senate*, 1027.
11. Cox and Stoiko, *Spacepower*, 69. Sputnik was so widely known and discussed in American society that the name influenced other names. The writer Herb Caen coined the term "beatnik" in an article published in the *San Francisco Chronicle* by adding the Russian suffix *-nik* to the term "beat," an adjective derivative of the Beat Culture of post–World War II, encompassing a rejection of societal standards, rejection of materialism, drug experimentation, and attraction to Eastern philosophies and religions.
12. Dickson, *Sputnik*, 5–6.
13. Wilson, "How the U.S. Space Act Came to Be," 49. Gerald W. Siegel was a staff policy adviser for Johnson during his Senate years and later served as vice president and general counsel of *The Washington Post.*
14. Dethloff, *Suddenly, Tomorrow Came*, 1.
15. Caro, *Master of the Senate*, 1022.
16. Caro, *Master of the Senate*, 1021.
17. "Conversation with Willis H. Shapley," 9.
18. "Conversation with Willis H. Shapley," 10.
19. There was renewed anxiety on November 3 when the USSR launched Sputnik II, of larger size and carrying the dog Laika. See "Sputnik II."
20. Dethloff, *Suddenly, Tomorrow Came*, 4.
21. Galloway, "Additional Comments," 57.
22. Wilson, "How the U.S. Space Act Came to Be," 50.
23. Wilson, "How the U.S. Space Act Came to Be," 51.
24. Wilson, "How the U.S. Space Act Came to Be," 52.
25. Dethloff, *Suddenly, Tomorrow Came*, 1.
26. Dethloff, *Suddenly, Tomorrow Came*, 1. Lippman was a respected writer and intellectual leader who previously was a confidant and close aide to Houstonian Edward House. Lippman later helped shape the notion of a Cold War. Neu, *Colonel House*, 318, 359, 369.
27. Dethloff, *Suddenly, Tomorrow Came*, 3.
28. Dethloff, *Suddenly, Tomorrow Came*, 53. The Senate version was first passed on June 16, but the White House was concerned about a strong Space Policy Board that could "usurp the authority of the President" (D. Day, "A New Space Council?"). Johnson believed a powerful board was necessary to advance the national interest, but when meeting with Eisenhower, suggested that the president himself chair the board. This compromise satisfied all parties.
29. Wilson, "How the U.S. Space Act Came to Be," 54.
30. Galloway, "Additional Comments," 59.
31. Wilson, "How the U.S. Space Act Came to Be," 54.
32. Hurley, *Decisive Years for Houston*, 179.

33. "Apollo 11 Plaque Left on the Moon."
34. Historian Robert Caro takes the position that Johnson was not genuinely interested in the space program and was pursuing the matter only at the insistence of his staff. Caro contends that Johnson had no real interest in space until he was vice president and President Kennedy placed him in charge of the Space Council. Caro, *Master of the Senate*, 1030.
35. Ken Belieu, Memo to Lyndon B. Johnson, December 22, 1960, Pre-Presidential Papers, Lyndon Baines Johnson Presidential Library (hereafter cited as LBJ Library).
36. Memo, "Role of National Aeronautics and Space Council in Coordinating US Space Activities," January 20, 1961, Pre-Presidential Papers, LBJ Library.
37. Webb had previously served as budget director and then as undersecretary of state under President Truman. Webb was selected after an internal discussion on the merits of placing a civilian rather than a military official in charge of the space program.
38. Meeting, White House Release, January 30, 1961, MS. Vice Presidential File, LBJ Library.
39. McDougall, *The Heavens and the Earth*, 311. Gavin was instead appointed ambassador to France. Henry Dethloff believes Johnson killed the Gavin nomination by convincing Kennedy that it was a mistake to have a military man heading NASA.
40. McDougall, *The Heavens and the Earth*, 309.
41. Caro, *Master of the Senate*, 138, 149–50, 645, 806, 932, 1035.
42. Kerr was the founder of Kerr-McGee Industries and made a fortune in the oil business. He used his wealth to launch his political career, first as governor of Oklahoma and then later in the US Senate.
43. McDougall, *The Heavens and the Earth*, 311.
44. Lyndon B. Johnson, Memo to John F. Kennedy, February 14, 1961, MS. Vice Presidential File, LBJ Library.
45. Meeting Agenda for NASA conference, March 22, 1961, MS. Vice Presidential File, LBJ Library.
46. John F. Kennedy, Special Message to Congress, April 4, 1961, MS. Vice Presidential File, LBJ Library.
47. John F. Kennedy, Letter to Lyndon B. Johnson, April 4, 1961, MS. Vice Presidential File, LBJ Library. Only the draft letter is in the archive, but it was presumably sent.
48. Ed Welsh, Memo to Lyndon B. Johnson, April 6, 1961, MS. Vice Presidential File, LBJ Library.
49. John F. Kennedy, Letter to Lyndon B. Johnson, April 20, 1961, MS. Vice Presidential File, LBJ Library.
50. McDougall, *The Heavens and the Earth*, 319.
51. The report was authored by leading Soviet space expert Charles S. Sheldon II, who later authored books on the space race, and George J. Feldman, who was later appointed by President Johnson as ambassador to Malta, 1965–67, and ambassador to Luxembourg, 1967–69.
52. "Report on Space Policy," April 24, 1961, Box 17, 13–14, Vice Presidential Security File, LBJ Library.
53. White House Press Release, April 25, 1961, MS. Vice Presidential File, LBJ Library.
54. Lyndon B. Johnson, Letter to James Webb, May 5, 1961, MS. Vice Presidential File, LBJ Library.

55. James Webb, Personal Statement, June 2, 1972, MS. Vice Presidential File, LBJ Library.
56. Hurley, *Decisive Years for Houston*, 207.
57. George Low was an Austrian Jew who had fled to the United States with his family in 1938 after the Nazi occupation of his country. He studied at Rensselaer Polytechnic Institute (RPI) and served in the army in World War II. Later in his career, he was president of RPI.
58. Dethloff, *Suddenly, Tomorrow Came*, 36.
59. Lyndon B. Johnson, Memo to John F. Kennedy, May 8, 1961, MS. Vice Presidential File, LBJ Library.
60. Lyndon B. Johnson, Letter to Melvin Price, May 8, 1961, MS. Vice Presidential File, LBJ Library.
61. This 1961 Asian tour included South Vietnam, where Johnson famously called South Vietnamese President Ngo Dinh Diem the "Churchill" of Asia and committed US support for the fight against communism.
62. James Webb, Letter to Lyndon B. Johnson, May 23, 1961, MS. Vice Presidential File, LBJ Library.
63. James Webb, Letter to Lyndon B. Johnson, May 23, 1961, MS. Vice Presidential File, LBJ Library.
64. George R. Brown, Personal Statement, August 6, 1969, MS. Vice Presidential File, LBJ Library.
65. The scholar Walter A. McDougall, in his Pulitzer Prize–winning book, *The Heavens and the Earth*, references this same memo to Vice President Johnson but recounts it as "[Rep.] George [E.] Brown [D. Cal., on Space Committee] "(374). However, I am convinced from the context of the memo, the relationship between George R. Brown and Congressman Thomas, the mutual connection to Rice University, and the involvement with Lyndon Johnson, the memo must, in fact, be referring to Houstonian George R. Brown. Moreover, the oral history of George R. Brown confirms that he was involved with Congressman Thomas to secure the land for Rice, and ultimately for the manned space center (374).
66. McDougall, *The Heavens and the Earth*, 374. An additional plus for Houston was the planned $100 million research center at nearby Dallas funded by Lloyd Berkner and political support from officials like Senator Robert Kerr, who believed development projects might provide benefits as far away as his state of Oklahoma and the "Dallas-Houston axis would provide a great impetus to the intellectual and industrial base of this whole region" (374).
67. "The Decision to Go to the Moon."
68. Lyndon B. Johnson, Memo, June 3, 1961, MS. Vice Presidential File, LBJ Library.
69. McDougall, *The Heavens and the Earth*, 373–74.
70. Dethloff, *Suddenly, Tomorrow Came*, 36.
71. Dethloff, *Suddenly, Tomorrow Came*, 38.
72. Dethloff, *Suddenly, Tomorrow Came*, 39.
73. Dethloff, *Suddenly, Tomorrow Came*, 39.
74. Dethloff, *Suddenly, Tomorrow Came*, 40.
75. Hurley, *Decisive Years for Houston*, 208.
76. James Webb, Oral History, June 2, 1972, LBJ Library.

77. Dethloff, *Suddenly, Tomorrow Came*, 37. Abe Silverstein, a distinguished engineer, had joined NASA in 1958 to help the agency plan its new programs.
78. The West Mansion and the West Estate were built and formerly occupied by James Marion West Sr. and his family. West (1871–1941) made a fortune in lumber and ranching before entering the oil business and making another fortune. Governor O'Daniel appointed him to the Texas Highway Commission, but as a Republican, West could not get enough votes in the Democrat-controlled Senate to be confirmed. West later owned newspapers and one radio station, KBTC in Austin, which his son later sold to Lyndon Johnson, where it was rebranded as KLBJ.
79. Dethloff, *Suddenly, Tomorrow Came*, 37.
80. Dethloff, *Suddenly, Tomorrow Came*, 37.
81. McDougall, *The Heavens and the Earth*, 405.
82. James Webb, Oral History, June 2, 1972, 20, 21, LBJ Library.
83. McDougall, *The Heavens and the Earth*, 374.
84. Dethloff, *Suddenly, Tomorrow Came*, 37. It was not until July 7, 1961, that Administrator Webb "directed the establishment of preliminary site criteria and a site selection team." The documents in compliance with his directive appeared by August along with twenty-three possible locales. Johnson Space Center, History Office.
85. George Brown, Oral History, August 6, 1969, LBJ Library.
86. William Reynolds, Personal Statement, June 16, 1975, MS. Vice Presidential File, LBJ Library. Colonel Reynolds, a retired air force officer, was air force liaison to the Senate during the time Johnson was majority leader.
87. The Graduate Research Center is now known as the University of Texas at Dallas, following its addition to the University of Texas System in 1969.
88. James Webb, Letter to Lyndon B. Johnson, May 22, 1962, MS. Vice Presidential File, LBJ Library.
89. Sibley, *The Port of Houston*, 206.
90. Sibley, *The Port of Houston*, 206.
91. Nahas, *Houston, City of Destiny*, 32–33.
92. Sibley, *The Port of Houston*, 207.
93. Dethloff, *Suddenly, Tomorrow Came*, 42.
94. Joske's department stores were established in San Antonio in 1867 by Julius Joske, a Jewish immigrant from Germany. The business grew to twenty-six stores before it was acquired by Dillard's in 1987. The flagship store was located at Alamo Plaza in San Antonio and is still referred to as the Joske Building.
95. Dethloff, *Suddenly, Tomorrow Came*, 42.
96. Finger Furniture was established by Sam Finger in 1927 and was nationally regarded in the furniture industry. The business was operated for several generations of the family before dissolving in bankruptcy in 2014. Mulvaney and Kaplan, "Finger Furniture Files for Bankruptcy."
97. Dethloff, *Suddenly, Tomorrow Came*, 45.
98. Hurley, *Decisive Years for Houston*, 271.
99. Dethloff, *Suddenly, Tomorrow Came*, 146.
100. Apollo Series, NASA Budget and Planning, Johnson Space Center, History Office.
101. Dethloff, *Suddenly, Tomorrow Came*, 150, 257, 261.
102. Hurley, *Decisive Years for Houston*, 214.
103. "Final Relocation of Center Employees Begins Today."

104. Hurley, *Decisive Years for Houston*, 215.
105. Hurley, *Decisive Years for Houston*, 233.
106. Lynn Wyatt, interview.
107. Dethloff, *Suddenly, Tomorrow Came*, 314.
108. André Courrèges was born in France in 1923 and originally trained as a civil engineer. He joined Balenciaga as a designer in 1951 and then launched his own line in 1961. He has been described as the "designer who brought the space age to the catwalk" and was praised by President François Hollande for "using geometric shapes and new materials." Friedman, "André Courrèges."
109. Polan and Tredre, *The Great Fashion Designers*, 123–25. Although Courrèges is generally regarded as the inventor of the miniskirt, there is support to credit British designer Mary Quant, who certainly popularized the design in the Swinging Sixties in London.
110. Lynn Wyatt, interview.
111. Robert Sakowitz, interview.
112. Robert Sakowitz would repeat this success with Yves Saint Laurent, who launched a ready-to-wear line called Rive Gauche by YSL. It debuted in the United States in Houston at Sakowitz.
113. James Baker, interview.
114. Miller, *Ray Miller's Houston*, 190.
115. Mod, *Building Modern Houston*, 100.
116. "Capacity Crowd Views Dedication Ceremonies," *Space Center Roundup*, August 30, 1973.
117. Mrs. Johnson's Remarks, Space Center Houston, August 27, 1973, Box 23, MS. Vice Presidential File, LBJ Library.
118. Dethloff, *Suddenly, Tomorrow Came*, 333.
119. Fuermann, *Houston: The Once and Future City*, 90.
120. The voice-over of the opening of each *Star Trek* episode featured the voice of Captain Kirk (actor William Shatner) saying, "Space: the final frontier. These are the voyages of the starship *Enterprise*. Its five-year mission: to explore strange new worlds; to seek out new life and new civilizations; to boldly go where no man has gone before."
121. James Baker, interview.

CHAPTER 5

1. James Baker, interview.
2. K. Kirkland, *The Hogg Family*, xiii.
3. K. Kirkland, *The Hogg Family*, 160.
4. Muir, *William Marsh Rice*, 1.
5. Muir, *William Marsh Rice*, 10, 12.
6. Muir, *William Marsh Rice*, 26.
7. Muir, *William Marsh Rice*, 65.
8. Lipartito and Pratt, *Baker and Botts*, 2–3. The Houston law firm Baker Botts was originally established in 1840 by Peter Gray. It later became Gray and Botts and then Gray, Botts and Baker when the first Baker joined in 1872. Gray later left the firm, and it became Baker Botts. It is now an international law firm of over seven hundred lawyers in eight countries, including the major cities of London, Moscow, New York, and Beijing.

9. Lipartito and Pratt, *Baker and Botts*, 55–56.
10. Lipartito and Pratt, *Baker and Botts*, 56–59, 59.
11. That pattern would be repeated almost forty years later with the wealth and generosity of Monroe Dunaway Anderson and his lawyers at Fulbright who began MD Anderson Cancer Hospital and the Texas Medical Center complex.
12. Fenberg, *Unprecedented Power*, 1, 3.
13. Will, Jesse H. Jones Family and Personal Papers, Box 1, Folder 1, December 15, 1897, MS 252, Woodson Research Center, Fondren Library, Rice University (hereafter cited as Jones Family Papers). One of the other executors of the estate was T. W. House, brother of Edward Mandell House.
14. The estate of Jones's uncle was initially appraised at $1.07 million in 1898 but was at $1.758 million by the time of final dissolution in 1913, given the sale of certain assets and increase in value of others. Estate Settlement, Jones Family Papers, Box 1, Folders 2 and 10. One of the lawyers working on the case was Tom Ball of Andrews, Ball and Streetman (Folder 9).
15. Fenberg, *Unprecedented Power*, 39, 48.
16. Fenberg, *Unprecedented Power*, 43.
17. Timmons, *Jesse H. Jones*, 79.
18. The hotel remained a prestigious address and was occupied by many leading citizens, including Anson Jones, the last president of the Republic of Texas, who committed suicide in the hotel in 1858.
19. Johnston, *Houston, the Unknown City*, 181.
20. President Kennedy stayed at the Rice Hotel in Houston on November 21, 1963, before flying on to Fort Worth that evening. He was assassinated the next day in Dallas.
21. Timmons, *Jesse H. Jones*, 75.
22. Timmons, *Jesse H. Jones*, 116–17.
23. "The 2,500 seat theater looked like the inside of an Egyptian tomb. Enormous murals of kings, queens, sphinxes, and chariot races covered the walls. Colorful mosaic tiles resplendently wrapped drinking fountains, doorways, and massive carved columns. Over the stage, a mythical bird with outstretched wings the width of a movie screen watched over the audience." Fenberg, *Unprecedented Power*, 132.
24. "Brocade wallpaper, classical statuary, and enormous crystal chandeliers [that] gushed French Provincial instead of Egyptian tomb." Fenberg, *Unprecedented Power*, 134.
25. Allegro Letter of Membership, Jones Family Papers, Box 24, Folder 3, MS 252. Other members of Allegro at the time included Mike Hogg, St. John Garwood, and James A. Baker Jr.
26. Timmons, *Jesse H. Jones*, 158–59, 160.
27. George Strake Jr., interview.
28. "Spelling backwards was seen as trendy and fun in the early 1900's." Fenberg, *Unprecedented Power*, 39.
29. Cooper, *Woodrow Wilson*, 158.
30. Fenberg, *Unprecedented Power*, 51.
31. Richardson, *Colonel Edward M. House*, 59.
32. Letter from Governor Hogg to Senator Richard Coke, 1893, Edward Mandell House Papers, 1896–1938, Box 2R42, Folder 1, Dolph Briscoe Center for American History, University of Texas at Austin. The letter introduced Edward House, referring to him

as "one of my best friends" and "worthy of confidence and respect" and imploring the senator to "take an interest in him."

33. Jesse Jones described himself as a liberal and said he always voted the Democratic ticket (until Eisenhower) with the exception of the 1900 election, in which he voted for Republican nominee William McKinley rather than Democratic nominee William Jennings Bryan. Letter to Cordell Hull, January 5, 1949, Jones Family Papers, Folder 8, MS 252.
34. McAdoo became secretary of the treasury in 1913 and married President Wilson's daughter, Eleanor Wilson, the following year.
35. Fenberg, *Unprecedented Power*, 52.
36. Axson was an English professor and a noted Shakespearean scholar who taught at Princeton University from 1899 to 1914, overlapping with Woodrow Wilson's tenure as president of Princeton during 1902–10. Axson later joined the faculty at Rice Institute in 1914 to head the English Department. He continued at Rice until his death in 1935. Stockton Axson Papers, 1912–35, MS 338, Woodson Research Center, Fondren Library, Rice University.
37. Timmons, *Jesse H. Jones*, 105.
38. Timmons, *Jesse H. Jones*, 105–7.
39. Timmons, *Jesse H. Jones*, 108.
40. Timmons, *Jesse H. Jones*, 111.
41. Jones Family Papers, Box 24, Folders 1–28, MS 252.
42. Bohemian Grove, Jones Family Papers, Box 29, Folder 1, MS 252. The men-only encampment in California is perhaps the most elite summer gathering in the United States. Operated since 1878, its members have include the top political, business, and social leaders of the nation. Other members at the time of Jones included William Randolph Hearst and Herbert Hoover.
43. During this period the Democratic National Conventions were held in New York, Baltimore, St. Louis, Cincinnati, Chicago, Kansas City, Denver, and San Francisco, with some cities repeated more than once. Similarly, the Republicans did not meet in the South for over a century until the gathering in Miami in 1968 and in 1988 at New Orleans, a traditional Southern city.
44. Timmons, *Jesse H. Jones*, 134. Garner was a congressman from Uvalde, Texas, and later served as Speaker of the House and then vice president.
45. Timmons, *Jesse H. Jones*, 139.
46. Letter from Oveta Culp, September 9, 1935, Jones Family Papers, Box 38, Folder 1, MS 252.
47. Timmons, *Jesse H. Jones*, 143, 144.
48. This was obviously a distinctly different era when the host city was not chosen until the same year in which the convention would be held; the decision would be made by a small group of people who sat together in a hotel suite; and the person making an offer could commit a city without having first consulted the city and could further offer the construction of a new convention hall. The convention hall could be conceived and constructed in the next few months, ready for the just-announced convention! Timmons, *Jesse H. Jones*, 144, 145.
49. Timmons, *Jesse H. Jones*, 145.
50. Jones responded to Hogg and later incorporated many of his suggestions, including a trussless construction model for stability and speed. Telegram from Jesse Jones

to William Hogg, January 17, 1928, William Clifford Hogg Papers, 1897–1932, Box 2J345, Democratic National Convention 1928, Dolph Briscoe Center for American History, University of Texas at Austin (hereafter cited as W. C. Hogg Papers).

51. Letter from William Hogg to Ross Sterling, January 18, 1928, W. C. Hogg Papers, Box 2J345, Democratic National Convention 1928.
52. Final Report of Committee on Arrangements for Democratic National Convention, July 24, 1928, W. C. Hogg Papers, Box 2J345.
53. 1928 Convention, Jones Family Papers, Box 26, Folder 12, MS 252.
54. Nomination, Jones Family Papers, Box 26, Folder 19, MS 252.
55. Timmons, *Jesse H. Jones*, 147.
56. This may be seen in Jesse Jones's own attendance at the Gridiron Club in 1928, buying a benefactor table on behalf of himself and the *Houston Chronicle* with President Coolidge as the evening's featured speaker. Gridiron Club, Jones Family Papers, Box 24, Folder 17, MS 252.
57. Letter from H. B. Duval, July 6, 1928, W. C. Hogg Papers, Box 2J345.
58. Jones signed all the checks issued by the Democratic National Committee's Arrangement Committee for catering, flowers, and salaries to doormen, security, and other support personnel. Democratic National Committee Arrangements, Jones Family Papers, Box 26, Folder 14. There was one odd entry for a $100 check to a reporter, Ward Tinlin.
59. Democratic National Committee Arrangements, "City Is Lauded for Coliseum," June 19, 1928, Jones Family Papers, MS 252, Box 26, Folder 14.
60. Letter from FDR, April 21, 1954, Jones Family Papers, Box 37, Folder 40, MS 252.
61. Letter from FDR, January 7, 1929, Jones Family Papers, Box 37, Folder 40, MS 252.
62. McComb, *Houston, the Bayou City*, 168.
63. Correspondence with William Hobby, March 14, 1933, Jones Family Papers, Box 36, Folder 2, MS 252.
64. Herbert Hoover first appointed Jones to the RFC, although Roosevelt, realizing Jones's talents, not only retained but promoted him. Jones maintained regular contact and cordial ties with Hoover the rest of his life. Telegram from Jones to Hoover, January 5, 1936, inviting Hoover to share his private Pullman to Chicago and enjoy turkey his chef was preparing. Hoover wrote a note to Jones on March 3, 1933, the day before leaving the White House, to thank Jones "for the cooperation which you have shown to me in these difficult times." Correspondence with Herbert Hoover, Jones Family Papers, Box 37, Folder 4, MS 252.
65. In 1932, John Nance Garner had just become US Speaker of the House. He asked Jesse Jones to come up with some names to head the soon-to-be-created Reconstruction Finance Corporation. He then ignored all the names Jones suggested and instead submitted only Jones's name to the White House. President Hoover called Jones and asked him to accept the nomination. The two had known each other since World War I when Hoover served as food administrator and Jones was director of the Red Cross. Timmons, *Jesse H. Jones*, 164–65.
66. Timmons, *Jesse H. Jones*, 231–32. Some of the loans to Brazil to modernize railroads, construct steel mills, and purchase American ships for international cargo were worked out between Jones and Ambassador Carlos Martins "over the bridge table at the Brazilian Embassy" in Washington (233).

67. The proposal was made to Jesse Jones on a train ride from Florida to New York by President Roosevelt accompanied by Secretary of State Cordell Hull. Timmons, *Jesse H. Jones*, 248.
68. Telegram to Ambassador William Bullitt from Jesse Jones, August 2, 1938, requesting reservations at the Ritz Hotel. Bullitt previously served as the first American ambassador the Soviet Union during 1933–36. Jones Family Papers, Box 29, Folder 8.
69. The idea was vigorously attacked by Senator William E. Borah of Idaho. Jones went to Borah and explained the rationale of building up American relationships in the region to strengthen American diplomacy and bolster security in the event of war. Only on Jones's personal assurance did Borah relent and agree to appropriations. Timmons, *Jesse H. Jones*, 265–66.
70. Poem by FDR, Jones Family Papers, Box 30, Folder 5, MS 252.
71. Poem by FDR, Jones Family Papers, Box 30, Folder 7, MS 252.
72. Letter from FDR, June 27, 1939, and Letter from LBJ, June 26, 1939, Jones Family Papers, Box 31, Folder 1, MS 252.
73. Letter to FDR, March 7, 1940, Jones Family Papers, Box 311, Folder 9, MS 252. The relationship between Jones and Lyndon Johnson is not always clear. In 1941, there was a special election for an open US Senate seat in Texas. Johnson lost the contest to the sitting governor, W. Lee O'Daniel, in a hard-fought Democratic primary. White House aide James Rowe Jr. sent a memo to President Roosevelt on May 5, 1941, complaining that Jesse Jones was helping O'Daniel, that Johnson was a New Deal supporter and Jones was not, and that it was unacceptable that Jones as a cabinet member from Texas was taking sides against Johnson in the race. FDR rejected these charges against Jones (Memo from James Rowe Jr. to President Roosevelt, May 5, 1941, LBJ Senatorial Campaign, Jones Family Papers, Box 32, Folder 15). Roosevelt obviously shared Rowe's memo with Jones, because Jones sent a two-page letter rejecting the "misinformation" and giving a detailed response on the charges and the political situation in Texas. Letter to FDR, May 31, 1941, Jones Family Papers, Box 32, Folder 15, MS 252.

    Rowe would later manage LBJ's 1960 presidential campaign until Johnson lost the nomination to Kennedy. Rowe served under Jones at the RFC until coming to the Roosevelt White House. S. King, "James Rowe."
74. Undated Handwritten Notes from FDR, Jones Family Papers, Box 32, Folder 16, MS 252.
75. The plan was that James A. Farley would nominate Jesse Jones for vice president and Elliott Roosevelt would second the nomination. Farley was chairman of the Democratic National Committee. Eleanor Roosevelt also tried to dissuade her husband from supporting Henry Wallace for vice president, urging that Jones would attract business support. But President Roosevelt insisted he had given his word to Wallace. In the end, Wallace barely drew enough support from the convention and then only after Jones and Rayburn had declined nomination and urged Texans and the rest of the delegation to support Wallace. Timmons, *Jesse H. Jones*, 278–79.
76. It is interesting to note that Jones had designed the cabinet table at which he then sat and then presented it to the White House as a gift. Prior to that, the seating arrangement since President Washington had the president sitting at the head of the table, where he could see only part of his cabinet. "So Jones had the new table built and

sent to the White House. The table proved very practical and [has] remained in use at the White House in succeeding administrations." Timmons, *Jesse H. Jones*, 282.

77. Timmons, *Jesse H. Jones*, 286.
78. Memo to FDR, September 16, 1940, Jones Family Papers, Box 31, Folder 9, MS 252; Memo to FDR January 31, 1941, Jones Family Papers, Box 31, Folder 9.
79. Jones Family Papers, Box 40, Folder 4, MS 252.
80. Timmons, *Jesse H. Jones*, 287.
81. Memo on Netherlands Loan Application, August 24, 1943, Jones Family Papers, Box 32, Folder 19, MS 252.
82. Letter to FDR, April 10, 1941, Jones Family Papers, Box 31, Folder 9, MS 252.
83. Letter from Roosevelt, November 29, 1944, Jones Family Papers, Box 32, Folder 21, MS 252.
84. Letter from Roosevelt, January 20, 1945, Jones Family Papers, Box 33, Folder 9, MS 252.
85. Letter from Jones to Roosevelt, January 20, 1945, Jones Family Papers, Box 33, Folder 9, MS 252.
86. Jesse Jones Memo to the File, March 20, 1945, Jones Family Papers, Box 33, Folder 9, MS 252.
87. In a letter to Cordell Hull in 1949, Jones wrote, "Notwithstanding all the many good things that Roosevelt did, I am afraid he started the American people on a course that is apt to destroy our way of life." Cordell Hull Correspondence, Jones Family Papers, Box 37, Folder 8, MS 252.
88. Letter from E. Roosevelt, July 1, 1947, Jones Family Papers, Box 31, Folder 1, MS 252.
89. The Joneses presented the Eisenhowers with a carved ivory elephant, symbol of the GOP, as a Christmas gift in 1954. Correspondence with Eisenhower, Jones Family Papers, Box 36, Folder 15, MS 252.
90. Kelley, *Foundations of Texan Philanthropy*, 33–45.
91. Opening Jones Hall, January 1945, Jones Family Papers, Box 57, Folder 8, MS 252.
92. Fossedal, *Our Finest Hour*.
93. Fuermann, *Houston: Land of the Big Rich*, 125.
94. William Lockhart Clayton Papers, 1897–1966, Oral History, Box 96, Folder 6, 1, 37, 40, MS 007, Woodson Research Center, Fondren Library, Rice University (hereafter cited as Clayton Papers).
95. Timmons, *Jesse H. Jones*, 291.
96. Letter from William Clayton, June 19, 1933, Jones Family Papers, Box 36, Folder 8, MS 252.
97. Letter from William Clayton, July 24, 1943, Jones Family Papers, Box 31, Folder 16, MS 252.
98. Clayton Papers, Oral History, Box 96, Folder 6, 96, MS 007.
99. Letter to Harry Hopkins, January 14, 1942, Clayton Papers, Box 85, MS 007.
100. Clayton Papers, Oral History, Box 96, Folder 6, 104, MS 007; Telegram from FDR, November 29, 1944, Clayton Papers, Box 85, Folder 6.
101. It was a nice turn of events for Clayton because he originally opposed Roosevelt in the 1930s. He even joined, contributed money, and got placed on the board of directors of the Liberty League, a group of Democrats and some Republicans who sought to oust Roosevelt. After Roosevelt's landslide victory in 1936, the group melted away. Clayton's wife, Susan Vaughn Clayton, supported Roosevelt and sent money to his campaign in 1936 at the same time her husband was opposing him.

Clayton believes Roosevelt's fondness for his wife probably got him in the political door later. Clayton Papers, Oral History, Box 96, Folder 6, 81, MS 007.

102. Oil Pipeline Negotiations, October 1945, Clayton Papers, Diplomatic, Box 85, Folder 1, MS 007; Meeting with Lord Halifax, Clayton Papers, Box 96, Folder 6, 110.
103. Clayton Papers, 1897–1966, Oral History, Box 96, Folder 6, 144, MS 007.
104. Clayton Papers, Oral History, Box 96, Folder 6, 158, MS 007.
105. Memo on Financial Assistance to the Government of Saudi Arabia, April 7, 1945, Clayton Papers, Diplomatic, Box 85, MS 007.
106. Memo from W. W. Rostow, September 18, 1945, re Westphalia, Clayton Papers, Diplomatic, Box 85, MS 007.
107. Memo on American Interests in China, November 1, 1945, Clayton Papers, Diplomatic, Box 85, MS 007.
108. Clayton Papers, Oral History, Box 96, Folder 6, MS 007, 180–81.
109. Clayton Papers, Oral History, Box 96, Folder 6, MS 007, 227, 228. Susan Vaughn Clayton died in Houston in 1960, and W. L. Clayton, in 1966.
110. Statement to Senate, December 12, 1944, Clayton Papers, Box 85, MS 007.
111. Her father was elated with the birth of his daughter and wrote to his brother John that "our cup of joy is now overflowing." Letters 1882–1990, Ima Hogg Papers, 1824–1977, Box 4ZG89, Folder 1, July 13, 1882, Dolph Briscoe Center for American History, University of Texas at Austin (hereafter cited as Ima Hogg Papers).
112. Letters 1882–1990, Ima Hogg Papers, Box 4ZG89, Folder 3; Draft of Chapter 2 in letter from Kate Leader, September 16, 1975, Ima Hogg Papers, Box 4ZG89, Folder 3.
113. Jim Hogg ran for governor on a platform that called for the establishment of a railroad commission in Texas to protect the public from unfair consumer practices. After his election, the Railroad Commission was established, which later assumed regulatory power over the oil and gas industry and continues to this day, while jurisdiction over railroads ended in 2005.
114. Letters 1882–1990, Ima Hogg Papers, Box 4ZG89, Reminiscences of the Governor's Mansion, Dictated by Ima Hogg 1944–1945.
115. Letters 1882–1990, Ima Hogg Papers, Box 4ZG89, Reminiscences of the Governor's Mansion, Dictated by Ima Hogg 1944–1945, 2, 3.
116. Letters 1882–1990, Ima Hogg Papers, Box 4ZG89, Reminiscences of the Governor's Mansion, Dictated by Ima Hogg 1944–1945, 5, 9, 15, 37.
117. Letters 1882–1990, Ima Hogg Papers, Box 4ZG89, Reminiscences of the Governor's Mansion, Dictated by Ima Hogg 1944–1945, 35.
118. Bernhard, *Ima Hogg*, 43.
119. Ima Hogg Papers, Box 4Zg86, Folder: Personal Papers and Travel Diaries.
120. Bernhard, *Ima Hogg*, 53.
121. Ima Hogg Papers, Box 4Zg86, Folder: Personal Papers and Travel Diaries, 1898, 1908, 1912, 1930.
122. Neeley, *Miss Ima and the Hogg Family*, 36.
123. One problem was Houston musicians going off to military service with no idea when they would return. K. Kirkland, *The Hogg Family*, 173.
124. Roussel, *The Houston Symphony Orchestra*, 3.
125. Letters for the German Grand Opera, February 8, 1930, Ima Hogg Papers, Box 2.324/D31a.
126. K. Kirkland, *The Hogg Family*, 175.

127. Article from *Cleveland Plain Dealer*, August 19, 1933, Ima Hogg Papers, Box 2.324/D31a.
128. "If the Hogg millions should ever vanish, Miss Hogg would not have to worry about making a living [for people] have long respected her worth as a musician." Newspaper Clippings, Ima Hogg Papers, Box 4W201.
129. Nespoli had originally been brought to Houston by Noma Graham, a voice teacher and the choir director of the First United Methodist Church. She was able to secure a visa for him but could not sustain her operatic vision. K. Kirkland, *The Hogg Family*, 177–78.
130. Roussel, *The Houston Symphony Orchestra*, 191.
131. As part of that dream, Ima decided to look for a replacement for conductor Ernst Hoffman. This led to a sharp conflict with Hugh Roy Cullen, who sent a telegram to Ima Hogg while she was in New York on symphony business and said he was done and was withdrawing his support. Ima handwrote a long letter to him asking him to reconsider and pointing out that "Houston has a great future [and that] the Symphony [is part] of its development." Houston Activities, Symphony Correspondence, undated letter to Hugh Roy Cullen from Ima Hogg on Waldorf-Astoria stationery, Ima Hogg Papers, Box 2.325/D31a.
132. Symphony Correspondence, Hugh Roy Cullen, March 5, March 10, April 23, and May 18, 1947, Ima Hogg Papers, Box 21.324/D31a.
133. Roussel, *The Houston Symphony Orchestra*, 114–18.
134. The term "International Set" soon gave way to "Jet Set," attributed to Igor Cassini, who wrote society columns under the name Cholly Knickerbocker and was the brother of designer Oleg Cassini.
135. Roussel, *The Houston Symphony Orchestra*, 125.
136. "The Passing Show," *Dallas Morning News*, November 9, 1951, Ima Hogg Papers, Box 2.324/D31a. However, the same reporter in a column the next day was critical of the just-released book *Houston: Land of the Big Rich*, by George Feuermann, which the reporter says makes unfair or unfounded comparisons with Dallas on the arts and society.
137. Letter from Sir Thomas Beecham, May 15, 1956, Ima Hogg Papers, Box 2.325/D31a.
138. Letter from Leopold Stokowski, April 23, 1956, Ima Hogg Papers, Box 2.325/D31a.
139. Letter from Van Cliburn, January 20, 1956, Hogg Papers, Box 2.325/D31a. Van Cliburn had played with the Houston Symphony while still a teenager. At the time he wrote this letter to Ima Hogg, he had not yet won the 1958 International Tchaikovsky Piano Competition, which brought him international fame.
140. Hirsch was Jewish but was able to enter society at the highest levels, including membership in the River Oaks Country Club.
141. Symphony Correspondence, Ima Hogg Papers, Box 2.325/D31a.
142. Bernhard, *Ima Hogg*, 63.
143. K. Kirkland, *The Hogg Family*, 200.
144. Houston Activities; River Oaks Owners Association, Ima Hogg Papers, Box 4W201, Folder 1, 5. Will Hogg's prejudice against black citizens living in the same neighborhood was apparently not as harsh as some sentiments of the time. When Hogg published his *Garden Book* to distribute to Houstonians and instruct them on how to make the city more beautiful, he provided it free to black and white citizens alike. Additionally, he financed thousands of crape myrtle bushes to be given to

citizens to plant in their own yards. When he "learned that the white folks were getting all the shrubs, [he purchased] thousands more which were given out only at Emancipation Park, the Negroes recreation center." J. A. Lomax, *Will Hogg*, 29–30.

145. Houston Activities, River Oaks Owners Association, Ima Hogg Papers, Box 4W201, Folder 1, 7, 9.
146. Bernhard, *Ima Hogg*, 78.
147. Houston Activities, River Oaks Owners Association, Ima Hogg Papers, Box 4W201, Folder 1, 8–10.
148. *Houston Post* Texas Sunday Magazine, February 20, 1966, Ima Hogg Papers, Box 2.325/V26; see also *Bayou Bend: Collection and Gardens*.
149. Warren, *Bayou Bend Gardens*, vii.
150. One 1956 shopping trip in Pennsylvania resulted in a circa 1750 cherrywood pipe box for $285, a Staffordshire pottery figure of Benjamin Franklin made in 1775 for $900, and a pair of Queen Anne wing chairs with original needlework for $15,000. Typed Shopping List with Handwritten Notes, March 22, 1956, Ima Hogg Papers, Box 2.325/D31a.
151. "The saying in Houston was that newcomers realized they were becoming real Houstonians when Miss Ima's name no longer seemed odd." Iscoe, *Ima Hogg*, 43.
152. Neeley, *Miss Ima and the Hogg Family*, 8.
153. There have been critics who claim the public service and philanthropy of Ima Hogg, and others like her, are actually self-serving ways to promote their own interests and status. However, such people fail "to illuminate the synergistic nature of public-private interaction that was particularly powerful during the Hoggs' lifetimes." K. Kirkland, *The Hogg Family*, xiii.
154. Oveta Culp Hobby Papers, 1817–1995, MS #459, Box 19, Folder 4, Woodson Research Center, Fondren Library, Rice University (hereafter cited as Hobby Papers).
155. Letter from Marshall Hobby, January 14, 1958, Hobby Papers, Box 19, Folder 5.
156. Letter from Jones to Eisenhower, November 12, 1952, Hobby Papers, Box 12, Folder 2.
157. Official Biography, Hobby Papers, Box 1, Folder 1.
158. Official Biography, Hobby Papers, Box 1, Folder 5.
159. Official Biography, Hobby Papers, Box 1, Folder 5.
160. Letter to Chiang Kai-shek, March 16, 1953, Hobby Papers, Box 12, Folder 1.
161. Letter from Sargent Shriver, April 20, 1961, Hobby Papers, Box 19, Folder 6.
162. Cook, "Fraying Empire of Bobby Sakowitz," 135, 136.
163. The Gulf Building, at thirty-seven stories, remained the tallest building in Houston until 1963, when it was surpassed by the Exxon Building. The names Gulf and Exxon make clear the importance of oil to Houston, and vice versa.
164. Cook, "Fraying Empire of Bobby Sakowitz," 132.
165. "A Confederate flag flew at the entrance as if to emphasize that Sakowitz—with its old-school patriarchs, and its starchy, determinedly patrician air—was very much a Southern store." Bernard Sakowitz himself chose a plantation-house look with white columns and a country club atmosphere. Cook, "Fraying Empire of Bobby Sakowitz," 232.
166. Another side to Oscar is his role in the rescue of American hostages held by Saddam Hussein in 1990. Along with former Texas Governor John Connally, and relying on his contacts with Saddam over the years through oil purchases, Oscar traveled

to Baghdad to secure the hostages' release, much to the approval of the American public and the annoyance of the American government.

167. Hurt, "Oscar's Follie."

168. Lynn Sakowitz Wyatt was not only named to the International Best Dressed list but in 1978 was named to the International Best Dressed List Hall of Fame, along with Jacqueline Kennedy Onassis and the Duchess of Windsor. Swartz, "River Oaks 77019," 89.

169. Remarks by Carolina Herrera on February 16, 2013, at Houston Ballet Gala honoring Lynn Wyatt. Observation by the author.

170. See generally, Wolfe, *Blood Rich*.

171. Cook, "Fraying Empire of Bobby Sakowitz," 132.

172. The deal with Courrèges was especially trendsetting with "iconoclastic inventor of the miniskirt." Robert Sakowitz, hearing that Courrèges planned to open his own ready-to-wear line, had "flown to Paris, and cajoled Courrèges in French; he touted the Space City as the perfect launching pad for the futuristic couture." Cook, "Fraying Empire of Bobby Sakowitz," 234; Robert Sakowitz, interview.

173. Cook, "Fraying Empire of Bobby Sakowitz," 238, 246.

174. Good evidence of Lynn Wyatt's popularity and continued iconic status came with her eightieth birthday in 2015. A series of celebrations occurred throughout the year: a glittering party in Paris, lunch with the Prince of Wales in London, cocktail party and dinner in New York. But it was to Houston that she returned for the main event: a Truman Capote–inspired black-and-white Grand Gala Ball at Houston's Museum of Fine Arts. The birthday bash was also a fundraiser raking in a record $2 million for a single event. The museum's Cullinan Hall was "decorated in a stunning recreation of Lynn and Oscar Wyatt's River Oaks dining room" with "walls covered in 6,000 yards of black and white silk stripes [and] crystal chandeliers wrapped in black shades hung overhead while massive arrangements of white orchids sprung from tabletops." The elite crowd included Shirley MacLaine, the Duchess of York, and Sir Elton John, albeit by video appearance to wish Lynn a happy birthday. Hodge, "Elton John's Gift to MFAH."

175. Sheehy, *Texas Big Rich*, 57–67.

176. Also in 1979, a deranged man claiming to be the Madi took over the holy mosque of Mecca, violently resisting all Saudi Arabian attempts to restore order. Finally, he was killed by French special forces acting on a desperate appeal by the Saudi monarchy. To receive blessing for the entire operation, the Saudi royal family sought the official permission of the Wahabi sect of Sunni Muslims, a bargain that set in motion the rise of Islamic extremism, including Al-Qaeda. Wright, *The Looming Tower*, 88–93.

177. This political coalition would be skillfully tapped by Ronald Reagan the following year as he united traditional Republicans with many conservative, especially Southern, Democrats and independents disillusioned with the stagnant economy, the failing foreign policy, or both.

178. Naftali, *George H. W. Bush*, 12.

179. Moore, *Houston Legends*, 36.

180. For biographical information, see generally, Herring and Dorman-Hickson, *Diplomacy and Diamonds*. Still in impeccable condition, the home was moved to

Joanne Herring's country place, where it has been occupied by her son Robin King since then. Herring and Dorman-Hickson, *Diplomacy and Diamonds.*

181. Joanne later married and resettled in Houston. She raised two sons and for years had a television show interviewing leading local and visiting personalities. Herring and Dorman-Hickson, *Diplomacy and Diamonds.*
182. Zia had deposed Prime Minister Zulfikar Ali Bhutto in 1977 in a military coup followed by a declaration of martial law. Zia feared the Soviet Union and worked hard to create alliances against further incursions in South Asia, particularly Pakistan. Herring and Dorman-Hickson, *Diplomacy and Diamonds*, 183.
183. Robert Herring was an international oilman and traveled frequently to secure new deals. Joanne frequently traveled with him on business trips. She arranged this trip to Islamabad. Joanne Herring, interview.
184. Herring and Dorman-Hickson, *Diplomacy and Diamonds*, 184.
185. Although personally close and fond of each other, Joanne Herring denies there was a romantic relationship between her and President Zia. She says, in fact, that all of their calls were monitored by one of his aides and that they were never alone for a meeting—someone was always present from his staff. Joanne Herring, interview.
186. Crile, *Charlie Wilson's War*, 67–71.
187. Charlie Wilson was born in Trinity in deep East Texas. He attended the US Naval Academy and then served four years in the navy, including a stint at the Pentagon as part of a naval intelligence unit assessing Soviet nuclear capabilities. He served first in the Texas legislature before being elected to the first of twelve terms in the US Congress. When he read reports of Afghan refugees fleeing the Soviet occupation, he used his position on the Appropriations Committee to secure additional funding to help Afghan resistance. Wilson believed the Soviet action was dangerous and wrong, and he wanted to help Afghanistan resist it. But it was Joanne Herring who focused his attention on the details of the challenge and the best options for success.
188. Fellow Houstonian George H. W. Bush was serving as vice president, and James Baker III was serving as White House chief of staff.
189. Joanne Herring had her own objections to the movie's accuracy, even hiring a lawyer who threatened to sue the studio, although her concerns dealt more with her proposed portrayal as a foul-mouthed and superficial personality rather than the more cautious and strategic character in the final script. Joanne Herring, interview.
190. At least the literary and film world was convinced, as were many political leaders who credited the joint efforts of Charlie Wilson, Joanne Herring, and CIA officer Gust Avrakotos and nominated them for the Congressional Gold Medal.
191. James Baker also pointed out that Joanne still looked fantastic in an evening gown, drawing approving laughs and applause from a familiar crowd. Observation by the author, 2008.
192. Fuermann and Johnson, *The Face of Houston*, 3–7.
193. Haqqani, *Magnificent Delusions*, 256.
194. Joanne Herring had no official US position, but ironically she did have an official Pakistani position. President Zia appointed her honorary consul of Pakistan in Houston and gave her the rank of ambassador-at-large. Further, he presented her with Pakistan's highest civilian honor, the Jinnah Medal.
195. Haqqani, *Magnificent Delusions*, 256.
196. Crile, *Charlie Wilson's War*, 68.

197. Joanne Herring, interview.
198. Abram, "Cecil Blaffer 'Titi' von Furstenberg."
199. Carolyn Shulman Farb is the granddaughter of Jake Freedman, a Texas oilman who founded the Sands Hotel and Casino in Las Vegas. She was married from 1977 to 1983 to Houston real estate developer Harold Farb, who built tens of thousands of apartments. Harold later married Diane Lokey in 1995 and died in 2006.
200. Margaret Alkek Williams's father, Albert Alkek, was a fabulously successful oilman who established the state's first petroleum pipeline. With his wife, Margaret, he established the Alkek Foundation, which has directed tens of millions to Baylor College of Medicine, the MD Anderson Cancer Hospital, Texas Children's Hospital, and the Texas Heart Institute. Their daughter, Margaret Alkek Williams, has chaired the foundation since 2005.
201. Mickey Leland was chair of the Congressional Black Caucus and tireless promoter of Houston. He died in a plane crash in Ethiopia in 1989. The international terminal is named for him at the George Bush Intercontinental Airport.
202. The US government charged the consulate with espionage in 2020 and ordered it closed.
203. Roy Huffington was a successful international oilman based in Houston. He served as ambassador to Austria in the George H. W. Bush administration. He and his wife, Phyllis, endowed the Huffington Center on Aging at the Texas Medical Center. Their son, Michael Huffington, was previously married to Arianna Huffington, creator of the *Huffington Post*. Ambassador Huffington died in 2008.
204. *The Dynamo*, published by Houston Junior Chamber of Commerce, July 1965.
205. *The Dynamo*, July 20, 1948.
206. *The Dynamo*, April 5, 1949.
207. "Andre A. Crispin Obituary."
208. Crispin would also be named to Five Outstanding Young Texans in 1953. *The Dynamo*, January 1, 1954, 1.
209. *The Dynamo*, May 15, 1953, 1.
210. *The Dynamo*, January 1, 1954.
211. *The Dynamo*, January 15, 1953.
212. *The Dynamo*, December 15, 1953, 3.
213. *The Dynamo*, December 15, 1957. Marvin Zindler was then a Houston news reporter and photographer who would become famous in 1973 for exposing the Chicken Ranch brothel at La Grange. The story was told by Larry L. King and Peter Masterson in the musical *The Best Little Whorehouse in Texas*, which opened on Broadway in 1978. The movie version was released in 1982, starring Dolly Parton and Burt Reynolds.
214. *The Dynamo*, December 15, 1957, 5.
215. *The Dynamo*, December 15, 1957.
216. *The Dynamo*, December 15, 1957, 27.
217. *The Dynamo*, July 1960, 1.
218. *The Dynamo*, August 1960, 1.
219. *The Dynamo*, October 1960.
220. *The Dynamo*, October 1961, 10. Carla was a Category 5 Hurricane that caused widespread damage between Port O'Connor and Corpus Christi. The then-unknown

reporter Dan Rather reported live from a building in Texas City, the first live hurricane coverage.

221. *The Dynamo*, October 1961, 10.
222. *The Dynamo*, November 1961, 4.
223. *The Dynamo*, November 1961, 5.
224. *The Dynamo*, May 1961, 3.
225. *The Dynamo*, December 1961, 31.
226. *The Dynamo*, December 1961, 32.
227. Taken from program for the 2012 ball honoring Turkey.
228. George H. W. Bush served as honorary chair of the event three times, most recently in 2007 for Germany.
229. The 2001 Consular Ball and the visit of Princess Alexandra occurred on November 3, 2001, soon after the 9/11 attack and just three weeks after the United States and United Kingdom launched a coordinated attack on Afghanistan and began the process of ousting the Taliban and searching for bin Laden. The ball included tributes to the British and American soldiers in the fight. Observation by the author.
230. These sashes are made specifically according to protocol standards recognized internationally and modeled on the colors and design of the nation's flag. Where the colors are the same, for example, the flags of the United States, United Kingdom, Netherlands, and Russian Federation, only the trained eye can distinguish the country from the color layout of the sash.
231. This was true even though Shell is a joint Anglo-Dutch corporation.

CONCLUSION

1. Bernhard, *Ima Hogg*, 89–91. Furthermore, Ima Hogg herself served a term on the Houston School Board from 1943 to 1947. Ima Hogg ran for the school board because she felt it was wrong that there were no women on the board and because she wanted the district to develop programs for emotionally disturbed students who struggled with normal classroom routines. And naturally, she made sure all the students had access to the arts, including special Houston Symphony events.
2. Spencer, *Globalization and Urbanization*, 1.

AFTERWORD

1. Swayze was a star before 1990 but continued in spectacular fashion after the release of the film *Ghost* the same year. He was married to Houstonian Lisa Niemi, an actress and dancer, until his death in 2009.
2. Tilman Fertitta served as chairman of the University of Houston System Board of Regents. In 2025, he was nominated by President Trump to be ambassador to Italy.

Bibliography

COLLECTIONS

Dolph Briscoe Center, University of Texas at Austin
  Bickett, John H. Papers
  Connally, Tom. Papers
  Hogg, Ima. Papers
  Hogg, William Clifford. Papers
  House, Edward Mandell. Papers
  Rainey, Homer Price. Papers
Johnson Space Center, History Office
Lyndon Baines Johnson Presidential Library
Rice University, Woodson Research Center
  Axson, Stockton. Papers
  Barnes, Marguerite Johnston. Collection
  Clayton, William Lockhart. Papers
  Dillingham Family. Papers
  Fondren, Ella. Papers
  Hobby, Oveta Culp. Papers
  Jones, Jesse H. Family and Personal Papers
Texas Medical Center, McGovern Historical Collections and Research Center
  Schiflett, Mary. Papers
  Smythe, Cheves. Papers
  Tinsley Narrative

INTERVIEWS

Baker, James. Interview by author. October 19, 2016.
Hartsell, Don. Interview by author. June 20, 2015; October 7, 2016.
Herring, Joanne. Interview by author. April 28, 2016.
Sakowitz, Robert. Interview by author. October 20, 2016.
Strake, George, Jr. Interview by author. October 20, 2016.
Wyatt, Lynn. Interview by author. October 7, 2016.

NEWSPAPERS AND PERIODICALS

Dynamo
Economist
Forbes
Houston Chronicle
New York Times
Port of Houston Magazine (*Houston Port Book, Houston Port*)
Space Center Roundup
Texaco Star
Texas Monthly

BOOKS AND ARTICLES

Abram, Lynwood. "Cecil Blaffer 'Titi' von Furstenberg, a Patron of the Arts and a Member of a Family That Combined Two Great Texas Oil Fortunes." *Houston Chronicle*, November 26, 2006. https://www.chron.com/news/houston-deaths/article/cecil-blaffer-titi-von-furstenberg-a-patron-1862043.php.

Abram, Lynwood. "Deaths: William Fields, Neurologist, Pioneer in Stroke Treatment." *Houston Chronicle*, March 26, 2004. http://www.chron.com/news/houston-deaths/article/Deaths-William-Fields-neurologist-pioneer-in-1988923.php.

Allen, Frederick. *Atlanta Rising: The Invention of an International City 1946–1996*. Atlanta: Longstreet Press, 1996.

Altman, Lawrence K. "In Moscow in 1996, a Doctor's Visit Changed History." *New York Times*, May 1, 2007.

Altman, Lawrence K. "Michael DeBakey, Rebuilder of Hearts, Dies at 99." *New York Times*, July 13, 2008.

"Andre A. Crispin Obituary." *New York Times*, October 28, 2012. http://www.legacy.com/obituaries/nytimes/obituary.aspx?pid=160696445.

"Apollo 11 Plaque Left on the Moon." NASA Marshall Center, Houston, TX, July 1969. https://science.nasa.gov/resource/apollo-11-plaque/#:~:text=The%20plaque%20says%3A%20%22Here%20men,in%20peace%20for%20all%20mankind.%22.

Barnstone, Howard. "Staub, John Fanz." *Handbook of Texas Online*. Accessed April 16, 2025. https://www.tshaonline.org/handbook/entries/staub-john-fanz.

Baughman, James P. *Charles Morgan and the Development of Southern Transportation*. Nashville, TN: Vanderbilt University Press, 1968.

Becker, Ann Dunphy. *Houston, 1860–1900*. Charleston, SC: Arcadia Publishing, 2010.

"Ben Love Obituary." *Houston Chronicle*, January 15, 2006. http://www.legacy.com/obituaries/houstonchronicle/obituary.aspx?n=ben-love&pid=16313113.

Bernanke, Ben S. "Monetary Policy and the Global Economy." Speech, London, March 21, 2013. Board of Governors of the Federal Reserve System. https://www.federalreserve.gov/newsevents/speech/bernanke20130325a.htm.

Bernhard, Virginia. *Ima Hogg: The Governor's Daughter*. Austin: Texas Monthly Press, 1984.

Bernreider, William. "The U.S.S. Houston, Port Houston's Latest Asset." *Houston Port and City*, June 1927.

Best, Hugh. *Debrett's Texas Peerage*. New York: Coward-McCann, 1983.

Blake, Eric S., and Ethan G. Gibney. *The Deadliest, Costliest, and Most Intense United States Tropical Cyclones from 1851 to 2010 (and Other Frequently Requested Hurricane Facts).* August 2011. https://www.nhc.noaa.gov/pdf/nws-nhc-6.pdf.

Boutwell, Bryant. *John P. McGovern, MD: A Lifetime of Stories.* College Station: Texas A&M University Press, 2014.

Boutwell, Bryant. "Two Bachelors, a Vision and the Texas Medical Center." *Houston Review* 2, no. 1 (2004): 8.

Bredeson, Carmen. *The Spindletop Gusher.* Brookfield, CT: Millbrook Press, 1996.

Bryan, L. R. "In the Development of Houston's Foreign Trade." *Houston Port Book,* May 1947.

Bryce, Robert. *Cronies: Oil, the Bushes, and the Rise of Texas, America's Superstate.* New York: PublicAffairs, 2004.

Buenger, Walter L., and Joseph A. Pratt. *But Also Good Business: Texas Commerce Banks and the Financing of Houston and Texas, 1886–1986.* College Station: Texas A&M University Press, 1986.

Burrough, Bryan. *The Big Rich: The Rise and Fall of the Greatest Texas Oil Fortunes.* New York: Penguin Press, 2009.

Burrows, Edwin G., and Mike Wallace. *Gotham: A History of New York City to 1898.* New York: Oxford University Press, 1999.

Bush, Barbara. *Barbara Bush: A Memoir.* New York: Scribner's Sons, 1994.

Campbell, C. J. *Oil Crisis.* Brentwood, Essex, England: Multi-Science Publishing, 2005.

Caro, Robert A. *Master of the Senate.* New York: Alfred A. Knopf, 2002.

Cartwright, Gary. *Galveston: A History of the Island.* New York: Atheneum, 1991.

Chernow, Ron. *Titan: The Life of John D. Rockefeller, Sr.* New York: Random House, 1998.

Chesnar, Lynne. *February Fever: Historical Highlights of the First Sixty Years of the Houston Livestock Show and Rodeo, 1932–1992.* Houston: Houston Livestock Show and Rodeo, 1991.

Chipman, Donald E. "In Search of Cabeza de Vaca's Route Across Texas: An Historiographical Survey." *Southwestern Historical Quarterly* 91 (July 1987): 127–49.

Clancy, Tom. *Red Storm Rising.* New York: G. P. Putnam's Sons, 1986.

Clayton, W. L. "Clayton Urges More Trade as Best Hope for World." *Houston Port Magazine,* May 1962.

"Company History." Gulf Oil. Accessed April 14, 2025. https://gulfoil.com/AboutGulf/CompanyHistory.aspx.

Conaway, James. *The Texans.* New York: Knopf, 1976.

Congressman Stephen Lee Fincher, speaking on Bill honoring M. D. Anderson, on March 30, 2011. 112th Cong., 1st sess., *Congressional Record* 157, pt. 4:4756.

"Conversation with Willis H. Shapley." Interview by John M. Longsdon. *Legislative Origins of the National Aeronautics and Space Act of 1958,* April 3, 1992. https://lawcat.berkeley.edu/search?f1=author&as=1&sf=title&so=a&rm=&m1=p&p1=United%20States.%20National%20Aeronautics%20and%20Space%20Administration.%20History%20Office.&ln=en.

Cook, Alison. "The Fraying Empire of Bobby Sakowitz." *Texas Monthly,* December 1985.

Cooley, Denton A. "A Brief History of the Texas Heart Institute." *Texas Heart Institute Journal* 35, no. 3 (2008): 235–39.

Cooper, John Milton. *Woodrow Wilson: A Biography.* New York: Alfred A. Knopf, 2009.

Cotner, Robert Crawford. *James Stephen Hogg: A Biography.* Austin: University of Texas Press, 1959.

Cox, Donald, and Michael Stoiko. *Spacepower: What It Means to You*. Philadelphia: John C. Winston, 1958.

Crile, George. *Charlie Wilson's War: The Extraordinary Story of the Largest Covert Operation in History*. New York: Atlantic Monthly Press, 2003.

Cronon, William. *Nature's Metropolis: Chicago and the Great West*. New York: W. W. Norton, 1991.

Crowley, Carolyn Hughes. "The Man Who Invented Elsie, the Borden Cow." *Smithsonian*, September 1999.

Cummins, Light. "History, Memory, and Rebranding Texas as Western for the 1936 Centennial." In *This Corner of Canaan: Essays on Texas in Honor of Randolph B. Campbell*, edited by Richard B. McCaslin, Donald E. Chipman, and Andrew J. Torgelt, 37–57. Denton: University of North Texas Press, 2013.

"Daniel Harrison, III: Profile." *Forbes*. Accessed July 11, 2016. http://www.forbes.com/profile/daniel-harrison-iii/.

Davis, Wallace. *Corduroy Road: The Story of Glenn H. McCarthy*. Houston: A. Jones Press, 1951.

Day, Dwayne A. "A New Space Council?" *Space Review*, June 21, 2004. http://www.thespacereview.com/article/163/1.

Day, James M. *The Black Giant: A History of the East Texas Oil Field and Oil Industry Skulduggery and Trivia*. Austin: Eakin Press, 2003.

"The Decision to Go to the Moon: President John F. Kennedy's May 25, 1961 Speech Before Congress." National Aeronautics and Space Administration, September 22, 1988. http://history.nasa.gov/moondec.html.

Dethloff, Henry C. *Suddenly, Tomorrow Came—: A History of the Johnson Space Center*. Houston: National Aeronautics and Space Administration, Lyndon B. Johnson Space Center, 1993.

Dickson, Paul. *Sputnik: The Shock of the Century*. New York: Walker Publishing, 2001.

Divine, Robert A. *The Sputnik Challenge: Eisenhower's Response to the Soviet Satellite*. New York: Oxford University Press, 1993.

Dyll, Remi S. *Bayou Bend: Collection and Gardens*. Houston: Museum, 1997.

Elliott, Frederick C., and William Henry Kellar. *The Birth of the Texas Medical Center: A Personal Account*. College Station: Texas A&M University Press, 2004.

Ely, Glen Sample. *Where the West Begins: Debating Texas Identity*. Lubbock: Texas Tech University Press, 2011.

Emmett, Chris. "Pierce, Abel Head [Shanghai]." *Handbook of Texas Online*. Accessed July 13, 2016. https://tshaonline.org/handbook/online/articles/fpi08.

"*Esso Houston*: A Challenger Is Launched. Largest Tanker Ever Christened Here." *Shipyard Bulletin*, 1964.

"Facts and Figures—Texas Medical Center." Texas Medical Center. Accessed July 1, 2016. http://www.tmc.edu/about-tmc/facts-and-figures/.

"The Famous San Jacinto Battleground." *Houston Port and City*, November 1927, 29.

Fenberg, Steven. *Unprecedented Power: Jesse Jones, Capitalism, and the Common Good*. College Station: Texas A&M University Press, 2011.

Ferris, Sylvia Van Voast, and Eleanor Sellers Hoppe. *Scalpels and Sabers: Nineteenth Century Medicine in Texas*. Austin: Eakin Press, 1985.

"Final Relocation of Center Employees Begins Today." *Space Center Roundup*, June 24, 1964.

Fisher, James. "Deep Water Houston: From the *Laura* to the Deep Water Jubilee." *Houston History*, October 5, 2014.
Fleming, Richard T. "Peddy, George Edwin." *Handbook of Texas Online*. Accessed August 14, 2016. https://tshaonline.org/handbook/online/articles/fpe13.
Fossedal, Gregory A. *Our Finest Hour: Will Clayton, the Marshall Plan, and the Triumph of Democracy*. Stanford, CA: Hoover Institution Press, 1993.
Friedman, Vanessa. "André Courrèges, Fashion Designer Who Redefined Couture, Dies at 92." *New York Times*, January 8, 2016. http://www.nytimes.com/2016/01/09/business/andre-courreges-fashion-designer-who-redefined-couture-dies-at-92.html?_r=0.
Fuermann, George. *Houston: The Feast Years, an Illustrated Essay*. Houston: Premier Printing, 1962.
Fuermann, George. *Houston: Land of the Big Rich*. Garden City, NY: Doubleday, 1951.
Fuermann, George. *Houston: The Once and Future City*. Garden City, NY: Doubleday, 1971.
Fuermann, George, and Owen Johnson. *The Face of Houston*. Houston: Press of Premier, 1963.
Garwood, Ellen. *Will Clayton, a Short Biography*. Austin: University of Texas Press, 1958.
Gesick, John. "Weinert, Hilmar Herman." *Handbook of Texas Online*. Accessed July 31, 2016. http://www.tshaonline.org/handbook/online/articles/fwe73.
Getty, J. Paul. *As I See It: The Autobiography of J. Paul Getty*. Englewood Cliffs, NJ: Prentice-Hall, 1976.
Gresham, Newton, and James A. Tinsley. "Crooker, John Henry." *Handbook of Texas Online*. Accessed November 15, 2016. http://www.tshaonline.org/handbook/online/articles/fcr63.
Halverton, H. A. "Houston—the City." *Houston Port Magazine*, November 1927.
Hamilton, Thomas W. "The Launch of Sputnik." Columbia250, 2004. http://c250.columbia.edu/c250_perspectives/write_history/161.html.
Hamrick, Peggy, Robert Gutierrez, and Tom Craddick. "Relief from Severance Taxes: Incentive or Windfall?" Texas Legislature, House, Steering Committee, 77th Cong. H. Rept.
Haqqani, Husain. *Magnificent Delusions*. New York: PublicAffairs, 2013.
Helgesen, Sally. *Wildcatters: A Story of Texans, Oil, and Money*. Garden City, NY: Doubleday, 1981.
Herring, Joanne King, and Nancy Dorman-Hickson. *Diplomacy and Diamonds: My Wars from the Ballroom to the Battlefield*. New York: Center Street, 2011.
"Historical Population: 1900 to 2017, City of Houston," 2017, https://www.houstontx.gov/planning/Demographics/docs_pdfs/Cy/hist_pop_1900_2017.pdf.
Hochschild, Adam. *Spain in Our Hearts: Americans in the Spanish Civil War, 1936–1939*. Boston: Houghton Mifflin Harcourt, 2016.
Hochschild, Adam. "The Untold Story of the Texaco Oil Tycoon Who Loved Fascism." *The Nation*, March 21, 2016. https://www.thenation.com/article/archive/the-untold-story-of-the-texaco-oil-tycoon-who-loved-fascism/.
Hodge, Shelby. "Elton John's Gift to MFAH in Honor of Chair Lynn Wyatt Takes Grand Gala Ball to $2 Million Mark." *Houston Culture Map*, October 4, 2015. https://houston.culturemap.com/news/society/10-04-15-elton-johns-gift-to-mfah-in-honor-of-chair-lynn-wyatt-takes-grand-gala-ball-to-2-million-mark/.

Houghton, Dorothy Knox Howe. *Houston's Forgotten Heritage: Landscape, Houses, Interiors, 1824–1914*. Houston: Rice University Press, 1991.

Howie-Willis, Ian. "Willis, Rupert Allan (1898–1980)." *Australian Dictionary of Biography*, National Centre of Biography, Australian National University. Accessed June 17, 2016. http://adb.anu.edu.au/biography/willis-rupert-allan-12039/text21597.

Hurley, Marvin. *Decisive Years for Houston*. Houston: Houston Magazine, 1966.

Hurt, Harry, III. "Oscar's Folly." *Texas Monthly*, December 1981.

Hurt, Harry. *Texas Rich: The Hunt Dynasty, from the Early Oil Days Through the Silver Crash*. New York: W. W. Norton, 1981.

Iscoe, Louise Kosches. *Ima Hogg, First Lady of Texas: Reminiscences and Recollections of Family and Friends*. Austin: Hogg Foundation for Mental Health, 1976.

James, Marquis. *The Texaco Story: The First Fifty Years 1902–1952*. New York: Texas Company, 1953.

Johnston, Marguerite. *Houston, the Unknown City, 1836–1946*. College Station: Texas A&M University Press, 1991.

Keith, Gary. *Eckhardt: There Once Was a Congressman from Texas*. Austin: University of Texas Press, 2007.

Kellar, William. *Enduring Legacy: The M. D. Anderson Foundation & the Texas Medical Center*. College Station: Texas A&M University Press, 2014.

Kelley, Mary L. *The Foundations of Texan Philanthropy*. College Station: Texas A&M University Press, 2004.

Kilman, Edward W., and Theon Wright. *Hugh Roy Cullen: A Story of American Opportunity*. New York: Prentice-Hall, 1954.

King, Edward. *The Great South*. Baton Rouge: Louisiana State University Press, 1972.

King, John O. *Joseph Stephen Cullinan: A Study of Leadership in the Texas Petroleum Industry, 1897–1937*. Nashville, TN: Published for the Texas Gulf Coast Historical Association by Vanderbilt University Press, 1970.

King, Seth. "James Rowe, New Deal Aide and an Assistant to Roosevelt." *New York Times*, June 19, 1984.

Kirkland, Kate Sayen. *Captain James A. Baker of Houston, 1857–1941*. College Station: Texas A&M University Press, 2012.

Kirkland, Kate Sayen. *The Hogg Family and Houston: Philanthropy and the Civic Ideal*. Austin: University of Texas Press, 2009.

Kirkland, William A. "Cruiser Houston Comes Home for Navy Day." *Houston Port Book*, November 1945.

Klein, Kyle. "T. P. Lee." *Texas Oil Magazine*, May 2005.

Kotkin, Joel. *The City: A Global History*. London: Weidenfeld and Nicolson, 2005.

Kraemer, Richard H., and Charldean Newell. *Texas Politics*. St. Paul, MN: West Publishing, 1979.

Krebs, Michael. "Her Name Still Rings a Bell." *New York Times*, October 19, 2001. http://www.nytimes.com/2001/10/19/automobiles/her-name-still-rings-a-bell.html.

Lanoy, George. "Southern Steamship Company Began Service Ten Years Ago." *Port Houston*, November 1925.

Lardas, Mark. *Port of Houston*. Charleston, SC: Arcadia Publishing, 2013.

Launius, Roger D. "Sputnik and the Origins of the Space Age." NASA, October 10, 2007. http://history.nasa.gov/sputnik/.

Lezon, Dale. "Oil Firm Chief, Arts Patron Paul N. Howell Dies at 82." *Houston Chronicle*, September 2, 2001. http://www.chron.com/news/houston-texas/article/Oil-firm-chief-arts-patron-Paul-N-Howell-dies-2050336.php.

Lipartito, Kenneth, and Joseph A. Pratt. *Baker & Botts in the Development of Modern Houston*. Austin: University of Texas Press, 1991.

Lomax, John A. *Will Hogg, Texan*. Austin: Published for the Hogg Foundation University of Texas Press, 1956.

Lomax, John N. "Is Texas Southern, Western, or Truly a Lone Star?" *Texas Monthly*, March 3, 2015.

"Lord Beaverbrook." Beaverbrook Foundation. Accessed August 14, 2016. https://beaverbrookfoundation.org/history/.

Macon, Don N. *Monroe Dunaway Anderson, His Legacy*. Houston: Texas Medical Center, 1994.

Macon, Don N. *South from Flower Mountain: A Conversation with William B. Bates*. Houston: Texas Medical Center, 1975.

"Malcolm McLean." *The Economist*, 2001. http://www.economist.com/node/638561. https://www.economist.com/obituary/2001/05/31/malcolm-mclean.

Marshall, J. Howard, and Robert L. Bradley. *Done in Oil: An Autobiography*. College Station: Texas A&M University Press, 1994.

Martin, Douglas. "Roy M. Huffington, Independent Oilman, Is Dead at 90." *New York Times*, July 17, 2008. http://www.nytimes.com/2008/07/17/business/worldbusiness/17huffington.html.

Mattox, Kenneth L., and Joseph S. Coselli. *The History of Surgery in Houston: Fifty-Year Anniversary of the Houston Surgical Society*. Austin: Eakin Press, 1998.

Maxwell, Robert S., and Baker Robert D. *Sawdust Empire: The Texas Lumber Industry, 1830–1940*. College Station: Texas A&M University Press, 1983.

McAshan, Marie Phelps. *A Houston Legacy: On the Corner of Main and Texas*. Houston: Hutchins House, 1985.

McCaslin, Richard B., Donald E. Chipman, Andrew J. Torget, and Randolph B. Campbell. *This Corner of Canaan: Essays on Texas in Honor of Randolph B. Campbell*. Denton: University of North Texas Press, 2013.

McComb, David G. *Houston, the Bayou City*. Austin: University of Texas Press, 1969.

McDougall, Walter A. *The Heavens and the Earth: A Political History of the Space Age*. New York: Basic Books, 1985.

Miller, Ray. *Ray Miller's Houston*. Houston: Cordovan Press, 1982.

Mod, Anna. *Building Modern Houston*. Charleston, SC: Arcadia Publishing, 2011.

Moore, Hank. *Houston Legends: History and Heritage of Dynamic Global Capitol: Back Stories of Companies, Community Leaders & Innovators in Energy, Medicine, Space, Technology and Entrepreneurship*. New York: Morgan James Publishing, 2015.

Morris, Jan. *Journeys*. New York: Oxford University Press, 1984.

Morse, Clarence G. "A Study of American Merchant Marine Legislation." *Law and Contemporary Problems* 25, no. 1 (1960): 61–62.

Muir, Andrew Forest. *Texas in 1837: An Anonymous, Contemporary Narrative*. Austin: University of Texas Press, 1958.

Muir, Andrew Forest. *William Marsh Rice and His Institute: A Biographical Study*. Houston: William Marsh Rice University, 1972.

Mulvaney, Erin, and David Kaplan. "Finger Furniture Files for Bankruptcy." *Houston Chronicle*, February 28, 2014. http://www.houstonchronicle.com/business/retail/article/Finger-Furniture-files-for-bankruptcy-5277462.php.

Mumsford, Lewis. *The Culture of Cities*. New York: Harcourt Brace, 1938.

Naftali, Timothy J. *George H. W. Bush*. New York: Times Books, 2007.

Nahas, Fred, ed. *Houston, City of Destiny*. New York: Macmillan, 1980.

NASA's Origins and the Dawn of the Space Age. Monographs in Aerospace History #10. Accessed April 20, 2025. https://www.nasa.gov/history/monograph10/korspace.html#:~:text=The%20IGY%20science%20satellite%20program,with%20high%2Dpriority%20missile%20programs.&text=On%20May%2027%2C%20Eisenhower%20approved,science%20satellite%20during%20the%20IGY.

Neeley, Gwendolyn Cone. *Miss Ima and the Hogg Family*. Dallas: Hendrick-Long Publishing, 1992.

Neu, Charles E. *Colonel House: A Biography of Woodrow Wilson's Silent Partner*. New York: Oxford University Press, 2015.

"New Deal Trade Policy: The Export-Import Bank & the Reciprocal Trade Agreements Act, 1934." Department of State. https://history.state.gov/milestones/1921-1936/export-import-bank.

Olien, Diana Davids, and Roger M. Olien. *Oil in Texas: The Gusher Age, 1895–1945*. Austin: University of Texas Press, 2002.

Osborne, James. "Oil Boom Sends Gusher of Cash to Texas Universities." *Dallas Morning News*, May 2014. http://www.dallasnews.com/business/energy/2014/05/31/oil-boom-sends-gusher-of-cash-to-texas-universities.

Peden, E. A. "A Brief Survey." *Port Houston*, June 1923.

Platell, Amanda. "A Navy Single-Breasted Suit, String of Pearls, Black Court Shoes and Magnificent Hair: How Margaret Thatcher Taught Me Powerful Women Never Wear Trousers." *Daily Mail*, November 4, 2015. http://www.dailymail.co.uk/femail/article-3304242/A-navy-single-breasted-suit-string-pearls-black-court-shoes-magnificent-hair-Margaret-Thatcher-taught-powerful-women-never-wear-trousers.html.

Polan, Brenda, and Roger Tredre. *The Great Fashion Designers*. Oxford: Berg Publishers, 2009.

Pomery, C. David, Jr. "Allen Ranch." *Handbook of Texas Online*. Accessed July 13, 2016. https://tshaonline.org/handbook/online/articles/apa01.

"The Port of Houston." *Port Houston*, November 1924, 5–6.

Pratt, Joseph A., Martin V. Melosi, and Kathleen A. Brosnan. *Energy Capitals: Local Impact, Global Influence*. Pittsburgh: University of Pittsburgh Press, 2014.

Presley, James. *A Saga of Wealth: The Rise of the Texas Oilmen*. Toronto, Canada: Longman Canada, 1978.

Prichard, Walter. "George Graham's Mission to Galveston in 1818: Two Important Documents Bearing upon Louisiana History." *Louisiana Historical Quarterly* 20 (July 1937): 619–50.

"Privately Owned Terminal and Industrial Facilities." *Port Houston*, November 1925.

Ramsdell, Charles. "Why Lafitte Became a Pirate." *Southwestern Historical Quarterly* 43 (July 1939): 465–72.

Rawson, Michael. *Eden on the Charles: The Making of Boston*. Cambridge, MA: Harvard University Press, 2010.

Reed, S. G. "Houston Direct Navigation Company." *Handbook of Texas Online*. Accessed February 28, 2025. https://tshaonline.org/handbook/online/articles/eth01.
Reginato, James. "The Legend of Lynn Wyatt, the Best Little Socialite in Texas." *Vanity Fair*, February 2016.
Richardson, Rupert Norval. *Colonel House: The Texas Years*. Abilene, TX: Hardin-Simmons University Press, 1964.
Roemer, Ferdinand, and Oswald Mueller. *Texas; with Particular Reference to German Immigration and the Physical Appearance of the Country; Described Through Personal Observation, by Dr. Ferdinand Roemer; Translated from the German by Oswald Mueller*. San Antonio: Standard Print, 1935.
Roosevelt, Franklin D. "Letter to Henry A. Wallace and Jesse H. Jones on Economic Warfare." July 15, 1943. Online by Gerhard Peters and John T. Woolley, The American Presidency Project. https://www.presidency.ucsb.edu/documents/letter-henry-wallace-and-jesse-h-jones-economic-warfare.
Roussel, Hubert. *The Houston Symphony Orchestra: 1913–1971*. Austin: University of Texas Press, 1972.
Sampson, Anthony. *The Seven Sisters: The Great Oil Companies and the World They Shaped*. New York: Viking Press, 1975.
Sanguily, R. P. "International Houston." *Houston Port Book*, May 1948.
Saxon, Wolfgang. "Lee Clark, Doctor Who Helped Build Cancer Center, Dies at 87." *New York Times*, May 5, 1994. http://www.nytimes.com/1994/05/05/obituaries/lee-clark-doctor-who-helped-build-cancer-center-dies-at-87.html.
Schull, William J. *Song Among the Ruins*. Cambridge, MA: Harvard University Press, 1990.
Sheehy, Sandy. *Texas Big Rich: Exploits, Eccentricities, and Fabulous Fortunes Won and Lost*. New York: Morrow, 1990.
Sibley, Marilyn McAdams. *The Methodist Hospital of Houston: Serving the World*. Austin: Texas State Historical Association, 1989.
Sibley, Marilyn McAdams. *The Port of Houston: A History*. Austin: University of Texas Press, 1968.
Siegel, Stanley, and John Moretta. *Houston: A Chronicle of the Bayou City*. Sun Valley, CA: American Historical Press, 2005.
Smyrl, Frank H. "Mayfield, Earle Bradford." *Handbook of Texas Online*. Accessed November 14, 2016. https://tshaonline.org/handbook/online/articles/fma91.
Spencer, James H. *Globalization and Urbanization: The Global Urban Ecosystem*. Lanham, MD: Rowman and Littlefield, 2015.
Spratt, John S. *The Road to Spindletop: Economic Change in Texas, 1875–1901*. Austin: Published in Cooperation with the Texas State Historical Association University of Texas Press, 1970.
"Sputnik II." NASA Space Science Data Coordinated Archive, October 28, 2022. https://nssdc.gsfc.nasa.gov/nmc/spacecraft/display.action?id=1957-002A.
Swartz, Mimi. "River Oaks 77019." *Texas Monthly*, July 1992.
Taylor, Harvey Grant, N. Don Macon, and John P. McGovern. *Remembrances & Reflections*. Houston: University of Texas Health Science Center at Houston, 1991.
"Texas Almanac: City Population History from 1850–2000." *Texas Almanac*. Accessed April 13, 2025. https://www.texasalmanac.com/drupal-backup/images/CityPopHist%20web.pdf.

Texas Department of Transportation, Planning and Programming Division. *2005 Gulf Intercoastal Waterway*. Austin: Texas Department of Transportation, 2005.
"Texas Medical Center Celebrating 50 Years of Vision." *Texas Medical Center News*, January 15, 1995.
Tierney, Dominic. *FDR and the Spanish Civil War: Neutrality and Commitment in the Struggle That Divided America*. Durham, NC: Duke University Press, 2007.
Tierney, Gene, and Mickey Herskowitz. *Self-Portrait*. New York: Wyden Books, 1979.
Timmons, Bascom N. *Jesse H. Jones: The Man and the Statesman*. New York: Holt, 1956.
Turner, Frederick Jackson. *The Frontier in American History*. Exton, PA: Franklin Library, 1977.
"Upper Texas Coast Tropical Cyclones in the 1910s." National Weather Service Forecast Office, January 30, 2007. https://www.weather.gov/hgx/hurricanes_climatology_1910s.
"Uses in Industry." NaturalGas.org, September 20, 2013. http://naturalgas.org/overview/uses-industrial/.
Vandiver, Frank Everson. *The Southwest: South or West?* College Station: Texas A&M University Press, 1975
Vela, Lee, and Maxine Edward. *Reaching for the Sea: The Story of the Port of Houston*. Houston: Port of Houston Authority, 1989.
Warren, David B. *American Decorative Arts and Paintings in the Bayou Bend Collection*. Houston: Museum of Fine Arts, Houston in Association with Princeton University Press, 1998.
Warren, David B. *Bayou Bend Gardens: A Southern Oasis*. London: Scala, 2006.
White, Graham J., and J. R. Maze. *Harold Ickes of the New Deal: His Private Life and Public Career*. Cambridge, MA: Harvard University Press, 1985.
Williams, Amelia W. "Allen, Augustus Chapman." *Handbook of Texas Online*. Accessed February 28, 2025. https://tshaonline.org/handbook/online/articles/fal17.
Williamson, Harold F. *The American Petroleum Industry*. Evanston, IL: Northwestern University Press, 1963.
Williamson, Harold F., and Arnold Daum. *The American Petroleum Industry*. Evanston, IL: Northwestern University Press, 1959.
Wilson, Glen P. "How the U.S. Space Act Came to Be." *Legislative Origins of the National Aeronautics and Space Act of 1958*, April 3, 1992.
Wolfe, Jane. *Blood Rich: When Oil Billions, High Fashion, and Royal Intimacies Are Not Enough*. Boston: Little, Brown, 1993.
Wright, Lawrence. *The Looming Tower: Al-Qaeda and the Road to 9/11*. New York: Knopf, 2006.
Wygant, Larry J. "Aynesworth, Kenneth Hazen." *Handbook of Texas Online*. Accessed August 15, 2016. http://www.tshaonline.org/handbook/online/articles/fayo2.
"Yellow Fever Virus." Centers for Disease Control and Prevention. Accessed November 14, 2016. http://www.cdc.gov/yellowfever/index.html.
Yergin, Daniel. *The Prize: The Epic Quest for Oil, Money, and Power*. New York: Simon and Schuster, 1991.
Young, Samuel Oliver. *A Thumb-Nail History of the City of Houston from Its Founding in 1836 to the Year 1912*. Houston: Press of Rein, 1912.

Index

Note: Page numbers for images are in *italics*, maps in **bold.** Italic *n* indicates endnote.